ESSENTIALS

Microsoft® Office Word 2003

Level Two

ESSENTIALS

Microsoft® Office Word 2003

Level Two

Keith Mulbery
Utah Valley State College

PEARSON
Prentice Hall

Prentice Hall
Upper Saddle River, New Jersey 07458

Library of Congress Cataloging-in-Publication Data

Mulbery, Keith.
    Essentials Microsoft Office Word 2003. Level two / Keith Mulbery.
        p. cm.—(Essentials)
    Includes index.
    ISBN 0-13-143547-7
    1. Microsoft Word. 2. Word processing. I. Title. II. Essentials
(Prentice-Hall, inc.)

    Z52.5.M52M8463   2004
    005.52—dc22   2004001203

Publisher and Vice President: Natalie E. Anderson
Executive Editor: Jodi McPherson
Acquisitions Editor: Melissa Sabella
Editorial Assistant: Alana Meyers
Developmental Editor: Patricia O'Shea
Senior Media Project Manager: Cathleen Profitko
Marketing Manager: Emily Knight
Senior Managing Editor: Gail Steier de Acevedo
Senior Project Manager, Production: April Montana
Project Manager, Production: Vanessa Nuttry
Manufacturing Buyer: Natacha St. Hill Moore
Design Manager: Maria Lange
Interior Design: Kevin Kall
Cover Design: OX Design
Manager, Print Production: Christy Mahon
Composition and Design Services: Kinetic Publishing Services, LLC
Full-Service Management: Thistle Hill Publishing Services, LLC
Cover Printer: Coral Graphics
Printer/Binder: Quebecor World

Credits and acknowledgments borrowed from other sources and reproduced, with permission, in this textbook appear on the appropriate page within the text.

Microsoft, Windows, Windows NT, MSN, The Microsoft Network, PowerPoint, Outlook, FrontPage, Hotmail, the MSN logo, and/or other Microsoft products referenced herein are either trademarks or registered trademarks of Microsoft Corporation in the United States and/or other countries. Screen shots and icons reprinted with permission from the Microsoft Corporation. This book is not sponsored or endorsed by or affiliated with Microsoft Corporation.

Microsoft and the Microsoft Office Specialist Logo are either trademarks or registered trademarks of Microsoft Corporation in the United States and/or other countries. Pearson Education is independent from Microsoft Corporation, and is not affiliated with Microsoft in any manner. This text may be used in assisting students to prepare for a Microsoft Office Specialist (MOS) Exam. Neither Microsoft, its designated review company, nor Pearson Education warrants that use of this text will ensure passing this exam.

Use of the Microsoft Office Specialist Approved Courseware Logo on this product signifies that it has been independently reviewed and approved in complying with the following standards: Acceptable coverage of all content related to the Specialist and Expert Level Microsoft Office exams entitled "Word 2003" when used in combination with the following books—Essentials Word 2003 Level 1, Essentials Word 2003 Level 2, and Essentials Word 2003 Level 3.

Copyright © 2004 by Prentice Hall, Inc., Upper Saddle River, New Jersey, 07458. All rights reserved. Printed in the United States of America. This publication is protected by Copyright and permission should be obtained from the publisher prior to any prohibited reproduction, storage in a retrieval system, or transmission in any form or by any means, electronic, mechanical, photocopying, recording, or likewise. For information regarding permission(s), write to: Rights and Permissions Department.

PEARSON
Prentice Hall

10 9 8 7 6 5 4 3 2 1

ISBN 0-13-143547-7

What does this logo mean?

It means this courseware has been approved by the Microsoft® Office Specialist Program to be among the finest available for learning **Microsoft® Office Word 2003, Microsoft® Office Excel 2003, Microsoft® Office PowerPoint® 2003,** and **Microsoft® Office Access 2003.** It also means that upon completion of this courseware, you may be prepared to take an exam for Microsoft Office Specialist qualification.

What is a Microsoft Office Specialist?

A Microsoft Office Specialist is an individual who has passed exams for certifying his or her skills in one or more of the Microsoft Office desktop applications such as Microsoft Word, Microsoft Excel, Microsoft PowerPoint, Microsoft Outlook, Microsoft Access, or Microsoft Project. The Microsoft Office Specialist Program typically offers certification exams at the "Specialist" and "Expert" skill levels.* The Microsoft Office Specialist Program is the only program approved by Microsoft for testing proficiency in Microsoft Office desktop applications and Microsoft Project. This testing program can be a valuable asset in any job search or career advancement.

More information:

To learn more about becoming a Microsoft Office Specialist, visit **www.microsoft.com/officespecialist**

To learn about other Microsoft Specialist approved courseware from Pearson Education, visit **www.prenhall.com/computing**

---

*The availability of Microsoft Office Specialist certification exams varies by application, application version, and language. Visit www.microsoft.com/officespecialist for exam availability.

Microsoft, the Microsoft Office Logo, PowerPoint, and Outlook are trademarks or registered trademarks of Microsoft Corporation in the United States and/or other countries, and the Microsoft Office Specialist Logo is used under license from the owner.

Dedication

This book is dedicated to Mrs. Penny Sumpter, my high school business education teacher. She is the one who inspired me to major in business education in college. Through her teaching, I learned attention to detail, the importance of formatting, effective teaching strategies, and passion for teaching.

Acknowledgments

This book is a result of collaborative effort from the *Essentials* team. First, I'd like to express sincere appreciation to Jodi McPherson, Executive Editor; Melissa Sabella, Acquisitions Editor; Trisha O'Shea, Developmental Editor; Alana Meyers, Editorial Assistant; April Montana, Senior Project Manager; and Vanessa Nuttry, Project Manager, for their dedication to the *Essentials* series and their drive for developing one of the strongest Microsoft Office series available.

A special thanks to Marianne Fox and Lawrence Metzelaar for their strong leadership as series editors and developmental editors. Their feedback on the organization of the manuscript helped strengthen this particular book, as well as the entire *Essentials* series. The successful pedagogy of the *Essentials* series is a result of their ongoing efforts.

Furthermore, sincere appreciation is extended to Angela Williams Urquhart, John Ferguson, and the staffs at Thistle Hill Publishing Services and Kinetic Publishing Services, for converting manuscript and image files into the exquisitely typeset book you are currently reading.

Finally, I appreciate the valuable feedback from Colette Eisele, Joyce Nielsen, and Michael Myers, Technical Editors, for their meticulous review of the manuscript to ensure clarity and accuracy.

About the Series Editors

Marianne Fox—Series editor of *Essentials Microsoft Office 2003* and coauthor of *Essentials Microsoft Office Excel 2003 Level 1, Level 2,* **and** *Level 3.* Marianne Fox is a CPA with B.S. and M.B.A. degrees in Accounting from Indiana University. For 24 years she enjoyed teaching full-time—10 years teaching accounting in Indiana University's School of Business and 14 years teaching accounting and microcomputer applications in the College of Business Administration at Butler University. Currently she retains adjunct faculty status at Butler University. As the co-owner of a consulting firm, Marianne has extensive experience consulting and training in the corporate and continuing education environments. Since 1984, she has coauthored more than 40 computer-related books and has given presentations on accounting, computer applications, and instructional development topics at numerous seminars and conferences.

Lawrence C. Metzelaar—Series editor of *Essentials Microsoft Office 2003* and coauthor of *Essentials Microsoft Office Excel 2003 Level 1, Level 2,* **and** *Level 3.* Lawrence C. Metzelaar earned a B.S. degree in Business Administration and Computer Science from the University of Maryland, and an Ed.M. and C.A.G.S. in Human Problem Solving from Boston University. Lawrence has more than 35 years of experience with military and corporate mainframe and microcomputer systems. He has taught courses on computer science and Management Information Systems (MIS) at the University of Hawaii, Control Data Institute, Indiana University, and Purdue University; currently, he is an adjunct faculty member in the College of Business Administration at Butler University. As the co-owner of a consulting firm, he has extensive experience consulting and training in the corporate and continuing education environments. Since 1984, he has coauthored more than 40 computer-related books and has given presentations on computer applications and instructional development topics at numerous seminars and conferences.

About the Author

Keith Mulbery—Author of *Essentials Microsoft Office Word 2003 Level 1, Level 2,* and *Level 3.* Keith Mulbery is an Associate Professor in the Business Computer Information Systems department and the Business Systems Administration and Education department at Utah Valley State College (UVSC), where he teaches Visual Basic programming and computer applications. He is the lead instructor of the required business computer proficiency course. Keith received his B.S. and M.Ed. (majoring in Business Education) from Southwestern Oklahoma State University. He is currently working toward a Ph.D. with a specialization in Business Information Systems at Utah State University. Keith has written over 15 software textbooks and business communication test banks. In January 2001, he received the Utah Valley State College Board of Trustees Award of Excellence for authoring *MOUS Essentials Word 2000*. In addition, he served as the developmental editor of *Essentials Word 2000 Intermediate* and *Essentials Word 2000 Advanced*. Keith also conducts hands-on computer application workshops at the local, state, and national levels, including the National Business Education Association convention.

Contents at a Glance

PROJECT 1	Refining Documents	1
PROJECT 2	Creating and Formatting Columns	41
PROJECT 3	Automating Work with Autotext, Styles, and Templates	75
PROJECT 4	Collaborating with Others	119
PROJECT 5	Performing Mail Merge	163
PROJECT 6	Using Drawing Tools and Special Effects	201
PROJECT 7	Creating Charts and Diagrams	237
PROJECT 8	Using Word with Other Applications	275
	Integrating Projects	309
	File Guide	319
	Task Guide	327
	Glossary	339
	Index	343

Table of Contents

PROJECT 1 — REFINING DOCUMENTS 1

Lesson 1	Finding and Replacing Text	4
Lesson 2	Finding and Replacing Formatting	8
Lesson 3	Sorting Lists, Paragraphs, and Tables	13
Lesson 4	Creating Different Headers and Footers for Odd- and Even-Numbered Pages	15
Lesson 5	Splitting the Document Window and Arranging Panes	17
Lesson 6	Using the Research Tool to Locate Information	21
Lesson 7	Creating and Modifying a Document Style	24
	Summary	27
	Key Terms	28
	Checking Concepts and Terms	28
	Skill Drill	30
	Challenge	34
	Discovery Zone	38

PROJECT 2 — CREATING AND FORMATTING COLUMNS 41

Lesson 1	Setting the Page Orientation	43
Lesson 2	Formatting Text into Columns	45
Lesson 3	Revising Column Structure	48
Lesson 4	Inserting Section Breaks, Column Breaks, and Files	50
Lesson 5	Balancing Column Length	54
Lesson 6	Creating Drop Caps	55
Lesson 7	Hyphenating Text	57
	Summary	60
	Key Terms	61
	Checking Concepts and Terms	61
	Skill Drill	63
	Challenge	66
	Discovery Zone	72

PROJECT 3 — AUTOMATING WORK WITH AUTOTEXT, STYLES, AND TEMPLATES 75

Lesson 1	Using a Template to Create a New Document	77
Lesson 2	Creating and Inserting AutoText Entries	81
Lesson 3	Editing and Deleting AutoText Entries	85
Lesson 4	Applying Built-In Word Styles	88
Lesson 5	Creating a Paragraph Style	92
Lesson 6	Creating a Character Style	97
Lesson 7	Copying Styles to the Normal Template	100
Lesson 8	Attaching a Word Template to a Document	103

Summary 105
Key Terms 106
Checking Concepts and Terms 106
Skill Drill 108
Challenge 112
Discovery Zone 116

PROJECT 4 — COLLABORATING WITH OTHERS 119

Lesson 1	Inserting, Viewing, and Editing Comments	121
Lesson 2	Tracking Changes	125
Lesson 3	Customizing Track Changes Options	128
Lesson 4	Reviewing Changes by Type and Reviewer	132
Lesson 5	Saving Versions and Accepting and Rejecting Changes	135
Lesson 6	E-Mailing a Document as an Attachment for Review	142
Lesson 7	Comparing and Merging Documents	147

Summary 149
Key Terms 150
Checking Concepts and Terms 150
Skill Drill 152
Challenge 155
Discovery Zone 160

PROJECT 5 — PERFORMING MAIL MERGE 163

Lesson 1	Starting the Mail Merge Process	166
Lesson 2	Creating a Recipient List	170
Lesson 3	Sorting Records in a Data Source	176
Lesson 4	Creating a Main Document	178
Lesson 5	Merging the Main Document and the Data Source	182
Lesson 6	Creating Mailing Labels	184

Summary 187
Key Terms 188
Checking Concepts and Terms 188
Skill Drill 190
Challenge 193
Discovery Zone 197

PROJECT 6 — USING DRAWING TOOLS AND SPECIAL EFFECTS 201

Lesson 1	Drawing and Sizing Shapes	204
Lesson 2	Drawing Lines	209
Lesson 3	Inserting Text with a Text Effect	212
Lesson 4	Positioning Shapes	214
Lesson 5	Formatting Shapes and Lines	216
Lesson 6	Layering and Grouping Shapes	218

xi

Summary 221
Key Terms 222
Checking Concepts and Terms 222
Skill Drill 223
Challenge 228
Discovery Zone 234

PROJECT 7 CREATING CHARTS AND DIAGRAMS 237

Lesson 1 Creating a Chart 240
Lesson 2 Formatting a Chart Object 244
Lesson 3 Inserting Titles 246
Lesson 4 Formatting Chart Elements 248
Lesson 5 Importing Excel Data to Create a Chart in Word 251
Lesson 6 Creating an Organization Chart 253
Lesson 7 Adding Positions to an Organization Chart 255
Lesson 8 Designing Diagrams 258
Summary 262
Key Terms 263
Checking Concepts and Terms 263
Skill Drill 264
Challenge 268
Discovery Zone 273

PROJECT 8 USING WORD WITH OTHER APPLICATIONS 275

Lesson 1 Inserting and Modifying Hyperlinks 277
Lesson 2 Inserting an Excel Workbook as an Object 281
Lesson 3 Embedding Excel Data into Word 284
Lesson 4 Modifying Embedded Data 288
Lesson 5 Linking Excel Data into Word 290
Lesson 6 Saving Documents in Different Formats 293
Summary 295
Key Terms 296
Checking Concepts and Terms 296
Skill Drill 298
Challenge 302
Discovery Zone 306

INTEGRATING PROJECTS 309

FILE GUIDE 319

TASK GUIDE 327

GLOSSARY 339

INDEX 343

xii

Introduction

Essentials courseware from Prentice Hall Information Technology is anchored in the practical and professional needs of all types of students.

The *Essentials* series is conceived around a learning-by-doing approach that encourages you to grasp application-related concepts as you expand your skills through hands-on tutorials. As such, it consists of modular lessons that are built around a series of numbered, step-by-step procedures that are clear, concise, and easy to review.

The end-of-project exercises have likewise been carefully constructed, from the routine Checking Concepts and Terms to creative tasks in the Discovery Zone that prod you into extending what you've learned into areas beyond the explicit scope of the lessons proper.

How to Use This Book

Typically, each *Essentials* book is divided into eight projects. A project covers one area (or a few closely related areas) of application functionality. Each project consists of six to nine lessons that are related to that topic. Each lesson presents a specific task or closely related set of tasks in a manageable chunk that is easy to assimilate and retain.

Each element in the *Essentials* book is designed to maximize your learning experience. A list of the *Essentials* project elements and a description of how each element can help you follows. To find out more about the rationale behind each book element and how to use each to your maximum benefit, take the following walk-through.

Essentials Series 2003 Walk-Through

Project Objectives. Starting with an objective gives you short-term, attainable goals. At the beginning of each project are objectives that closely match the titles of the step-by-step tutorials. ▶

OBJECTIVES
IN THIS PROJECT, YOU LEARN HOW TO
- Explore the Word screen
- Use menus and toolbars
- Enter text in a document
- Save a document in a new folder
- Correct spelling and grammatical errors
- Preview and print a document
- Get Help
- Close a document and exit Word

◀ **Why Would I Do This?** Introductory material at the beginning of each project provides an overview of why these tasks and procedures are important.

Visual Summary. An illustrated introductory feature graphically presents the concepts and features you will learn, including the final results of completing the project.

Step-by-Step Tutorials. Hands-on tutorials let you "learn by doing" and include numbered, bold, step-by-step instructions. ▶

◀ **If You Have Problems.** These short troubleshooting notes help you anticipate or solve common problems quickly and effectively.

◀ **To Extend Your Knowledge.** These features at the end of most lessons provide extra tips, shortcuts, alternative ways to complete a process, and special hints about using the software.

◀ **Creative Solution Exercises.** Special icons mark selected end-of-project exercises. The creative solution exercises enable you to make choices that result in a unique solution.

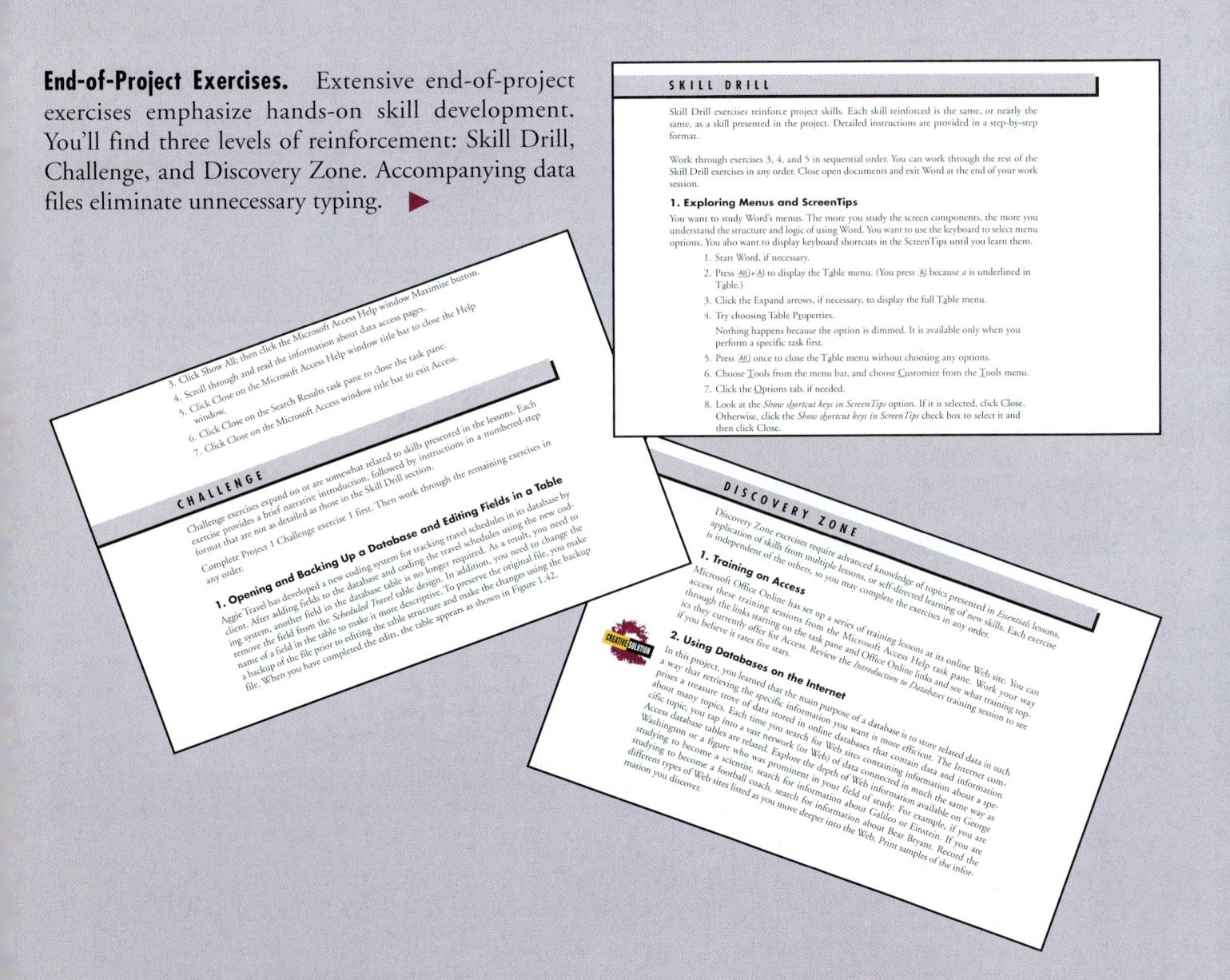

End-of-Project Exercises. Extensive end-of-project exercises emphasize hands-on skill development. You'll find three levels of reinforcement: Skill Drill, Challenge, and Discovery Zone. Accompanying data files eliminate unnecessary typing. ▶

Integrating Projects Exercises. Hands-on activities provide an opportunity to apply skills from two or more projects.

File Guides. Convenient reference tables list the student and solution files for each project.

Task Guides. These charts, found at the end of each book, list alternative ways to complete common procedures and provide a handy reference tool.

Typeface Conventions Used in This Book

Essentials Microsoft Office 2003 uses the following typeface conventions to make it easier for you to understand the material.

Key terms appear in ***italic and bold*** the first time they are defined in a project.

Monospace type appears frequently and `looks like this`. It is used to indicate text that you are instructed to key in.

Italic text indicates text that appears onscreen as (1) warnings, confirmation, or general information; (2) the name of a file to be used in a lesson or exercise; and (3) text from a menu or dialog box that is referenced within a sentence, when that sentence might appear awkward if it were not set off.

Hotkeys are indicated by underline. Hotkeys are the underlined letters in menus, toolbars, and dialog boxes that activate commands and options, and are a quick way to choose frequently used commands and options. Hotkeys look like this: File, Save.

Student Resources

Companion Web Site (www.prenhall.com/essentials). This text-specific Web site provides students with additional information and exercises to reinforce their learning. Features include: additional end-of-project reinforcement material; online Study Guide; easy access to *all* project data files; and much, much more!

Accessing Student Data Files. The data files that students need to work through the projects can be downloaded from the Companion Web site (www.prenhall.com/essentials). Data files are provided for each project. The filenames correspond to the filenames called for in this book. The files are named in the following manner: The first character indicates the book series (E = *Essentials*), the second character denotes the application (W = Word, E = Excel, etc.), and the third character indicates the level (1 = Level 1, 2 = Level 2, and 3 = Level 3). The last four digits indicate the project number and the file number within the project. For example, the first file used in Project 3 would be 0301. Therefore, the complete name for the first file in Project 3 in the *Word Level 1* book is *EW1_0301*. The complete name for the third file in Project 7 in the *Excel Level 2* book is *EE2_0703*.

Instructor's Resources

Customize Your Book (www.prenhall.com/customphit). The Prentice Hall Information Technology Custom PHIT Program gives professors the power to control and customize their books to suit their course needs. The best part is that it is done completely online using a simple interface.

xvii

Professors choose exactly what projects they need in the *Essentials Microsoft Office 2003* series, and in what order they appear. The program also enables professors to add their own material anywhere in the text's presentation, and the final product will arrive at each professor's bookstore as a professionally formatted text.

To learn more about this new system for creating the perfect textbook, go to www.prenhall.com/customphit, where the online walk-through demonstrates how to create a book.

Instructor's Resource CD-ROM. This CD-ROM includes the entire Instructor's Manual for each application in Microsoft Word format. Student data files and completed solutions files are also on this CD-ROM. The Instructor's Manual contains a reference guide of these files for the instructor's convenience. PowerPoint slides, which give more information about each project, are also available for classroom use.

Companion Web Site (www.prenhall.com/essentials). Instructors will find all of the resources available on the Instructor's Resource CD-ROM available for download from the Companion Web site.

TestGen Software. TestGen is a test generator program that lets you view and easily edit test bank questions, transfer them to tests, and print the tests in a variety of formats suitable to your teaching situation. The program also offers many options for organizing and displaying test banks and tests. A built-in random number and text generator makes it ideal for creating multiple versions of tests. Powerful search and sort functions let you easily locate questions and arrange them in the order you prefer.

QuizMaster, also included in this package, enables students to take tests created with TestGen on a local area network. The QuizMaster utility built into TestGen lets instructors view student records and print a variety of reports. Building tests is easy with TestGen, and exams can be easily uploaded into WebCT, Blackboard, and CourseCompass.

Prentice Hall has formed close alliances with each of the leading online platform providers: WebCT, Blackboard, and our own Pearson CourseCompass.

WebCT and Blackboard. Each of these custom-built distance-learning course features exercises, sample quizzes, and tests in a course management system that provides class administration tools as well as the ability to customize this material at the instructor's discretion.

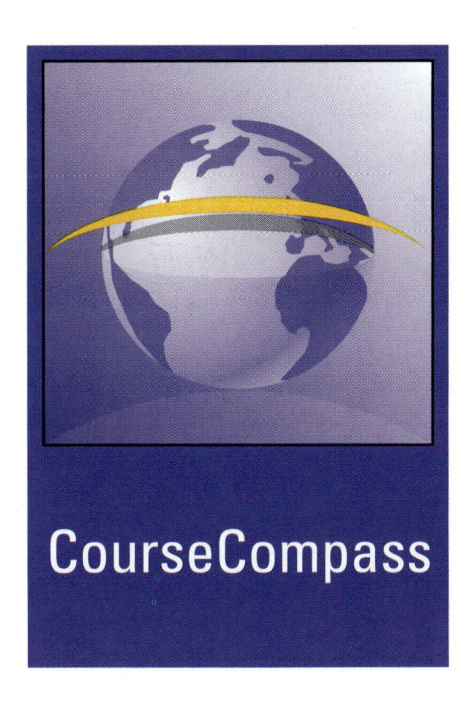

CourseCompass. CourseCompass is a dynamic, interactive online course management tool powered by Blackboard. It lets professors create their own courses in 15 minutes or less with preloaded quality content that can include quizzes, tests, lecture materials, and interactive exercises.

Performance-Based Training and Assessment: Train & Assess IT. Prentice Hall offers performance-based training and assessment in one product—Train & Assess IT.

The Training component offers computer-based instruction that a student can use to preview, learn, and review Microsoft Office application skills. Delivered via Web or CD-ROM, Train IT offers interactive multimedia, computer-based training to augment classroom learning. Built-in prescriptive testing suggests a study path based not only on student test results but also on the specific textbook chosen for the course.

The Assessment component offers computer-based testing that shares the same user interface as Train IT and is used to evaluate a student's knowledge about specific topics in Word, Excel, Access, PowerPoint, Windows, Outlook, and the Internet. It does this in a task-oriented, performance-based environment to demonstrate students' proficiency and comprehension of the topics. More extensive than the testing in Train IT, Assess IT offers more administrative features for the instructor and additional questions for the student. Assess IT also enables professors to test students out of a course, place students in appropriate courses, and evaluate skill sets.

PROJECT 1

LEVEL 2

REFINING DOCUMENTS

OBJECTIVES

In this project, you learn how to

- Find and replace text
- Find and replace formatting
- Sort lists, paragraphs, and tables
- Create different headers and footers for odd- and even-numbered pages
- Split the document window and arrange panes
- Use the Research tool to locate information
- Create and modify a document summary

WHY WOULD I DO THIS?

As you work with a long document, you might want to make global changes throughout the file. For example, you might want to find all occurrences of a particular word and replace those occurrences with a different word. Or you might want to find particular formatting, such as italic and Red font color, and replace it with other formatting, such as bold and Blue font color. The Find and Replace feature automates the process of replacing text and formats.

Long documents often require other refinements. For instance, you might want to create different headers or footers for odd-numbered and even-numbered pages so that page numbers appear in the outside corners of the bound document. Furthermore, scrolling through a long document to review its contents as you write the conclusions and recommendations that appear at the end of the document can become monotonous. Instead of scrolling back and forth, you can split the window to display two locations of the document at the same time.

When you review a document, you might decide to rearrange a list or the rows of a table, so that the text is alphabetized or sorted in sequential order by date. To further improve the content of a document, you can conduct online research and insert additional information. Finally, you might want to create a document summary that contains information about who created the document, the subject of the document, and other pertinent data.

VISUAL SUMMARY

In this project, you refine a document that discusses Word formatting techniques. You find and replace text and formatting, and use the Research tool to locate and insert information into your document. Figure 1.1 shows a condensed version of the final document you modify in this project. It illustrates the results of finding *MS* and replacing it with *Microsoft;* the results of finding text formatted with bold, italic Times New Roman formatting and replacing it with bold, not italic, Arial Narrow, Blue font color formatting; and the results of finding and inserting a definition by using the Research tool.

Visual Summary | 3 | LEVEL 2

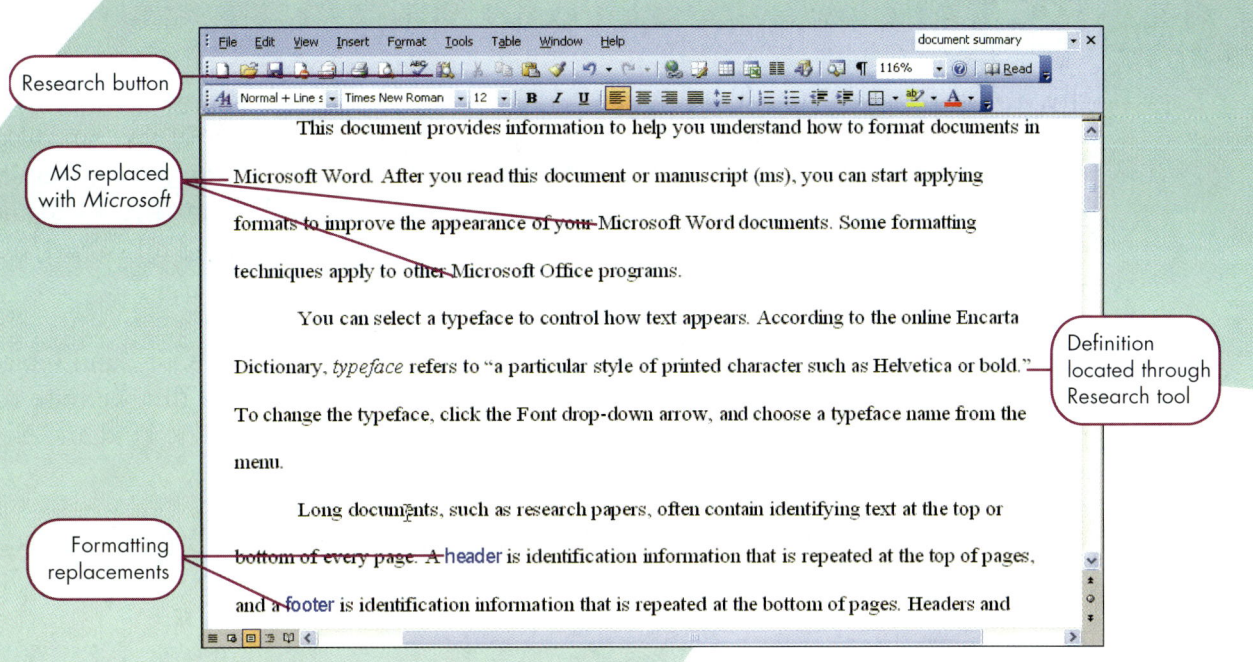

FIGURE 1.1

Callouts: Research button; MS replaced with *Microsoft*; Definition located through Research tool; Formatting replacements

You also learn how to split the window to show different areas of a document, create different footers for even-numbered and odd-numbered pages, and rearrange text in alphabetical order. Figure 1.2 displays a split document window, different footers, and an alphabetized bulleted list.

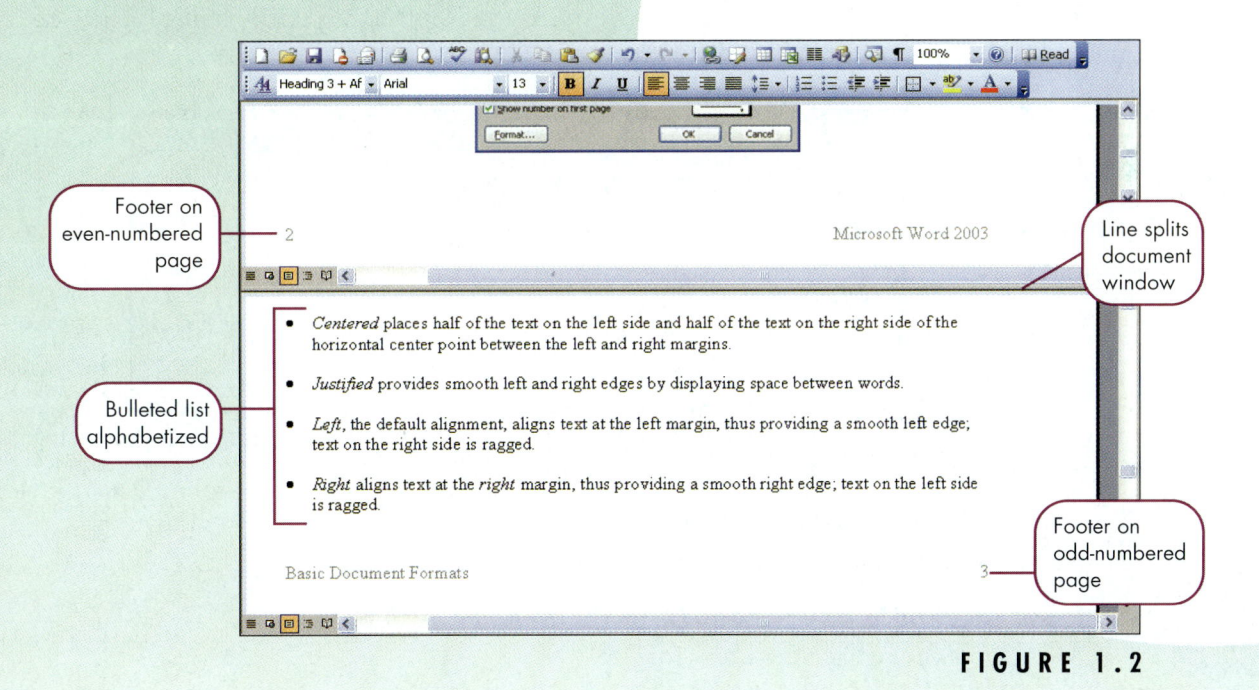

FIGURE 1.2

Callouts: Footer on even-numbered page; Bulleted list alphabetized; Line splits document window; Footer on odd-numbered page

LESSON 1: Finding and Replacing Text

After you create a document, you might decide to replace a certain phrase with a different phrase. For example, you might want to change "in my opinion" to "I believe" to make the text more concise. At other times, you might need to edit a report containing your team members' responsibilities. For example, assume that a manager assigned Brittany Beasley to another team and assigned Mohamed Amador to your team. You need to find all occurrences of Brittany's name and replace them with Mohamed's name.

The Find and Replace feature locates specific text (such as words or phrases) and replaces it with different text that you specify. Using Find and Replace saves a lot of time because you do not need to read the entire document and identify the text to change. The Find and Replace feature ensures that you do not overlook any text that you want to replace.

In this lesson, you decide to change the abbreviation *MS* to *Microsoft* in a document that discusses Microsoft Word formatting information.

To Find and Replace Text

1 Open *EW2_0101*, and save it as `Word_Formatting`.
You see occurrences of *MS* throughout the document.

2 Choose Edit, Replace.
The Find and Replace dialog box opens with the Replace tab options displayed (see Figure 1.3).

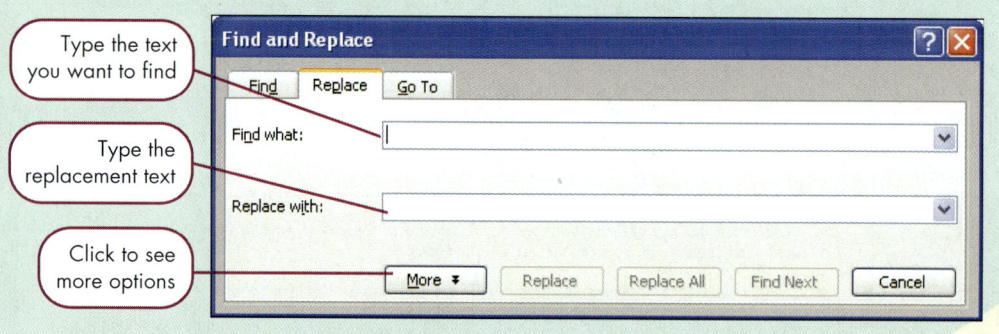

FIGURE 1.3

3 Type `MS` in the *Find what* box.
MS is the text that you want to find.

4 Press Tab and type `Microsoft` in the *Replace with* box.
Microsoft is the replacement text for *MS*.

5 Click Replace All at the bottom of the dialog box.
Word searches the entire document and replaces all occurrences of *MS* with *Microsoft*. You should see a message: *Word has completed its search of the document and has made 5 replacements.*

Lesson 1 Finding and Replacing Text

6 **Click OK, and then close the Find and Replace dialog box.**
Notice that Word replaces the capitalized occurrences of *MS* with capitalized *MICROSOFT* and occurrences of the lowercase abbreviation *ms* (for *manuscript*) with *Microsoft*. In addition to replacing the abbreviations *MS* and *ms*, Word also replaces *programs* with *programMicrosoft* (see Figure 1.4). These changes are not what you intended.

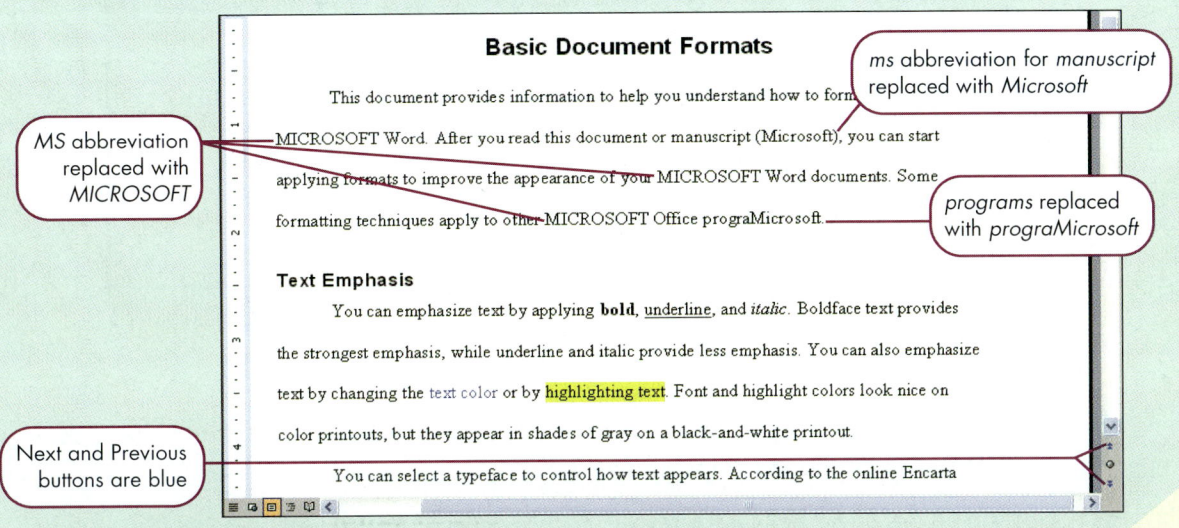

Basic Document Formats

This document provides information to help you understand how to form MICROSOFT Word. After you read this document or manuscript (Microsoft), you can start applying formats to improve the appearance of your MICROSOFT Word documents. Some formatting techniques apply to other MICROSOFT Office programMicrosoft.

Text Emphasis

You can emphasize text by applying **bold**, underline, and *italic*. Boldface text provides the strongest emphasis, while underline and italic provide less emphasis. You can also emphasize text by changing the text color or by highlighting text. Font and highlight colors look nice on color printouts, but they appear in shades of gray on a black-and-white printout.

You can select a typeface to control how text appears. According to the online Encarta

- MS abbreviation replaced with MICROSOFT
- *ms* abbreviation for *manuscript* replaced with *Microsoft*
- *programs* replaced with *programMicrosoft*
- Next and Previous buttons are blue

FIGURE 1.4

By default, Word does not look for *MS* as an individual word or for capitalized occurrences only. Therefore, any occurrence of *MS* or *ms* is found and replaced.

Because you do not want to replace *MS* with *MICROSOFT* in all capital letters, do not want to replace the abbreviation *ms* with *Microsoft*, and do not want the word *programs* changed to *programMicrosoft*, you need to undo the changes and set additional options in the Find and Replace dialog box.

7 **Undo the last action, and choose Edit, Replace.**
The Find and Replace dialog box displays the text you entered into the *Find what* and *Replace with* boxes.

8 **Click More at the bottom of the Find and Replace dialog box.**
The dialog box expands to display more options (see Figure 1.5).

Project 1   Refining Documents

More button changes to *Less* button

Search options

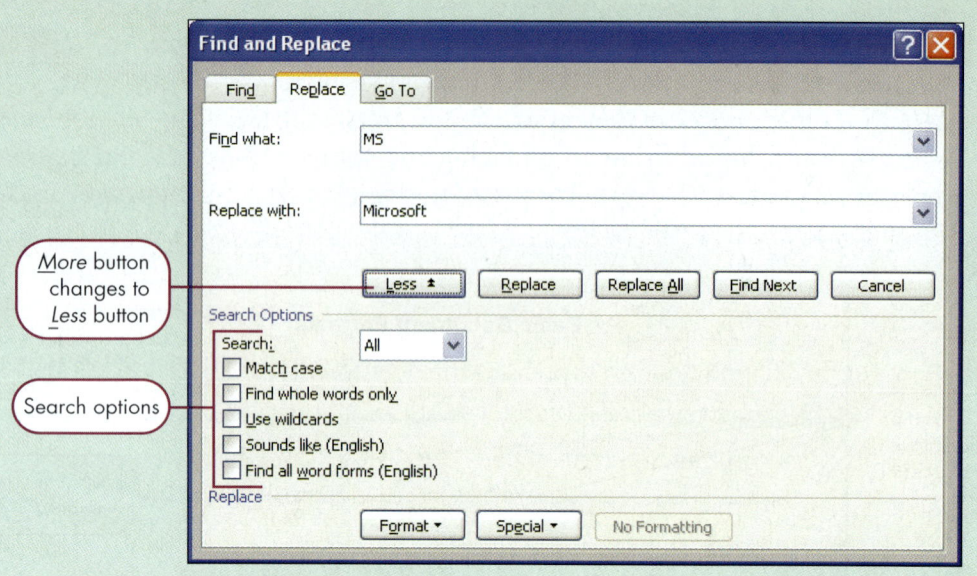

FIGURE 1.5

9 **Click the *Match case* check box.**
Match case restricts the Find and Replace process so that it finds only those occurrences with the same capitalization as *MS*.

10 **Click the *Find whole words only* check box.**
Find whole words only ensures that occurrences of *MS* are found only when they are individual words, not letters within other words—such as *programs*. You see *Options: Match Case, Whole Words* below the *Find what* box.

11 **Click Replace All.**
You see the message *Word has completed its search of the document and has made 3 replacements*.

12 **Click OK, and then close the Find and Replace dialog box.**
This time, Word finds and replaces only capitalized whole-word occurrences of *MS* (see Figure 1.6).

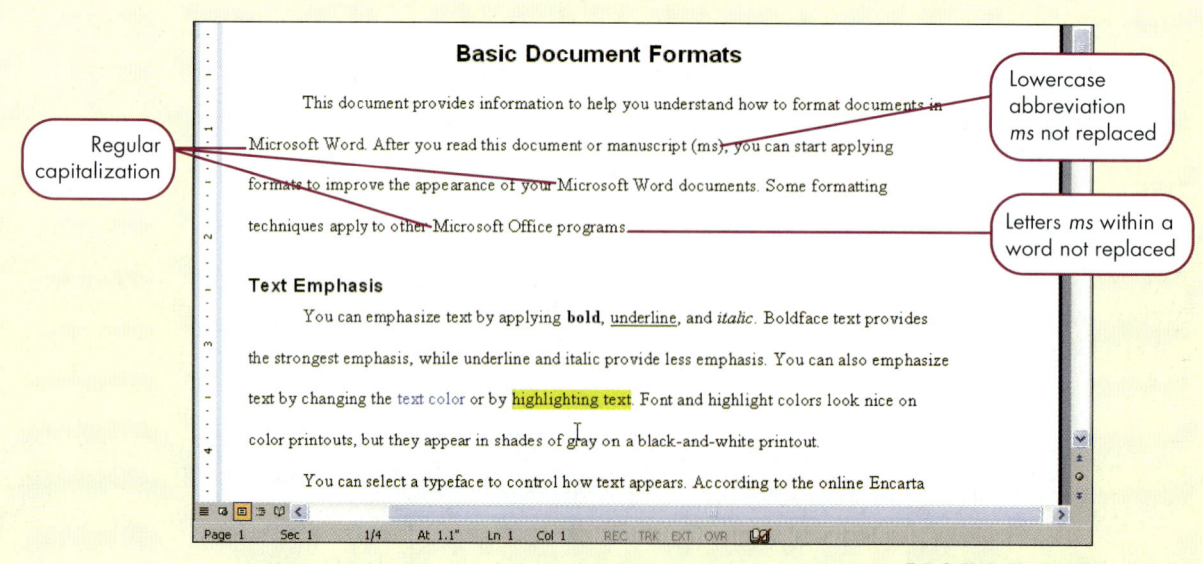

Regular capitalization

Lowercase abbreviation *ms* not replaced

Letters *ms* within a word not replaced

FIGURE 1.6

Lesson 1 Finding and Replacing Text

13. Save the *Word_Formatting* document, and keep it onscreen to continue with the next lesson.

TO EXTEND YOUR KNOWLEDGE . . .

USING KEYBOARD SHORTCUTS
Press Ctrl+F to find text, or press Ctrl+H to find and replace text.

SELECTIVELY FINDING AND REPLACING TEXT
You can select which occurrences to find and replace by clicking Find Next instead of Replace All in the Find and Replace dialog box. When you click Find Next, Word finds the next occurrence of the text you entered. If you want to replace that occurrence, click Replace. If you do not want to replace that text, click Find Next to continue searching.

USING THE PREVIOUS AND NEXT BUTTONS
When you find text, the Previous and Next buttons below the vertical scrollbar are blue (refer to Figure 1.4), indicating that clicking them goes to something besides the previous and next pages. Because you used the Find feature, these buttons now perform the related functions of going to the previous or next find. You can click the Select Browse Object button and choose *Browse by Page* to change the browse function back to page.

SELECTING SEARCH OPTIONS
Table 1.1 describes the options in the *Search Options* area of the Find and Replace dialog box.

TABLE 1.1

OPTION	DESCRIPTION
Search	Specifies the direction in which Word searches through the document. *All*, the default option, searches the entire document. *Up* searches from the insertion point toward the top of the document. *Down* searches from the insertion point to the end of the document.
Match case	When selected, Word searches for only those occurrences that appear with the same casing as the text you entered in the *Find what* box. Otherwise, Word finds all occurrences, regardless of capitalization. For example, Word finds *ms, MS,* and *Ms* if you do not choose this option.
Find whole words only	When selected, Word ignores text that is part of another word. If you want to find *man*, this option ignores words such as *manuscript* and *manipulate*.

TABLE 1.1 (continued)

OPTION	DESCRIPTION
Use wildcards	When selected, Word enables you to find text, even if you are not sure of the spelling, by using operators (such as * for any number of characters or ? for one character) rather than letters. For example, searching for *w?n* finds *win* and *won*. After selecting this option, click *Special* to see a list of search operators.
Sounds like (English)	When selected, Word stops on text that sounds like or is spelled similarly to the Search text.
Find all word forms (English)	When selected, Word finds all forms or tenses of a word. For example, searching for *swim* also finds *swam* and *swimming*.
Format	Displays list of formatting styles from which you choose specific formats to replace.
Special	Displays list of special nontext characters, such as paragraph marks or nonbreaking spaces, that you can search and replace.
No Formatting	Turns off any formatting options that you selected, so you can search for text regardless of formatting.

LESSON 2: Finding and Replacing Formatting

In addition to finding and replacing text, you can find and replace certain types of formatting. For example, you might want to replace Arial text with Century Gothic text. Furthermore, you might want to replace regular spaces with nonbreaking spaces between courtesy titles (such as *Dr.*) and people's last names. Figures 1.7 and 1.8 show you the menus that appear when you click the Format and Special buttons in the Find and Replace dialog box.

Lesson 2 Finding and Replacing Formatting   9   LEVEL 2

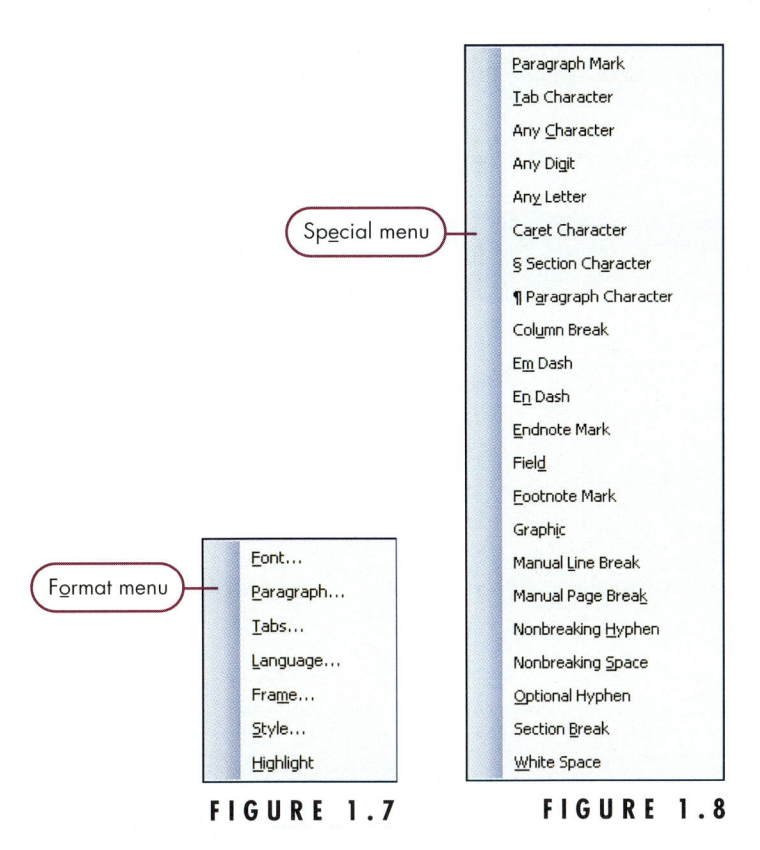

```
                              Paragraph Mark
                              Tab Character
                              Any Character
                              Any Digit
                              Any Letter
         Special menu         Caret Character
                              § Section Character
                              ¶ Paragraph Character
                              Column Break
                              Em Dash
                              En Dash
                              Endnote Mark
                              Field
                              Footnote Mark
                              Graphic
                   Font...    Manual Line Break
   Format menu     Paragraph… Manual Page Break
                   Tabs...    Nonbreaking Hyphen
                   Language…  Nonbreaking Space
                   Frame…     Optional Hyphen
                   Style…     Section Break
                   Highlight  White Space

        FIGURE 1.7            FIGURE 1.8
```

In this lesson, you find Times New Roman, bold, italic formatting and replace it with Arial Narrow, bold, no italic, Blue font color formatting.

To Find and Replace Formatting

1 **In the *Word_Formatting* document, choose Edit, Replace.**
Because you want to find any text with a specific format, you need to delete the contents of the *Find what* and *Replace with* boxes.

2 **Delete the text in the *Find what* and *Replace with* boxes.**
You also need to deselect the current search options to expand the search beyond particular casing and whole words.

3 **Deselect the *Match case* and *Find whole words only* options.**
You are ready to specify the formatting characteristics you want to find and replace.

If you have problems . . .

If you do not deselect the *Match case* and *Find whole words only* options, you might not get the desired results for finding and replacing formats.

4 Click in the *Find what* box, click F**o**rmat at the bottom of the dialog box, and choose **F**ont.

The Find Font dialog box opens (see Figure 1.9).

Select Times New Roman → [Find Font dialog box] ← *Choose Bold Italic*

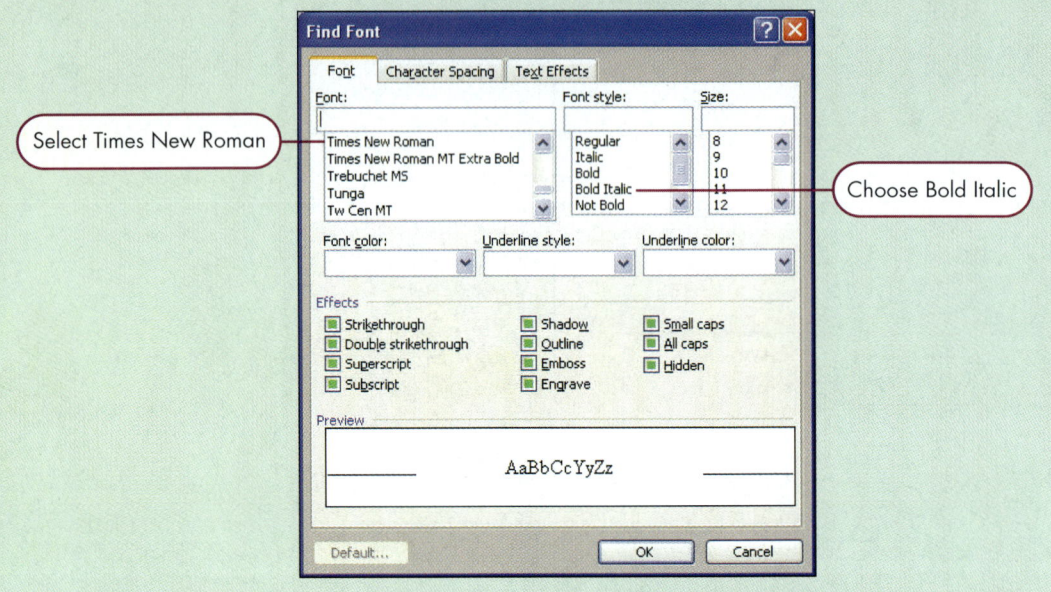

FIGURE 1.9

5 Select Times New Roman in the *Font* list, select Bold Italic in the *Font style* list, and click OK.

If you have problems . . .

If you select Bold or Italic instead of Bold Italic, your results will differ. You want to find the combination of Bold Italic font style.

You see *Format: Font: Times New Roman, Bold, Italic* below the *Find what* box. Now you need to specify the replacement formatting.

6 Click in the *Replace with* box, click F**o**rmat, and choose **F**ont.

The Replace Font dialog box opens with the same options.

7 Scroll through the *Font* list, and choose Arial Narrow.

You selected Arial Narrow font to replace Times New Roman.

8 Scroll down in the *Font style* list and choose Not Italic.

Choosing *Not Italic* ensures that the replacement formatting does not include italic.

Lesson 2   Finding and Replacing Formatting   **11**   LEVEL 2

If you have problems . . .

Do not assume that selecting Bold simply replaces Bold Italic with the Bold only font style. If you choose Bold instead of Not Italic, Word does not remove the italic formatting during the Find and Replace process.

9 **Click the *Font color* drop-down arrow, choose Blue, and click OK.**
Figure 1.10 shows the Find and Replace dialog box with the formatting specifications.

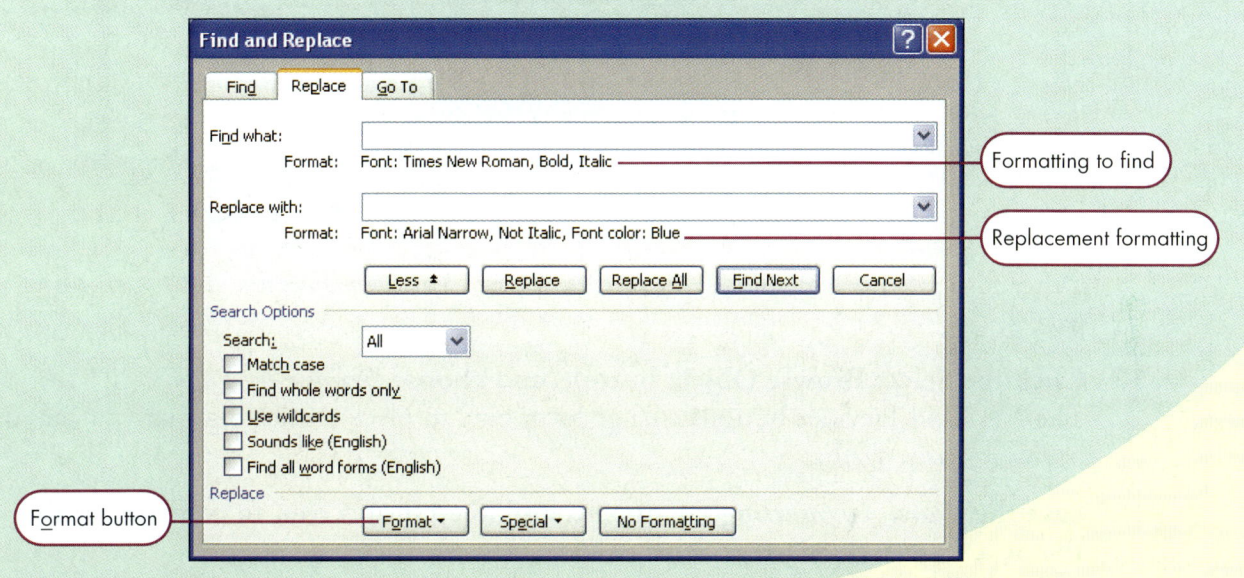

FIGURE 1.10

10 **Click Replace All.**
You see the message *Word has completed its search of the document and has made 6 replacements.*

11 **Click OK, and then close the Find and Replace dialog box.**

12 **Scroll through the document to see some of the replacement formatting.**
The word *Margins* is formatted in Arial Narrow, bold, Blue font color, but not italic at the bottom of the first page. Figure 1.11 shows two replacements on page 2.

Project 1   Refining Documents

Replacement formatting

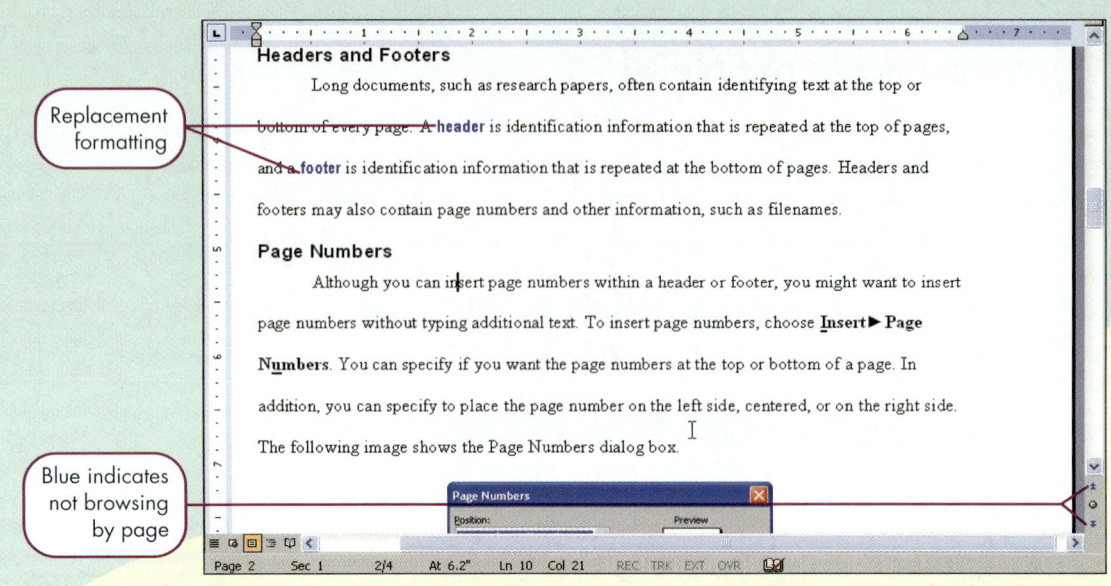

Blue indicates not browsing by page

FIGURE 1.11

Other formatted text includes *Alignment* on page 3 and *Indentation* and *Spacing* on page 4.

13 **Click the Select Browse Object button, and choose *Browse by Page*.**
The Next and Previous buttons change from blue to black, indicating that you can browse by page again.

14 **Save the *Word_Formatting* document, and keep it onscreen to continue with the next lesson.**

TO EXTEND YOUR KNOWLEDGE...

UNDOING REPLACEMENTS
If you do not get the results you expect from using Find and Replace, undo the action. Study the options and formatting selections in the Find and Replace dialog box and try again.

REMOVING FORMATTING OPTIONS
Word maintains the options you set in the Find and Replace dialog box until you exit Word. If you need to find and replace other text, you might need to remove the formatting options you selected previously. To do this, click *No Formatting* at the bottom of the dialog box.

FINDING AND REPLACING PARAGRAPH FORMATS
If you want to find and replace paragraph formats, click Special and choose Paragraph Mark. Word inserts **^p** in the *Find what* box. You can then click Format and choose Paragraph to specify the type of formatting you want to find and replace.

Lesson 3 Sorting Lists, Paragraphs, and Tables   13   LEVEL 2

LESSON 3: Sorting Lists, Paragraphs, and Tables

After you type a tabulated list, paragraphs, or table data, you might decide to rearrange the text. For example, you might want to organize a tabulated list in alphabetical order by name or organize table rows by price with the highest price listed first. **Sorting** is the process of rearranging tabulated text, table data, or paragraphs.

You can sort data in either ascending or descending order. When you sort in **ascending order,** Word arranges the text in alphabetical or sequential order, starting with the lowest letter or number and continuing to the highest letter or number (A–Z or 0–9). When you sort in **descending order,** Word arranges text from the highest letter or number to the lowest letter or number (Z–A or 9–0).

In this lesson, you sort the bulleted list of alignment options in alphabetical order.

To Sort a Bulleted List

1 In the *Word_Formatting* document, select the four paragraphs of the bulleted list at the bottom of page 3.

2 Choose T**a**ble, **S**ort.
The Sort Text dialog box opens so that you can choose how to sort, the type of text to sort, and the sort order (see Figure 1.12).

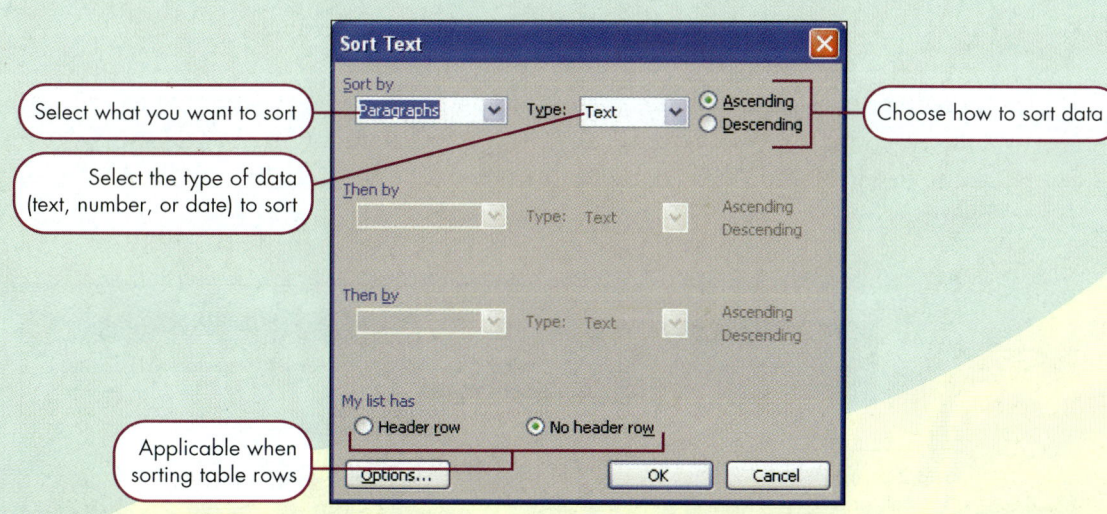

- Select what you want to sort
- Select the type of data (text, number, or date) to sort
- Applicable when sorting table rows
- Choose how to sort data

FIGURE 1.12

3 Click OK, and then deselect the bulleted list.
The bulleted list is sorted in alphabetical order by the first word of each item in the list (see Figure 1.13).

LEVEL 2 14   Project 1   Refining Documents

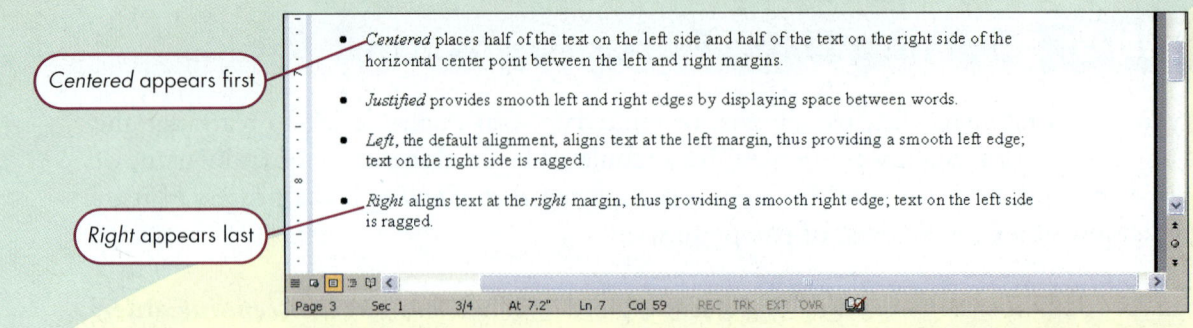

Centered appears first → *Centered* places half of the text on the left side and half of the text on the right side of the horizontal center point between the left and right margins.

• *Justified* provides smooth left and right edges by displaying space between words.

• *Left*, the default alignment, aligns text at the left margin, thus providing a smooth left edge; text on the right side is ragged.

Right appears last → *Right* aligns text at the *right* margin, thus providing a smooth right edge; text on the left side is ragged.

FIGURE 1.13

4 Save the *Word_Formatting* document, and keep it onscreen to continue with the next lesson.

TO EXTEND YOUR KNOWLEDGE . . .

SORTING TABLE ROWS AND TABULATED TEXT

You can also sort table rows and tabulated text. Depending on what type of data you select (table rows or tabulated text), Word provides different *Sort by* options.

When you sort table rows, the *Sort by* option enables you to choose which table column you want to sort by. It lists column number, such as *Column 1* and *Column 2,* or it lists text contained in the first row of the table. If the first row of the table contains column headings, make sure you click the *Header row* option to prevent that row from being sorted with the rest of the data.

If you sort tabulated text, the *Sort by* option enables you to select which tabulated column you want to sort by. *Field 1* is text at the left margin. *Field 2* applies to text at the first tab stop, *Field 3* applies to text at the second tab stop, and so on (see Figure 1.14).

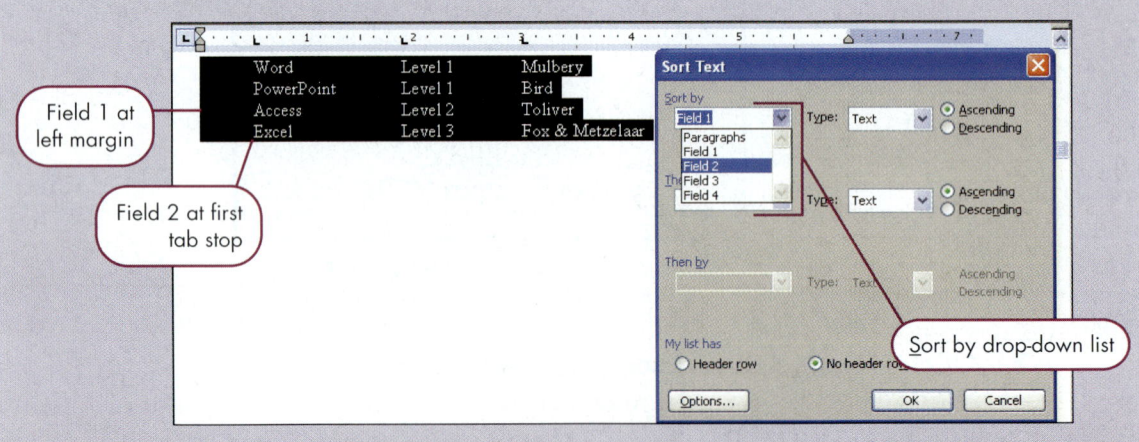

FIGURE 1.14

SETTING THE SORT TYPE

The *Type* option changes, based on the data you select. The different options are *Text, Number,* and *Date.* Refer to Help to learn about the sort order rules for text, numbers, dates, fields, and so on.

PERFORMING A MULTIPLE-LEVEL SORT

You can perform a multiple-level sort by using the *Then by* options. For example, a table contains data listing various companies, the city in which they are headquartered, and the state in which they are headquartered. You can sort the table by state, and then by city, and then by company. Word first sorts the table by state. Within each state, Word further sorts the table by city. Finally, within each city, Word sorts the table by company name.

LESSON 4: Creating Different Headers and Footers for Odd- and Even-Numbered Pages

Published manuals and booklets often have different header text for odd-numbered and even-numbered pages. For example, this textbook uses different headers on the pages. The header on even-numbered pages displays the *Level 2*, the page number, the project number, and the project title. The header on odd-numbered pages displays the topic—such as the lesson number and lesson title—the page number, and the level number. Notice also that the header on even-numbered pages is left-aligned, while the header on odd-numbered pages is right-aligned. This type of alignment helps you see the information as you quickly flip through pages in the book.

In this lesson, you create different footers for odd-numbered and even-numbered pages.

To Create Footers for Odd- and Even-Numbered Pages

1. In the *Word_Formatting* document, position the insertion point at the beginning of the document.

2. Choose **V**iew, **H**eader and Footer.
   The header window and the Header and Footer toolbar appear onscreen.

3. Click *Switch Between Header and Footer* on the Header and Footer toolbar.
   You see the footer window at the bottom of the first page.

4. Click Page Setup on the Header and Footer toolbar, and click the Layout tab, if needed.
   Figure 1.15 shows the header and footer options on the Layout tab of the Page Setup dialog box.

Page Setup dialog box callouts

- Click to set different headers and footers for odd- and even-numbered pages
- Enables user to set a header/footer on the first page within a section that is different from the header/footer for the rest of the section
- Controls the amount of space from the edge of the paper to the header and footer

FIGURE 1.15

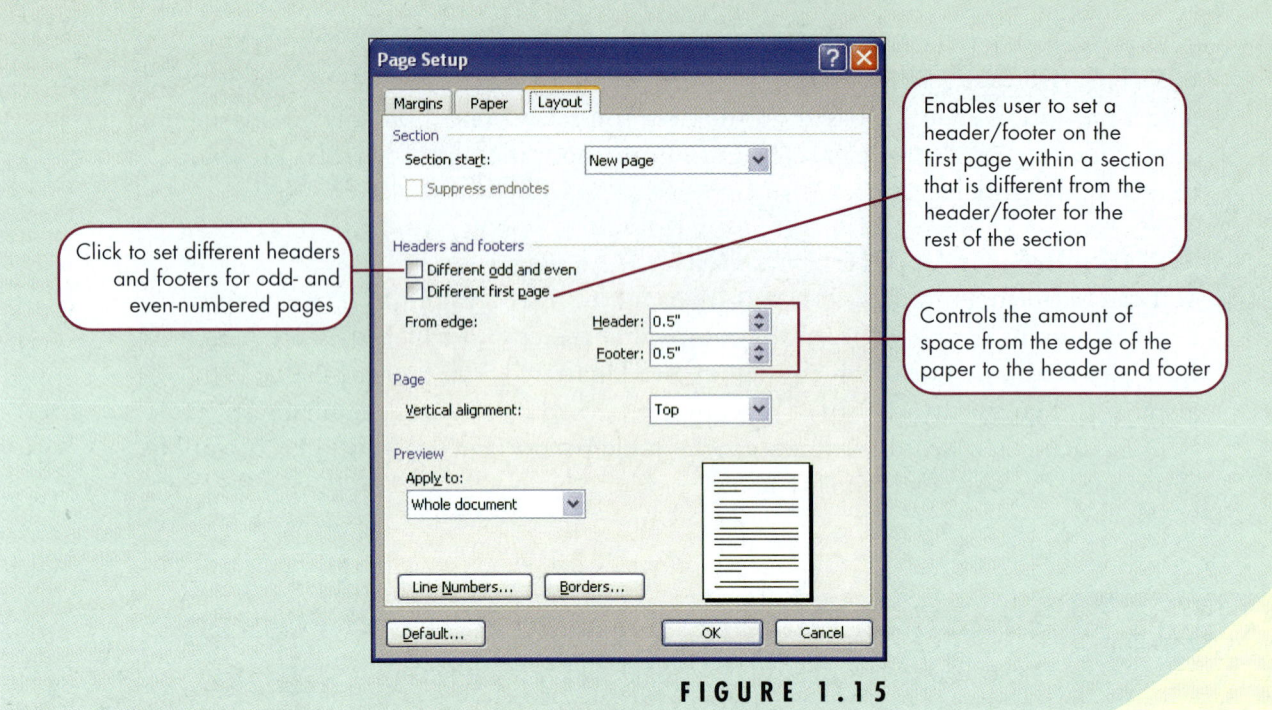

5 Click the *Different odd and even* check box, and then click OK.
Odd Page Footer appears above the footer window, indicating the footer content you enter will appear on odd-numbered pages only.

6 Type `Basic Document Formats`, press Tab twice, and click Insert Page Number on the Header and Footer toolbar.
The text appears on the left side of the footer, and the page number appears on the right side of the footer, so that the page number will be in the outside corner of the duplex-printed document.

7 Click Show Next on the Header and Footer toolbar.
Even Page Footer appears above the footer window, indicating the footer content you enter will appear on even-numbered pages only.

8 Click Insert Page Number on the Header and Footer toolbar, press Tab twice, and type `Microsoft Word 2003`.
The text appears on the right side of the footer, and the page number appears on the left side of the footer so that the page number will be in the outside corner of the duplex-printed document.

9 Click Close on the Header and Footer toolbar.
You see the different footers in the next lesson.

10 Save the *Word_Formatting* document and keep it onscreen to continue with the next lesson.

Lesson 5   Splitting the Document Window and Arranging Panes   17   **LEVEL 2**

TO EXTEND YOUR KNOWLEDGE . . .

CREATING SECTIONAL HEADERS AND FOOTERS
If you insert section breaks in a document, you can create different headers and footers for each section. The header and footer windows display information (such as *Footer –Section 2–*) so that you know what section contains the footer or header you create.

In addition, when a document is divided into sections, you typically see *Same as Previous* above the header or footer window when you click Show Next to display the header or footer window for the next section. By default, Word continues the previous header or footer for the next section unless you click Link to Previous to use different headers or footers in different sections.

CREATING A DIFFERENT HEADER OR FOOTER ON THE FIRST PAGE
To create a different header or footer for the first page, click Page Setup on the Header and Footer toolbar before you start typing the header or footer text. Click the *Different first page* check box, and then click OK. Word displays the appropriate note (*First Page Header* or *First Page Footer*) above the header or footer window. The text you type appears on the first page only. To create a header or footer for the remaining pages of the section, click Show Next.

LESSON 5: Splitting the Document Window and Arranging Panes

Sometimes you need to view two areas of the same document or two different documents simultaneously. The Window menu enables you to arrange document windows onscreen.

A **split document window** displays two different areas of a document at the same time so that you can scroll separately within each window pane. Splitting the document window is helpful when you need to see one part of the document while you work on another part of the document. **Arranged windows** display two or more document windows onscreen at the same time. This arrangement is helpful when you need to review the contents of one document while you compose or edit contents of another document.

In this lesson, you split the *Word_Formatting* document window to see the footers on an odd-numbered page and an even-numbered page at the same time, and then you open another document and arrange windows onscreen.

Project 1   Refining Documents

To Split the Document Window and Arrange Windows

1 In the *Word_Formatting* document, position the insertion point on the first page.

2 Choose <u>W</u>indow, <u>S</u>plit.
You see a horizontal line in the middle of the screen. The mouse pointer appears as a two-headed arrow on the horizontal line (see Figure 1.16).

Horizontal line to split window

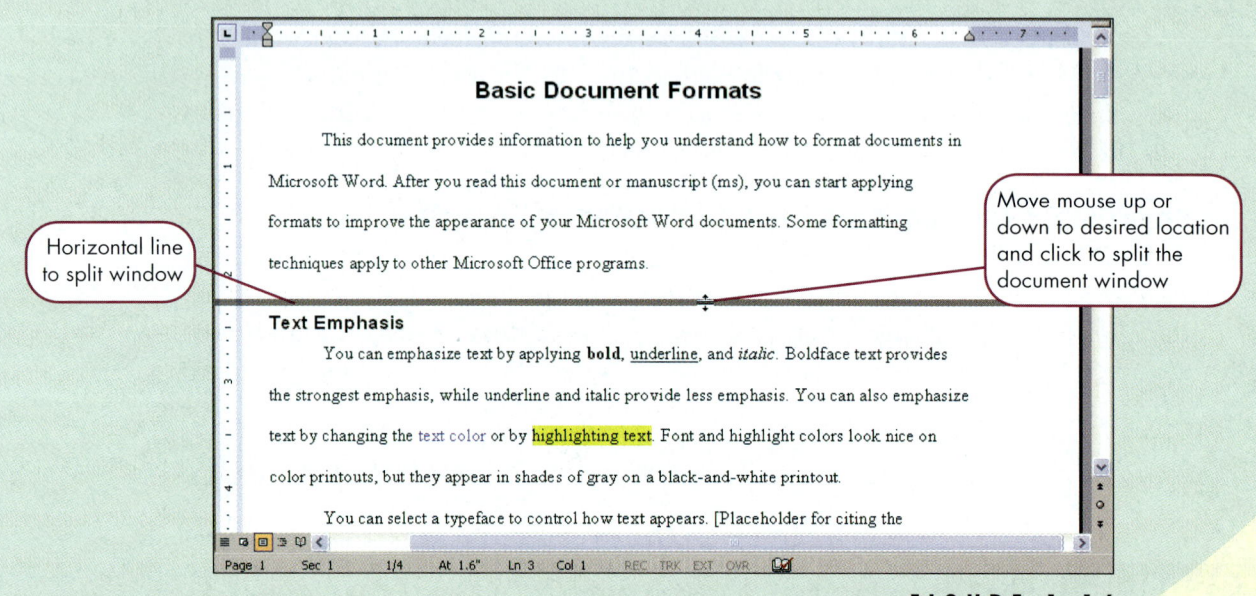

Move mouse up or down to desired location and click to split the document window

FIGURE 1.16

3 Click the horizontal line.
Clicking the horizontal line anchors it to a particular location onscreen. A horizontal scrollbar and ruler bar appear for each window pane. You see different parts of the document in each window.

4 Scroll down in the top window pane until you see the footer on page 1 of your document.

5 Scroll down in the bottom window pane until you see the footer on page 2 of your document.
You can see the different footers you created. Figure 1.17 shows the split window panes: *Basic Document Formats* on page 1 (an odd-numbered page) and *Microsoft Word 2003* on page 2 (an even-numbered page).

Lesson 5   Splitting the Document Window and Arranging Panes

Footer text on odd-numbered page

Page number on right side of odd-numbered page

Page number on left side of even-numbered page

Footer text on even-numbered page

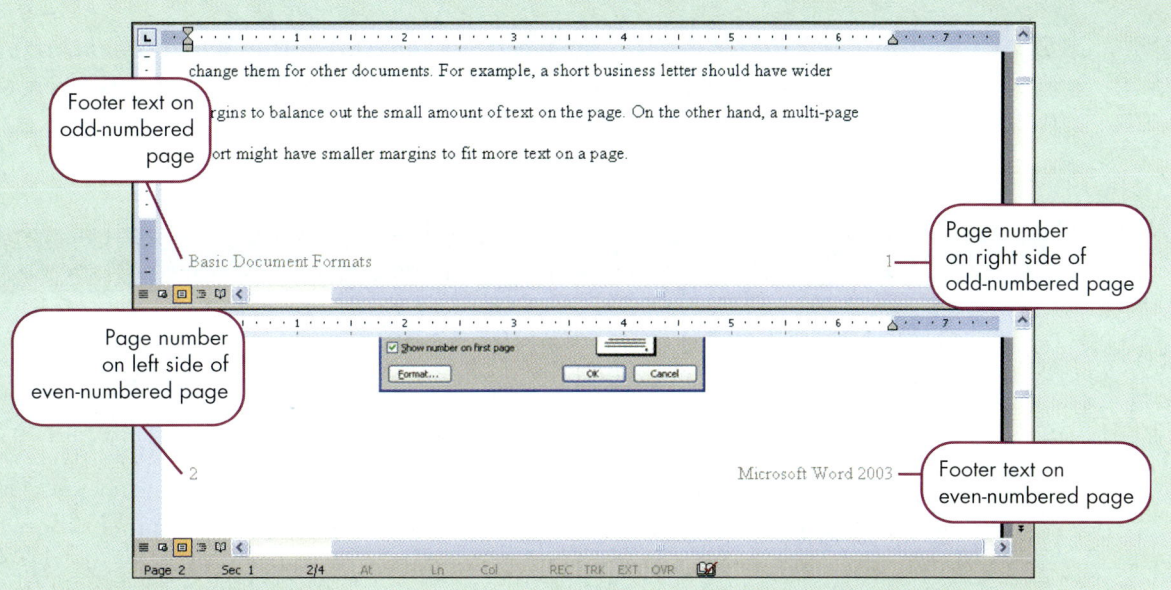

FIGURE 1.17

6 **Choose Window, Remove Split, and then position the insertion point at the top of the document.**

Word displays one document window for the document again.

7 **Open *EW2_0102*, and display it in Normal view.**

EW2_0102 is in the active document window.

8 **Choose Window, Arrange All.**

Word displays the *EW2_0102* document in the top half of the screen and the *Word_Formatting* document in the bottom half of the screen. Each document window has its own title bar, toolbars, and menu bar (see Figure 1.18).

EW2_0102 document window

Word_Formatting document window

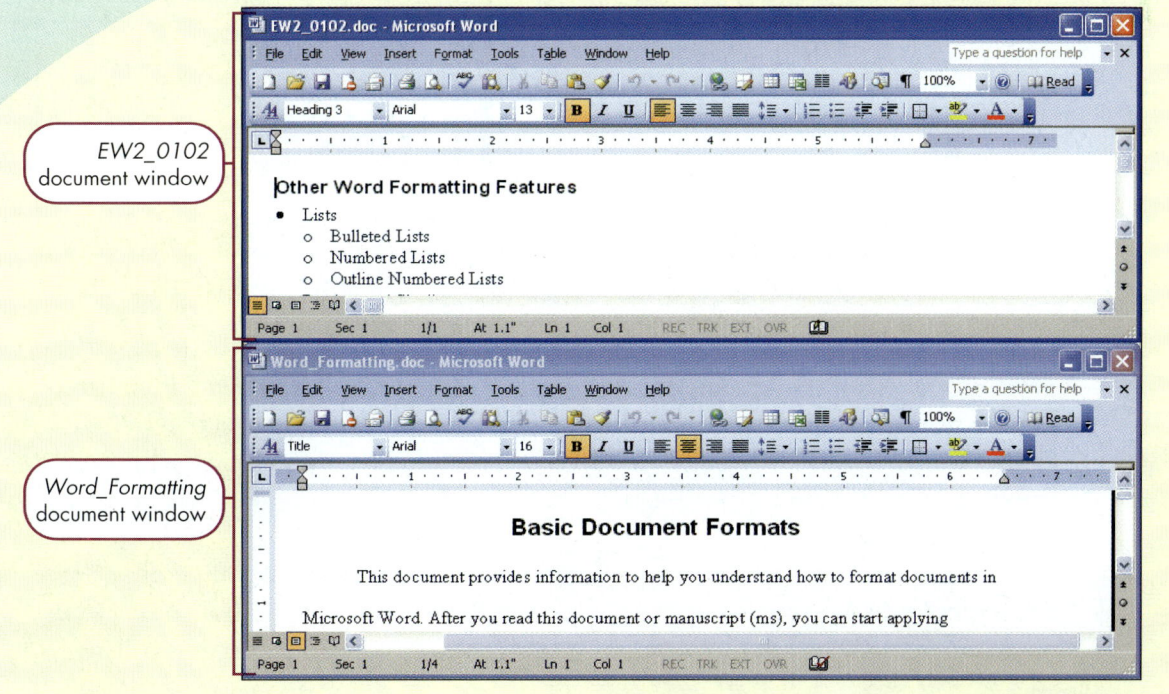

FIGURE 1.18

Project 1 Refining Documents

9 Close the *EW2_0102* document window, maximize the *Word_Formatting* document window, and keep the *Word_Formatting* document onscreen to continue with the next lesson.

TO EXTEND YOUR KNOWLEDGE...

COMPARING TWO WINDOWS SIDE BY SIDE

If you have three or more open document windows, arranging windows may not be the best option to view documents because each open Word document is displayed onscreen. If you want to compare only two open documents, choose Window, Compare Side *by* Side with. When you have three or more open documents, the Compare Side by Side dialog box opens so that you can choose which open document to display with the currently active document window. Figure 1.19 shows an example of two documents compared side by side.

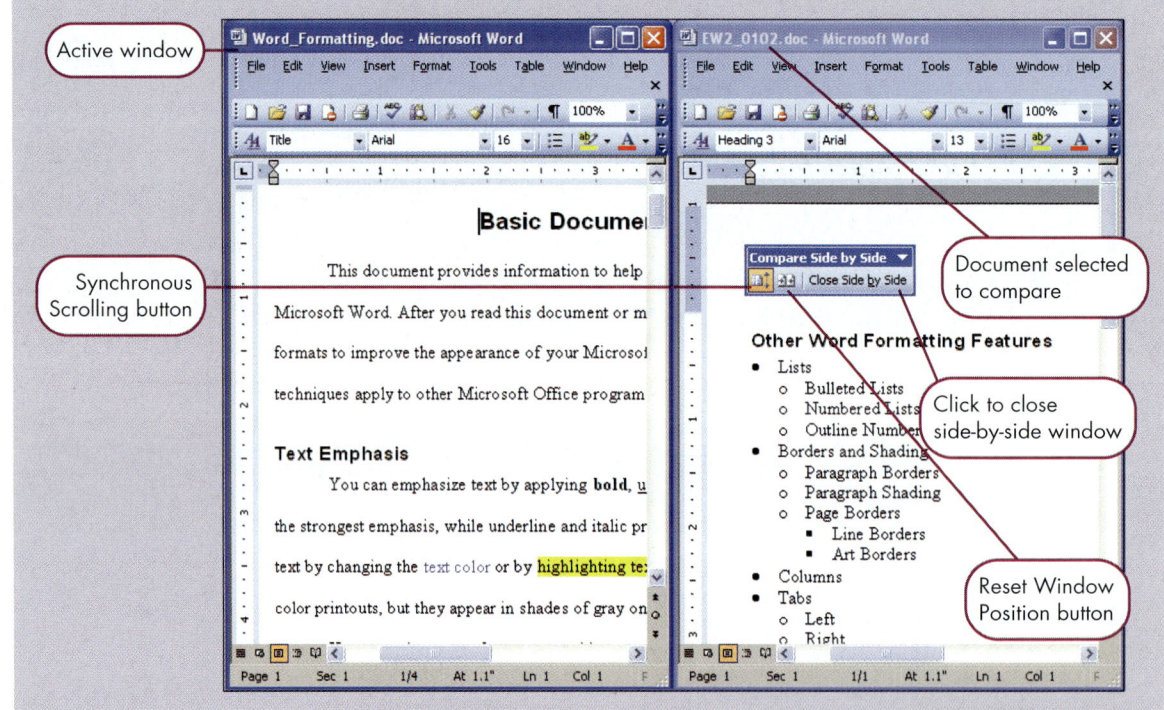

FIGURE 1.19

You can scroll through both documents at the same time by clicking the Synchronous Scrolling button on the Compare Side by Side toolbar. The button appears with an orange background when synchronous scrolling is active (refer to Figure 1.19). To scroll through documents individually, click the Synchronous Scrolling button again to deselect it.

You can display document windows back to their previous size before comparing documents side by side. To do this, click the Reset Window Position button on the Compare Side by Side toolbar.

LESSON 6: Using the Research Tool to Locate Information

The ***Research tool*** enables you to conduct research investigations to find information. You can use it to look up definitions of words, identify synonyms, read encyclopedia articles, and find language translation services. In addition, you can find information through an MSN Search, identify fee-based research sites, and look up business and financial information, such as an organization's revenue. When you insert research findings into your documents, be sure to include the proper citations.

In this lesson, you use the Research tool to look up the definition of *typeface* in an online dictionary and then insert the definition into your document.

To Use the Research Tool to Locate and Insert a Definition

1. Make sure you have a live Internet connection.

2. In the *Word_Formatting* document, select and delete the placeholder *[Placeholder for citing the definition of typeface from an online dictionary. Include the citation info and quotation marks.]* located on the first page of the document in the middle of the second paragraph in the *Text Emphasis* section.
   This is where you want to insert the definition.

3. With the insertion point where you deleted the placeholder, click Research on the Standard toolbar.
   The Research task pane opens on the right side of the screen (see Figure 1.20). By default, Word displays the text to the right of the insertion point to suggest the word you may want to use in the search.

Project 1 Refining Documents

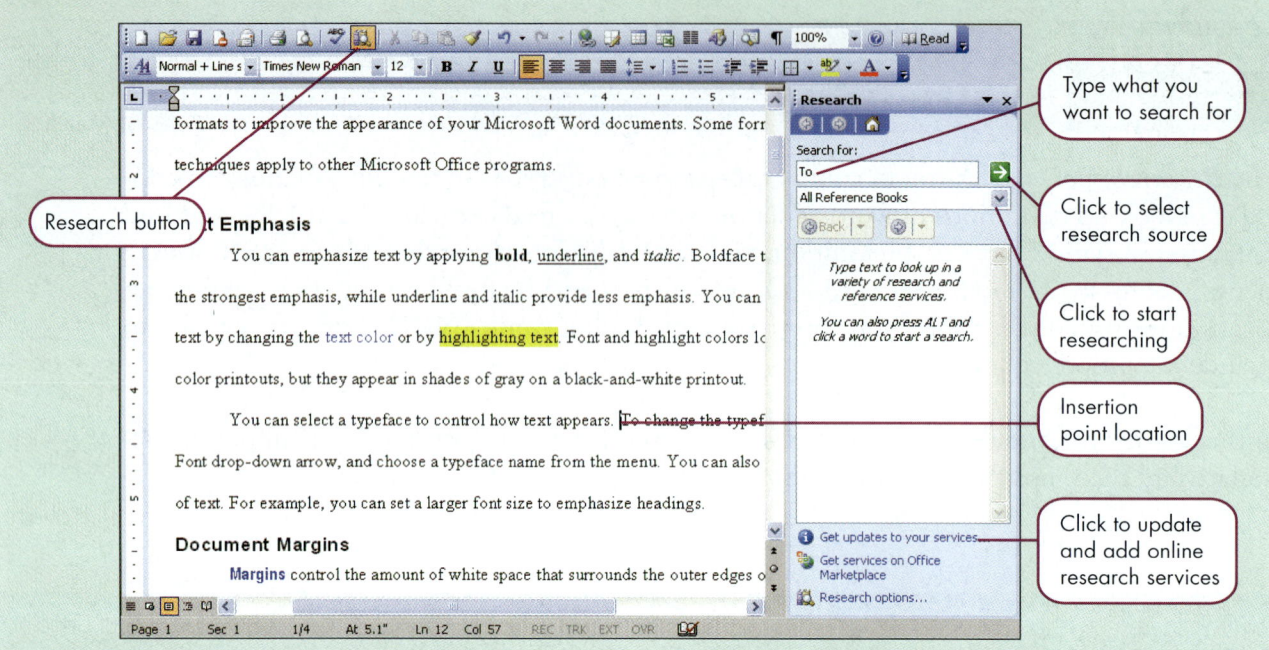

FIGURE 1.20

Callouts on the figure:
- Research button
- Type what you want to search for
- Click to select research source
- Click to start researching
- Insertion point location
- Click to update and add online research services

4 Click in the *Search for* box, delete existing text, and type `typeface`.

5 Click the All Reference Books drop-down arrow.
Word displays a list of research sources to choose from (see Figure 1.21). The default, *All Reference Books,* performs an extensive search through all sources. Your list may vary based on how Office 2003 was installed on your computer and based on previous use of the Reference tool.

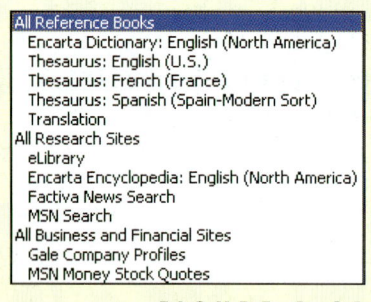

Drop-down list contents:
- All Reference Books
-   Encarta Dictionary: English (North America)
-   Thesaurus: English (U.S.)
-   Thesaurus: French (France)
-   Thesaurus: Spanish (Spain-Modern Sort)
-   Translation
- All Research Sites
-   eLibrary
-   Encarta Encyclopedia: English (North America)
-   Factiva News Search
-   MSN Search
- All Business and Financial Sites
-   Gale Company Profiles
-   MSN Money Stock Quotes

FIGURE 1.21

6 Choose *Encarta Dictionary: English (North America)* or a respective dictionary for your continent.
After you choose a research source, Word automatically starts the search process and displays results that match the keyword you typed (see Figure 1.22).

Lesson 6 Using the Research Tool to Locate Information   23   LEVEL 2

Callouts on figure: Keyword typed • Research source selected • Research results • Scroll down to see more options

FIGURE 1.22

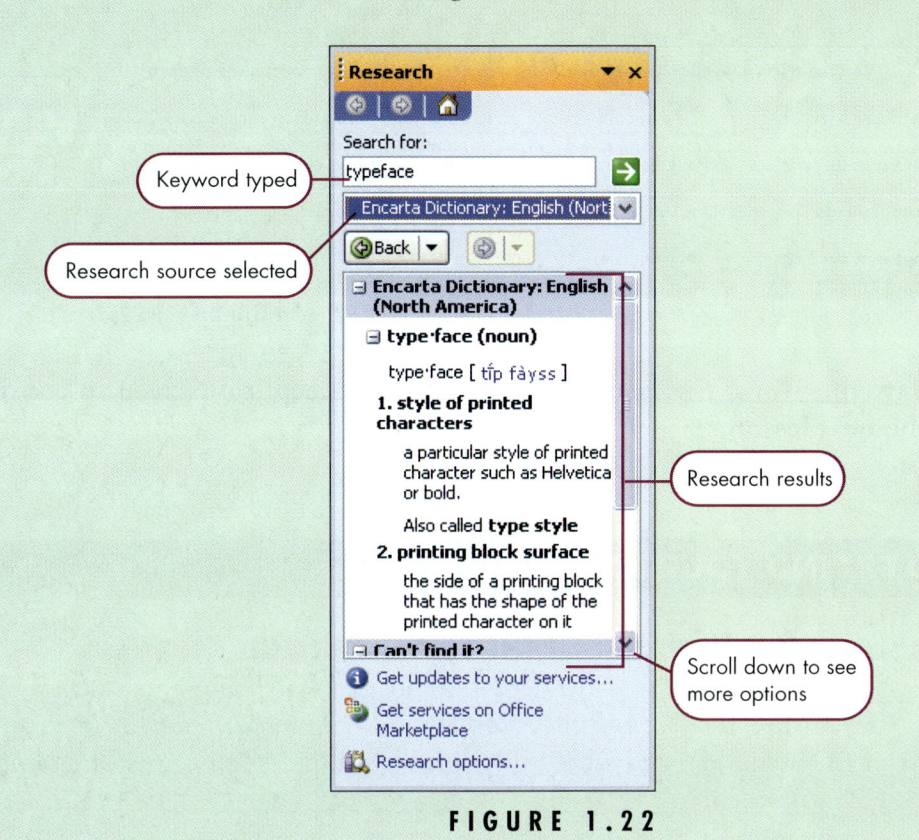

If you have problems . . .

If you do not have a live Internet connection, your results are not as comprehensive. If you do not see the definitions shown in Figure 1.22, connect to the Internet and start this exercise again.

7 Click and drag to select the phrase *a particular style of printed character such as Helvetica or bold.* within the first definition, and then press Ctrl+C.
You copied the selected definition to the Clipboard. Notice that the Copy button is not available to copy from the Research task pane.

8 Click to the left of *To change the typeface* in the document window, and then click Paste on the Standard toolbar.
The definition is pasted at the insertion point location. Now you need to provide a short citation for the definition, enclose the exact definition in quotation marks, and ensure that a space separates the sentences.

9 Close the Research task pane, and edit the sentence as shown in Figure 1.23.

Project 1   Refining Documents

> You can select a typeface to control how text appears. According to the online Encarta Dictionary, *typeface* refers to "a particular style of printed character such as Helvetica or bold."
>
> To change the typeface, click the Font drop-down arrow, and choose a typeface name from the menu. You can also control the size of text. For example, you can set a larger font size to emphasize headings.

— Type citation wording and quotation marks

FIGURE 1.23

10 Save the *Word_Formatting* document, and keep it onscreen to continue with the next lesson.

TO EXTEND YOUR KNOWLEDGE...

LEARNING MORE ABOUT THE RESEARCH TOOL
The Research tool provides access to valuable search engines. To learn more about this feature, type **Research tool** in the *Type a question for help* box to the right of the menu bar, and search through Help topics. You can even complete online Help tutorials.

LESSON 7: Creating and Modifying a Document Summary

Sometimes, people want to record information about a document but do not want to include the information directly in the document window. For example, you might want to record some notes to yourself about a document, such as the document's purpose or intended audience. At other times, you might want to include keywords to help locate a file, similar to the way you typed keywords in the Research task pane to find definitions and other information. To help maintain documents, you can create a ***document summary*** that provides descriptive information about a document, such as a title, subject, author, keywords, and comments.

When you create a document summary and save the document, Word saves the document summary with the document. You can modify the document summary at any time by opening the Properties dialog box for the respective document.

In this lesson, you create a document summary from within Microsoft Word and then you modify the document summary from the Open dialog box.

Lesson 7 Creating and Modifying a Document Summary 25 LEVEL 2

To Create and Modify a Document Summary

1 **In the *Word_Formatting* document, choose File, Properties.**
The *Word_Formatting.doc Properties* dialog box opens (see Figure 1.24). By default Word uses the first line of the document to suggest the title property, and it displays the name of the author as stored in the Options dialog box (accessible through Tools, Options).

Type your name here, if needed

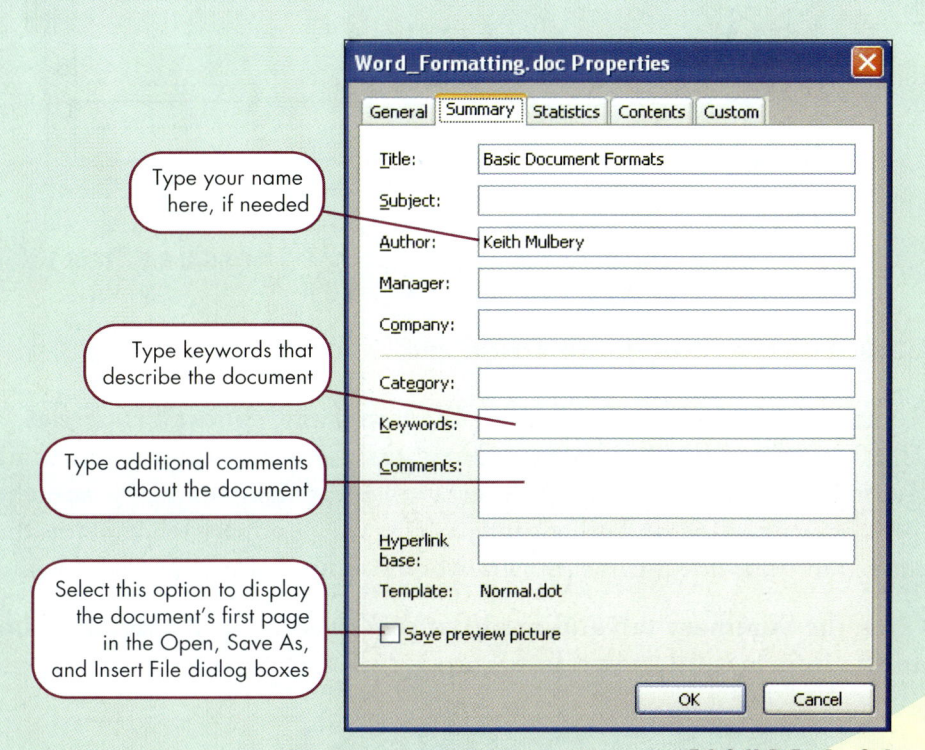

Type keywords that describe the document

Type additional comments about the document

Select this option to display the document's first page in the Open, Save As, and Insert File dialog boxes

FIGURE 1.24

2 **Type your name in the *Author* box, if it does not already display your name.**

3 **Type `Microsoft Word` in the *Category* box, and type `formatting, paragraph formats` in the *Keywords* box.**
The content of the *Keywords* box is helpful when you perform an advanced search within the Open dialog box to find a particular document.

4 **Click the *Save preview picture* check box, and click OK.**
Selecting the *Save preview picture* check box enables you to view the first page of the document in the Open dialog box.

5 **Save the *Word_Formatting* document, and close it.**
Now, let's see how the document summary is useful in the Open dialog box.

6 **Display the Open dialog box, select the *Word_Formatting* filename, click the Views drop-down arrow on the dialog box toolbar, and choose Preview.**
The right side of the dialog box displays a preview of the first page of the document because you selected *Save preview picture* in the Properties dialog box (see Figure 1.25).

Project 1 Refining Documents

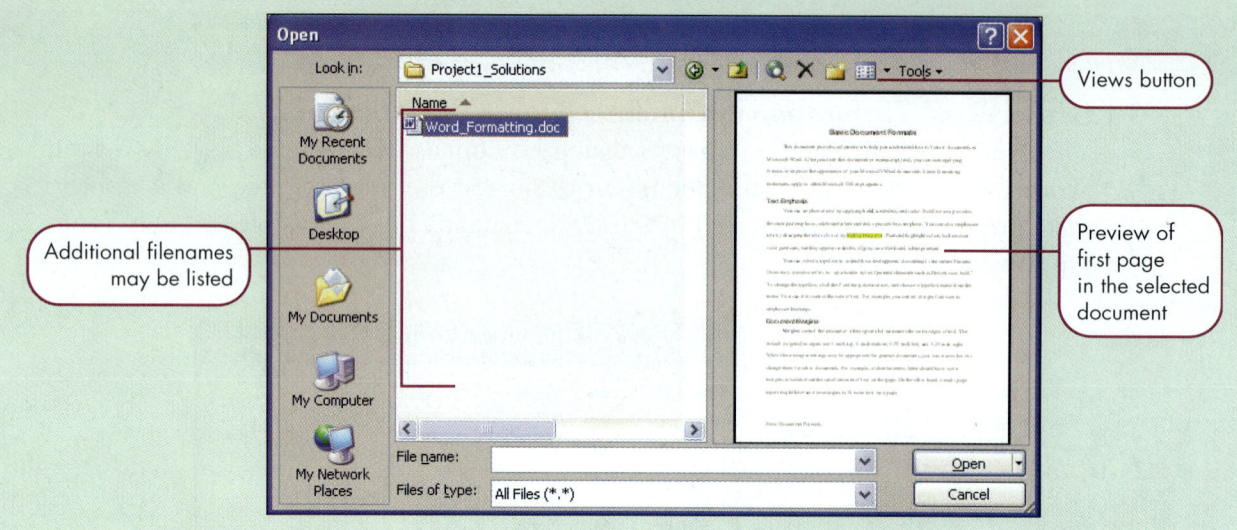

FIGURE 1.25

Callouts: Views button; Preview of first page in the selected document; Additional filenames may be listed

7 Click the Views drop-down arrow, and choose <u>D</u>etails.

8 Right-click the *Word_Formatting* filename, and choose Properties.
The Properties dialog box contains three tabs: General, Custom, and Summary. The General tab contains data about the creation and revision dates, file size, the program used to open the file, and other general data. The Summary tab contains the data you entered into the document summary when you first created the document summary.

9 Click the Summary tab and modify the *Keywords* and *Comments* boxes based on the information shown in Figure 1.26.

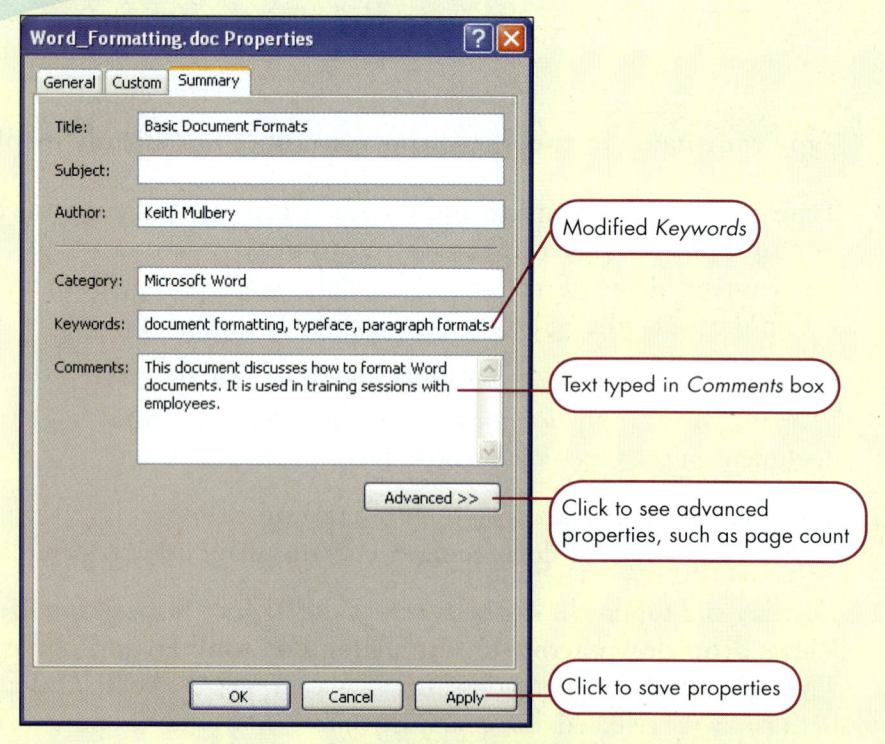

Word_Formatting.doc Properties — Summary tab:
- Title: Basic Document Formats
- Subject:
- Author: Keith Mulbery
- Category: Microsoft Word
- Keywords: document formatting, typeface, paragraph formats
- Comments: This document discusses how to format Word documents. It is used in training sessions with employees.

Callouts: Modified *Keywords*; Text typed in *Comments* box; Click to see advanced properties, such as page count; Click to save properties

FIGURE 1.26

10 Click Apply, click OK, and then open the *Word_Formatting* document.

11 Choose **F**ile, Proper**t**ies.
The *Word_Formatting.doc Properties* dialog box contains the modifications you made from within the Open dialog box.

12 Close the *Word_Formatting.doc Properties* dialog box, and then close the document.

TO EXTEND YOUR KNOWLEDGE . . .

CREATING AND MODIFYING DOCUMENT PROPERTIES
You can create and modify document summaries directly from the Open dialog box, through Windows Explorer, or in the Windows file management windows. You do not have to create the document summary with the document open within Microsoft Word.

CHANGING THE DEFAULT AUTHOR NAME FOR DOCUMENT PROPERTIES
You can change the default user information that appears in places such as the document summary. To do this, choose **T**ools, **O**ptions, click the User Information tab, type your name in the *Name* box, and click OK.

PRINTING DOCUMENT PROPERTIES
You can print document properties to have hard copies to store in a filing cabinet for easy reference. To do this, display the Print dialog box, click the *Print what* drop-down arrow, choose *Document properties*, and click OK.

SEARCHING FOR FILES BY KEYWORDS
Use Help to learn how to perform an advanced search by keywords within the Open dialog box.

SUMMARY

In this project, you used the Find and Replace feature to locate specific text and formats and replace these occurrences with other text and specific formats, such as a different font and font color. You also rearranged a bulleted list by sorting the list in alphabetical order. So that page numbers will be on the outside corners of a duplex-printed document, you created different footers for odd-numbered and even-numbered pages and then split the document window to see both types of footers at the same time. Furthermore, you learned how to use the Research tool to locate information, such as definitions or other topical information, and then insert or paraphrase that information to support the content of your own document. Finally, you created a document summary that provides details about a document, such as the author's name, keywords, and comments.

Project 1   Refining Documents

You can extend your learning by reviewing concepts and terms, and by practicing variations of skills presented in the lessons. Use the following table as a guide to the numbered questions and exercises in the end-of-project learning opportunities.

LESSON	MULTIPLE CHOICE	DISCUSSION	SKILL DRILL	CHALLENGE	DISCOVERY ZONE
Finding and Replacing Text	1	1	1	1, 2, 3	
Finding and Replacing Formatting	2, 3		1, 2	1, 2, 3, 4	1
Sorting Lists, Paragraphs, and Tables	5, 6		3	1, 2, 3, 4	1, 2
Creating Different Headers and Footers for Odd- and Even-Numbered Pages	7		4	1, 2, 4	1
Splitting the Document Window and Arranging Panes	4, 10		4	2	1, 3
Using the Research Tool to Locate Information	8	2	6	1, 3, 4	2, 3
Creating and Modifying a Document Summary	9	3	5	2, 3, 4	

KEY TERMS

arranged windows   document summary   sorting
ascending order   Research tool   split document window
descending order

CHECKING CONCEPTS AND TERMS

MULTIPLE CHOICE

Circle the letter of the correct answer for each of the following.

1. What search option prevents *CTC* from finding *ctc* or *Ctc*? [L1]
   a. Match case
   b. Find whole words only
   c. Use wildcards
   d. Special

2. Assume you want to replace a regular space with a nonbreaking space. Which button do you click within the Find and Replace dialog box to be able to choose the Nonbreaking Space option? [L2]
   a. Use wildcards
   b. Format
   c. Special
   d. No Formatting

3. What notation appears below the *Find what* box if you select options to find text formatted with Arial font face, Italic font style, and 12-point size? [L2]
   a. Format: Font: Arial, 12 pt, Italic
   b. Format: Arial, Italic, 12 pt
   c. Format: Font, Font Style, Size
   d. Arial font, 12 pt size, Italic style

4. To see two different parts of the same document so that you can easily read the text in one part while composing or editing text in the other, you should _____. [L5]
   a. split the document window
   b. open the document twice so that it appears in two document windows
   c. display the document into a multiple-pane print preview window
   d. select the option that arranges window panes onscreen

5. Which of the following is an example of text sorted in descending order? [L3]
   a. apple, apricot
   b. 0, 1
   c. apricot, 10
   d. apricot, apple

6. When you sort text columns separated by tab settings, where is Field 2 located? [L3]
   a. At the left margin
   b. At the first column of tabulated text
   c. At the second column of tabulated text
   d. On the second horizontal row within the tabulated text

7. Which of the following would you most likely expect to see in a bound document or book that has different headers on odd-numbered and even-numbered pages? [L4]
   a. Page numbers on the right side of even-numbered pages
   b. Text positioned to the left of page numbers on even-numbered pages
   c. Page numbers centered on odd-numbered pages
   d. Page numbers on the right side on odd-numbered pages

8. You can use the Research tool to help you do which of the following? [L6]
   a. Find definitions of words
   b. Find and insert stock prices
   c. Find information on particular topics
   d. All of the above

9. What tab in a document Properties dialog box do you use to enter descriptive information about the document, such as the document's author, keywords, and comments? [L7]
   a. General
   b. Summary
   c. Statistics
   d. Contents

10. Which option from the Window menu do you choose to display two or more document windows onscreen at the same time? [L5]
    a. New Window
    b. Compare Side by Side with
    c. Arrange All
    d. Split

DISCUSSION

1. Why should you use caution when clicking Replace All within the Find and Replace dialog box? [L1]
2. When and for what purposes might you use the Research tool in Word? [L6]
3. What are the benefits of typing keywords into a document summary? [L7]

SKILL DRILL

Skill Drill exercises reinforce project skills. Each skill reinforced is the same, or nearly the same, as a skill presented in the project. Detailed instructions are provided in a step-by-step format.

Work through exercise 1 first and then work exercises 2–5 in any order. Exercise 6 is independent of the other exercises, so you can do it at any time. Be sure to save your changes and close the document if you need more than one work session to complete the desired exercises. Continue working on *Training_Proposal* instead of starting over in the original *EW2_0103* file. After you complete all of the exercises, print a copy of the document (optional). Figure 1.27 is a split document window in Full Screen view to show you the odd-numbered page footer, sorted tabulated text, sorted paragraphs, and text and formatting replacements after you complete the first four exercises.

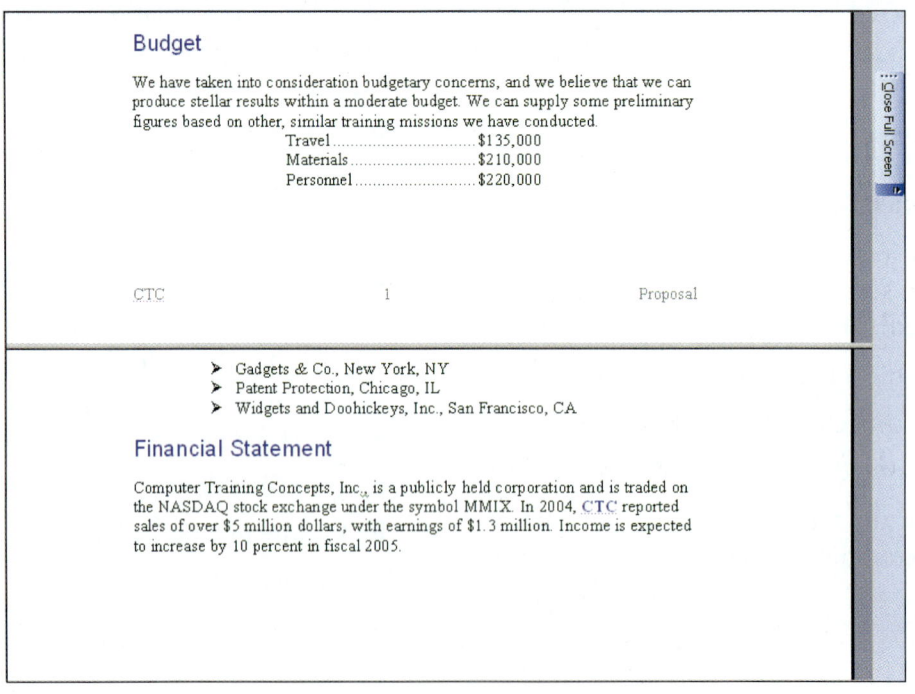

FIGURE 1.27

1. Finding and Replacing Text and Formats

You work for Computer Training Concepts, Inc., a company that provides training to small and large businesses. After creating a proposal for a potential new client, you decide to find and replace some occurrences of *Computer Training Concepts* with *CTC* in Indigo font color and bold font style.

1. Open *EW2_0103* and save it as **Training_Proposal**.
2. Choose Edit, Replace.
3. Type **Computer Training Concepts** in the *Find what* box.
4. Press Tab and type **CTC** in the *Replace with* box.
5. Click More at the bottom of the dialog box, if needed, to display additional options.
6. Click No Formatting, if necessary, to clear the formats for the *Find what* and *Replace with* formatting criteria.
7. Make sure the insertion point is inside the *Replace with* box.
8. Click Format at the bottom of the dialog box, and choose Font.
    a. Click the *Font color* drop-down arrow, and choose *Indigo,* the second color from the right on the first row of the color palette. Watch the ScreenTip to identify the color before choosing Indigo.
    b. Click *Bold* in the *Font style* list.
    c. Click OK.
9. Selectively find and replace text by completing the following steps:
    a. Click Find Next to start searching for text.
    b. Click Find Next to skip the main title and keep searching.
    c. Click Find Next to skip the first occurrence of *Computer Training Concepts* at the beginning of the first paragraph.
    d. Click Replace to replace the second occurrence in the first paragraph.
    e. Click Replace to replace the next occurrence.
    f. Click Find Next to skip the next occurrence.
    g. Click Replace to replace the next occurrence.
    h. Click Find Next to skip the next occurrence.
    i. Click Replace to replace the next occurrence.
    j. Click Find Next to display the next occurrence, which is in the footer.
    k. Click Find Next, and then click OK when Word informs you that it has searched the document.
10. Close the Find and Replace dialog box.
11. Save the *Training_Proposal* document.

2. Finding and Replacing Formats

As you review the *Training_Proposal* document, you want to increase the font size of some headings, and you also want to increase the paragraph spacing before and after these headings. To do this efficiently, you decide to use the Find and Replace feature to find text formatted in 14-point size and replace it with text in 16-point size, with 12-point spacing before and after paragraphs.

1. In the *Training_Proposal* document, choose Edit, Replace.
2. Delete the text in the *Find what* box.
3. Click Format and do the following:
   a. Choose Font.
   b. Click *14* in the *Size* box, and click OK.
4. Delete the text in the *Replace with* box.
5. Click No Formatting to remove the previous replacement formatting.
6. Click Format and do the following:
   a. Choose Font.
   b. Click *16* in the *Size* box.
   c. Click the *Font color* drop-down arrow, choose *Indigo,* and click OK.
7. Click Format and do the following:
   a. Choose Paragraph.
   b. Click in the *Before* box and type **12 pt**.
   c. Click in the *After* box and type **12 pt**; click OK.
8. Click Replace All, and then click OK when Word informs you that it made seven replacements.
9. Close the Find and Replace dialog box.
10. Save the *Training_Proposal* document.

3. Sorting Tabulated Data and Bulleted List Data

You decide to rearrange the tabulated list in ascending order by cost. In addition, you want to rearrange the items in the bulleted list so that the text is alphabetized.

1. In the *Training_Proposal* document, select the three lines of tabulated text within the *Budget* section at the bottom of the first page. The first line of tabulated text is *Materials*.

   Notice that no text is at the left margin (Field 1), budget categories appear at the first tab stop (Field 2), and the costs appear at the second tab stop (Field 3).

2. Choose Table, Sort and do the following:
   a. Click the *Sort by* drop-down arrow, and choose *Field 3* to sort by the tabulated column that contains the costs.
   b. If needed, click the *Type* drop-down arrow, and choose *Number*.
   c. If needed, click the *Ascending* option.
   d. Click OK and then deselect the text.

3. Select the three lines of bulleted text in the *Background Information* section on the second page.

4. Choose T<u>a</u>ble, <u>S</u>ort and do the following:

   a. Click the <u>Sort by</u> drop-down arrow, and choose *Paragraphs*.
   b. Make sure the *Type* option displays *Text*.
   c. Make sure the <u>Ascending</u> option is selected.
   d. Click OK, and then deselect the bulleted list.

5. Save the *Training_Proposal* document.

4. Creating Odd-Numbered and Even-Numbered Footers and Splitting the Document Window

Although the proposal contains a footer, you want to modify it to have one footer on the first page and a different footer on the second page.

1. In the *Training_Proposal* document, position the insertion point on the first page.
2. Choose <u>V</u>iew, <u>H</u>eader and Footer, and switch to the footer window.
3. Click Page Setup and click the Layout tab, if needed.
4. Click the *Different <u>o</u>dd and even* check box, and then click OK.
5. Do the following in the *Odd Page Footer* window:

   a. Delete existing footer text.
   b. Type **CTC**, press `Tab`, click Insert Page Number, press `Tab`, and type **Proposal**.
   c. Click and drag the 6" right tab marker to 5.5" on the ruler.

6. Click Show Next to display the *Even Page Footer* window and then do the following:

   a. Make sure the original footer appears in the *Even Page Footer* window. If not, type **Computer Training Concepts, Inc.**, press `Tab` twice, type **Page -,** and click Insert Page Number.
   b. Click and drag the 6" right tab marker to 5.5" on the ruler.

7. Close the footer window.
8. Type **split window** in the *Type a question for help* box, press `Enter`, click the *View two parts of a document simultaneously* link, and read the information about a different method for splitting windows than you learned in Lesson 5.
9. Print (optional) the Help topic, close the Help window, and close the Search Results task pane.
10. Use the Split Window method discussed in the Help topic to split the document window in the middle of the screen.
11. Click in the top window, and scroll down to see the footer at the bottom of page 1.
12. Click in the bottom window, and scroll down to see the footer at the bottom of page 2.
13. Double-click the split window horizontal line to remove the split document window.
14. Save the *Training_Proposal* document.

5. Creating a Document Summary

Because you have an extensive number of documents on your computer, you want to create a document summary for the *Training_Proposal* document, with general information and keywords.

1. In the *Training_Proposal* document, choose File, Properties, and click the Summary tab, if needed.
2. Type **Training Proposal** in the *Title* box.
3. Type your name in the *Author* box.
4. Type **CTC** in the *Company* box.
5. Type **budget, proposal, company, CTC** in the *Keywords* box.
6. Click OK to close the dialog box.
7. Save the *Training_Proposal* document.

6. Using Help and the Research Tool

You want to learn more about the Research tool and how you can use it to locate information. In this exercise, you use Help to read through an online tutorial about the Research tool and complete hands-on activities to explore the capabilities of the Research tool.

1. Make sure you have a live Internet connection.
2. Type **Research tool** in the *Type a question for help* box, and press ⏎Enter.
3. In the Search Results task pane, click *See what you can do with the Research service*.
   The Microsoft Office Online Training Web site opens to a tutorial on the Research service.
4. Read the overview, goals, course content, and information on the first page.
5. Click Next to continue with the training.
6. Download the practice document from the *How to research* pane on the left side of the screen, and print the list of exercise tasks.
7. Complete the exercises.
8. Return to the online training and complete the rest of the training.
9. Be prepared to discuss your knowledge of the Research service with your classmates.

CHALLENGE

Challenge exercises expand on or are somewhat related to skills presented in the lessons. Each exercise provides a brief narrative introduction, followed by instructions in a numbered-step format that are not as detailed as those in the Skill Drill exercises. You can work through one or more exercises in any order.

1. Editing and Completing an Internet Report

You need to make some adjustments to an Internet report you prepared for clients. You want to replace some text and formats, create footers, sort tabulated text, and use the Research tool to find information to include in the report.

1. Open *EW2_0104,* and save it as **Internet_Information**.
2. Find **Internet Protocol** and replace all occurrences, except the first three occurrences, with **IP**. (Clear formatting options, if needed.)
3. Find the lowercase word **inform** and replace it with **notify**.
4. Find headings formatted with Green font color, solid underline, and center horizontal alignment. Replace with these formats: Arial, bold font style, Blue font color, left horizontal alignment, 12-point spacing before, and 12-point spacing after the paragraph.
5. Delete the red sentence on page 1 and use the Research tool to do the following:
   a. Find a definition of **IP Address** in the encyclopedia.
   b. Copy and paste the definition to your document window where the red sentence was located.
   c. Type **According to the online Encarta Encyclopedia, an IP address is** before the pasted definition, and then type quotation marks around the quoted definition.
   d. Format the sentence in Blue font color.
   e. Close the Research task pane.
6. Select the tabulated list on page 2 and do the following:
   a. Sort the tabulated text by domain name in alphabetical order.
   b. Clear the existing Find and Replace settings. Find occurrences of bold font style and replace them with these formats: Arial, bold font style, 10-point size, and Blue font color.
   c. Apply a Blue paragraph border and Pale Blue paragraph shading.
7. Apply Blue font color to the main title.
8. Create a footer on odd-numbered pages that displays your name at the left side, the page number field in the center, and the filename field at the right side.
9. Create a footer on even-numbered pages that displays **Using the Internet** on the left side, the page number field in the center, and the date field on the right side.
10. Save, print (optional), and close the *Internet_Information* document.

2. Modifying an Annual Report

As the executive assistant to the president of Seatek-Parkway Enterprises, you are responsible for preparing and distributing the corporate annual report to employees and stockholders. The annual report is almost ready. You need to find and replace text and formatting, sort tabulated text, and create a footer to complete the document.

Project 1   Refining Documents

1. Open *EW2_0105,* and save it as **2004_Annual_Report**.
2. Find all occurrences of the word **SP** and replace them with **Seatek-Parkway**. Choose the *Match case* option to ensure that the replacements do not appear in all capital letters.
3. Find occurrences of **costs** and replace them with **expenditures**. Deselect all other options in the Find and Replace dialog box.
4. Find occurrences of **company** and replace them with **organization** using these specifications:
    a. Do not replace capitalized occurrences, when used as *the Company.*
    b. Find and replace all word forms so that **companies** is replaced with **organizations**. Choose the appropriate replacement—*organization* or *organizations*—as needed. Use Find Next to skip occurrences you should not replace.
    c. Find the phrase **a organization** and replace it with **an organization**.
5. Find all occurrences and word forms of **decrease** and replace them with word forms of **reduce**. Edit the word where necessary by changing it to **reduction**.
6. Find single spacing with justified paragraph formatting and replace it with single spacing and left-aligned paragraph formatting. Deselect other options and do not search for any text.
7. In the *Acquisition of Parkway Industries* section, sort the tabulated list in descending order by number of employees.
8. Create an odd-numbered page footer with the text **Seatek-Parkway Enterprises**, a space, and a page number field on the right side of the footer window.
9. Create an even-numbered page footer with the page number field, a space, and **Annual Report 2004** on the left side of the footer window.
10. Edit the footer windows by applying Arial Narrow font and a top paragraph border line.
11. Split the document window and scroll through the windows to see an odd-numbered page footer in one window and an even-numbered page footer in the other window. Then remove the split document window.
12. Modify the existing document summary by changing the author's name to your name and by typing **annual report** in the Keyword text box.
13. Save, print (optional), and close the *2004_Annual_Report* document.

3. Completing a Headache Informational Document

As a secretary for a physician, you have been asked to prepare an information sheet about headaches. You started the document yesterday, and now you need to conduct some online research to complete the descriptions. In addition, you want to find italicized headings and replace them with the built-in Heading 1 style, use the Research tool to activate a thesaurus to change some wording, and then create a document summary.

1. Open *EW2_0106* and save it as **Headache_Types**.
2. Position the mouse pointer within each of the respective highlighted words (listed below), and use the Research tool to identify and insert an appropriate replacement from the online thesaurus. Apply the Bright Green highlight to the replacements you insert. After replacing the words, edit surrounding text, if necessary, to make sure the sentences make sense.
   a. unsuccessful
   b. continuous
   c. incapacitate
3. Find occurrences of headings formatted in italic and replace the formatting with the Heading 3 built-in style, no italic, and Blue font color.
4. Find the word **dollars** with a preceding space, and delete all occurrences.
5. Use the Research tool to find information about headaches. Limit the research to MSN searches. Read information and replace the placeholders indicated by text highlighted in square brackets. Copy and paste the URLs to the end of the document in the *Sources* section. Correctly format the sources you insert (hanging indent and construction). Sort the sources in alphabetical order.
6. Format the URLs into bibliographic entries.
7. Create a document summary with your name as the author, **Dr. Nelson** as the manager, and **City Clinic** as the company. Insert at least five appropriate keywords. Print (optional) the document properties.
8. Save, print (optional), and close the *Headache_Types* document.

4. Researching and Sorting Computer Terminology

You work as a sales associate in the computer department of a local electronics store. A lot of customers want to purchase a computer but have little or no computer literacy. You decide to prepare a sheet of definitions that you can give to customers shopping for a computer, so they can improve their computer literacy.

1. Open *EW2_0107*, and save it as **Computer_Terminology**.
2. Use the Research tool to look up **computer terminology** definitions through MSN. Use the links to find definitions.
3. Type definitions and explanations for each computer term in the document. Paraphrase the information you read about online.
4. Find bold formatting and replace it with Arial font, bold font style, Blue font color.
5. Sort the terminology in alphabetical order.
6. Apply hanging indents to the definitions and 12-point spacing after paragraphs.
7. Create an odd-numbered page footer that contains your name on the left side and the date on the right side.
8. Create an even-numbered page footer that contains a statement about where you obtained the information.

9. Create a document summary with an appropriate title, your name as the author, and comments about the purpose of the document.

10. Save, print (optional), and close the *Computer_Terminology* document.

DISCOVERY ZONE

Discovery Zone exercises require advanced knowledge of topics presented in the lessons or self-directed learning of new skills. You can work through one or more exercises in any order.

1. Customizing Headers for a Design Guidelines Document

You created a document that discusses design guidelines, and now you want to modify it. Open *EW2_0108* and save it as `Design_Information`. Open *EW2_0109*. Display the two open documents in side-by-side document windows. (Refer to the To Extend Your Knowledge section at the end of Lesson 5 to do this.) Compare the content of the first page of Section 2 in the *Design_Information* document to the first page in the *EW2_0109* document. Copy any extra information in the *EW2_0109* document and paste it into the appropriate location in the *Design_Information* document, and then close *EW2_0109*.

Use Help to learn about built-in styles, such as Heading 1. Use Find and Replace to find occurrences of Heading 3 style and replace them with Heading 2 style.

Sort each of the respective bulleted lists in the *Font Faces* section in alphabetical order.

Create headers for Section 1 based on these characteristics:

- Empty header for the first page of Section 1 (Hint: Study the header options in the Page Setup dialog box to decide how to create an empty header for the first page.)
- `Desktop Publishing Design Guidelines`, the round bullet symbol, and the page number field for the remaining odd-numbered pages
- The page number field, the round bullet symbol, and `Introduction` for even-numbered pages
- Header text alignment similar to the header alignments for odd-numbered and even-numbered pages in this textbook

Create headers for Section 2 based on these characteristics:

- Same header for odd-numbered pages as in Section 1
- Similar header for even-numbered pages except use the text `Selecting Font Characteristics`
- Header displayed on the first page of this section
- Same alignment that you used in Section 1

Create headers for Section 3 based on these characteristics:

- Same header for odd-numbered pages as in Sections 1 and 2
- Similar header for even-numbered pages, except use the text `Setting the Spacing`
- Same alignment that you used in Sections 1 and 2

View the headers page by page to ensure that you met all requirements. Save; display the Print dialog box, select the *2 pages* option for *Pages per sheet,* and print (optional). Then close the *Design_Information* document.

2. Researching Company Stocks

You are interested in investing money in the stock market. Open *EW2_0110* and save it as `Stock_Information`.

Below the first *Sorted by* heading, create a table to store stock data for 10 publicly traded companies of your choice, one row per company. Include enough columns to list the company names, tickers, current price, change in price, and two other columns of data, such as previous closing prices. Type the company names in the first column. Use the Research tool to identify the official company names and their tickers. Edit company names as needed and type the tickers in the second column.

Use the Research tool to look up current stock information based on the tickers. Type the information in the respective cells in your table. After entering the data, delete the asterisk placeholders and type appropriate reference information at the top of the document in the space provided. Modify the table by inserting column headings, formatting the table appropriately, setting decimal tabs to format monetary values, and making other table adjustments.

Copy and paste the table below the other bolded headings. Sort each respective table as indicated by the headings. Use Help as needed to learn how to create a multiple-level sort. Make sure that the column headings on the first row are not sorted with the rest of the data.

Save, print (optional), and close the *Stock_Information* document.

3. Using the Research Tool to Translate Languages

Your company has a division in Germany, and you want to translate the annual report from English to German. Use Help to learn how to use the translation option through the Research tool. Open *EW2_0105,* and make sure you have a live Internet connection to process the translation.

Select the entire content and use the Research tool to convert the entire document text from English to German. When the Web browser window displays the translated document, copy and paste the document text into a new Word document, and save the document as `Report_EnglishtoGerman`.

Now select the entire content of *Report_EnglishtoGerman* and use the Research tool to convert German to English. When the Web browser window displays the translated document, copy and paste the document text into a new Word document, and save the document as `Report_GermantoEnglish`.

Use Help to learn how to display two different document windows side by side, and then display *EW2_0105* and *Report_GermantoEnglish.* Compare the two English versions to identify differences when the document is converted back to English.

Save, print (optional), and close the *Report_GermantoEnglish* document. Print (optional) and close the *Report_EnglishtoGerman* document. Close *EW2_0105* without saving it, and close all Web browser windows.

PROJECT 2
LEVEL 2

CREATING AND FORMATTING COLUMNS

OBJECTIVES

IN THIS PROJECT, YOU LEARN HOW TO

- Set the page orientation
- Format text into columns
- Revise column structure
- Insert section breaks, column breaks, and files
- Balance column length
- Create drop caps
- Hyphenate text

Project 2   Creating and Formatting Columns

WHY WOULD I DO THIS?

Many organizations prepare periodic newsletters for their employees, customers, or members. Because newsletters contain several short articles, the text is easier to read when you format the page with two or more columns, rather than one wide column that spans all the way across from the left to the right margin. *Columns* format a section of a document into side-by-side vertical blocks in which the text flows down the first column and then continues at the top of the next column. The length of a line of columnar text is shorter, enabling people to read through each article faster.

You can format a newsletter in either portrait or landscape orientation, insert section breaks to format sections differently, and insert the contents of an entire file into the current document. After formatting text into columns, you can change the number of columns and insert column breaks to control the text that appears at the top of a column. In addition, you can enlarge and format the first letter of a paragraph to enhance the visual effectiveness, and you can hyphenate words to smooth out the right margin.

VISUAL SUMMARY

As an owner of a condominium in the Mountain Grove Condominiums complex, you prepare the quarterly newsletter. The newsletter contains articles that provide relevant information for the condominium owners. In this project, you format a document into columns and then insert column and section breaks in desired locations. Then, you insert the contents of another file—the newsletter name—at the top of the document. Figure 2.1 shows the first page of the completed newsletter, complete with a drop cap character and hyphenated text.

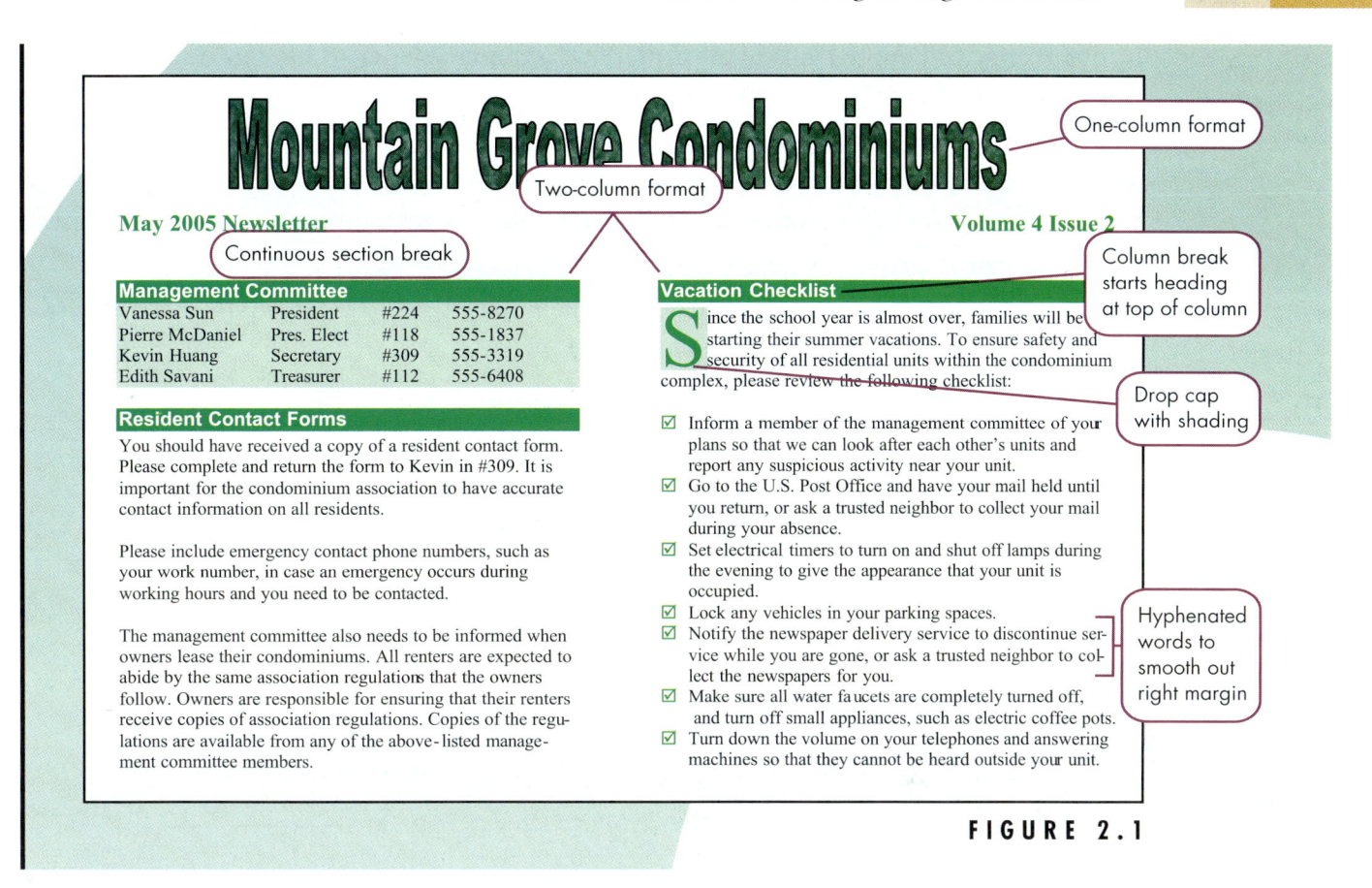

Mountain Grove Condominiums

One-column format
Two-column format

May 2005 Newsletter *Continuous section break* **Volume 4 Issue 2**

Column break starts heading at top of column

Management Committee
Vanessa Sun	President	#224	555-8270
Pierre McDaniel	Pres. Elect	#118	555-1837
Kevin Huang	Secretary	#309	555-3319
Edith Savani	Treasurer	#112	555-6408

Resident Contact Forms

You should have received a copy of a resident contact form. Please complete and return the form to Kevin in #309. It is important for the condominium association to have accurate contact information on all residents.

Please include emergency contact phone numbers, such as your work number, in case an emergency occurs during working hours and you need to be contacted.

The management committee also needs to be informed when owners lease their condominiums. All renters are expected to abide by the same association regulations that the owners follow. Owners are responsible for ensuring that their renters receive copies of association regulations. Copies of the regulations are available from any of the above-listed management committee members.

Vacation Checklist

Since the school year is almost over, families will be starting their summer vacations. To ensure safety and security of all residential units within the condominium complex, please review the following checklist:

Drop cap with shading

- ☑ Inform a member of the management committee of your plans so that we can look after each other's units and report any suspicious activity near your unit.
- ☑ Go to the U.S. Post Office and have your mail held until you return, or ask a trusted neighbor to collect your mail during your absence.
- ☑ Set electrical timers to turn on and shut off lamps during the evening to give the appearance that your unit is occupied.
- ☑ Lock any vehicles in your parking spaces.
- ☑ Notify the newspaper delivery service to discontinue service while you are gone, or ask a trusted neighbor to collect the newspapers for you.
- ☑ Make sure all water faucets are completely turned off, and turn off small appliances, such as electric coffee pots.
- ☑ Turn down the volume on your telephones and answering machines so that they cannot be heard outside your unit.

Hyphenated words to smooth out right margin

FIGURE 2.1

LESSON 1: Setting the Page Orientation

Page orientation refers to the way printed text appears on a sheet of paper. You can choose between portrait and landscape. ***Portrait orientation*** produces a printed page taller than it is wide, so named because it is similar to a regular large-framed portrait. ***Landscape orientation*** produces a printed page wider than it is tall, as in a wide picture of the landscape. Figure 2.2 illustrates portrait and landscape orientations.

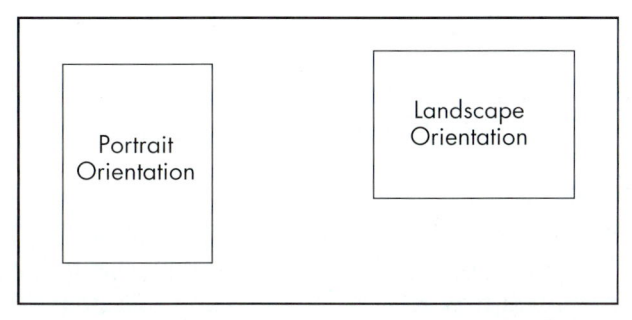

FIGURE 2.2

Typically, most correspondence and business reports are formatted in portrait orientation. Newsletters, brochures, and advertisements, however, are often formatted in landscape orientation. You can set the page orientation before or after formatting text into columns; however, choosing the page orientation first can prevent columnar formatting problems.

44   Project 2   Creating and Formatting Columns

In this lesson, you apply landscape orientation to the newsletter to have a wider amount of space from the left to the right margin.

To Select Landscape Orientation

1 **Open *EW2_0201* and save it as `May_Newsletter`.**
This document contains the basic text for the newsletter. In Lesson 4, you insert the name of the newsletter at the top of the document.

2 **Choose File, Page Setup, and click the Margins tab, if needed.**
The default page orientation is Portrait (see Figure 2.3).

Current page orientation — *Produces a printed page wider than it is tall* — *Preview of page orientation*

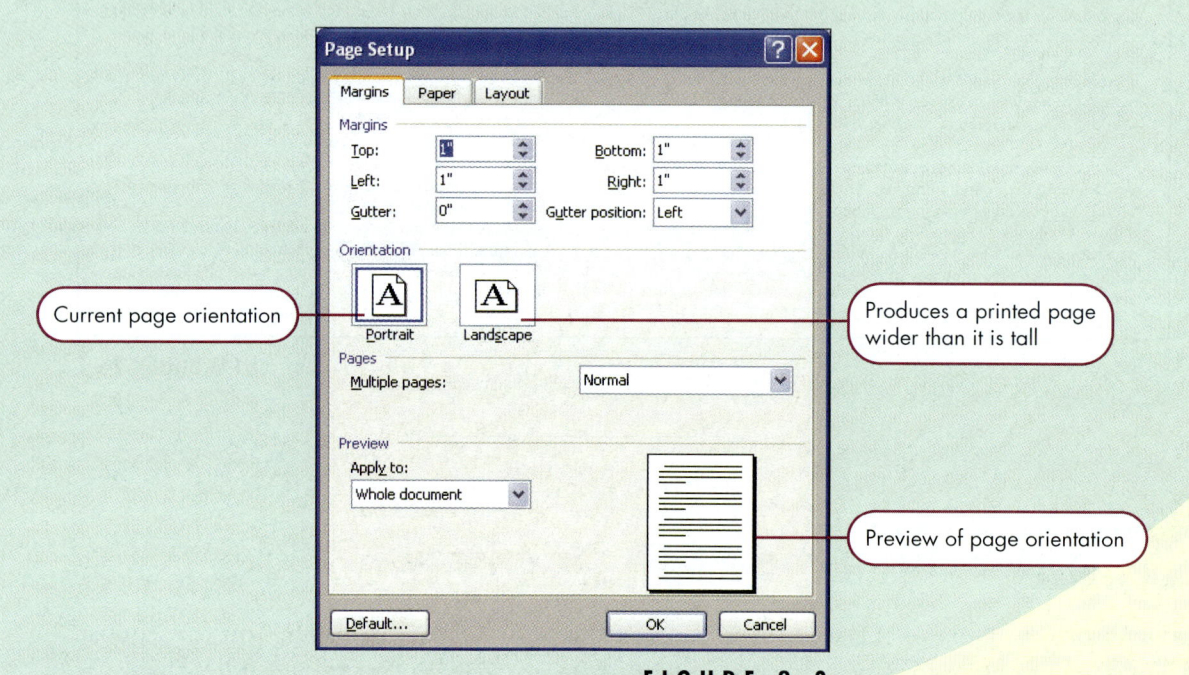

FIGURE 2.3

3 **Click *Landscape* and click OK.**
Word formats the document in landscape orientation. The pages are now wider (11″) than they are tall (8.5″).

4 **Click the Zoom drop-down arrow, and choose Whole Page.**   `100%`
You can see the entire page now, but the page is small onscreen.

5 **Choose View, Full Screen.**
The title bar, menu bar, toolbars, scrollbars, and status bar disappear to use the full screen to display the document. Figure 2.4 shows the whole page in landscape orientation, which displays more text between the left and right margins.

Lesson 2   Formatting Text into Columns   45   LEVEL 2

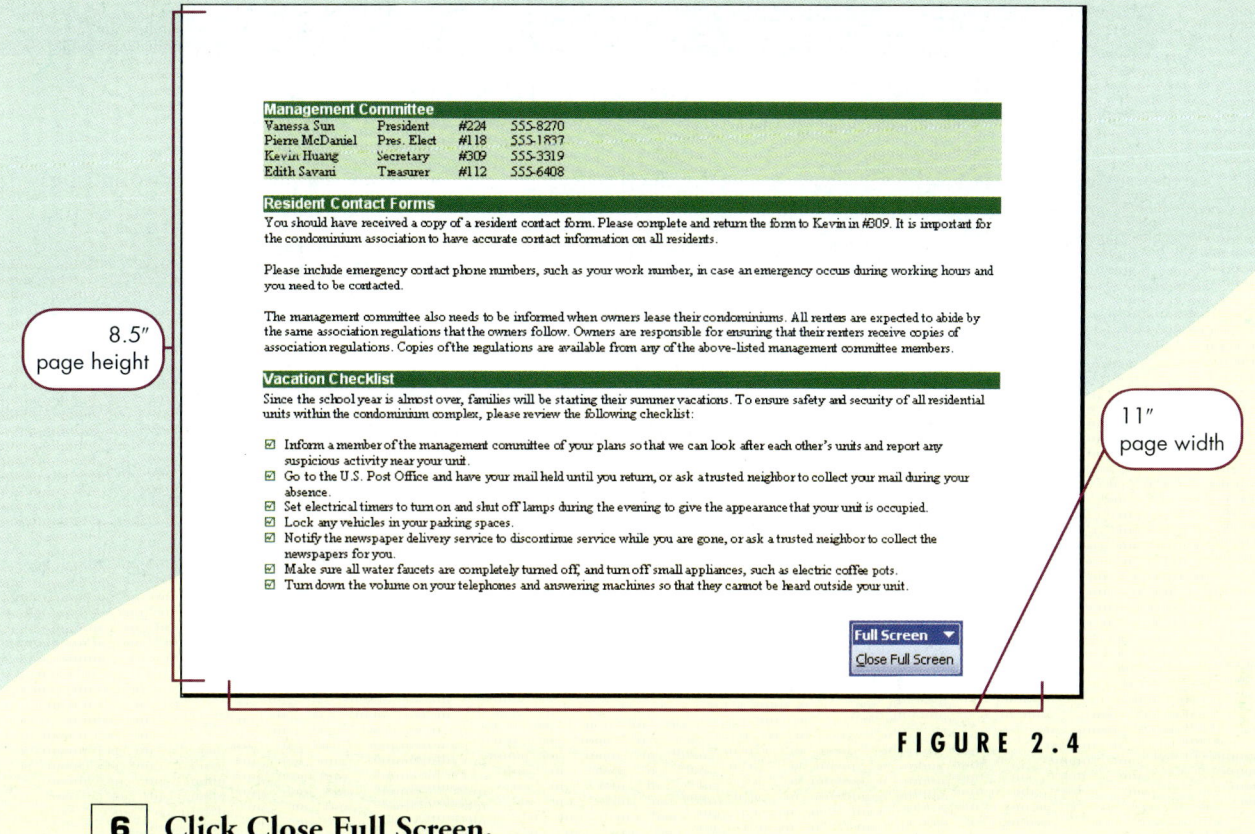

(8.5" page height)

(11" page width)

FIGURE 2.4

6 Click **C**lose Full Screen.
The document is still displayed in Whole Page view.

7 Save the *May_Newsletter* document, and keep it onscreen to continue with the next lesson.

TO EXTEND YOUR KNOWLEDGE...

APPLYING DIFFERENT ORIENTATIONS IN A DOCUMENT

You can set multiple page orientations in a document if your document is divided into sections. Choose *I*nsert, *B*reak; choose *N*ext page, *E*ven page, or *O*dd page; and click OK to create a section break. After creating the section break, choose *F*ile, Page Set*u*p; then click the Margins tab, click Land*s*cape, and click OK.

LESSON 2: Formatting Text into Columns

You can apply columnar format either before or after you compose the text for a document. However, many people prefer composing text first and then applying columnar format. You can apply column formatting to the entire document, an entire section, or part of the document. Table 2.1 guides you in formatting text into columns.

TABLE 2.1

IF YOUR DOCUMENT CONTAINS...	AND YOU WANT TO APPLY COLUMN FORMATTING TO...	DO THIS:
only one section	the entire document	Apply column formatting from anywhere within the document.
two or more sections	only one section	Position the insertion point in that section, and apply column formatting.
one or more sections	only part of the document within a section	Select the text you want to format, and then apply column formatting.

In this lesson, you use a toolbar button to apply a three-column format to the entire document.

To Format Text into Columns

1 **In the *May_Newsletter* document, click Columns on the Standard toolbar.**
A grid appears so you can specify how many columns you want.

2 **Position the mouse pointer over the third column on the grid.**
Figure 2.5 shows three columns selected on the grid.

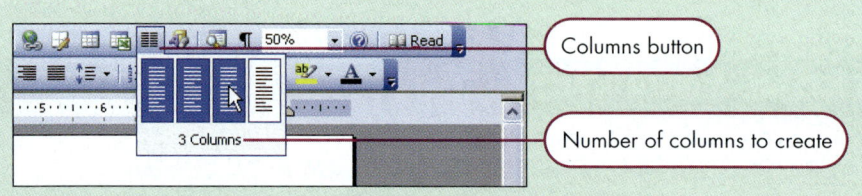

- Columns button
- Number of columns to create

FIGURE 2.5

3 **Click the third column on the grid.**
The document is now formatted into three columns. You can see that text runs down the first column and then continues at the top of the second column (see Figure 2.6). When the third column is full, text continues in the first column on the next page.

Lesson 2   Formatting Text into Columns

Text continues at top of second column

Bottom of first column

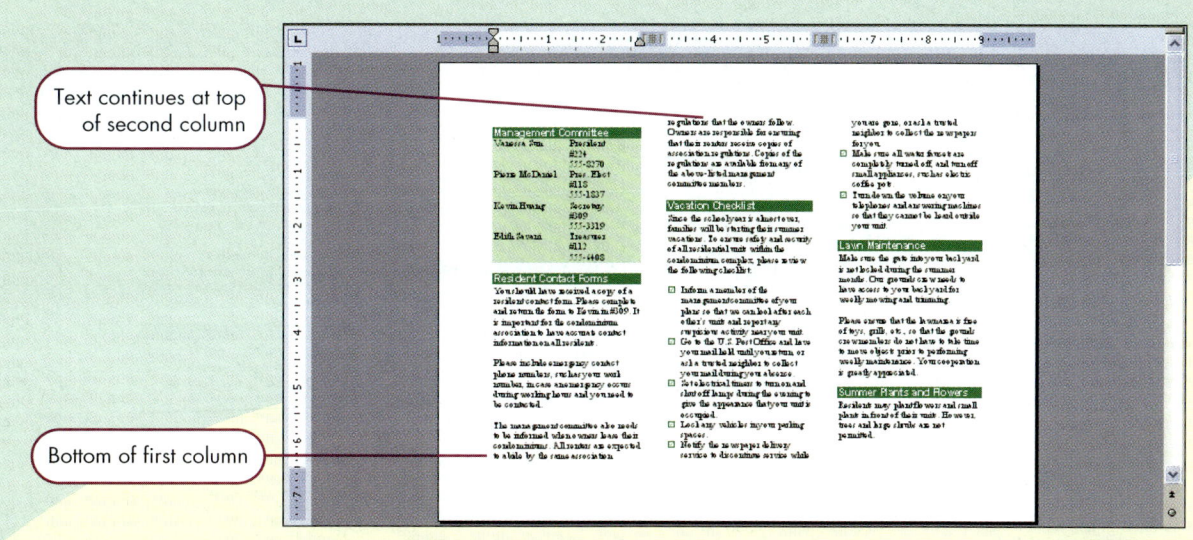

FIGURE 2.6

4 Save the *May_Newsletter* document, and keep it onscreen to continue with the next lesson.

TO EXTEND YOUR KNOWLEDGE...

REMOVING COLUMNS
If you decide that you do not want multiple columns, click Columns and choose *1 Column* on the grid. This formats the document back as one column, which is how regular text appears.

SEEING TEXT BOUNDARIES
You can display dotted-line boundaries, indicating the text area for the columns; the boundaries do not print. To show or hide the text boundaries, choose Tools, Options; then click the View tab, click the *Text boundaries* option in the *Print and Web Layout options* section, and click OK. Figure 2.7 shows text boundaries around columnar text.

Project 2   Creating and Formatting Columns

Text boundaries for columns

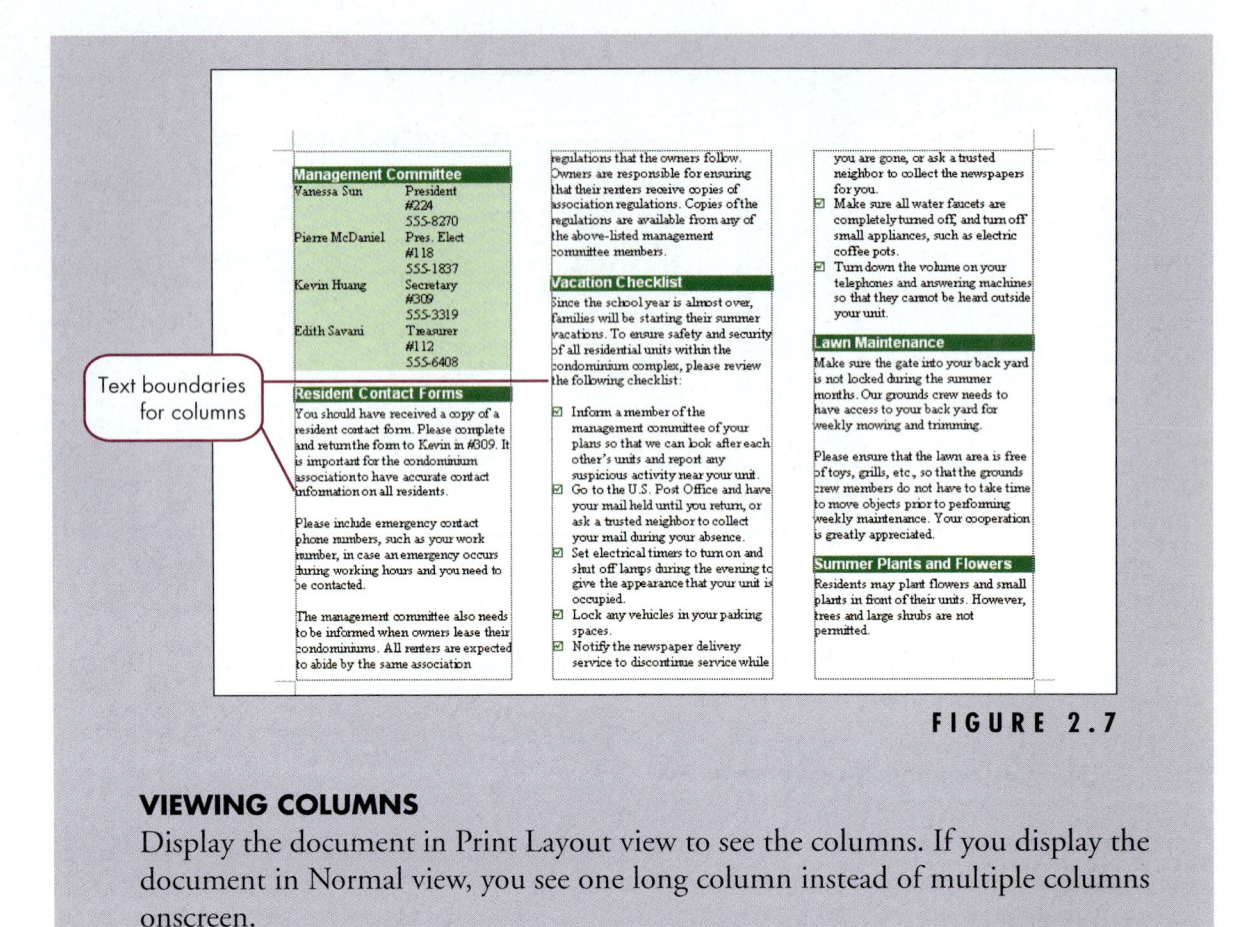

FIGURE 2.7

VIEWING COLUMNS
Display the document in Print Layout view to see the columns. If you display the document in Normal view, you see one long column instead of multiple columns onscreen.

LESSON 3: Revising Column Structure

After you apply column formatting to text, you might want to change it. For example, you might want to format the text into two columns instead of three columns. You can open the Columns dialog box to change the number of columns and specify different widths for each column instead of using equal column width. You can specify the size of the ***gutter***—the space between columns—if you want more or less space than the default 0.5". Finally, you can insert a vertical line between columns to separate them.

In this lesson, you use the Columns dialog box to apply two columns to the newsletter. In addition, you set a 0.75" gutter.

Lesson 3 Revising Column Structure

To Revise Column Structure

1 In the *May_Newsletter* document, choose F**o**rmat, **C**olumns.
The Columns dialog box opens, enabling you to choose one of five preset column formats or specify more columns in the *Number of columns* box (see Figure 2.8).

- Preset options
- Specify number of columns
- Click to insert a vertical line between columns
- Set space between columns

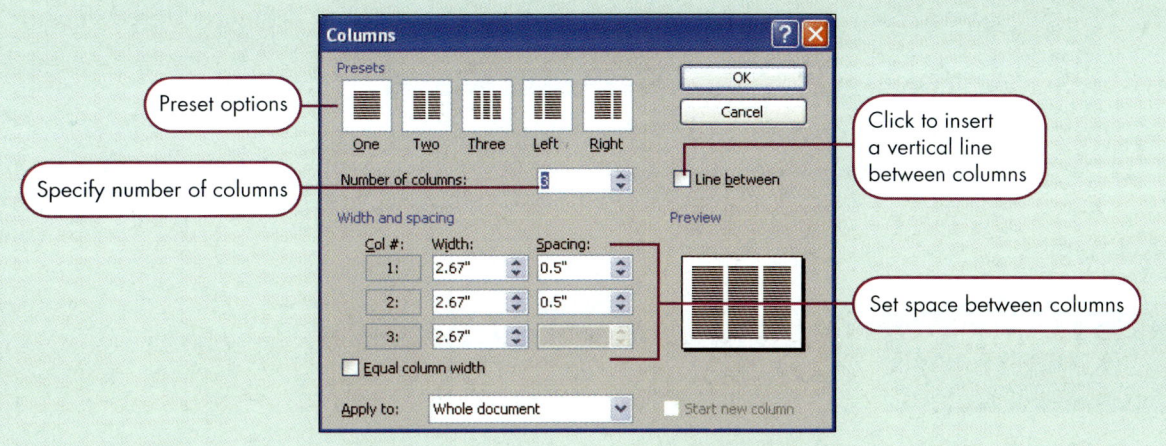

FIGURE 2.8

2 Click *T**w**o* in the Presets section.
This formats your document text into two columns of equal width.

3 Change the *Spacing* setting to **0.75** and click OK.
You increased the space between the columns, which results in slightly narrower column widths. The text is formatted into two columns with 0.75" space between them (see Figure 2.9).

- Ruler indicates 0.75" space between columns
- 0.75" space between columns
- Two columns

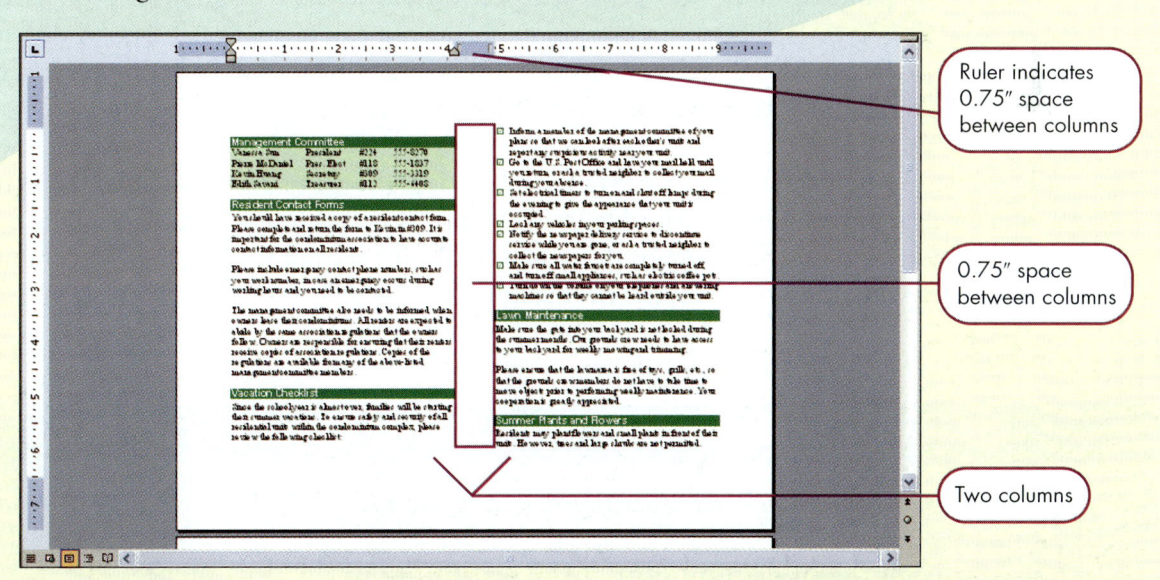

FIGURE 2.9

4 Click the Zoom drop-down arrow, and choose 100%.

5 Save the *May_Newsletter* document, and keep it onscreen to continue with the next lesson.

TO EXTEND YOUR KNOWLEDGE...

SETTING DIFFERENT COLUMN WIDTHS

If you want to specify different widths for columns, deselect *Equal column width* in the Columns dialog box. You can set the exact width of each column in the *Width* box and control the space between columns by entering a value in the *Spacing* box.

APPLYING PRESET UNEVEN COLUMN WIDTHS

You can select a preset column format with different column widths. The *Left* preset option creates a smaller left column with a bigger right column. The *Right* preset option creates a smaller right column with a bigger left column.

LESSON 4: Inserting Section Breaks, Column Breaks, and Files

When you create a newsletter, you probably want a **masthead** (also known as a **nameplate**), which is the area on the first page that contains the title, date, and volume information. The masthead usually spans all columns. Because the masthead is almost identical for all newsletters, it is saved in a different file so that you can insert it directly into the current document without opening the masthead document into a separate window.

To have a one-column format for the masthead and multiple columns on the rest of the page, you must insert continuous section breaks. A **continuous section break** divides a document into sections but continues with the next section on the same page instead of starting a new page. After you insert a continuous section break, you can format each section differently. You can format the masthead section with one column while keeping the two-column format for the body of the newsletter, which is in a different section.

In this lesson, you complete two sets of hands-on steps. In the first set, you insert a continuous section break at the beginning of the document, apply a one-column format to the new first section, and then insert a file that contains the masthead. In the second set, you insert a column break to start a news article at the top of the next column.

To Insert a Masthead That Spans Columns of Text

1 In the *May_Newsletter* document, click Show/Hide ¶ on the Standard toolbar.

2 Position the insertion point at the beginning of the document.
You need to insert a continuous section break before the first paragraph mark.

3 Choose Insert, Break.
The Break dialog box opens (see Figure 2.10).

Lesson 4 Inserting Section Breaks, Column Breaks, and Files

Starts text at top of next column

Inserts section break on same page

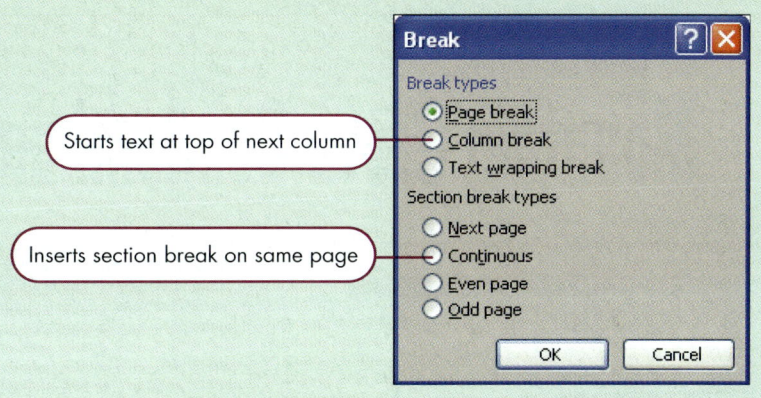

FIGURE 2.10

4 **Click *Continuous,* and click OK.**
Word inserts a section break but begins the new section on the same page. You see two dotted lines with *Section Break (Continuous)* to indicate the continuous section break.

5 **Press Ctrl+Home to position the insertion point within Section 1.**
The insertion point is to the left of the *Section Break (Continuous)* indicator, and the status bar displays *Sec 1,* indicating that the insertion point is in the first section. The new first section takes on the formats from the original section, which is set up for two columns. You need to remove column formatting in the first section.

6 **Click Columns on the Standard toolbar, and choose *1 Column.***
The *Section Break (Continuous)* indicator spans across both columns now. You are ready to insert the file that contains the masthead.

7 **With the insertion point in the first section (as shown by *Sec 1* on the status bar), choose Insert, File.**

8 **Choose *EW2_0202,* and click Insert.**
Word inserts the entire contents of *EW2_0202* in the first section, which is formatted for only one column.

9 **With the insertion point in the first section, choose File, Page Setup; then set a 0.75" top margin, and make sure the *Apply to* option is *This section.* Click OK.**
Figure 2.11 shows the masthead file inserted into the first section.

Project 2   Creating and Formatting Columns

[Screenshot of newsletter document with annotations:
- Masthead in Section 1
- Continuous section break
- Body of newsletter in two-column format in Section 2]

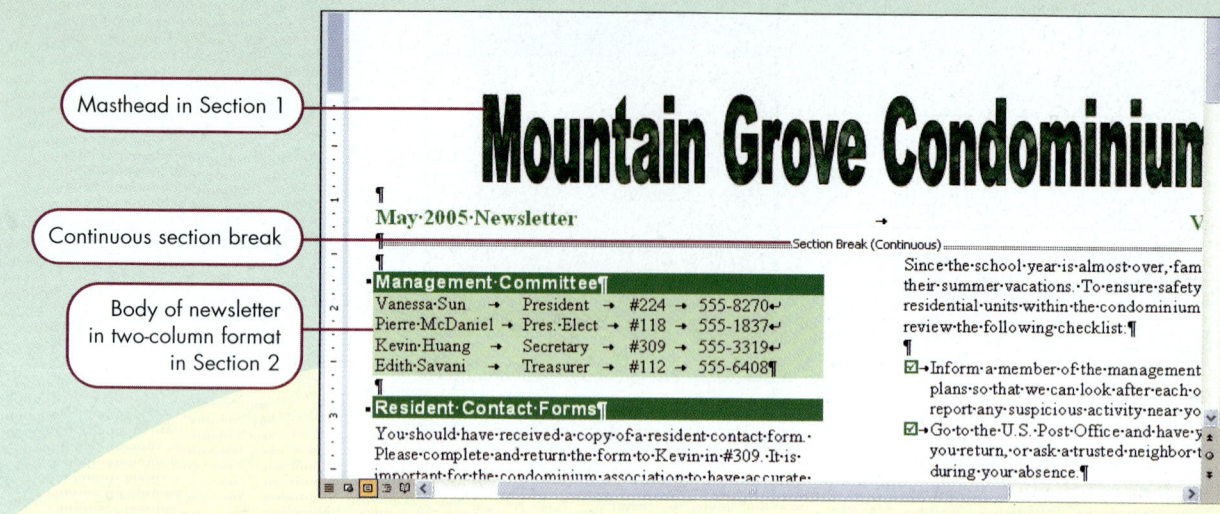

FIGURE 2.11

10 Save the *May_Newsletter* document, and keep it onscreen to continue with the next set of steps.

As you review your newsletter, you might want to start a new column to balance text more evenly. For example, the heading *Vacation Checklist* is isolated at the bottom of the first column, while the article continues at the top of the second column. In the next set of steps, you insert a column break to start the heading at the top of the second column.

To Insert a Column Break

1 In the *May_Newsletter* document, position the insertion point at the bottom of the first column on the blank line above the heading *Vacation Checklist*.
You need to insert the column break so that the blank line is at the top of the second column to match the blank line at the top of the first column.

2 Choose **I**nsert, **B**reak.

3 Click *Column break,* and click OK.
Word inserts a column break and places the heading at the top of a column.

If you have problems . . .

If you insert the column break at the beginning of the *Vacation Checklist* heading instead of on the blank line above it, Word duplicates the paragraph shading and font attributes at the bottom of the first column. If this happens, click Undo, position the insertion point on the blank line above the *Vacation Checklist* heading, and then insert the column break again.

Lesson 4 Inserting Section Breaks, Column Breaks, and Files   53   LEVEL 2

4 **Click and drag across the Zoom percentage on the Standard toolbar, type 85, press Enter, and adjust the view to see both the top and bottom of the columns on the first page.**

With the nonprinting symbols displayed, you see a *Column Break* note at the bottom of the first column. The heading appears at the top of the second column (see Figure 2.12).

Blank line at top of both columns

Heading aligns with heading in first column

Column break inserted here

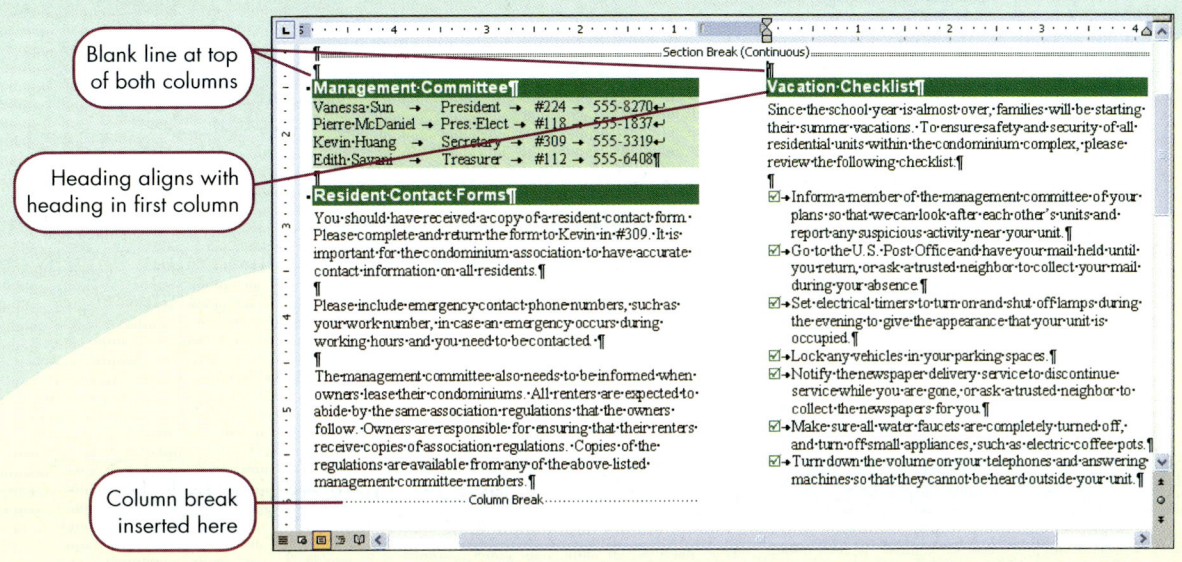

FIGURE 2.12

5 **Save the *May_Newsletter* document, and keep it onscreen to continue with the next lesson.**

TO EXTEND YOUR KNOWLEDGE...

APPLYING COLUMN FORMATTING TO SELECTED TEXT
When you apply column formatting to selected text, Word automatically inserts continuous section breaks between the selected text and the text before and after the selected text in addition to formatting the selected text into columns.

DELETING SECTION AND COLUMN BREAKS
You can delete a section or column break in any view mode *except* Reading Layout. In Normal view, you see the dotted break lines; in Web Layout, Print Layout, or Outline view, you must click Show/Hide ¶ to see the dotted break lines. Position the insertion point to the immediate left of the single or double dotted line and then press Del.

When you delete a section break, you delete the formats associated with that section, and it takes on the formats of the next section. For example, if you delete the section break after the masthead, the masthead takes on the two-column formatting of the second section.

USING THE COLUMN BREAK KEYBOARD SHORTCUT
You can also insert a column break by pressing Ctrl+Shift+Enter.

LESSON 5: Balancing Column Length

If the columns take up more than one page, the columns on the first page are balanced. That means that the bottom of all columns end at about the same place. However, the last page that contains columns might not be full. If this is the case, the column lengths are not balanced. The last column might be shorter than the others. You can balance the column lengths on the last page by inserting a continuous section break at the end of the last column.

In this lesson, you balance the columns on the last page of the newsletter.

To Balance Column Length

1. **In the *May_Newsletter* document, press Ctrl+End.**
   The insertion point is at the end of the document. Notice that the last column is shorter than the first column on the last page (see Figure 2.13).

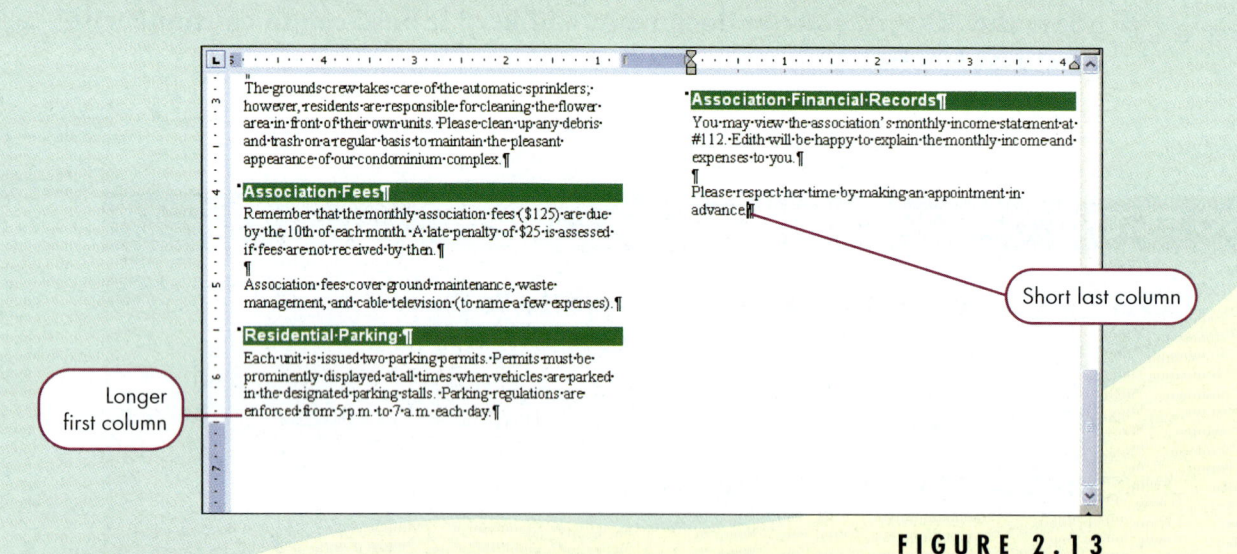

FIGURE 2.13

2. **Choose Insert, Break.**

3. **Click *Continuous,* and click OK.**
   Word tries to balance the column lengths the best it can, based on the type of text in the columns. Figure 2.14 shows that the second column ends at the same place that the first column ends.

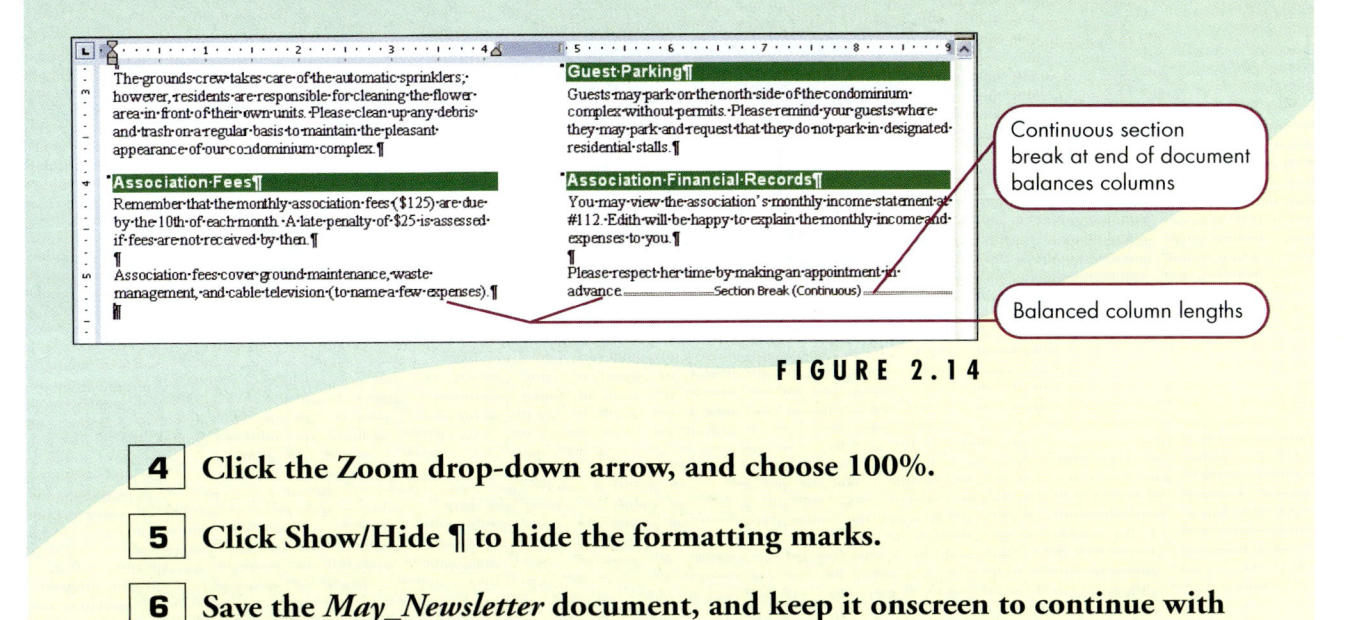

Lesson 6 Creating Drop Caps   55   LEVEL 2

Continuous section break at end of document balances columns

Balanced column lengths

FIGURE 2.14

4 Click the Zoom drop-down arrow, and choose 100%.

5 Click Show/Hide ¶ to hide the formatting marks.

6 Save the *May_Newsletter* document, and keep it onscreen to continue with the next lesson.

LESSON 6: Creating Drop Caps

You can enhance the appearance of a newsletter by adding color, graphics, and drop caps. A *drop cap* is a big character that drops below the current line of text. Publishers often use a drop cap for the first letter of the first paragraph in a chapter or section.

In this lesson, you add a drop cap to the first paragraph in the second column. After creating the drop cap, you change its font color and shading color.

To Create a Drop Cap

1 In the *May_Newsletter* document, position the insertion point in the first paragraph of the second column on page 1.
The paragraph starts with *Since the school year is almost over.*

2 Choose F**o**rmat, **D**rop Cap.
The Drop Cap dialog box opens so you can specify its position and set other options (see Figure 2.15).

Project 2 Creating and Formatting Columns

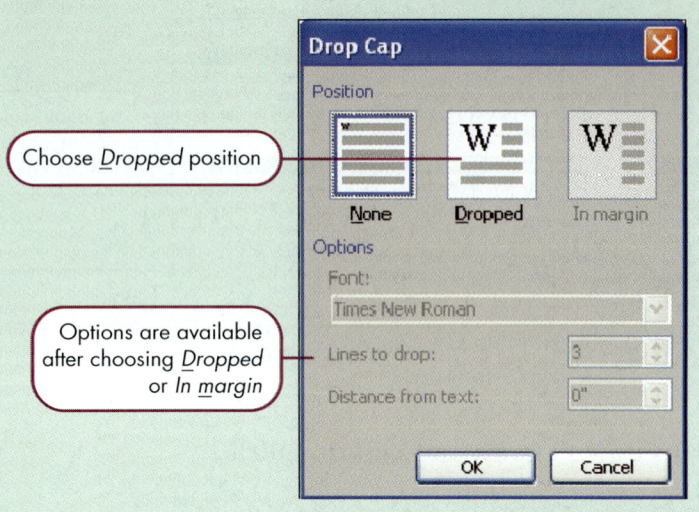

Choose *Dropped* position

Options are available after choosing *Dropped* or *In margin*

FIGURE 2.15

3 Click *Dropped,* and click OK.
Figure 2.16 shows the drop cap created from the first letter of that paragraph.

Drop cap

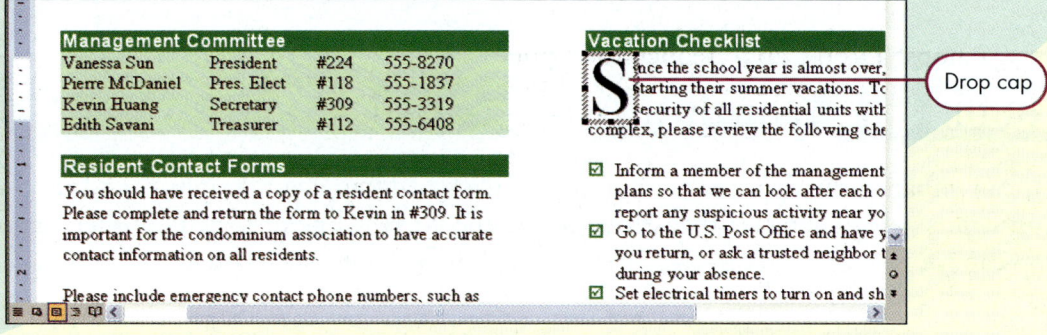

FIGURE 2.16

4 With the drop cap selected, click the Font Color drop-down arrow, and choose Green.
The drop cap text is now formatted with Green font color.

5 With the drop cap selected, choose F*o*rmat, *B*orders and Shading.
You want to add a Light Green shading color behind the drop cap letter.

6 Click the *S*hading tab in the Borders and Shading dialog box.

7 Click Light Green, the fourth color from the left on the last row, and then click OK.

If you have problems . . .

If the Light Green shading extends below the drop cap S and aligns with the bottom of the paragraph, select the outer edge of the drop cap area, open the Borders and Shading dialog box again, change the *Apply to* option to *Text,* and then click OK.

Lesson 7   Hyphenating Text   57   LEVEL 2

8 **Deselect the drop cap.**
The drop cap is visually appealing with its font color and shading (see Figure 2.17).

Management Committee			
Vanessa Sun	President	#224	555-8270
Pierre McDaniel	Pres. Elect	#118	555-1837
Kevin Huang	Secretary	#309	555-3319
Edith Savani	Treasurer	#112	555-6408

Vacation Checklist
Since the school year is almost over, starting their summer vacations. To security of all residential units with complex, please review the following che

Green font color for text and Light Green shading color

FIGURE 2.17

9 Save the *May_Newsletter* document, and keep it onscreen to continue with the next lesson.

TO EXTEND YOUR KNOWLEDGE . . .

REFORMATTING A DROP CAP
If you want to change drop cap options, select the drop cap as you would select an image and right-click the edge of the drop cap to display the shortcut menu. Choose Drop Cap to reopen the Drop Cap dialog box.

REMOVING A DROP CAP
If you decide to remove a drop cap, right-click it, choose Drop Cap from the shortcut menu, and choose None. Word removes the drop cap features and returns the drop cap text back to regular text.

If you press Del when a drop cap is selected, you delete the drop cap and the text that created it.

CREATING A DROP CAP FOR A WORD
By default, Word creates a drop cap from the first letter in the paragraph. You can create a drop for the first word in the paragraph by selecting the entire word before displaying the Drop Cap dialog box.

LESSON 7: Hyphenating Text

By now, you know that the word-wrap feature wraps a word to the next line if it cannot fit at the end of the existing line. However, word-wrap sometimes causes a large gap at the right margin when it wraps a long word to the next line. You can smooth out the right margin by hyphenating words. The Hyphenation feature identifies words that can partially fit at the end of the line; it fits as much of the word at the end of the line as possible, inserts a hyphen, and continues the rest of the word on the next line.

When you hyphenate words at the end of text lines, you should ensure readability and ease of flow from one line to the next. The following guidelines improve the appearance of hyphenated text:

Project 2   Creating and Formatting Columns

- Do not hyphenate words that start with a capital letter, such as *Microsoft, November,* or the first word of a sentence.
- Do not hyphenate the last word of a paragraph or the last word on a page when a paragraph continues to another page.
- Do not hyphenate words that are already hyphenated.
- Make sure at least three letters appear before and after the hyphen. Do not hyphenate words such as *re-port* or *ad-vance* where only two letters appear before the hyphen.

In this lesson, you hyphenate words to make the newsletter look more professional.

To Hyphenate Words

1   In the *May_Newsletter* document, position the insertion point at the beginning of the document.

2   Choose **T**ools, **L**anguage, **H**yphenation.
The Hyphenation dialog box appears (see Figure 2.18).

Deselect this option

Click for Word to prompt you to approve hyphenation locations

Set the number of consecutive lines ending with hyphens

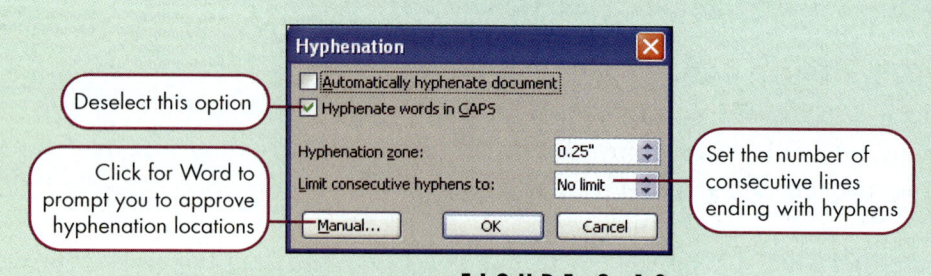

FIGURE 2.18

3   Deselect *Hyphenate words in **C**APS,* if it is selected.
Hyphenating capitalized words, such as *November,* creates an unprofessional-looking document. Deselecting *Hyphenate words in CAPS* prevents capitalized words from being hyphenated automatically.

4   Click the ***L**imit consecutive hyphens to* increment button to *2*.
The default allows unlimited number of consecutive lines ending with hyphenated words. This effect detracts from the overall appearance. Limiting the number of consecutive hyphens to two is more professional.

5   Click **M**anual.
Clicking *M*anual lets you decide hyphenation locations instead of letting Word hyphenate the document automatically.

The Manual Hyphenation dialog box opens with the first word that can be hyphenated (see Figure 2.19).

Lesson 7 Hyphenating Text 59 LEVEL 2

Location of word within document

Suggested hyphen location

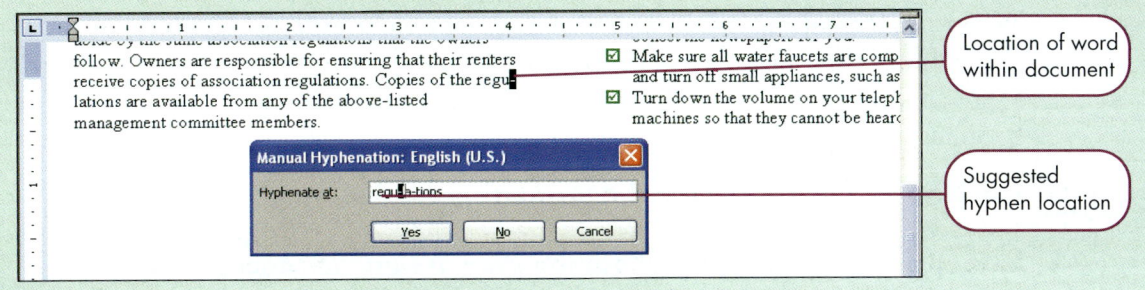

FIGURE 2.19

If you have problems . . .

You may see different potential words to hyphenate based on your computer system and the current printer. Choose hyphenation locations based on the guidelines presented at the beginning of this lesson.

---

6 Click <u>Y</u>es to hyphenate the word *regu-lations* as suggested.
The Manual Hyphenation dialog box appears again, prompting you to hyphenate another word.

7 Click <u>Y</u>es to hyphenate most words based on the rules presented at the beginning of this lesson.

8 Click OK when you see the message *Hyphenation is complete*.

9 Click Show/Hide ¶, change the zoom to Text Width, and scroll to the bottom of the second page.
Figure 2.20 shows hyphenation locations on the second page of the newsletter.

enforced not hyphenated

Hyphen inserted by Hyphenation feature

advance not hyphenated

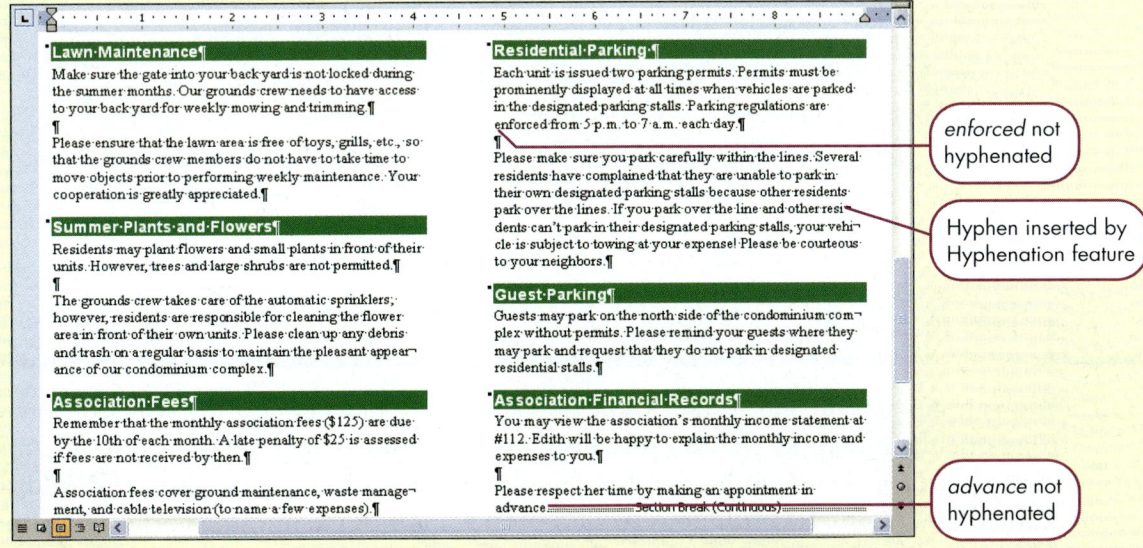

FIGURE 2.20

Project 2   Creating and Formatting Columns

When the formatting marks are displayed, you see a little vertical line on the right side of hyphens inserted by the Hyphenation feature; this helps you identify a Hyphenation hyphen from a typed hyphen or nonbreaking hyphen. However, all hyphens print the same.

10 Click Show/Hide ¶ to hide the formatting marks.

11 Save, print (optional), and close the *May_Newsletter* document.

TO EXTEND YOUR KNOWLEDGE . . .

CHANGING THE HYPHENATION ZONE
The ***hyphenation zone*** is the area at the end of a line that determines whether a word can potentially be hyphenated. If a word starts on or before the zone and extends past it, Word prompts you to hyphenate that word. If a word starts after the zone, Word wraps it to the next line.

The default zone is 0.25". If you increase the zone, Word prompts you with *fewer* words to hyphenate. If you decrease the zone, Word prompts you with *more* words to hyphenate.

REMOVING HYPHENS INSERTED BY THE HYPHENATION FEATURE
If you change your mind about hyphenating a document, you can quickly remove the hyphens. Open the Find and Replace dialog box and complete these steps:

1. Clear current settings.
2. Click in the *Find what* box.
3. Click the More button, if needed, to see the full dialog box options.
4. Click the Special button at the bottom of the dialog box.
5. Choose Optional Hyphen from the menu.
6. Leave the *Replace with* box empty.
7. Click the Replace All button.

SUMMARY

You can now create and format professional-looking newsletters. You learned how to select page orientation, apply column formatting to text, and change the structure of column formatted text by changing the number of columns and adjusting the gutter. In addition, you learned how to insert continuous section breaks, insert a file into the current document, and insert a column break to start text at the top of a column. You added a drop cap, applied a different font color, and applied a shading background to enhance the visual effectiveness of the document. Finally, you hyphenated words to smooth out the right margin.

Checking Concepts and Terms

You can extend your learning by reviewing concepts and terms, and by practicing variations of skills presented in the lessons. Use the following table as a guide to the numbered questions and exercises in the end-of-project learning opportunities.

LESSON	MULTIPLE CHOICE	DISCUSSION	SKILL DRILL	CHALLENGE	DISCOVERY ZONE
Setting the Page Orientation	1, 10	1	2	4	1, 2
Formatting Text into Columns	2	1	2	1, 2, 3, 4, 5	1
Revising Column Structure	5	1	3	4	1
Inserting Section Breaks, Column Breaks, and Files	3, 9	1	1, 3	1, 2, 3, 4, 5	1, 2
Balancing Column Length	8	1		2, 4, 5	1
Creating Drop Caps	4	2	4	4	1
Hyphenating Text	6, 7	3	5	1, 2, 4	1

KEY TERMS

columns
continuous section break
drop cap
gutter
hyphenation zone
landscape orientation
masthead
nameplate
page orientation
portrait orientation

CHECKING CONCEPTS AND TERMS

MULTIPLE CHOICE

Circle the letter of the correct answer for each of the following.

1. What text orientation runs parallel with the long side of a printed page? [L1]
   a. Portrait
   b. Newspaper columns
   c. Section break
   d. Landscape

2. To remove multiple columns from a document, click Columns on the Standard toolbar and choose _____. [L2]
   a. 1 Column
   b. No Columns
   c. Delete Columns
   d. Remove Columns

3. What type of break must you insert to be able to have two types of column settings on the same page? [L4]
   a. Continuous section break
   b. Page break
   c. Column break
   d. Next page section break

4. You can set all of the following in the Drop Cap dialog box *except* _____. [L6]
   a. position
   b. font
   c. distance from text
   d. font color

5. What is the default space between columns? [L3]
   a. 0.25"
   b. 0.5"
   c. 0.75"
   d. 1"

6. Which of the following words is the most appropriate for being hyphenated? [L7]
   a. pro-grams
   b. Jan-uary
   c. re-source
   d. Jeffer-son

7. Which of the following Hyphenation option settings is the *least* appropriate? [L7]
   a. *Hyphenate words in CAPS* deselected
   b. *Automatically hyphenate document* selected
   c. *Limit consecutive hyphens to* 2
   d. *Hyphenation zone* 0.25"

8. What is the most effective method for balancing column endings on the last page of columnar text? [L5]
   a. Pressing ⏎Enter as needed within the shortest column until it ends at the same place as the other columns.
   b. Insert another column break within the last column.
   c. Insert a continuous section break at the end of the columnar text.
   d. Change column widths until all columns are balanced.

9. What is the most efficient method for including the contents of an entire document at the insertion point's location within the current document? [L4]
   a. Open the other file, select the entire contents, copy the contents, and paste them into the current document.
   b. Choose Insert, File, choose the file, and click Insert.
   c. Copy the contents of the current document, open the other document, and paste the Clipboard contents into the document you just opened.
   d. All of the above are equally efficient.

10. What is the width of a legal-sized piece of paper that is printed in landscape orientation? [L1]
    a. 8.5"
    b. 11"
    c. 14"
    d. 4.25"

DISCUSSION

1. Find a copy of a newsletter from an organization. Many utility companies include newsletters with the monthly statements. Evaluate the use of columns—appropriate number, too many, not enough for the paper size, and so forth. What type of alignment (left or justified) is used? Is the alignment appropriate? If not, why not? What are other characteristics of the columns? Bring a copy of the newsletter to class to discuss your critique. [L1–L5]

2. Look through newsletters and magazines to find examples of drop cap formatting. Critique them in terms of format and readability. Bring a copy to class to share your findings. [L6]

3. What are advantages and disadvantages of hyphenating a document? Provide specific examples. If possible, find examples of documents that support your answer. [L7]

SKILL DRILL

Skill Drill exercises reinforce project skills. Each skill reinforced is the same, or nearly the same, as a skill presented in the project. Detailed instructions are provided in a step-by-step format.

You modify one document—the *EW2_0203* file that you rename **TMG_Newsletter**. Work through exercise 1 first and exercise 5 last; you may work through the remaining exercises in any order. Be sure to save your changes and close the document if you need more than one work session to complete the desired exercises. Continue working on *TMG_Newsletter* instead of starting over in the original *EW2_0203* file. Figure 2.21 shows the newsletter after completing all five Skill Drill exercises.

Project 2 Creating and Formatting Columns

FIGURE 2.21

1. Inserting a File and a Continuous Section Break

Your assistant created a newsletter for your organization, The Millennium Group. Although your assistant composed the text and inserted some images, you need to finish formatting the newsletter. Your first task is to insert a continuous section break so that you can eventually format the document into newspaper columns.

1. Open *EW2_0203* and save it as **TMG_Newsletter**.
2. With the insertion point at the beginning of the document, do the following:
   a. Choose Insert, File.
   b. Select *EW2_0204* and click Insert.
3. Position the insertion point on the left side of the heading *Conference is Scheduled!*
4. Choose Insert, Break.
5. Click *Continuous,* and click OK.
6. Display the formatting marks to see *Section Break (Continuous)* between the horizontal line and the *Conference is Scheduled!* heading.
7. Save the *TMG_Newsletter* document.

2. Changing the Page Orientation and Formatting the Masthead

You realize that the masthead file was formatted in landscape orientation. Therefore, you decide to format the current newsletter in landscape orientation. After changing the orientation, you need to reapply a one-column format to the first section to center the WordArt and widen the existing horizontal line.

1. In the *TMG_Newsletter* document, press `Ctrl`+`Home`.
2. Choose File, Page Setup and do the following:
    a. Click the Margins tab, if needed.
    b. Click the *Landscape* option.
    c. Click the *Apply to* drop-down arrow and choose *Whole document,* and click OK.
3. Change the zoom to Page Width and do the following:
    a. Click Columns on the Standard toolbar.
    b. Click *1 Column.*

    The WordArt (which was set to center horizontal alignment) is now centered between the left and right margins in landscape orientation, and the horizontal line extends to the right margin.
4. Save the *TMG_Newsletter* document.

3. Formatting Text into Columns and Inserting a Column Break

You need to format the main part of the document into columns. Because you created a continuous section break, you can keep a one-column format for the first section and apply a multiple-column format for the second section. After formatting text into columns, you notice that a heading is isolated at the bottom of the first column; you need to insert a column break to start the heading at the top of the second column.

1. In the *TMG_Newsletter* document, position the insertion point anywhere within Section 2 (after the continuous section break).
2. Choose Format, Columns.
3. Click *Right* to set two columns with a smaller right column, and click OK.

   The *Dental Benefits* heading is isolated at the bottom of a column. You need to insert a column break so that it appears at the top of the next column.
4. Position the insertion point at the beginning of the heading *Dental Benefits.*
5. Choose Insert, Break.
6. Click *Column break* and then click OK.
7. Save the *TMG_Newsletter* document.

4. Creating a Drop Cap

You have noticed that several newsletters use a drop-cap character to start major sections or articles. You want to enhance your newsletter by adding a drop-cap character for the first paragraph.

1. In the *TMG_Newsletter* document, change the zoom to 100%.
2. Position the insertion point within the first paragraph, which begins with *The Technology Training Conference.*
3. Choose Format, Drop Cap.
4. Click the *Dropped* option, and then click OK.

5. With the drop cap selected, do the following:
   a. Click the Font Color drop-down arrow on the Formatting toolbar, and choose Yellow.
   b. Choose F̲ormat, B̲orders and Shading.
   c. Click the S̲hading tab, click Blue, and then click OK.
6. Deselect the drop cap.
7. Click after *October*, located at the end of the line, press Del to delete the soft space, and then press Ctrl+Shift+Spacebar to insert a nonbreaking space between the month and dates.
8. Save the *TMG_Newsletter* document.

5. Hyphenating the Newsletter

You notice several large gaps at the right margin of each column. Therefore, you decide to hyphenate the newsletter to smooth out the right side of each column. You want to control the hyphenation yourself, and you want to restrict hyphenation to avoid hyphenating capitalized words and to avoid having too many consecutive lines that end with hyphens.

1. In the *TMG_Newsletter* document, position the insertion point at the top of the document.
2. Choose T̲ools, L̲anguage, H̲yphenation and do the following:
   a. Make sure that *Hyphenate words in C̲APS* is not selected.
   b. Click the *L̲imit consecutive hyphens to* increment button to *2*.
   c. Click M̲anual.
3. Click Y̲es to hyphenate words when desired; click N̲o to avoid hyphenating proper nouns and words with only two letters before the hyphen.
4. Click OK when the hyphenation process is complete.
5. Save, print (optional), and close the *TMG_Newsletter* document.

CHALLENGE

Challenge exercises expand on or are somewhat related to skills presented in the lessons. Each exercise provides a brief narrative introduction, followed by instructions in a numbered-step format that are not as detailed as those in the Skill Drill exercises. You can work through one or more exercises in any order.

1. Preparing Course Descriptions for a College Catalog

You work as a curriculum assistant at the local university. Your job is to format incoming text to be published in the upcoming course catalog. You just received some course descriptions from the Information Systems Department and need to format the document.

1. Open *EW2_0205* and save it as **IS_Courses**.
2. Create a title for the document using these specifications:
   a. Delete the asterisk and type **Information Systems (IS) Courses**.
   b. Center the title.
   c. Apply 16-point Arial bold to the title.

3. Insert *EW2_0206* at the end of the document.

4. Sort the course descriptions in sequential order by course number.

5. Apply 12-point paragraph spacing after each course description paragraph. Do not press ⏎Enter; use the appropriate paragraph setting.

6. Insert a continuous section break at the beginning of the first course description.

7. Format the course descriptions with the following specifications:
   a. Two columns
   b. 0.75" top, bottom, left, and right margins
   c. 10-point Times New Roman
   d. Justify alignment

8. Hyphenate the document, using manual hyphenation, limiting the number of consecutive hyphens to three, and adhering to the specifications at the beginning of Lesson 7.

9. Make sure the tops of the columns align. If not, delete a blank line at the beginning of the second column. (Note: If you delete the blank line and then later edit the document, you might need to insert the blank line again. Always check formatting after making editing changes.)

10. Save, print (optional), and close the *IS_Courses* document.

2. Creating a Job Announcement Flyer

You work as an assistant in the Human Resources Department at your university. Because of your knowledge and skills in Microsoft Word, your supervisor asked you to create a job announcement flyer.

1. Open *EW2_0207* and save it as **Job_Announcement**.

2. Set 0.75" top and bottom margins.

3. Position the insertion point at the end of the document, insert a continuous section break, and then insert the file *EW2_0208* after the section break.

4. In the second section, apply two-column formatting, using unequal column widths with a 3.6" width for the first column and automatic width for the second column.

5. Insert a column break to the left of the *Opening Date* line.

6. Insert a continuous section break to the left of the *Mountaintop University* paragraph, and set a one-column format for the third section.

7. Insert a continuous section break to the left of the *Job Qualifications* heading, and set a two-column format with equal column widths for the fourth section.

8. Insert a column break to the left of the *Application Requirements* heading.

9. Adjust the font size of the last paragraph to match the font size of other paragraphs in the fourth section.

10. Insert a continuous section break at the end of the document, press ⏎Enter, and apply a one-column format to the fifth section.

11. Insert a paragraph border with these specifications:
    a. ninth paragraph border style (thick top line and thin bottom line)
    b. Dark Blue border color
    c. top border only (no lines on the left, right, or bottom)
12. Position the insertion point at the beginning of the document, and hyphenate the document, following the specifications listed at the beginning of Lesson 7 and limiting the consecutive hyphens to two.
13. Save, print (optional), and close the *Job_Announcement* document.

3. Creating a List of Job Descriptions

You work for a major publisher. Your supervisor asked you to prepare a document that lists key personnel and their job descriptions. This information sheet will be sent to each author on the Microsoft Office 2003 team, so they will know who is responsible for different aspects of the publication process.

1. In a new document window, set a 2" top margin, and save the document as **Publisher_Contacts**.
2. Type the title shown in Figure 2.22. Triple-space after the title. Select the title, and apply center horizontal alignment, 16-point Arial font, and bold.
3. At the end of the document, insert a continuous section break and create two columns, using the *Left* preset option.
4. Type the column heading **Publisher Contact** in boldface in the first column, set 12-point spacing after the paragraph, and then insert a column break. (The 12-point spacing after paragraph should continue for the rest of the document.)
5. Type the column heading **Job Description** in boldface in the second column. Then insert a continuous section break.
6. Finish typing the rest of the columnar text, inserting a column break after each person's name and inserting a continuous section break after each job description. The 12-point after paragraph spacing creates the equivalent of one blank line between rows.
7. Save, print (optional), and close the *Publisher_Contacts* document.

Office 2003 Series

Publisher Contact	Job Description
Gustavo Rosales	Executive Editor: Coordinate all books in the Office 2003 series. Contact potential authors and issue contracts to final authors. Work with all publishing personnel. Determine budgets, sales forecasts, etc.
Louise Hofheins	Developmental Editor: Work with author to organize topics for a final TOC. Review incoming chapters and provide suggestions for organization, content, and structure. Ensure that author correctly formats the manuscript according to series specifications.
Eleanor Wolhwend	Project Manager: Coordinate the publishing process with the authors, developmental editors, technical editors, copy editors, and production team members.
Damon Lamoreaux	Technical Editor: Review first-draft of manuscript to ensure technical accuracy of the step-by-step lessons. Make notes of any missing or extra steps. Point out inconsistencies with menu names, options, etc., including capitalization. Make other notes from a student's perspective.
Melody Fjerstad	Copy Editor: Proofread manuscript and correct errors in spelling, grammar, punctuation, wording, etc. Use the tracking feature in Word to make the online edits.

FIGURE 2.22

4. Creating a Graduation Announcement Flyer

You work as an administrative assistant in the Graduation Office at a local university. It is your responsibility to create, format, and mail a graduation information newsletter to all seniors. You just composed the information sheet, and now you want to format it into columns, insert an image, and insert WordArt.

1. Open *EW2_0209* and save it as `Graduation_Newsletter`.
2. Format the document in landscape orientation.
3. Create a WordArt object at the top of the document with the text `Graduation Information`. You may choose any WordArt style, but center it between the left and right margins and use a Top and Bottom text wrap.
4. Insert an appropriate section break at the beginning of the first paragraph so that the original and new sections appear on the same page.
5. Format the second section into two columns with a vertical line between columns. Use Help, if needed, to learn how to insert a line between columns.

6. Insert an appropriate clip art image next to the *Cap and Gown Orders* paragraph. Adjust the size and text wrapping, as needed, to accommodate the image.
7. Insert a column break, if needed, to balance text between the columns.
8. Insert a drop cap at the beginning of the first paragraph. Apply a different font color and shading color for the drop cap.
9. Insert nonbreaking spaces, as needed, within dates and times.
10. Use the Hyphenation feature to hyphenate words throughout the document. Use the specifications listed at the beginning of Lesson 7 and limit the number of consecutive hyphens to three.
11. Save, print (optional), and close the *Graduation_Newsletter* document.

5. Creating a Flyer to Sell a Condominium

You want to sell your condominium so that you can buy a house. You need to create an attractive flyer that displays a photograph of the condominium and lists some features of your condo in a two-column bulleted-list format.

1. In a new document window, type and center the title **Spacious Condominium for Sale**.
2. Save the document as **Condominium_Flyer**.
3. Refer to Figure 2.23 as you create the flyer. You will provide a different image and modify text as appropriate.
4. Apply a sans serif font of your choice, boldface, Dark Blue font color, and an appropriate font size for the title. Apply the same font face to the address, *Special Features* text, and the selling price line of text. Adjust font sizes as needed.
5. Use the Clip Art task pane to locate a photograph of an apartment complex or condominium complex and insert it into the document. Or if you prefer, take a digital photograph of a condominium and insert it into the document instead. Adjust the image's size, apply a Top and Bottom text wrapping style, and center the image.
6. Format the bulleted list with a customized blue symbol of a house; apply a two-column format to the bulleted list and insert a column break as needed to balance the bulleted list.
7. Type and format the last two lines within the document.
8. Adjust formatting, such as document margins, as needed to improve the appearance of the flyer.
9. Save, print (optional), and close the *Condominium_Flyer* document.

Challenge 71 LEVEL 2

Spacious Condominium for Sale

1018 East Village Parkway, #214

Special Features

- Over 1,600 Square Feet
- Three Stories
- Chef's Dream Kitchen
- Large Family Room
- Vaulted Ceilings in Upstairs Bedroom
- Remote-controlled Ceiling Fans
- Fenced-in Private Back Yard

- Two Covered Parking Stalls
- Three Large Bedrooms
- Master Bathroom w/ Jetted Tub
- Two Additional Bathrooms
- Central Heating/Air Conditioning
- High-Speed Internet Access
- Close to Mall and Schools

All of these features and more for ONLY $135,900!!

Call Kincaid @ 555-6432 for more information.

FIGURE 2.23

DISCOVERY ZONE

Discovery Zone exercises require advanced knowledge of topics presented in the lessons or self-directed learning of new skills. You can work through the exercises in any order.

1. Modifying a Newsletter

You recently created a newsletter for the local Parent Educator Association. Now you want to add a drop cap character, adjust the column formatting, and hyphenate the newsletter. Open *EW2_0210* and save it as **PEA_Newsletter_Update**.

Apply landscape orientation and set 0.75" left, right, and bottom margins to the entire document.

Center the WordArt object, and set a tab to align *September 2005 Edition* at the right margin.

Use Help to learn how to delete a section break. Delete the section page break and insert a continuous break instead. Make sure the first section is formatted with one column, and revise the structure of the second section to have these specifications: three-column format, 3.25" width for the first column, 2.5" width for the second column, 2.25" width for the third column, 0.75" space between columns, and a vertical line between columns. (Hint: After you change one setting, you might have to adjust another one.)

Format the first letter of the first paragraph as a drop cap. Apply a Green border, Light Green shading, and Green font color to the drop cap. Modify the drop cap format by dropping it four lines and applying Arial Narrow font.

Use the Help feature to learn about the hyphenation zone. Set a 0.15" hyphenation zone and manually hyphenate words when prompted. Observe the hyphenation rules mentioned in Lesson 7. After hyphenating the document, use the Find feature to find optional hyphens. If you see optional hyphens in the wrong locations, delete them.

Insert nonbreaking spaces as needed in the document, and insert an appropriate section break that balances the length of the columns. Adjust the position of the clip art and WordArt to ensure that the entire document fits on one page.

Save, print (optional), and close the *PEA_Newsletter_Update* document.

2. Creating a Program for an Awards Banquet

You are a member of the Regional Theatre Organization. You are holding your spring awards banquet to honor those receiving awards for theatrical performances. You are responsible for preparing the program for the event. In a new document window, set up the document for landscape orientation with 0.5" margins (all sides). Select the option to vertically center text in the document. Save the document as **Awards_Banquet_Program**.

Because you will fold the program like a greeting card, you need to plan this document carefully. Use the Help feature to learn how to create and print a book fold. Make sure the margins are still 0.5".

Refer to Figure 2.24 to create the front cover (page 1). Balance the space between lines of text as needed.

Regional Theatre Organization

(18-pt Script MT Bold or 20-pt Broadway font, White font color, Dark Blue highlight color)

Presents

10th Annual Awards Banquet

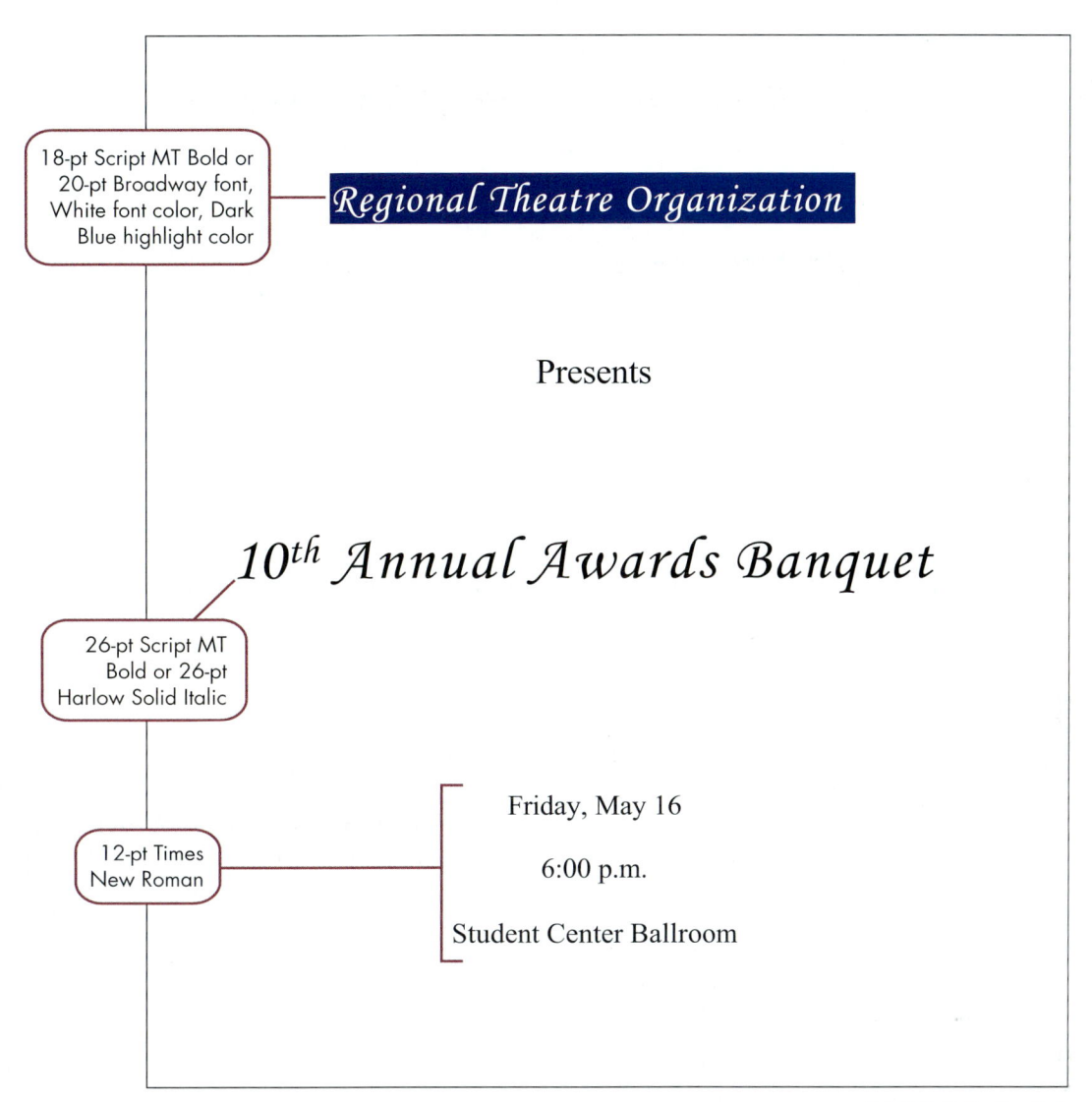

(26-pt Script MT Bold or 26-pt Harlow Solid Italic)

Friday, May 16

6:00 p.m.

Student Center Ballroom

(12-pt Times New Roman)

FIGURE 2.24

Insert a section page break. Use the Clip Organizer to search online for theatrical clip art. Download, insert, and format the image on page 2 of your document. Adjust the image's size and center it vertically and horizontally on the page.

Insert a manual page break and create page 3. Type and format the title **Awards Banquet Program** using the same font that you used for *10th Annual Awards Banquet* on the cover. Create a program that lists each activity on the left side and the announcer on the right side (with preceding dot leader tabs). Include a welcome, introductions, presentation of awards, closing remarks, and so forth. List several specific awards. See Figure 2.25 for a sample layout.

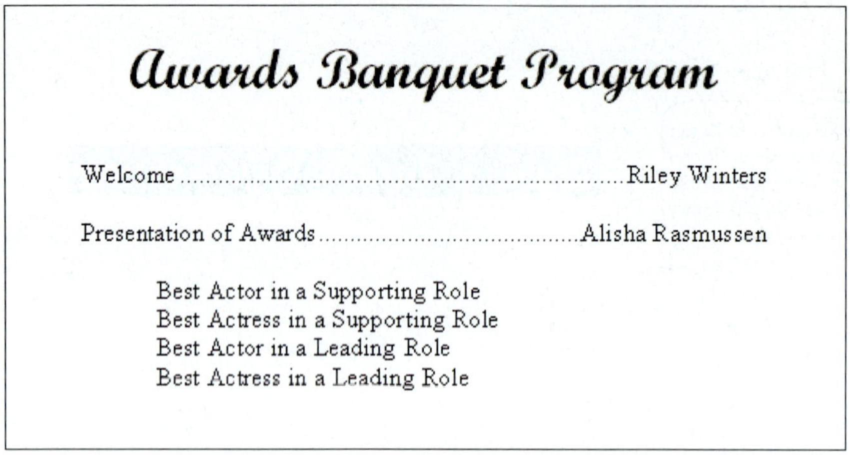

Awards Banquet Program

Welcome .... Riley Winters

Presentation of Awards .... Alisha Rasmussen

    Best Actor in a Supporting Role
    Best Actress in a Supporting Role
    Best Actor in a Leading Role
    Best Actress in a Leading Role

FIGURE 2.25

Insert a manual page break to create a blank fourth page. Save, print (optional) as a double-sided (duplexed) booklet, and close the *Awards_Banquet_Program* document. (Click Fix if you see the message *One or more margins are set outside the printable area of the page. Choose the Fix button to increase the appropriate margins.*)

Save, print (optional), and close the *Awards_Banquet_Program* document.

PROJECT 3

LEVEL 2

AUTOMATING WORK WITH AUTOTEXT, STYLES, AND TEMPLATES

OBJECTIVES

IN THIS PROJECT, YOU LEARN HOW TO

- Use a template to create a new document
- Create and insert AutoText entries
- Edit and delete AutoText entries
- Apply built-in Word styles
- Create a paragraph style
- Create a character style
- Copy styles to the Normal template
- Attach a Word template to a document

Project 3 Automating Work with AutoText, Styles, and Templates

WHY WOULD I DO THIS?

As you complete reports, assignments, and projects for other classes or in your job, you probably apply the same text, paragraph, table, and list formatting for similar documents. Instead of formatting each document individually, you can create a document based on a template to save time in setting particular formats, such as margins, headers, and paragraph indents. Another way to save time is by creating and using styles to format text, such as titles, headings, and paragraphs.

You already know that you can use AutoCorrect to automatically insert text such as *Internal Review Board* by typing a simple abbreviation such as *IRB*. Instead of expanding simple text abbreviations, you might want to insert formatted text, such as a memo heading or a signature block of a letter. With Word, you can create time-saving automatic text that you can quickly insert by typing just a few simple keys.

VISUAL SUMMARY

You can choose from a variety of predefined document types, such as memos, reports, and letters, to start creating your own documents. In the first lesson, you create a document based on a predefined memo format. You modify the memo heading and save it as automatic text you can quickly insert to start future memos. Figure 3.1 shows a memo heading based on a template and then inserted into a new document by typing a short abbreviation.

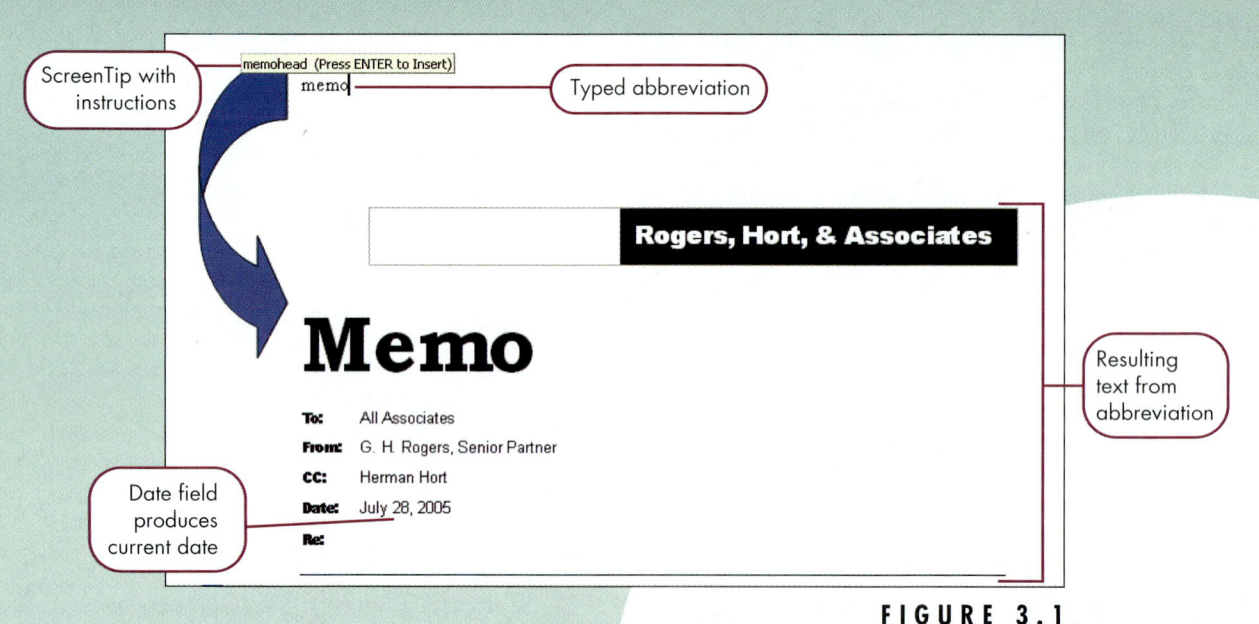

ScreenTip with instructions — memohead (Press ENTER to Insert)
Typed abbreviation — memo

Rogers, Hort, & Associates

Memo

To: All Associates
From: G. H. Rogers, Senior Partner
CC: Herman Hort
Date: July 28, 2005
Re:

Date field produces current date

Resulting text from abbreviation

FIGURE 3.1

To ensure consistency of headings throughout a document, you can create and apply styles to format the headings. You can also apply consistent formatting to other text, such as titles and names. Figure 3.2 shows a document formatted with styles.

FIGURE 3.2

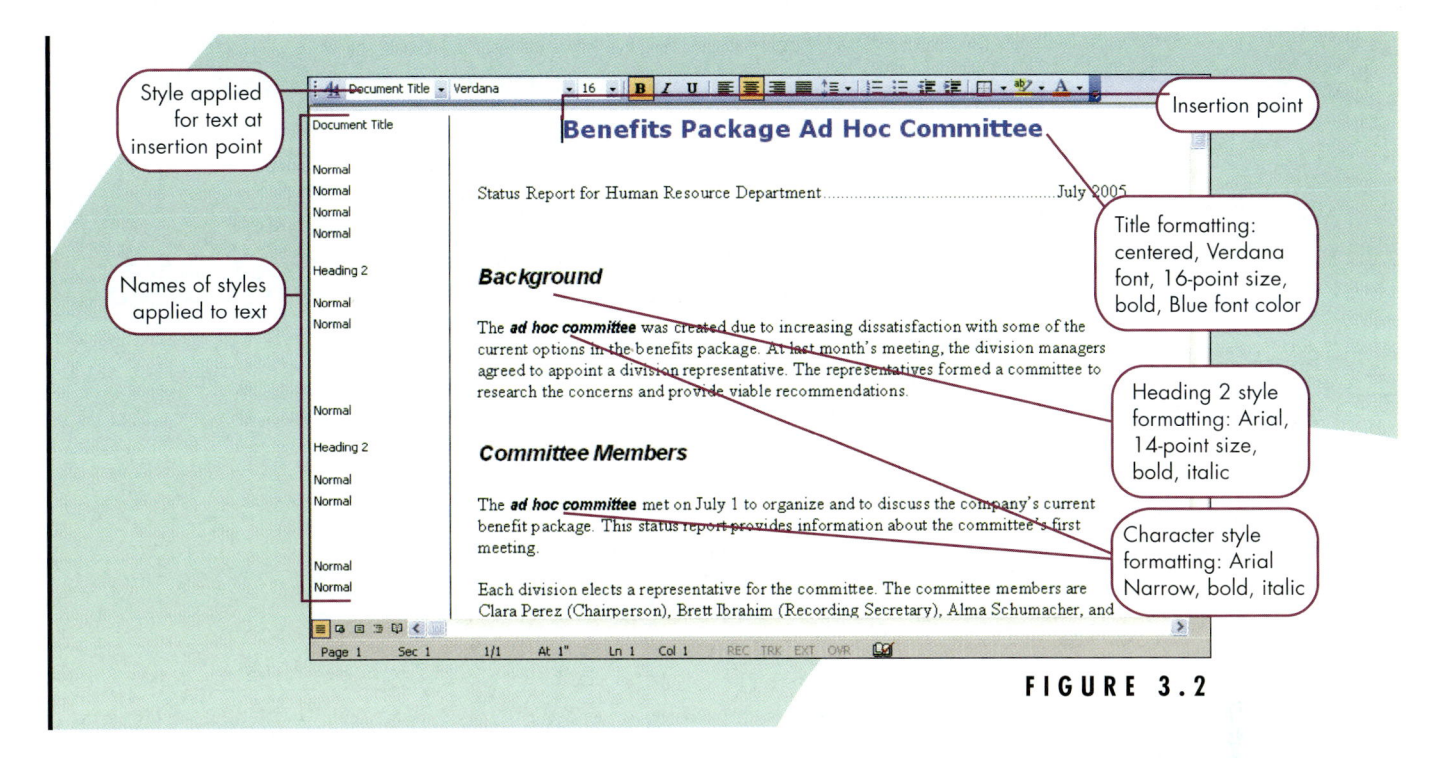

Callouts in figure:
- Style applied for text at insertion point
- Names of styles applied to text
- Insertion point
- Title formatting: centered, Verdana font, 16-point size, bold, Blue font color
- Heading 2 style formatting: Arial, 14-point size, bold, italic
- Character style formatting: Arial Narrow, bold, italic

LESSON 1: Using a Template to Create a New Document

If you are not sure how to format a certain type of document, or if you want to save time by using existing document formats, you can use a Word template. A *template* is a framework of specifications for creating a document; it specifies a document's formats—such as margins, font, and font size—and might include some text and graphics. Each time you create a new document, you use the *Normal template,* the framework that defines the 1.25″ left and right margins, 1″ top and bottom margins, Left horizontal alignment, 12-point Times New Roman font, and other settings.

Word provides other templates for specific types of documents. You can use Word templates to create letters, memos, reports, resumes, agendas, calendars, brochures, and other documents. Each template contains the framework of formats and text to decrease the time it takes you to create a document. You can even develop your own templates to use when you create certain types of documents, such as specialized reports.

In the first three lessons, you assume the role of an assistant for a legal firm. In this lesson, you complete two sets of hands-on steps. In the first set, you select the Professional Memo template to start a document. You save time doing so because you do not have to set tabs and type the main part of the memo heading. In the second set, you complete the memo heading and type the content for the memo.

To Create a Document from a Template

1 **Choose File, New.**

Figure 3.3 shows the New Document task pane so that you can start a new blank document or select a template to start a new document.

Callouts on Figure 3.3:
- Click to search for templates on Microsoft's Web site
- Click to see Word 2003 templates on your computer
- List of recently used templates, which will differ on your computer

FIGURE 3.3

2 **Click *On my computer* on the task pane.**

The Templates dialog box opens so that you can select a template category and a specific template.

3 **Click the Memos tab.**

You see several templates to help you create interoffice memos (see Figure 3.4).

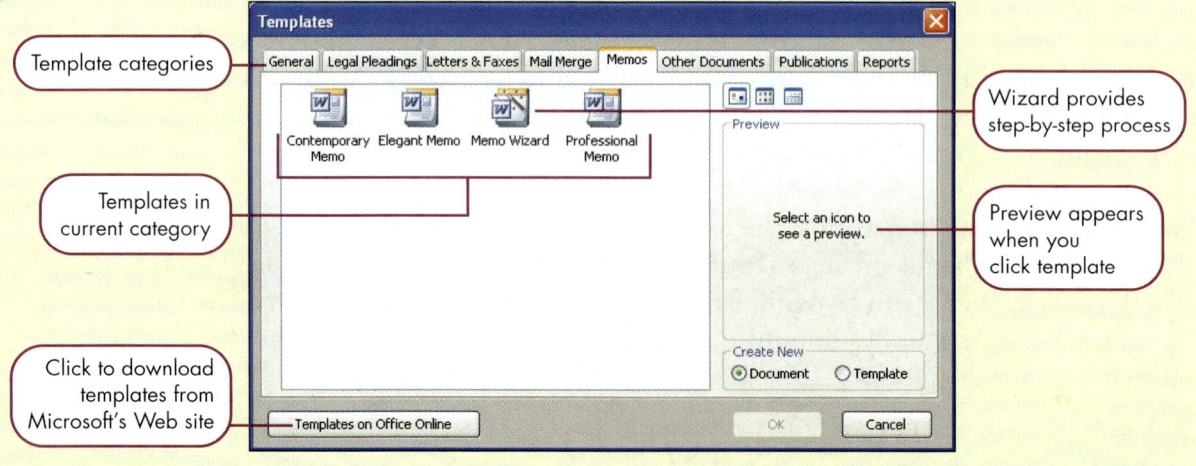

Callouts on Figure 3.4:
- Template categories
- Templates in current category
- Click to download templates from Microsoft's Web site
- Wizard provides step-by-step process
- Preview appears when you click template

FIGURE 3.4

Lesson 1   Using a Template to Create a New Document

4 **Click Professional Memo.**
The Preview window shows the overall formats and text for the selected template.

5 **Click OK.**
Word uses the template's specifications to create the document's framework for you, thus saving you valuable time (see Figure 3.5).

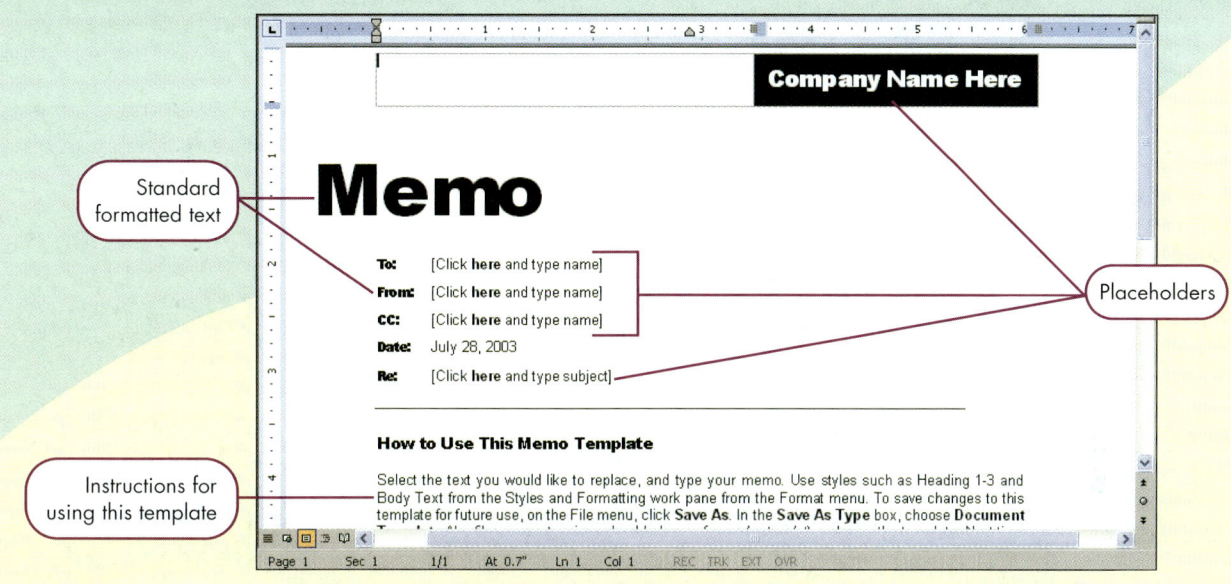

Standard formatted text
Placeholders
Instructions for using this template

FIGURE 3.5

6 Save the document as `Announcement_Memo` and keep it onscreen to continue with the next set of steps.

The document contains standard text, which is often referred to as ***boilerplate text.*** The text within brackets is simply a placeholder, indicating where you need to enter specific information. For example, *[Click here and type name]* is a placeholder for you to type the memo recipient's name. When you click a placeholder, that text is replaced with the text you type. In the next set of steps, you replace the placeholders with text and replace the paragraph with the content of your memo.

To Complete the Document

1 **In the *Announcement_Memo* document, select *Company Name Here* and type `Rogers, Hort, & Associates`.**
The text you type replaced the placeholder for the company name. Notice that it wraps the text within the table cell.

2 **Click in the first *[Click here and type name]* placeholder and type `All Associates`.**
The text you type replaces the placeholder.

3 **Click in the next placeholder to the right of *From*.**
Word highlights the next placeholder.

4 Use Figure 3.6 to replace the other three placeholders in the heading and to adjust the width of the cell containing the company name.

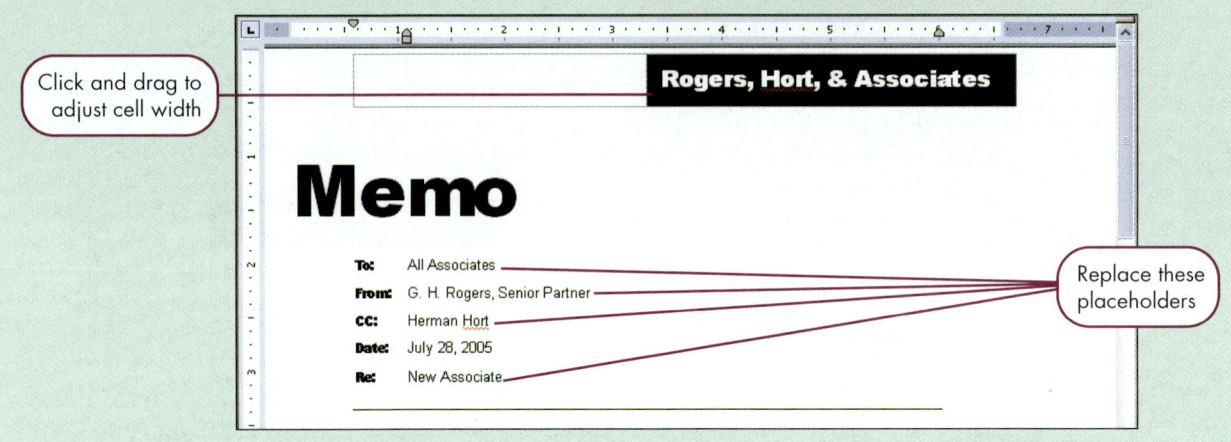

FIGURE 3.6

5 Select *How to Use This Memo Template* and type `Idelle Stearns`.
The text replaces the original heading and maintains the Heading 1 style formatting—Arial Black font and 11-point size.

6 Select the paragraph in the document and type the following paragraph:
`I'd like to extend a warm welcome to Idelle Stearns, the newest associate of our firm. She was a private corporate attorney for a large manufacturing company in New York. Her experience will help strengthen the services we provide to our clients. Please join me in welcoming Idelle at a small reception at 10 a.m. on Friday in the conference room.`

Figure 3.7 shows the completed memo.

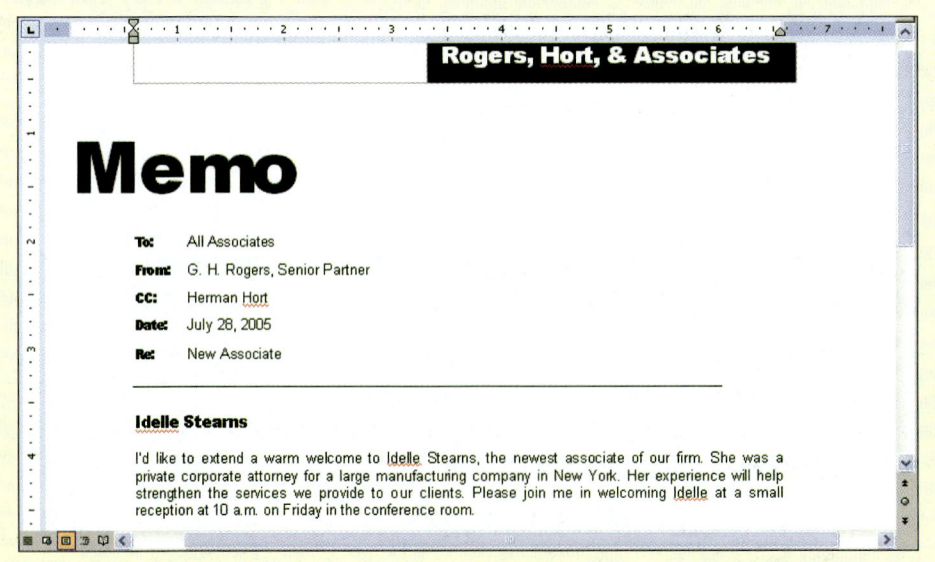

FIGURE 3.7

7 Save the *Announcement_Memo,* and keep it onscreen to continue with the next lesson.

TO EXTEND YOUR KNOWLEDGE . . .

DOWNLOADING ADDITIONAL TEMPLATES
Microsoft's Web site contains additional templates that you might find useful. To access these templates, first make sure you are connected to the Internet; then click *Templates on Office Online* on the New Document task pane or within the Templates dialog box. Follow the prompts to display a list of categories and then click a category to see specific templates. You can preview and download a template to edit within Word. You can then save the download as a document or as a template in the Save As dialog box.

PROTECTING THE NORMAL TEMPLATE AGAINST VIRUSES
Because the Normal template is the primary template for creating Word documents, it is a main target for computer viruses. Be careful when downloading unknown files from the Internet. As an extra precaution, you might want to create a backup of the Normal file in case the original template is corrupted.

USING A WIZARD TEMPLATE
Some templates are based on wizards. A *wizard* guides you through the process of completing a task, such as creating a document, by asking questions and enabling you to select various options. The wizard uses your responses to customize the document based on the template.

For example, you can choose the Calendar Wizard to guide you through creating a monthly calendar. The wizard enables you to choose the starting and ending months and years, along with specifying landscape or portrait orientation.

SAVING A DOCUMENT AS A TEMPLATE
You can save a regular Word document as a template. Choose File, Save As. Then click the *Save as type* arrow and choose *Document Template (*.dot)*, type a name for the template, and click Save. A template has a .dot extension. Templates you create appear in the General tab section of the Templates dialog box.

LESSON 2: Creating and Inserting AutoText Entries

An *AutoText entry* contains short text—such as a boilerplate paragraph and/or graphics—that you can quickly insert into a document. The default AutoText entries include attention lines, salutations, and closings. Creating and inserting AutoText entries is faster than inserting a file or typing the text each time you need it. For example, legal assistants create AutoText entries to store boilerplate paragraphs for legal documents.

You might want to create AutoText entries for text you use on a regular basis. For example, you can create an AutoText entry for your return address, a signature block for a letter, or a standard paragraph you plan to use in several documents.

Project 3 Automating Work with AutoText, Styles, and Templates

In this lesson, you complete two sets of hands-on steps. In the first set, you create an AutoText entry of the memo heading from the document you have onscreen. In the second set, you insert the AutoText entry into a new document window.

To Create an AutoText Entry

1 In the *Announcement_Memo* document, choose <u>V</u>iew, <u>T</u>oolbars, AutoText.
Displaying the AutoText toolbar helps you create, insert, and maintain AutoText entries.

2 Delete the text *New Associate,* but do not delete the paragraph mark after that line.
Before saving part of the memo as an AutoText entry, you want to delete the subject line since it changes for each memo. You must now select the text or graphic that you want to be the AutoText entry.

3 Select text from the beginning of the document through the horizontal line (see Figure 3.8).

Click to display the AutoText tab of AutoCorrect dialog box

Click to display list of current AutoText entries

Selected text

Click to create a new AutoText entry

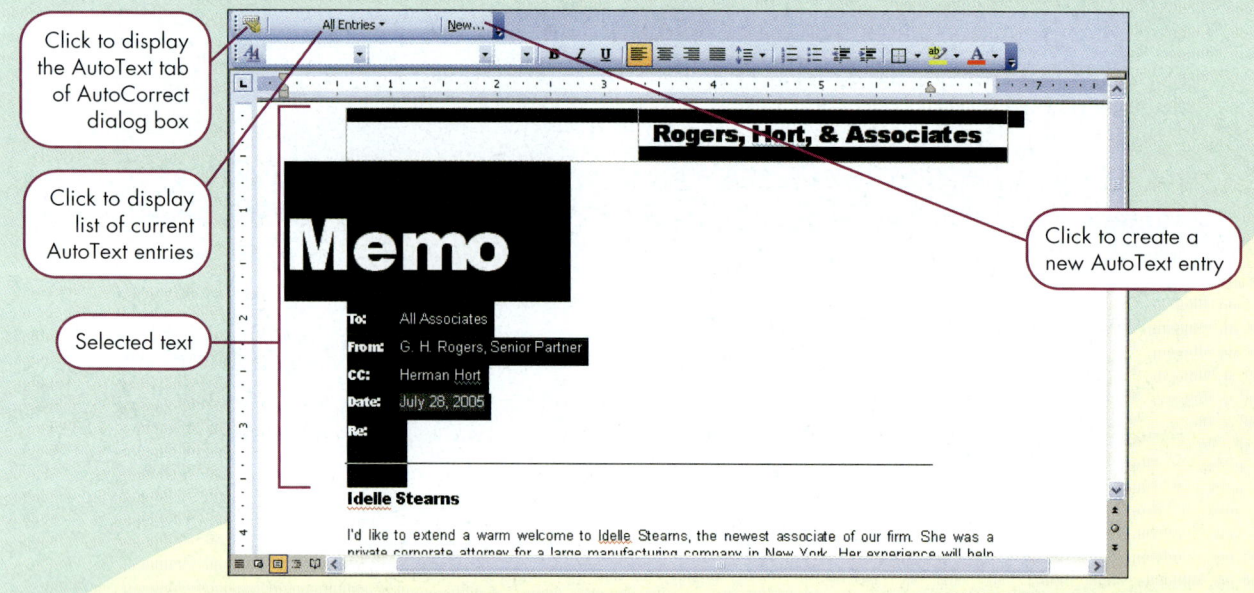

FIGURE 3.8

4 Click <u>N</u>ew on the AutoText toolbar.
The Create AutoText dialog box opens (see Figure 3.9).

FIGURE 3.9

Lesson 2 Creating and Inserting AutoText Entries   **83**   LEVEL **2**

5 **Type memohead and click OK.**

If you have problems . . .

If you see the message *Do you want to redefine the AutoText entry?* this means that an AutoText entry with the name you provide already exists. For this particular set of steps, click <u>Y</u>es to redefine the AutoText entry with the text you just selected.

6 **Close the *Announcement_Memo* document without saving the changes.**

You can insert the AutoText entries into any new or existing document. Word enables you to insert AutoText entries by using different methods. You can start typing the name of the AutoText entry. If you see a ScreenTip, press ⏎Enter to insert the AutoText. If you do not see a ScreenTip after typing the AutoText name, press F3 to insert the AutoText contents. You can also insert AutoText entries from the A<u>l</u>l Entries button on the AutoText toolbar or from the AutoCorrect dialog box.

In the next set of steps, you insert the *memohead* AutoText entry in a new document window.

To Insert an AutoText Entry

1 **Click New Blank Document on the Standard toolbar.**
You started a new document window after closing the *Announcement_Memo* document in the last set of steps.

2 **Type *memo*.**
Word displays the ScreenTip *memohead* with the instruction to press ⏎Enter to insert the AutoText entry (see Figure 3.10).

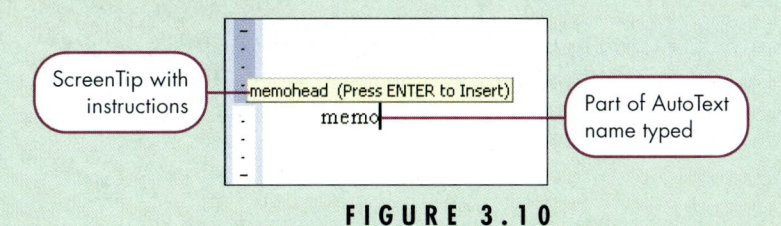

- ScreenTip with instructions → memohead (Press ENTER to Insert)
- memo| ← Part of AutoText name typed

FIGURE 3.10

If you have problems . . .

If you do not see the ScreenTip prompting you to press ⏎Enter to insert the AutoText entry, click AutoText on the AutoText toolbar to display the AutoCorrect dialog box. Select the *Show AutoComplete suggestions* check box. Then scroll through the list of AutoText entries, select *memohead,* and click <u>I</u>nsert.

3 **Press** ⏎Enter.

Word inserts the content of the *memohead* AutoText entry into the new document window. Notice that the text for the company name wraps in the table cell although you widened it earlier.

4 **Save the document as** `Memo_Heading`, **and keep it onscreen to continue with the next lesson.**

TO EXTEND YOUR KNOWLEDGE...

CREATING NEW AUTOTEXT ENTRIES
It is a good idea to create the AutoText text and graphics in a new document window so that you can edit it more easily before creating an AutoText entry from it. In addition to clicking New on the AutoText toolbar, you can also create a new AutoText entry by selecting the text and then choosing Insert, AutoText, New, or by pressing Alt+F3.

You might want to start an AutoText entry name with a backslash to avoid accidentally inserting an AutoText entry. For example, you can type **\ph** as a name for an AutoText entry that inserts a name such as *Prentice Hall*.

SAVING AUTOTEXT ENTRIES IN DIFFERENT TEMPLATES
By default, AutoText entries are saved to the Normal template so that they are available when you create new documents. However, you can save AutoText entries to other templates by using the Organizer dialog box. To learn more about how to do this, type **AutoText** in the *Type a question for help* box, press ⏎Enter, and click the *Copy AutoText entries to another template* option.

USING THE ALL ENTRIES BUTTON
You can insert an AutoText entry by clicking All Entries on the AutoText toolbar and choosing a category; then choose the AutoText entry name from the list (see Figure 3.11). The *memohead* AutoText entry you created is probably located under the *Return Address* category.

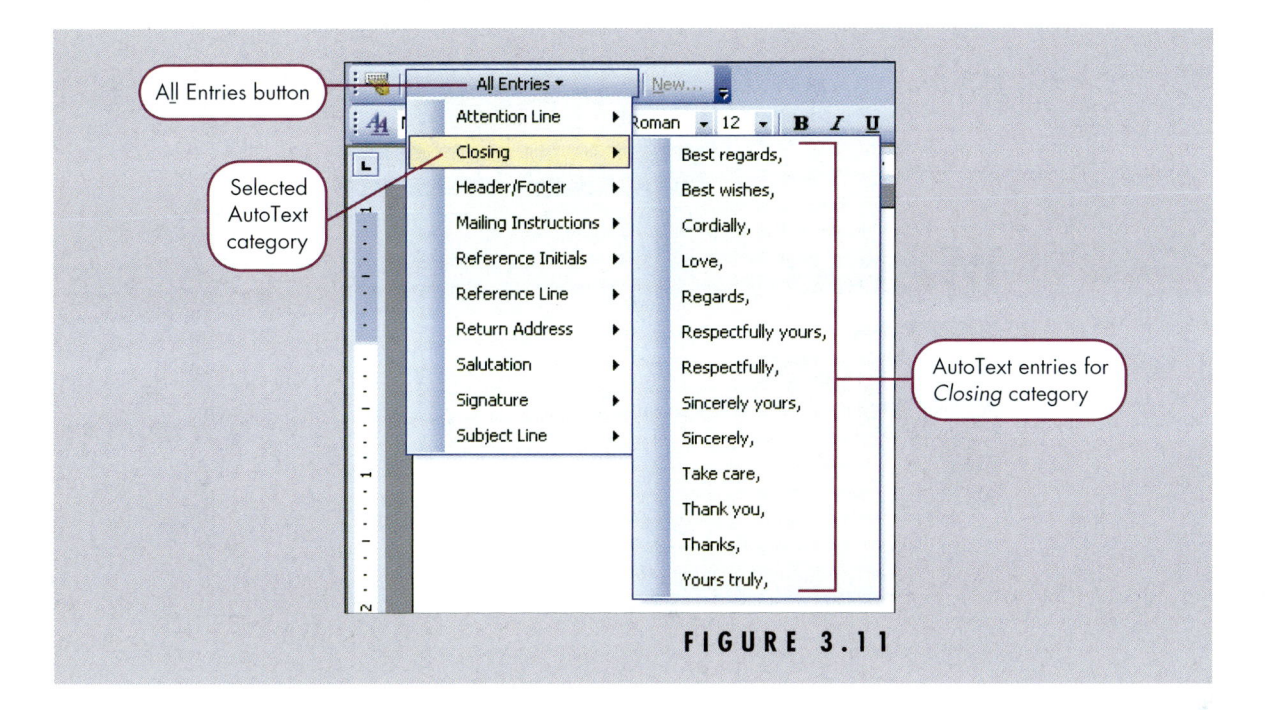

Lesson 3   Editing and Deleting AutoText Entries   **85**   LEVEL 2

- All Entries button
- Selected AutoText category
- AutoText entries for *Closing* category

FIGURE 3.11

LESSON 3: Editing and Deleting AutoText Entries

After creating an AutoText entry, you might need to change its results. For example, you might need to correct an error, change the text, or format the text. In addition, you might decide to delete an AutoText entry that you no longer use.

In this lesson, you modify the *memohead* AutoText entry by widening a table cell, changing the font of the Memo title, and eliminating the left indentation space for the memo heading text lines.

To Edit an AutoText Entry

1. **With the *Memo_Heading* document onscreen, adjust the cell containing the law firm name so that it does not wrap in its cell.**
   The name of the law firm appears on one line now.

2. **Select the title *Memo,* apply Bookman Old Style font, and apply bold.**
   The Bookman Old Style font adds more formality, appropriate for a law firm.

3. **Select the *To* line through the horizontal line after *Re:* but do not select the blank line below the horizontal line.**

4. **Choose Format, Paragraph, and click the Indents and Spacing tab, if needed.**
   The Indents and Spacing tab provides options for adjusting paragraph indentation.

5. **Set 0″ left and right indentations.**

6. **Click the Special drop-down arrow, choose *(none),* and click OK.**
   Figure 3.12 reflects the changes you made to the AutoText contents.

Project 3 Automating Work with AutoText, Styles, and Templates

Cell width adjusted

Click to redefine AutoText entry

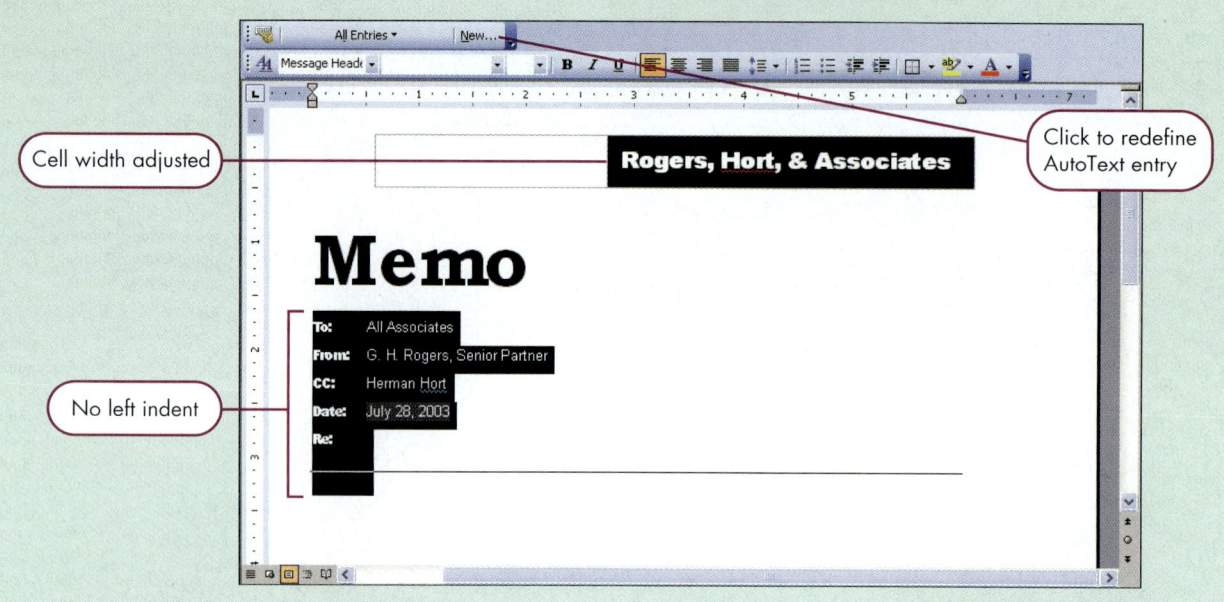

No left indent

FIGURE 3.12

7 Press Ctrl+A.
You just selected the entire document so that you can the redefine the AutoText entry.

8 Click **N**ew in the AutoText toolbar, type **memohead**, and click OK.
You see a message *Do you want to redefine the AutoText entry?* (see Figure 3.13).

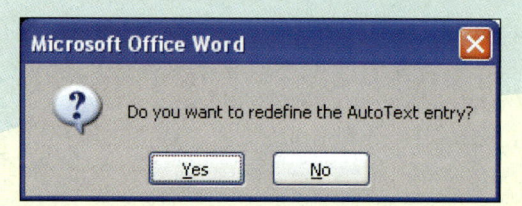

FIGURE 3.13

9 Click **Y**es.
Word redefines the *memohead* AutoText by saving the currently selected text with that name.

10 Close the document without saving it.

11 Open *EW2_0301* and save it as `Cell_Phone_Memo`.

12 With the insertion point at the beginning of the document, type **memo** and press ↵Enter when prompted by the ScreenTip.
Word inserts the *memohead* AutoText contents at the beginning of the document (see Figure 3.14).

Lesson 3   Editing and Deleting AutoText Entries   87   LEVEL 2

AutoText contents

Cell_Phone_Memo document contents

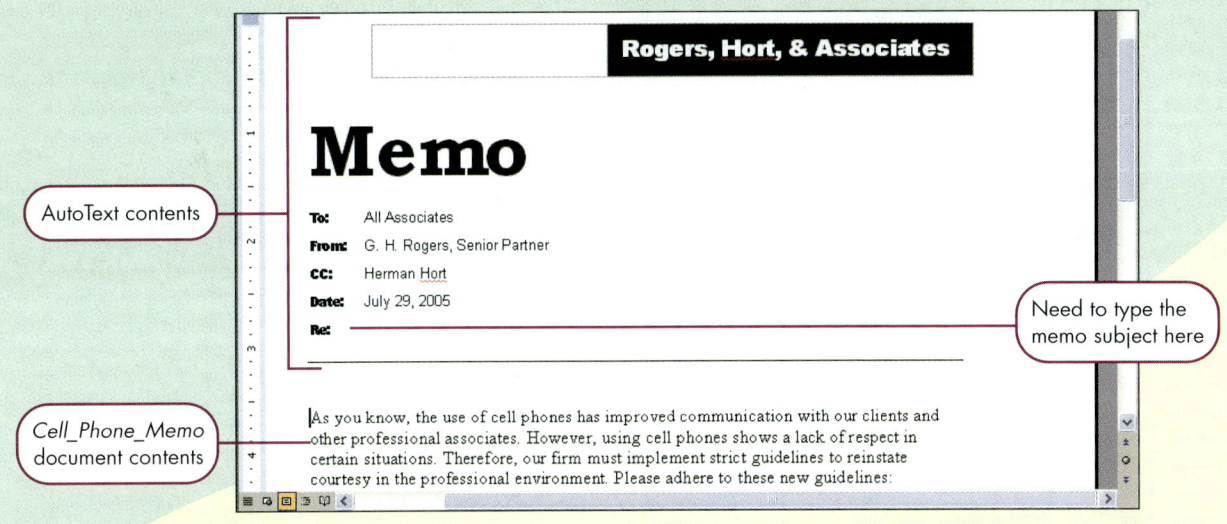

Need to type the memo subject here

FIGURE 3.14

13 Type `Cell Phone Usage` to the right of the *Re:* heading, aligned with the date.

14 Save, print (optional), and close the *Cell_Phone_Memo* document.

15 Hide the AutoText toolbar.

TO EXTEND YOUR KNOWLEDGE...

DELETING AN AUTOTEXT ENTRY

You can delete AutoText entries that you no longer use. Within an existing or new document window, click *AutoText* on the AutoText toolbar to display the AutoText tab of the AutoCorrect dialog box, and select the entry you want to delete (see Figure 3.15).

Project 3 Automating Work with AutoText, Styles, and Templates

FIGURE 3.15

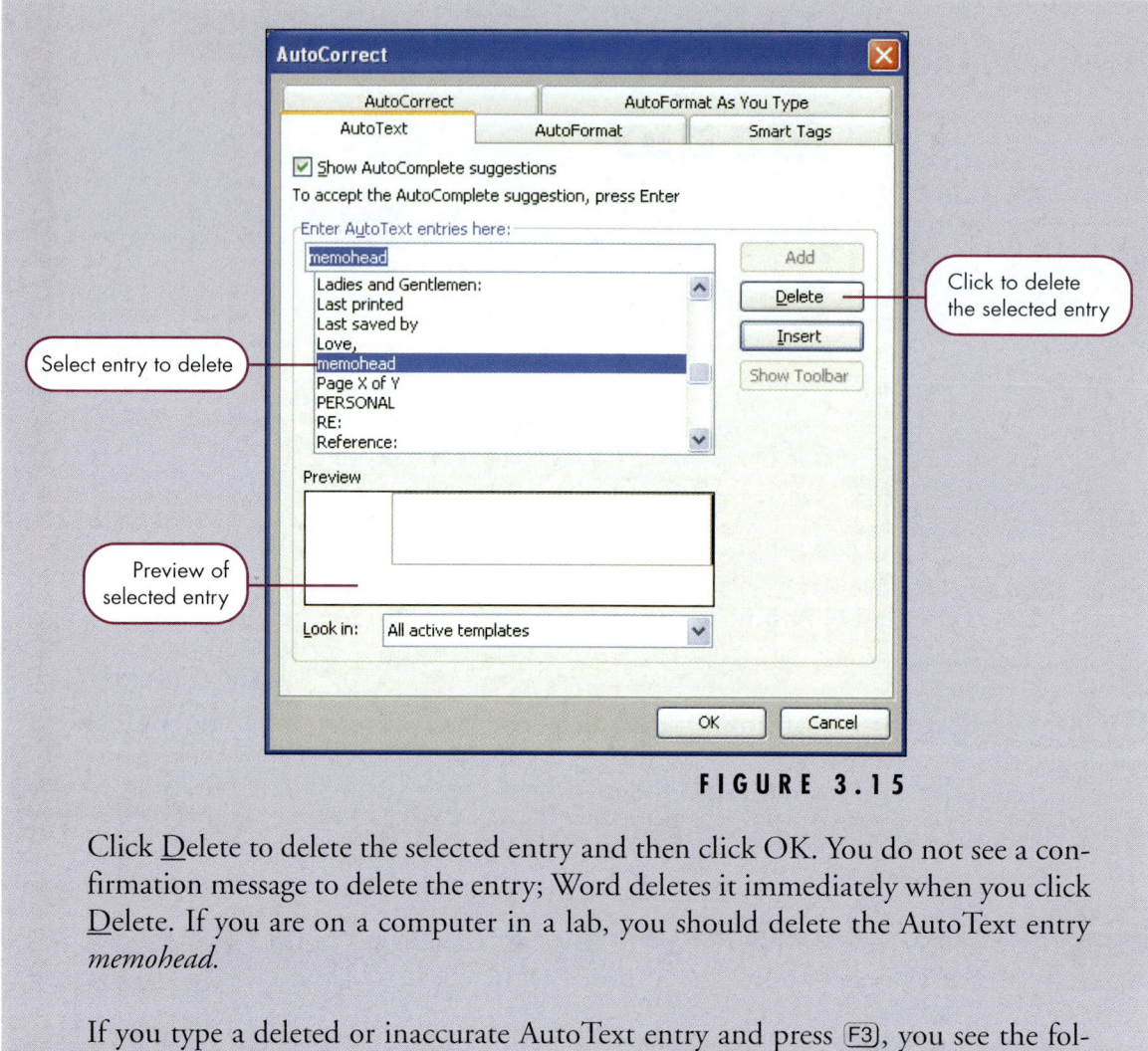

Click Delete to delete the selected entry and then click OK. You do not see a confirmation message to delete the entry; Word deletes it immediately when you click Delete. If you are on a computer in a lab, you should delete the AutoText entry *memohead*.

If you type a deleted or inaccurate AutoText entry and press F3, you see the following message on the status bar at the bottom of the screen: *The specified text is not a valid AutoText name. Use Insert AutoText to create AutoText entries.*

LESSON 4: Applying Built-In Word Styles

One of Word's most convenient and efficient attributes is the Style feature. A ***style*** is a group of formatting settings that you can apply to characters or paragraphs. Because a style contains several format settings, you exert less effort in formatting text, such as headings. For instance, a single style might apply 16-point Arial, Blue font color, Center horizontal alignment, and 12-point spacing after the paragraph. Instead of applying each of these settings individually, you apply the style that contains these formats.

Another benefit of using styles is consistency. Because you apply a style to headings instead of individually formatting headings, you know your headings are formatted consistently. Plus, if you change the style, all text formatted by that style is reformatted automatically.

Lesson 4 Applying Built-In Word Styles 89 LEVEL 2

The Normal template contains more than 100 styles. Unless you specify a style, Word uses the Normal style. The Normal style contains these settings: 12-point Times New Roman, English (U.S.) language, Single line spacing, Left horizontal alignment, and Widow/Orphan control.

In this lesson, you apply the default heading styles to an existing document.

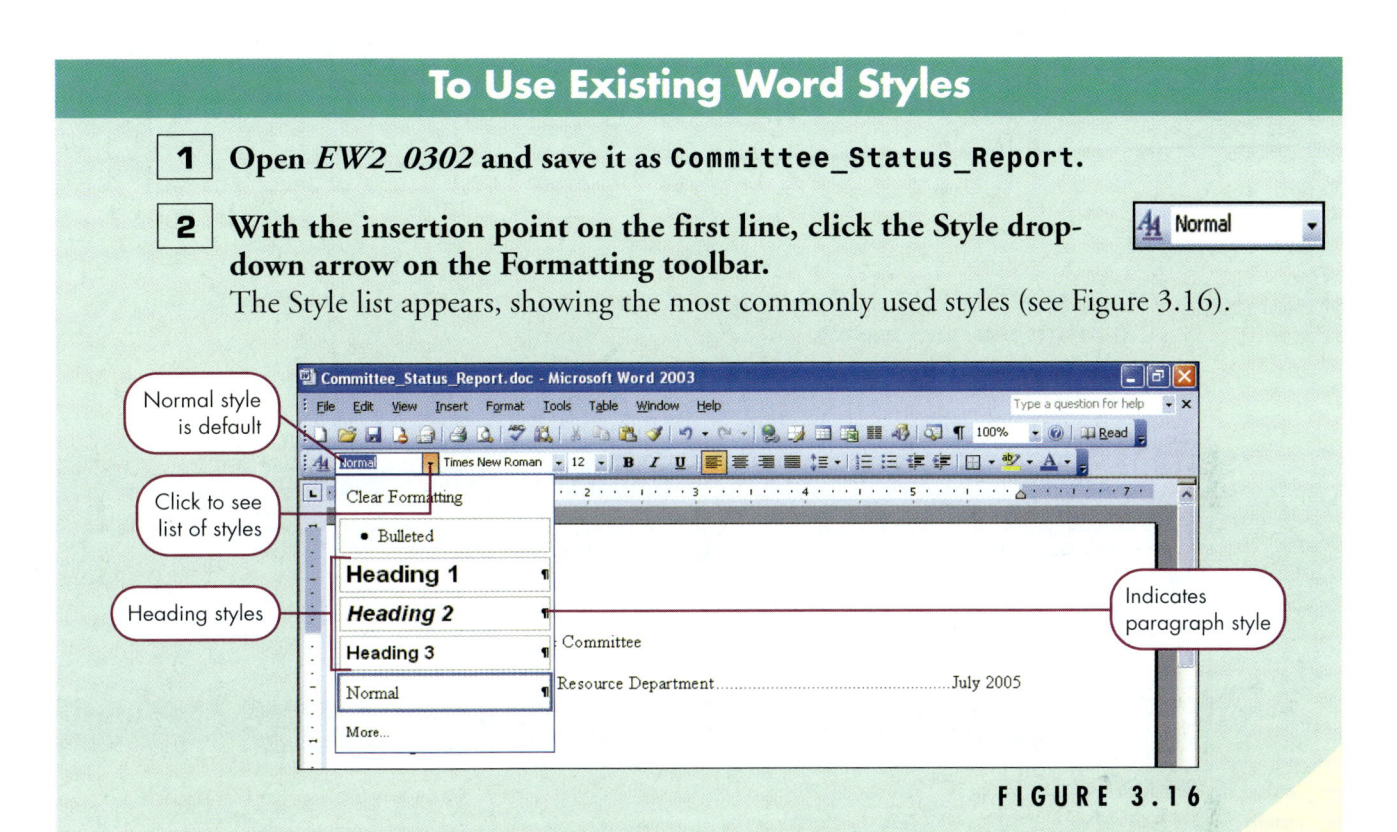

To Use Existing Word Styles

1 Open *EW2_0302* and save it as `Committee_Status_Report`.

2 With the insertion point on the first line, click the Style drop-down arrow on the Formatting toolbar.
The Style list appears, showing the most commonly used styles (see Figure 3.16).

FIGURE 3.16

3 Choose Heading 1 from the list.
When you choose a style, Word applies that style's formatting to the paragraph that contains the insertion point. The text is formatted in 16-point Arial font with bold attribute. Notice that the Style button on the toolbar displays Heading 1, the name of the style used for that paragraph.

4 Click in the heading *Background*.

5 Click the Style drop-down arrow, and choose Heading 2.
The Heading 2 style applies 14-point size, Arial font, bold, and italic attributes to the text.

6 Scroll down and apply the Heading 2 style to the *Committee Members, Employee Concerns,* and *Work in Progress* headings, and then scroll back to the top of the document and click in the *Background* heading.
Figure 3.17 shows the document after you apply the Heading 1 and Heading 2 styles.

Project 3 Automating Work with AutoText, Styles, and Templates

- Style button indicates style applied at insertion point location
- Heading 1 style
- Insertion point at text formatted with the Heading 2 style

Benefits Package Ad Hoc Committee

Status Report for Human Resource Department..................July 2005

Background

The ad hoc committee was created due to increasing dissatisfaction with some of the current options in the benefits package. At last month's meeting, the division managers agreed to appoint a division representative. The representatives formed a committee to research the concerns and provide viable recommendations.

Committee Members

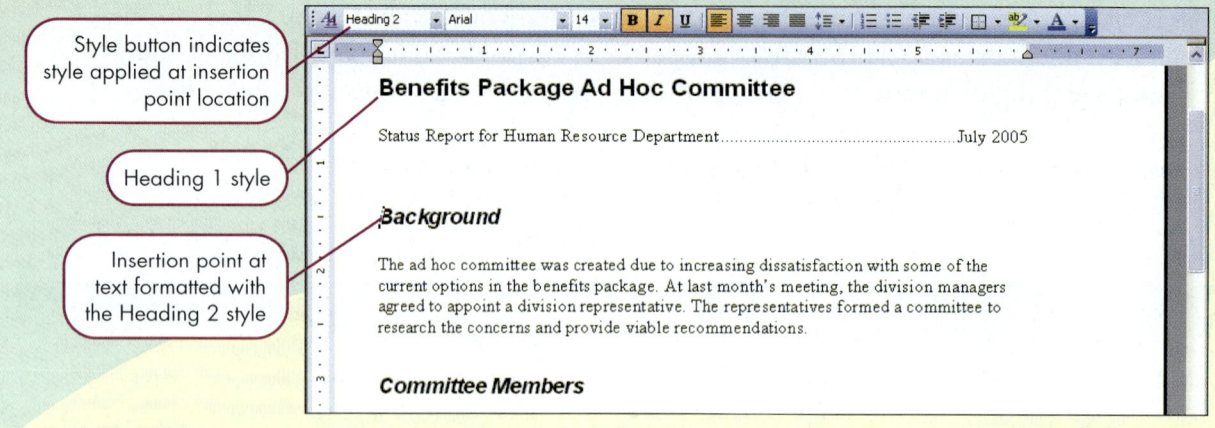

FIGURE 3.17

7 Save the *Committee_Status_Report* document, and keep it onscreen to continue with the next lesson.

TO EXTEND YOUR KNOWLEDGE . . .

USING KEYBOARD SHORTCUTS TO APPLY STYLES

You can apply some styles by using keyboard shortcuts. Table 3.1 lists the keyboard shortcuts for some of Word's default styles.

TABLE 3.1

KEYBOARD SHORTCUT	STYLE
Ctrl+Alt+1	Heading 1
Ctrl+Alt+2	Heading 2
Ctrl+Alt+3	Heading 3
Ctrl+Shift+L	List (for bullets)
Ctrl+Shift+N	Normal
Ctrl+Shift+S	Activates Style box on toolbar; press ↑ or ↓ to scroll through list

DISPLAYING ALL STYLES IN THE NORMAL TEMPLATE

When you click the Style drop-down arrow, you see only a few styles. If you want to see a list of all styles that are available in the Normal template, press Shift while you click the Style drop-down arrow.

USING HEADING STYLES

The heading styles also include space above and below the heading to visually separate the headings from the regular text. For example, Heading 2 includes 12-point spacing before and 3-point spacing after. Heading styles also contain the *Keep with next* pagination option (within the Paragraph dialog box) to make sure the heading is not isolated at the bottom of a page.

VIEWING PARAGRAPH FORMATS

You can view paragraph formats by choosing Format, Reveal Formatting. Figure 3.18 shows the Reveal Formatting task pane that details the formats for the *Background* heading formatted with the Heading 2 style.

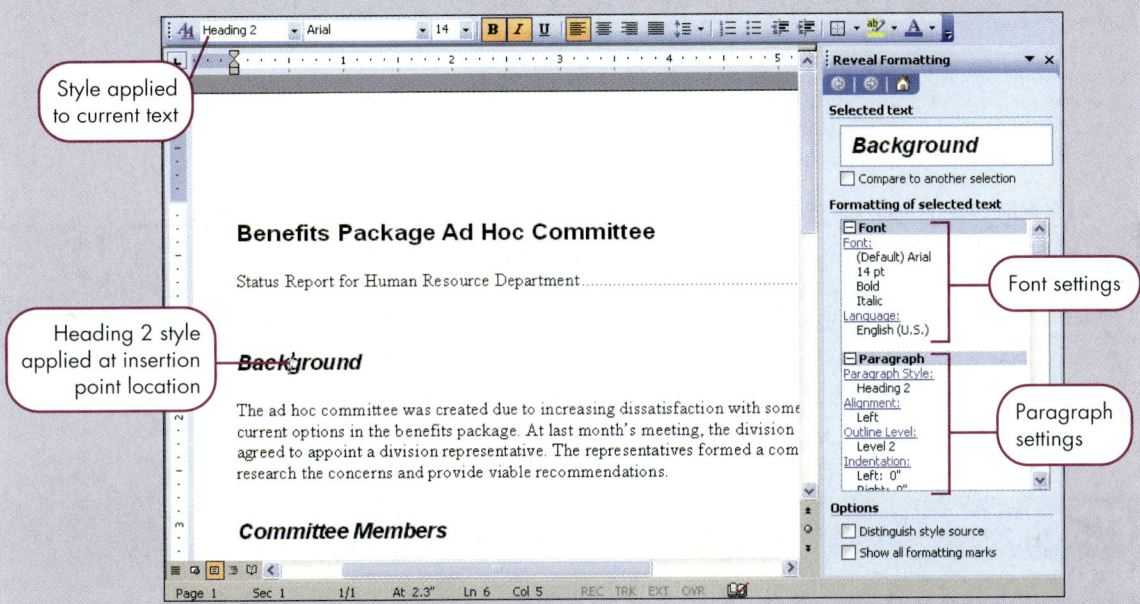

FIGURE 3.18

DISPLAYING STYLE NAMES IN NORMAL VIEW

You can display the ***style area***, the space on the left side of the screen that displays style names next to each paragraph in Normal and Outline views. To do this, choose Tools, Options to open the Options dialog box. In the *Outline and Normal options* section on the View tab, specify the amount of space in the *Style area width* box, and click OK. Figure 3.19 shows a 0.56" width for style names.

FIGURE 3.19

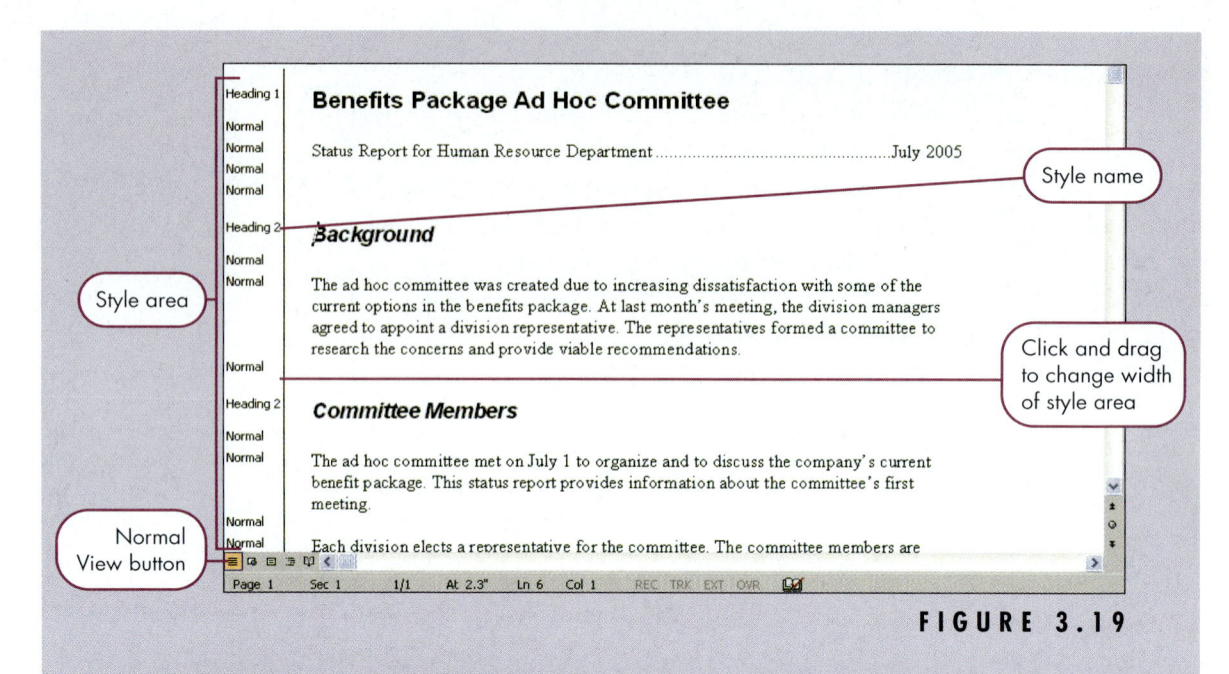

FINDING AND REPLACING STYLES

You can use the Find and Replace feature to locate text formatted with one style and replace it with another style. From within the Find and Replace dialog box, click More to display additional options, click Format at the bottom of the dialog box, and choose Style from the list. Choose the style you want to find. Then repeat the process to find the style you want to replace.

LESSON 5: Creating a Paragraph Style

Although Word contains a great number of styles, you might want to create your own. You can create four different types of styles: paragraph, character, table, and list. A *paragraph style* applies formats to an entire paragraph, or text separated by hard returns. Paragraph styles contain font formats and paragraph formats such as line spacing, indents, horizontal alignment, and spacing before and after the paragraph. The Heading 1 and Heading 2 styles you applied in the previous lesson are actually paragraph styles.

In this lesson, you create a paragraph style and apply it to the main heading in the status report.

To Create and Apply a Paragraph Style

1 In the *Committee_Status_Report* document, position the insertion point on the first line and then apply the Normal style again.

2 Click Styles and Formatting on the left side of the Formatting toolbar.
The Styles and Formatting task pane opens, displaying a list of available styles (see Figure 3.20).

Lesson 5   Creating a Paragraph Style   93   LEVEL 2

Styles and Formatting button

Click to create a new style

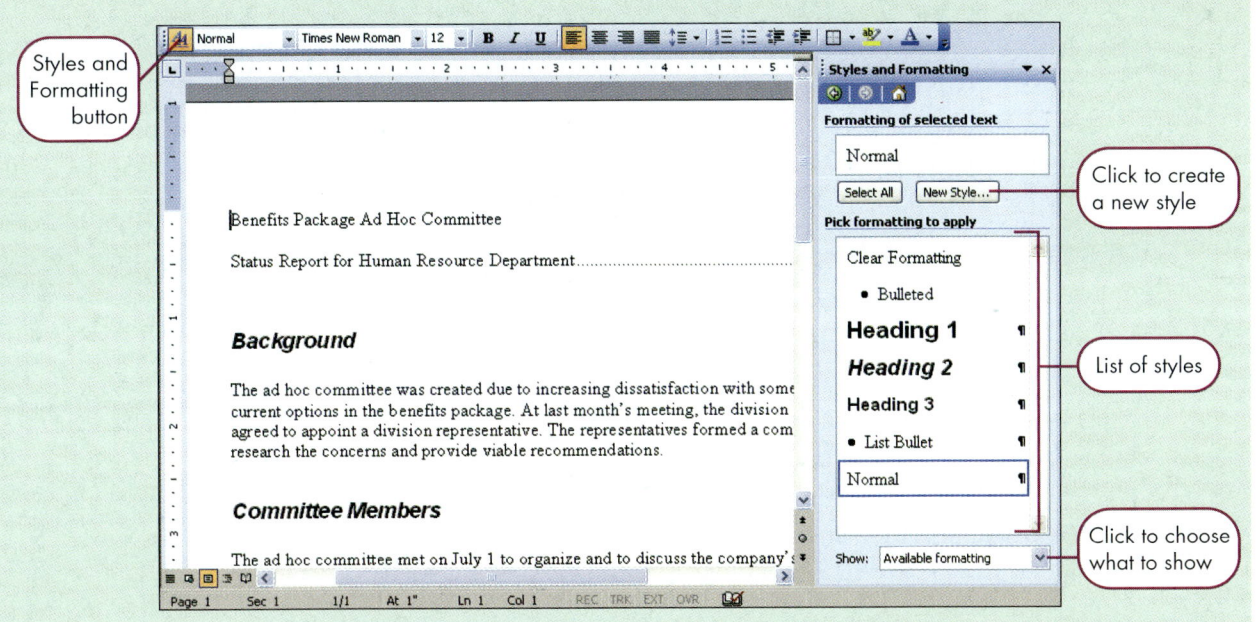

List of styles

Click to choose what to show

FIGURE 3.20

3 | **Click *New Style* on the task pane to create a new style.**
The New Style dialog box opens so that you can specify the style name, type, and format (see Figure 3.21).

Name your new style

Specify the type of style

Buttons to specify formats

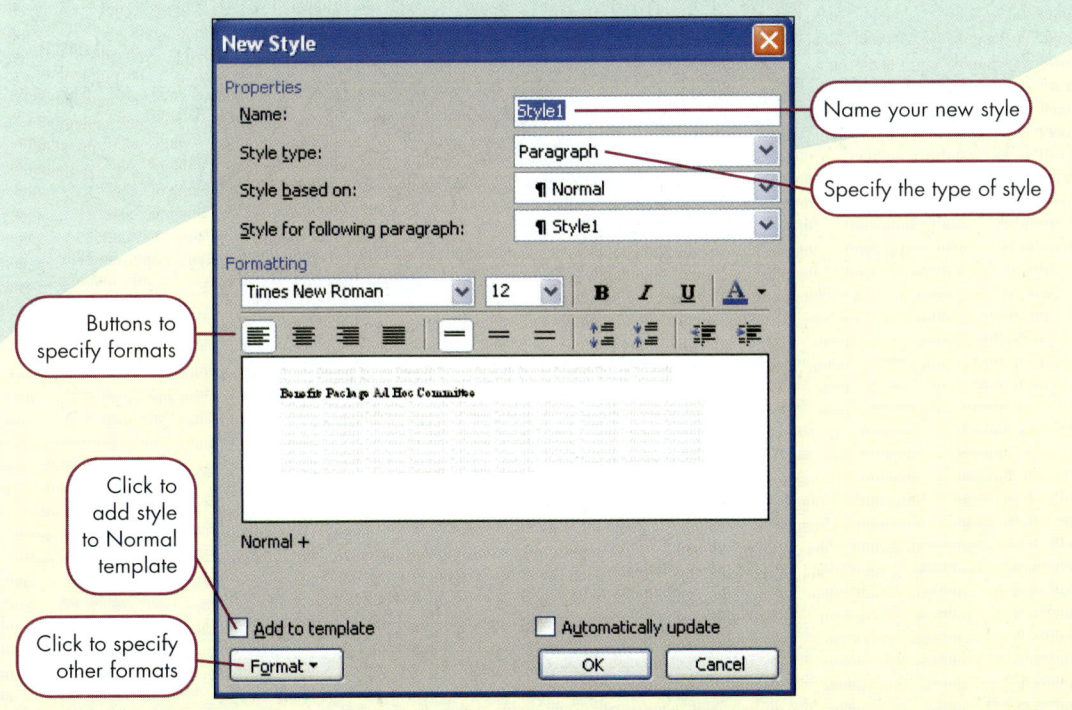

Click to add style to Normal template

Click to specify other formats

FIGURE 3.21

4 | **Type `Document Title` in the *Name* box.**
The default *Style type* setting is Paragraph, but you can change it to Character, Table, or List. Because you are creating a paragraph style in this lesson, leave the *Style type* as Paragraph.

5 Make sure the *Style type* is Paragraph, and make sure the *Style based on* option is Normal.

The *Style for following paragraph* option specifies what style is used for the next paragraph when you press ↵Enter. Because you do not typically apply two title styles on two consecutive lines, you should change the option to Normal.

6 Click the *Style for following paragraph* drop-down arrow, and choose Normal.

The New Style dialog box contains buttons to quickly select formats, such as fonts, sizes, and line spacing.

7 Make the following formatting changes:

- Verdana or Lucida Console font
- 16-point size
- Bold
- Blue font color
- Center alignment

8 Click F*o*rmat at the bottom of the New Style dialog box, and choose Paragraph.

The Paragraph dialog box opens so that you can choose additional paragraph formats. For example, the New Style dialog box contains a button that increases the spacing both before and after the paragraph by 6 points each time you click it, but you might want to set extra spacing only after the paragraph, which you can do by using the Paragraph dialog box.

9 Make sure the *I*ndents and Spacing tab is selected, click the Aft*e*r increment button to display *12 pt,* and then click OK.

Figure 3.22 shows the style's description after selecting the font and paragraph formats.

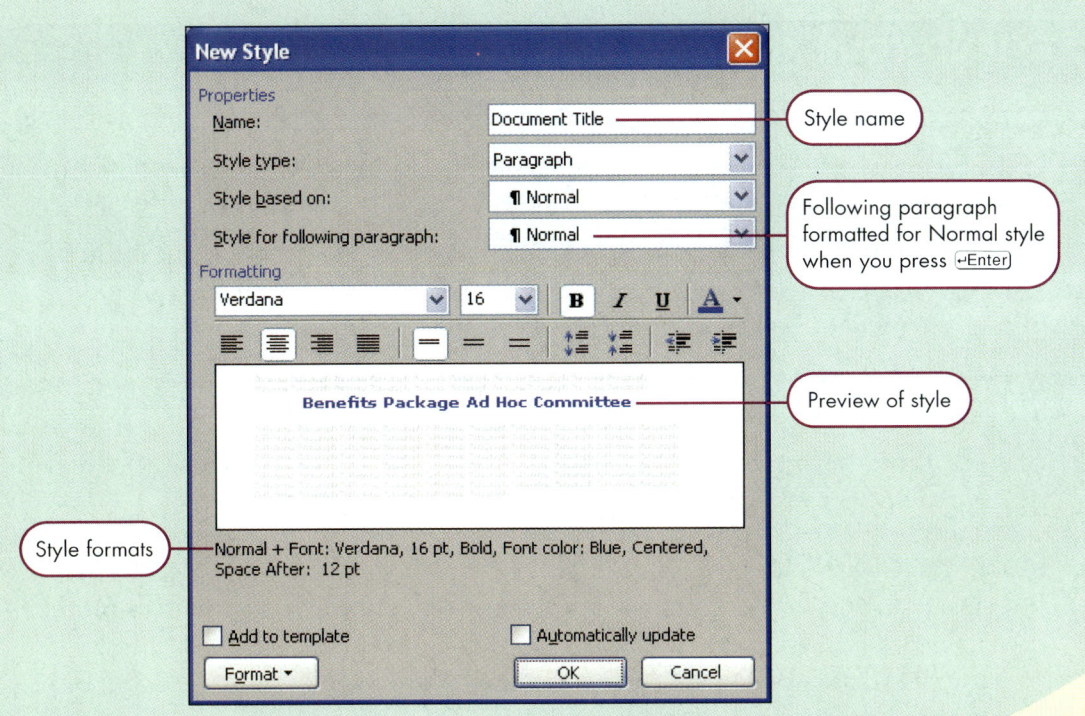

Lesson 5   Creating a Paragraph Style   95   LEVEL 2

FIGURE 3.22

Callouts on figure: Style name; Following paragraph formatted for Normal style when you press Enter; Preview of style; Style formats

10 Click OK to accept the style formats.

11 Click the Document Title style name from the Styles and Formatting task pane.
Figure 3.23 shows the Document Title style applied to the heading.

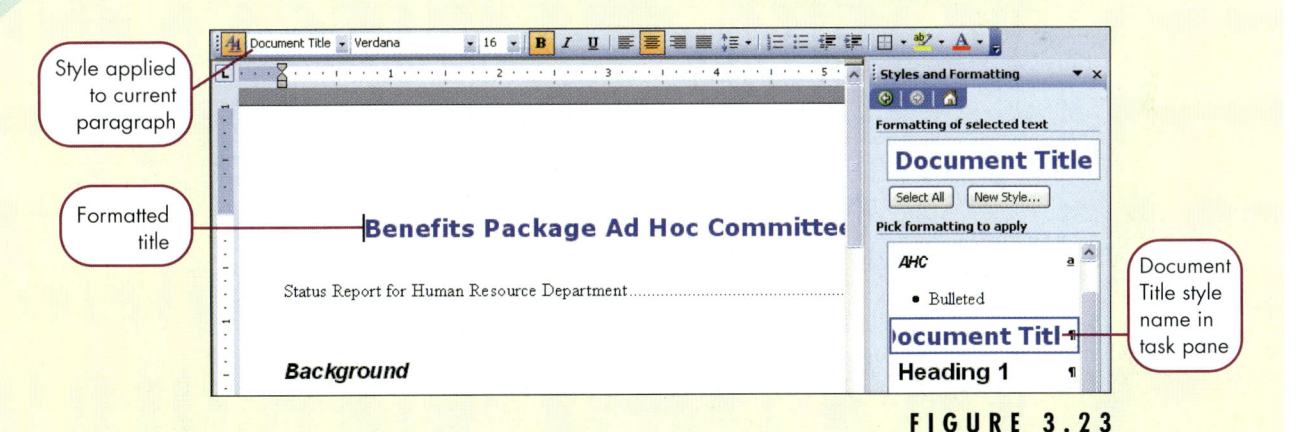

Callouts on figure: Style applied to current paragraph; Formatted title; Document Title style name in task pane

FIGURE 3.23

12 Save the *Committee_Status_Report* document, and keep it onscreen to continue with the next lesson.

TO EXTEND YOUR KNOWLEDGE...

BASING THE STYLE ON ANOTHER STYLE
If you want to include formats from an existing style, choose it from the *Style based on* drop-down list in the New Style dialog box. If you want to create a style from scratch without using existing styles, make sure the *Style based on* option is Normal. Use this option with caution: If you change the style on which you base other styles, the other related styles will also change.

DELETING A STYLE
To delete a style, position the mouse pointer on the style name in the task pane, click the drop-down arrow, and choose Delete. Click Yes when you see the message *Do you want to delete [style name]?*

MODIFYING A STYLE
If you want to edit a style to change its formats, position the mouse pointer on the style name on the task pane, click the drop-down arrow, and choose Modify. The Modify Style dialog box opens, which looks similar to the New Style dialog box. Change the format as needed.

You can also modify a style without opening the Modify Style dialog box. First, make the formatting changes to text affected by the style; then select that text, click the drop-down arrow by the style name in the task pane, and choose the *Update to Match Selection* option (see Figure 3.24).

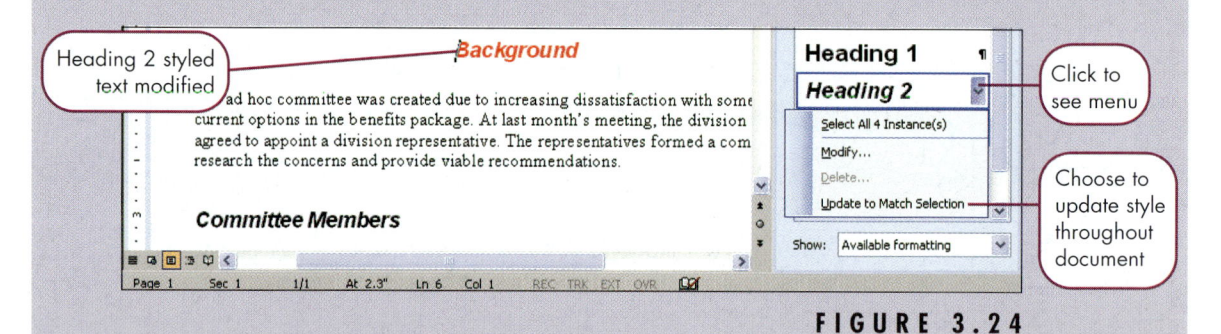

FIGURE 3.24

When you modify a style, Word automatically reformats text that is affected by that style. Using the Style feature saves you valuable time in reformatting text throughout the document.

USING STYLES IN OTHER DOCUMENTS
By default, Word will apply styles that you create to the current document only. However, you can click *Add to template* within the New Style dialog box to add a new style you create to the Normal template so that it is available for other new documents (refer to Figure 3.21 earlier in this lesson).

LESSON 6: Creating a Character Style

So far, you have applied paragraph styles using Word's heading styles and your own Document Title style; however, you might want to create and apply a *character style*—a style that formats a portion of the text within a paragraph. Unlike a paragraph style that can format font, border, language, line spacing, alignment, and indents, a character style can format only fonts, borders, and languages.

In this lesson, you create a character style named AHC and apply it to the text *ad hoc committee*.

To Create and Apply a Character Style

1. **In the *Committee_Status_Report* document, click on the blank line below the title.**
   The insertion point is positioned in an unformatted area of the document.

2. **If the Styles and Formatting task pane is not visible, click Styles and Formatting.**

3. **Click New Style on the task pane.**
   The New Style dialog box opens, enabling you to enter the new style's name and specify its formats.

4. **Type AHC in the *Name* box.**
   AHC is an abbreviation for *ad hoc committee*.

5. **Click the *Style type* drop-down arrow, and choose Character.**

6. **Make sure the *Style based on* option is Default Paragraph Font.**
   Now you are ready to specify the formats for the character style.

7. **Click the appropriate format buttons to set these formats: Arial Narrow font, bold, italic.**
   The description is *Default Paragraph Font+Font: Arial Narrow, Bold, Italic*.

8. **Click OK to close the New Style dialog box.**
   You are ready to apply the character style to the text *ad hoc committee* throughout the document.

9. **Select the text *ad hoc committee* in the first paragraph in the Background section.**
   Unlike applying a paragraph style, where you simply choose the style without selecting text, you must select text before applying a character style.

10. **Click the AHC style name from the *Pick formatting to apply* list box in the Styles and Formatting task pane.**
    Word applies the AHC style formats to the selected text.

11 Deselect this occurrence, and select *ad hoc committee* in the first paragraph in the Committee Members section. Apply the AHC style, and deselect the text.

Figure 3.25 shows the AHC style applied to text.

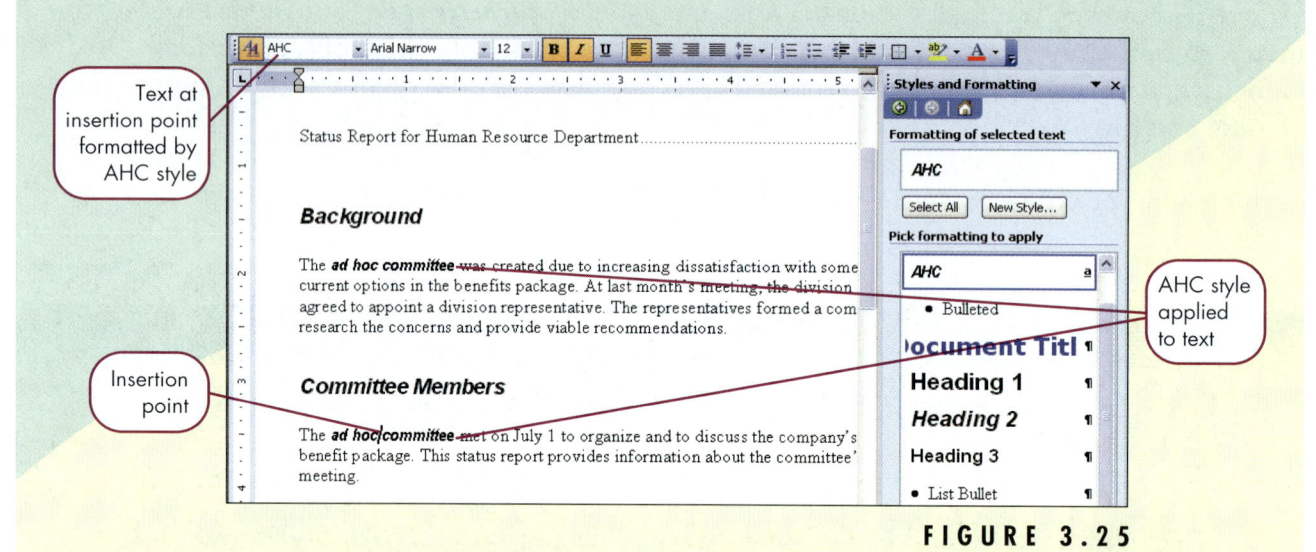

Text at insertion point formatted by AHC style

Insertion point

AHC style applied to text

FIGURE 3.25

12 Save the *Committee_Status_Report* document, and keep it onscreen to continue with the next lesson.

TO EXTEND YOUR KNOWLEDGE...

USING THE STYLES DIALOG BOX

Users of previous Word versions are accustomed to manipulating styles through the Styles dialog box. You can open this dialog box by clicking the *Show* drop-down arrow from the task pane, choosing *Custom* to open the Format Settings dialog box, and clicking the Styles button.

You can use the Style dialog box to create new styles, or to delete, modify, and apply styles (see Figure 3.26).

Lesson 6   Creating a Character Style   99   LEVEL 2

[Style dialog box with callouts: "Click to choose a category of styles to display", "Click to create new style", "List of styles", "Click to apply selected style to text at insertion point"]

FIGURE 3.26

CREATING TABLE AND LIST STYLES

You can create a table or list style by choosing Table or List from the *Style type* option in the New Style dialog box. When you create a table style, you can base it on a predefined Table AutoFormat style (refer to *Essentials Word 2003 Level 1* Project 7 Lesson 8). You can specify cell borders, shading, and other formats for the entire table, the header row, the first or last column, and so on. Figure 3.27 shows an example of options selected for a new table style.

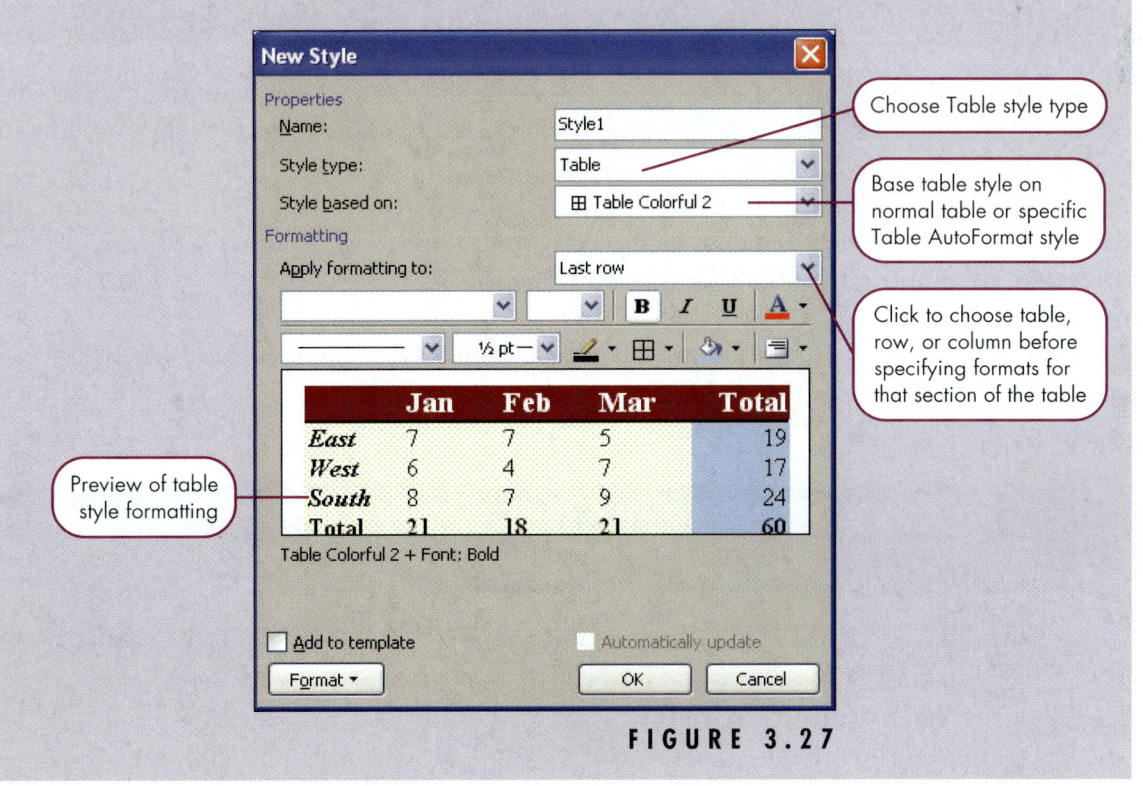

[New Style dialog box with callouts: "Choose Table style type", "Base table style on normal table or specific Table AutoFormat style", "Click to choose table, row, or column before specifying formats for that section of the table", "Preview of table style formatting"]

FIGURE 3.27

You can create a list style that is similar to the outline numbered list options in the Bullets and Numbering dialog box. A list style you create is similar to selecting the outline numbered list with a hierarchical structure to the list. You specify the level number and then choose the regular numbers, uppercase or lowercase Roman numerals, uppercase or lowercase alphabet, or bullet symbols. You can also choose fonts, font color, and other formatting for each level. Figure 3.28 shows the options available when creating a list style.

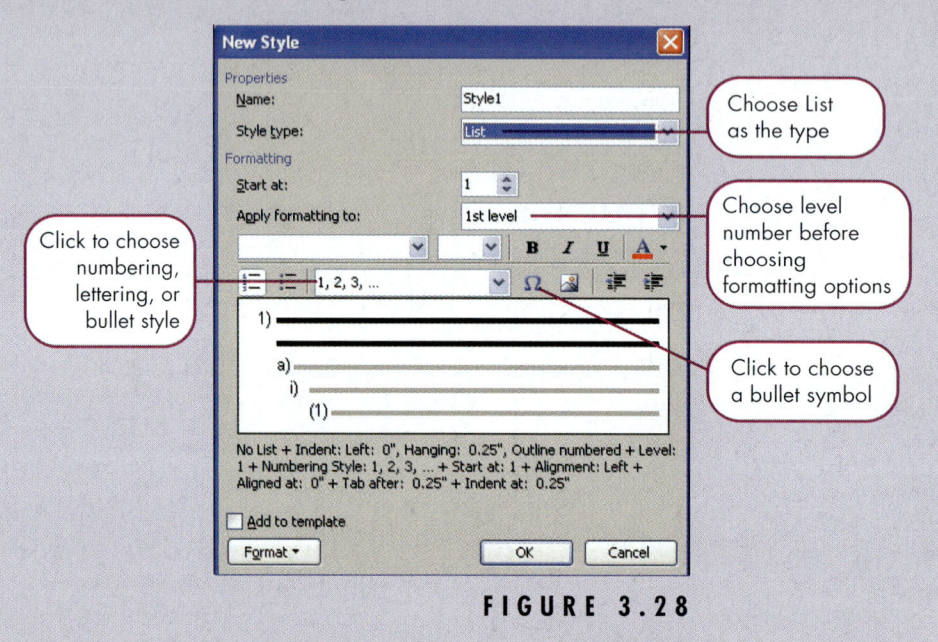

FIGURE 3.28

LESSON 7: Copying Styles to the Normal Template

Although you might create some styles only for a particular document, you might want to use other styles in other documents. For example, you might want to use the Document Title paragraph style in other documents you create. Instead of re-creating this style in new documents, you can copy the style to the Normal template, which is used when you create new documents. The ***Organizer*** enables you to copy styles, AutoText, toolbars, and macros from a document or template to another document or template.

In this lesson, you start a new document to see that the styles you created in Lessons 5 and 6 are not available to new documents, and then you copy the two styles you created to the Normal template to use in new documents you create based on that template.

To Copy Styles to the Normal Template

1 **Click New Blank Document on the Standard toolbar.**
A new blank document appears, based on the Normal template. You want to check the available styles.

2 **Click the Style drop-down arrow.**
The two styles you created—Document Title and AHC—are not listed; only Word's default styles are listed.

Lesson 7   Copying Styles to the Normal Template   **101**   LEVEL 2

3 **Close the document without saving it, and make sure the *Committee_Status_Report* document is open.**
You are ready to copy the new styles to the Normal template.

4 **Choose Tools, Templates and Add-Ins.**
The Templates and Add-ins dialog box opens.

5 **Click Organizer in the bottom-left corner of the dialog box.**
The Organizer dialog box opens (see Figure 3.29).

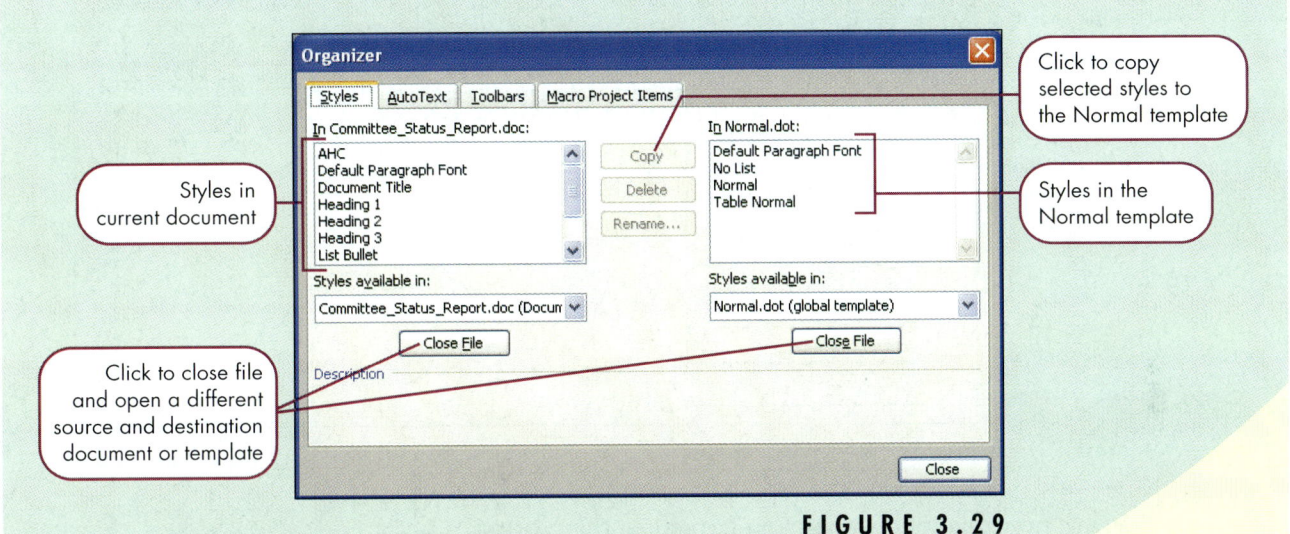

Styles in current document

Click to close file and open a different source and destination document or template

Click to copy selected styles to the Normal template

Styles in the Normal template

FIGURE 3.29

6 **In the *In Committee_Status_Report.doc* list, click *AHC* and press Ctrl while you click *Document Title*.**
Both the AHC and Document Title styles are selected. Notice that Copy, Delete, and Rename are available after selecting one style. However, Rename dims again when you select more than one style.

7 **Click Copy between the two lists.**
You just copied the two selected styles in the open document to the Normal template. These styles are listed in the *To Normal.dot* list (see Figure 3.30).

Selected styles

Click to copy to the Normal template

Styles copied to the Normal template

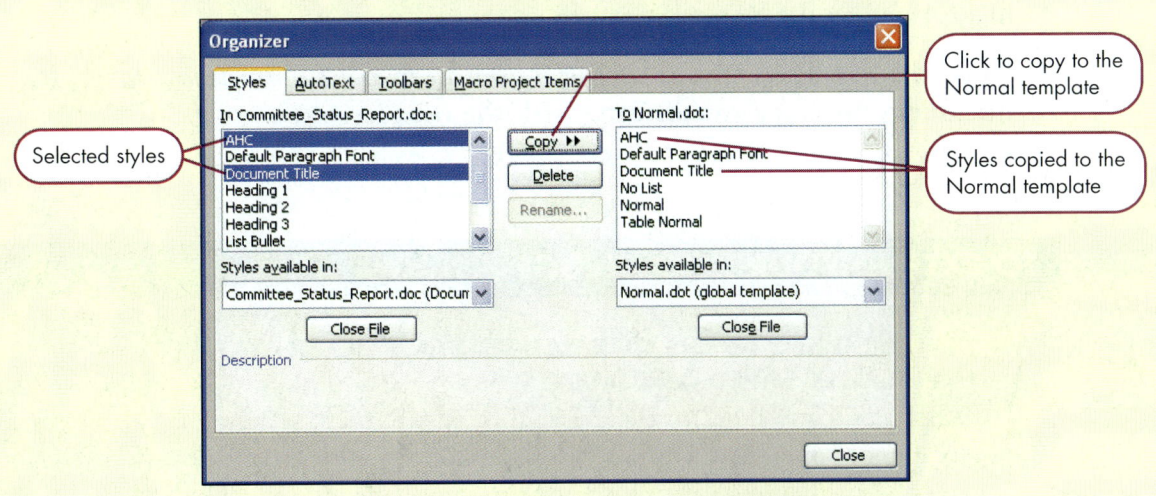

FIGURE 3.30

8 **Close the Organizer dialog box.**
You now want to create a new document to make sure the styles copied to Normal.

9 **Click New Blank Document on the Standard toolbar, and then click the Style drop-down arrow.**
The AHC and Document Title styles are now available for every new document you create (see Figure 3.31).

New document

Styles copied to the Normal template

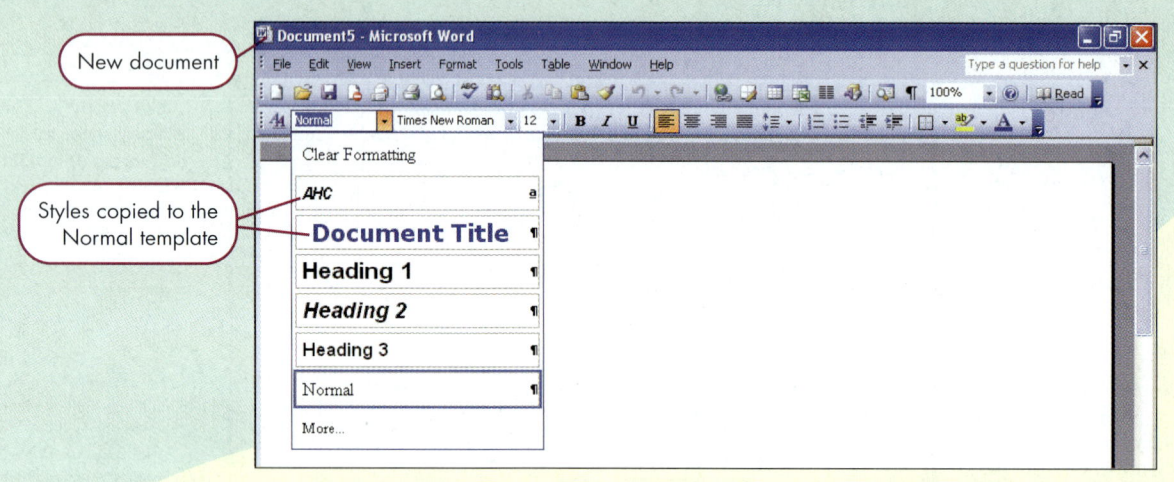

FIGURE 3.31

Let's now delete the styles you copied to the Normal template.

10 **Choose Tools, Templates and Add-Ins; then click Organizer within the Templates and Add-ins dialog box.**

11 **In the *In Normal.dot* list box on the right side of the dialog box, click AHC; then press and hold down Ctrl while you click Document Title.**
You selected the two styles in the Normal list so that you can delete them.

12 **Click Delete, click *Yes to All* to confirm the deletion, and close the Organizer dialog box.**
The AHC and Document Title styles are no longer available when you create documents based on the Normal template.

13 **Close the new file without saving it, and keep the *Committee_Status_Report* document onscreen to continue with the next lesson.**

TO EXTEND YOUR KNOWLEDGE . . .

STYLES COPIED TO THE NORMAL TEMPLATE DO NOT AFFECT PREVIOUSLY SAVED DOCUMENTS

When you copy styles to the Normal template, these styles are available for new documents only. The copied styles are not available in previously saved documents—even though those documents might have been based on the Normal template.

Lesson 8 Attaching a Word Template to a Document **103** LEVEL **2**

> **COPYING STYLES TO OTHER EXISTING DOCUMENTS**
>
> You can use the Organizer to copy styles from one document to another. Within the Organizer dialog box, click the Close File button to close the source file and then click the Open File button. Because the default option displays template files, you need to click the *Files of type* drop-down arrow, choose All Word Documents, and select and open the filename of the document that contains the styles you want to copy.
>
> Use a similar process to close and open a different destination document on the right side of the dialog box.
>
> The source and destination documents do not open into a document window; the document's styles are opened and displayed into the style list window on the left side of the Organizer dialog box. Use Help if you need additional information on copying styles between documents.

LESSON 8: Attaching a Word Template to a Document

Word contains a variety of templates, in addition to the Normal template. Although the Normal template is a good general template with general formatting styles, you might need a template with different styles. Even after you create a document, you can attach a different template to the document by using the Style Gallery. The ***Style Gallery*** is a window that enables you to select a template, see a preview of how its styles will affect your document, and then apply that template.

In this lesson, you attach the Professional Report template to your status report.

To Attach a Different Template to a Document

1. **With the *Committee_Status_Report* document onscreen, save it as `Committee_Status_Report_Version2`.**
   You want to keep a copy of the current file but use it to format a second version with another template.

2. **Click in the title and then apply the Heading 1 style again.**
   To see how your document looks with a different template, you need to use styles in the Normal template. The Document Title style you created is not in the Normal template, but the Heading 1 style is.

3. **Choose Format, Theme.**
   The Theme dialog box opens. You need to access the Style Gallery from here to choose a different template.

4. **Click Style Gallery at the bottom of the dialog box.**
   The Style Gallery dialog box opens, displaying a list of Word templates (see Figure 3.32).

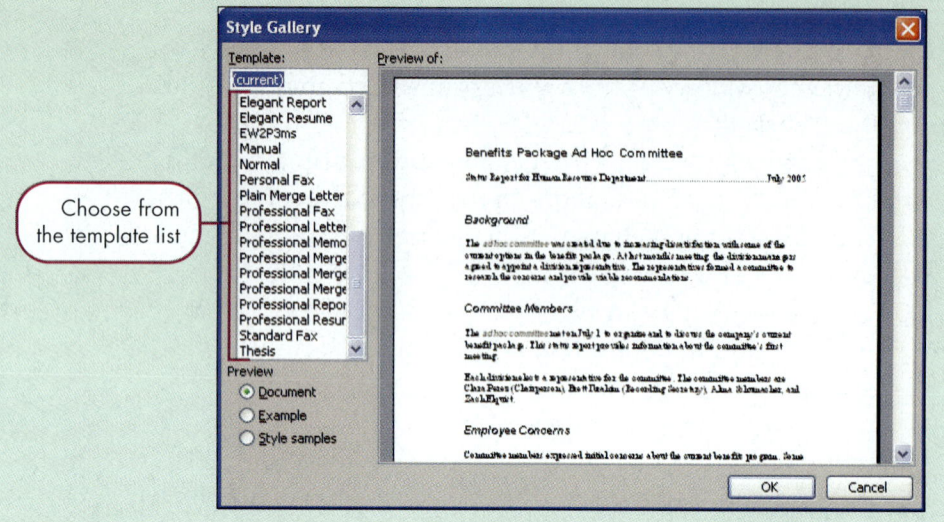

Project 3 Automating Work with AutoText, Styles, and Templates

Choose from the template list

FIGURE 3.32

5 Scroll to the bottom of the *Template* list box, click Professional Report, and click OK.

Figure 3.33 shows the document reformatted after you attach the Professional Report template; the styles within that template have different formats. Notice that the Normal style formatted text is Arial 10-point size with a 0.75" left paragraph indent.

Different format for Heading 1

Heading 2 format

Normal style

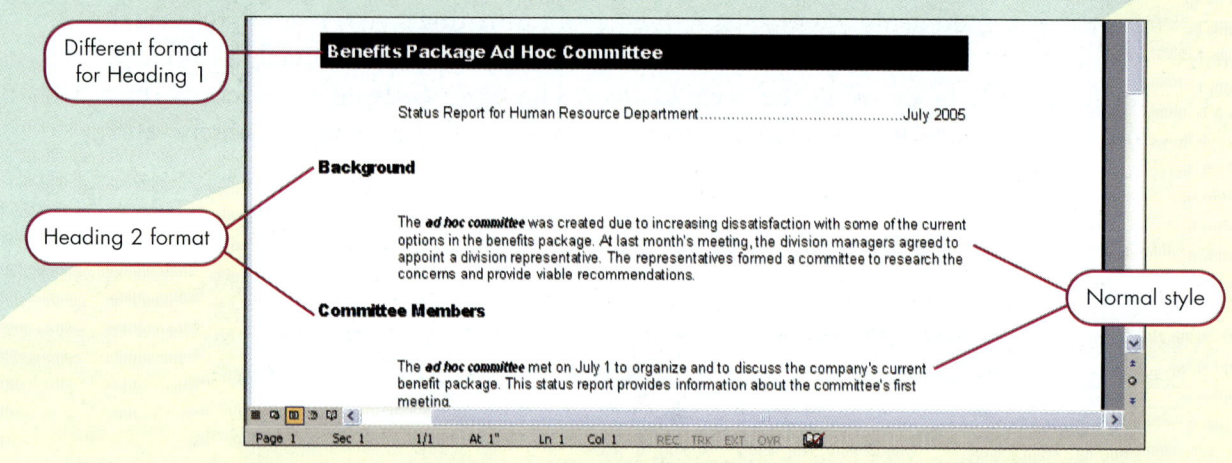

FIGURE 3.33

The bulleted list might be indented only 0.25" instead of aligning with the paragraphs.

6 Select the bulleted list, adjust the Left tab and Hanging Indent markers to 1" on the ruler, and adjust the First Line Indent marker to 0.75" on the ruler.

7 Save, print (optional), and close the *Committee_Status_Report_Version2* document.

TO EXTEND YOUR KNOWLEDGE...

ATTACHING OTHER TEMPLATES

You can create a template and then attach it to existing documents. Choose <u>T</u>ools, Templates and Add-<u>I</u>ns to display the Templates and Add-ins dialog box (see Figure 3.34).

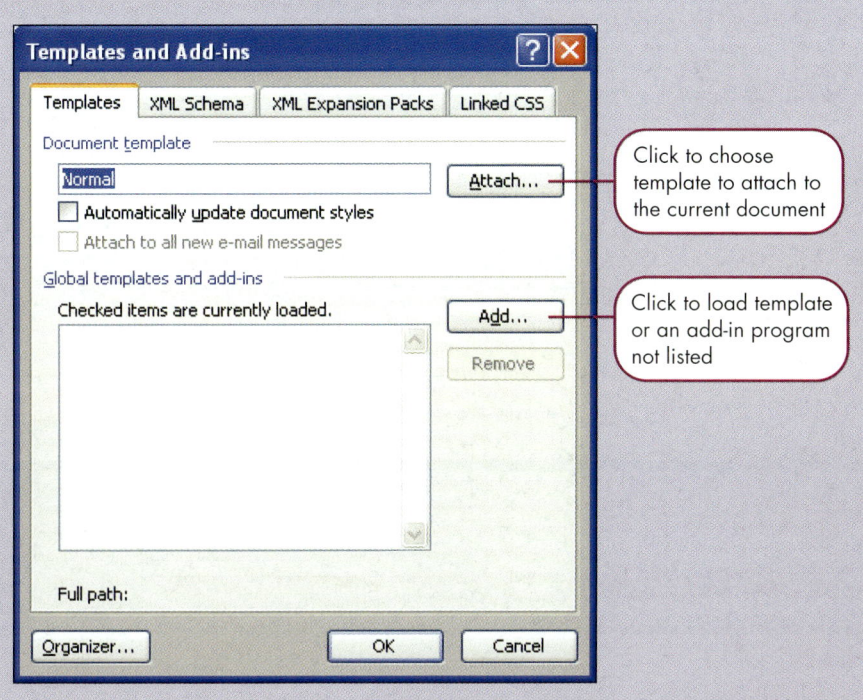

FIGURE 3.34

Click <u>A</u>ttach to attach another document template, or click A<u>d</u>d to load a template or a third-party add-in program.

SUMMARY

In this project, you learned how to use a template to create a new document. You then modified the document and used part of it to create an AutoText entry, so that you can quickly insert the memo heading in new documents with just a few keystrokes instead of having to access the Templates dialog box. Furthermore, you created paragraph and character styles to ensure consistent formatting throughout your document. You also learned how to copy those styles to the Normal template so that you can use them with other new documents. Finally, you learned how to attach a Word template to a document.

You can extend your learning by reviewing concepts and terms, and by practicing variations of skills presented in the lessons. Use the following table as a guide to the numbered questions and exercises in the end-of-project learning opportunities.

Project 3   Automating Work with AutoText, Styles, and Templates

LESSON	MULTIPLE CHOICE	DISCUSSION	SKILL DRILL	CHALLENGE	DISCOVERY ZONE
Using a Template to Create a New Document	1, 10	3	3	1, 2	2
Creating and Inserting AutoText Entries	2, 7	1	1	5	3
Editing and Deleting AutoText Entries	3	1	2	5	3, 4
Applying Built-In Word Styles	4	2	4	3	1, 2, 3
Creating a Paragraph Style	8	2	5	3	1, 2, 3
Creating a Character Style	5	2	5	3	
Copying Styles to the Normal Template	6		5	4	1, 3
Attaching a Word Template to a Document	9		4		

KEY TERMS

AutoText entry   Organizer   Style Gallery
boilerplate text   paragraph style   template
character style   style   wizard
Normal template   style area

CHECKING CONCEPTS AND TERMS

MULTIPLE CHOICE

Circle the letter of the correct answer for each of the following.

1. Which template is used when you create a new blank document? [L1]
   a. Normal
   b. General
   c. Professional Document
   d. Report Wizard

2. What is the first step for creating an AutoText entry? [L2]
   a. Click New on the AutoText toolbar.
   b. Press F9.
   c. Type the text from which to create the entry.
   d. Display the AutoText tab of the AutoCorrect dialog box.

3. How do you edit an AutoText entry? [L3]
   a. Select the AutoText entry in the dialog box, click Edit, make your changes in the Preview window, and click OK.
   b. Delete the AutoText entry, and start over.
   c. Insert the AutoText entry into a document window, edit the text in the document window, select it, and save it as an AutoText entry to replace the original one.
   d. None of the above

4. Which key should you press and hold to display all styles when clicking the Style drop-down arrow from the toolbar? [L4]
   a. Shift
   b. Ctrl
   c. Alt
   d. Spacebar

5. Which format option is *not* available when creating a character style? [L6]
   a. Arial font
   b. Red font color
   c. Bold
   d. Alignment

6. What feature enables you to copy styles from one document or template to another document or template? [L7]
   a. Style Gallery
   b. Organizer
   c. Templates
   d. Styles and Formatting task pane

7. Which feature lets you type a few letters and press Enter to insert a block of formatted text? [L2]
   a. AutoCorrect
   b. AutoText
   c. Templates
   d. Styles

8. What type of style is the most appropriate to create and format document headings? [L5]
   a. Character
   b. List
   c. Paragraph
   d. Table

9. What dialog box enables you to apply a template to the document in the current document window? [L8]
   a. New Style
   b. Organizer
   c. Templates
   d. Style Gallery

10. If you want Word to display a series of windows to help you select options for developing a new letter document, you should choose _____. [L1]
    a. Contemporary Letter
    b. Elegant Letter
    c. Professional Letter
    d. Letter Wizard

DISCUSSION

1. Based on your previous work with AutoCorrect entries, describe when to create AutoText entries and when to create AutoCorrect entries. Use examples, if needed. [L2, L3]
2. Make a list of at least three different items that are probably formatted with styles. Describe the formats included in each style. Bring a copy of your list to class to discuss your findings. [L4–L6]
3. Visit with an office manager or executive assistant at a local company to find out what types of templates the person uses or creates. Discuss your findings with the class. [L1]

SKILL DRILL

Skill Drill exercises reinforce project skills. Each skill reinforced is the same, or nearly the same, as a skill presented in the project. Detailed instructions are provided in a step-by-step format.

Work through exercises 1 and 2 in sequential order, and work through exercises 4 and 5 in sequential order. You can work exercise 3 at any time. Be sure to save your changes and close the document if you need more than one work session to complete the desired exercises. Continue working on the partially completed documents instead of the original *EW2_0303* through *EW2_0306* files.

1. Creating and Inserting an AutoText Entry

One of your coworkers created a logo with the company name and address. You want to create an AutoText entry from it to use frequently for business correspondence.

1. Open *EW2_0303*.
2. If the AutoText toolbar is not visible, choose View, Toolbars, AutoText.
3. Press Ctrl+A to select the entire document, which includes an image, the company name, address, phone number, and paragraph mark.
4. Click New on the AutoText toolbar, type **\cta** in the Create AutoText dialog box, and click OK.
5. Close the document without saving it.
6. Open *EW2_0304* and save it as **Jordan_Letter**.
7. With the insertion point at the top of the document, type **\cta**, and press F3 to insert the AutoText entry.
8. Save, print (optional), and close the *Jordan_Letter* document.

2. Editing an AutoText Entry

After using the *\cta* AutoText entry for a few days, you decide to add color to the letterhead. You need to insert the entry in a new document window, apply a font color, and save the edited entry. After editing the AutoText entry, you insert it into another letter that you need to send.

1. In a new document, type **\cta** and then press F3 to insert the AutoText entry.
2. Press Ctrl+A to select the entire document.
3. Click the Font Color drop-down arrow, and choose Dark Teal.
4. Click the image to select it and do the following:
    a. Click Format Picture on the Picture toolbar that appears.
    b. Click the Colors and Lines tab.
    c. Click the Fill Color drop-down arrow, choose Pale Blue (the third color from the right on the last row of the palette), and click OK.
5. Select the entire document again and display the AutoText toolbar, if needed.
6. Click New on the AutoText toolbar, type **\cta**, and click OK.
7. Click Yes when prompted to redefine the AutoText entry.
8. Close the document without saving it.
9. Open *EW2_0305* and save it as **Marjorie_Letter**.
10. Type **\cta** and press F3 to insert the AutoText entry.
11. Save, print (optional), and close the *Marjorie_Letter* document.

3. Creating a Document with the Fax Template

As a mortgage broker, you need to send a fax and other documents to a customer who will complete closing on her new home this week. Instead of formatting a new blank document as a fax, you decide to choose a fax template to save time. After starting the document with the fax template, you quickly replace placeholders with text and type a short paragraph.

1. Choose File, New and click *On my computer* on the New Document task pane to display the Templates dialog box.
2. Click the Letters & Faxes category tab.
3. Click *Professional Fax*, click OK, and save the document as **Mortgage_Closing_Fax**.
4. Click in the first placeholder, *[Click here and type return address and phone and fax numbers]*, type **840 North Main**, and press Spacebar.
5. Make sure the NumLock key is active; then press and hold down Alt while you type **0149** from the number keypad.

    When you release Alt, Word inserts a circular bullet so that you do not have to search through the Symbols dialog box to find the bullet symbol.
6. Press Spacebar, type **Bolivar, MO 65613**, and press Enter.
7. Type **Phone:**, press Ctrl+Tab, type **(417) 555-8000**, and press Enter.
8. Type **Fax:**, press Ctrl+Tab, and type **(417) 555-8500**.
9. Select *Company Name Here* and type **City Mortgage Corp.**
10. Replace the rest of the placeholders, except the date field, by entering the data shown in Figure 3.35.

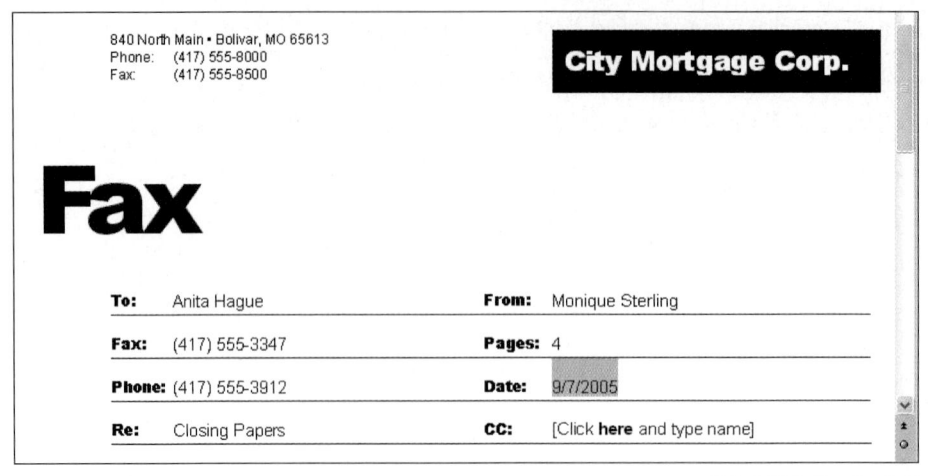

Project 3 Automating Work with AutoText, Styles, and Templates

```
                                                                City Mortgage Corp.
840 North Main • Bolivar, MO 65613
Phone:   (417) 555-8000
Fax:     (417) 555-8500

Fax

To:    Anita Hague              From:   Monique Sterling
Fax:   (417) 555-3347           Pages:  4
Phone: (417) 555-3912           Date:   9/7/2005
Re:    Closing Papers           CC:     [Click here and type name]
```

FIGURE 3.35

11. Delete the *CC* placeholder.

12. Select the text after the word *Comments* and type the following paragraph:

    `Anita, the following pages contain the preliminary closing papers for your loan. Please bring a cashier's check in the amount of $30,000 with you when you come to the closing on Friday. Please call me if you have any questions.`

13. Save, print (optional), and close the *Mortgage_Closing_Fax* document.

4. Applying Default Word Styles and Attaching a Template to a Document

You just created a status report to inform committee members about an upcoming conference of which you are in charge. Although you want it to look attractive and professional, you do not have time to create and apply your own styles; therefore, you want to apply some predefined heading styles. After applying the styles, you decide to use the Style Gallery to choose a template to attach to the current document.

1. Open *EW2_0306* and save it as **Training_Conference_Report**.

2. Press ⇧Shift while you click the Style drop-down arrow, scroll through the list of styles, and choose *Title* for the first line in the document.

3. Position the insertion point on the second line of the document, press ⇧Shift while you click the Style drop-down arrow, scroll through the list of styles, and choose *Subtitle* for the second line in the document.

4. Position the insertion point within *The Committee*, click the Style drop-down arrow, and choose Heading 3.

5. Repeat step 4 to format these headings: *Training Sessions* and *Training Goal*.

6. Choose Format, Theme.

7. Click Style Gallery to display the Style Gallery dialog box.

8. Choose Contemporary Report and then click OK.

9. Display the Style Gallery dialog box again.

10. Choose Professional Report and then click OK.

11. Save the *Training_Conference_Report* document.

5. Creating and Applying Styles

After reviewing your report, you decide to create and apply your own styles within the document. You create a paragraph style named Side Heading to format the headings and then you create a character style named Session to format the names of the conference sessions and apply these formats to text within the document. You then copy these two styles to the Normal template. Finally, you delete these two styles from the Normal template.

1. In the *Training_Conference_Report* document, click Styles and Formatting on the Formatting toolbar.
2. Click *New Style* on the Styles and Formatting task pane.
3. Set the following style properties:
   a. Type **Side Heading** in the *Name* box.
   b. Make sure the *Style type* is Paragraph.
   c. Click the *Style based on* drop-down arrow and choose Normal.
   d. Click the *Style for following paragraph* drop-down arrow and choose Normal.
4. Set these formats by clicking the appropriate buttons on the toolbar within the New Style dialog box:
   a. Arial 14-point size
   b. Bold
   c. Dark Red font color
5. Click F*o*rmat at the bottom of the dialog box, choose *P*aragraph, and then set the following paragraph formats:
   a. 12-point before paragraph spacing
   b. 6-point after paragraph spacing
6. Click OK within each open dialog box to close it.
7. Apply the Side Heading style to these three headings: *The Committee, Training Sessions,* and *Training Goal.*
8. Click New Style on the task pane and create a character style with the following specifications:
   a. Type **Session** in the *Name* box.
   b. Click the *Style type* drop-down arrow and choose Character.
   c. Click Bold on the dialog box toolbar.
   d. Choose Dark Red font color.
   e. Click OK.
9. In the bulleted list, do the following:
   a. Select the word *Word* and then apply the Session character style.
   b. Select the text *Web-Page Development* and then apply the Session character style.
   c. Apply the Session character style to the word *Multimedia* and the phrase *Presentations Graphics.*
10. Choose *T*ools, Templates and Add-*I*ns.
11. Click *Organizer* in the Templates and Add-Ins dialog box.

Project 3 Automating Work with AutoText, Styles, and Templates

12. In the Organizer dialog box, do the following:
    a. Click the Session style name; then press and hold down Ctrl while you click the Side Heading style name in the *In Training_Conference_Report.doc* list.
    b. Click *C*opy to copy the two styles to the *To Normal.dot* list.
    c. Close the Organizer dialog box.
13. Save, print (optional), and close the *Training_Conference_Report* document.
14. Click New Blank Document on the Standard toolbar.
15. Click the Style drop-down arrow to verify that the Session and Side Heading styles are listed.

    This proves that you copied the two styles to the Normal template so that they are available for new documents.
16. Choose *T*ools, Templates and Add-*I*ns, and click *O*rganizer in the Templates and Add-Ins dialog box.
17. In the Organizer dialog box, do the following:
    a. Click the Session style name, press and hold down Ctrl while you click the Side Heading style name in the *In Normal.dot* list.
    b. Click *D*elete to delete the two styles in the *In Normal.dot* list.
    c. Click Yes to *A*ll.
    d. Close the Organizer dialog box.
18. Close the blank document window without saving it.

CHALLENGE

Challenge exercises expand on or are somewhat related to skills presented in the lessons. Each exercise provides a brief narrative introduction, followed by instructions in a numbered-step format that are not as detailed as those in the Skill Drill exercises. You can work through one or more exercises in almost any order. However, you must complete exercise 3 to be able to work through exercise 4.

1. Creating a Monthly Calendar

You want to create a monthly calendar for the current year. Instead of manually creating 12 tables, one for each month, and typing dates within cells, you want to use the Calendar Wizard. After completing the wizard, you want to type information for important dates. For example, you want to enter birthdays and anniversaries on their respective dates.

1. Display the Templates dialog box.
2. Explore the categories and select the Calendar Wizard.
3. Select the *Boxes & borders* style option, and choose a page orientation of your choice, but do not leave room for a picture.
4. Specify the current month and year for the starting date and choose the appropriate month and year to complete a 12-month calendar.
5. Apply the *All* border style to create boxes within each monthly table.
6. Save the document as **Monthly_Calendar**.

7. Insert important information within the respective cells, formatting the text by changing the font size and font color as desired.

8. Insert, size, and format at least three images. Insert images on different months. Consider inserting images above the table, choosing the Behind Text wrapping option, and/or using the Washout appearance.

9. Make other changes as you want, such as changing date font colors, border colors, and so on.

10. Save, print (optional), and close the *Monthly_Calendar* document.

2. Using the Letter Wizard

You want to use the Letter Wizard to create a letter. The wizard asks you questions about how you want the letter formatted and provides boxes for you to enter data. After using the Letter Wizard, you want to insert the content of an existing document so that you do not have to retype it.

1. Display the Templates dialog box, and select the Letter Wizard to send one letter.

2. Click the Letter Format tab, and choose the Contemporary Letter page design and the Modified Block letter style.

3. Use this information in the Recipient Info section:

   a. Type **Ms. Isabel Kahn** as the recipient.
   b. Type her address:

   342 Maple Drive
   Laurel, MD 20708

   c. Use the Business salutation.

4. Type your name as the sender; choose the *Sincerely yours,* complimentary closing; type **Customer Service Director** as the job title; and specify one enclosure.

5. When the wizard is finished, save the document as **Customer_Survey_Response**.

6. Select the paragraph following the salutation, but do *not* include the paragraph mark. Insert the file *EW2_0307* to replace the selected paragraph.

7. Vertically center the document.

8. Apply 12-point Bookman Old Style font to the entire letter.

9. Save, print (optional), and close the *Customer_Survey_Response* document.

3. Creating and Applying Styles for Minutes of a Meeting

Yesterday, you typed the minutes for a condominium association meeting. Before distributing the minutes to residents of the condominium complex, you need to format it. To ensure consistency in formatting, you decide to create and apply paragraph and character styles for document components. In addition, you want to edit and apply the predefined Body Text paragraph style.

1. Open *EW2_0308* and save it as **September_Meeting_Minutes**.
2. Create a paragraph style with these specifications:
   a. Minutes Title (name)
   b. Normal (style basis)
   c. Body Text (style for following paragraph)
   d. 16-point size, Verdana or Tahoma font, Teal font color, bold
   e. 12-point spacing after paragraph, and centered horizontal alignment
3. Create a paragraph style with these specifications:
   a. Major Headings (name)
   b. Minutes Title (basis)
   c. Body Text (style for following paragraph)
   d. 14-point Verdana font
   e. 18-point spacing before paragraph, and left horizontal alignment
   f. All other formats to be carried over from the Minutes Title style
4. Apply the Minutes Title style to the first two lines of text in the document.
5. Apply the Major Headings style to the five major headings in the document.
6. Apply the Body Text style to the regular paragraphs.
7. Save and print (optional) the document.
8. Edit the Body Text style by setting a 0.5" first line indent, 0-point spacing after paragraph, and double-spacing.
9. Edit the Major Headings style by changing the font size to 12-point, choosing 12-point spacing before paragraph, clicking the *Keep with next* option, and setting a *(none)* special indent.
10. Set 1" left and right margins for the document.
11. Create a character style named Names that applies bold and Teal font color.
12. Apply the Names character style to people's names throughout the document except those listed in the Call to Order section.
13. Delete the blank line caused by a paragraph mark between the two main titles.
14. Save and print (optional) the *September_Meeting_Minutes* document; keep it onscreen to continue with the next exercise.

4. Copying Styles to the Normal Template and Applying Them in a New Document

You really like the styles you created for the condominium association newsletter. Because you might want to use them for new documents, you should copy them to the Normal template. After doing so, you can insert a file within the current (blank) document and apply the styles. (You must complete Challenge exercise 3 in order to work through this exercise.)

1. With *September_Meeting_Minutes* onscreen, display the Organizer dialog box.
2. Copy these formats from the current document to the Normal template: Major Headings, Minutes Title, and Names.

3. Close the *September_Meeting_Minutes* document and then start a new blank document.

4. Make sure your styles are displayed from the Style drop-down list.

5. Insert the *EW2_0309* file within the new document window, and save the document as **MG_Minutes**.

6. Apply the following styles:

   a. Minutes Title style to the document title

   b. Major Headings style to these four headings: Fall Training Conference, New Customer Service Branch, Just a Reminder, and Optical Benefits

   c. Names style to the following text: October 12–16, Riverfront Resort Center, Jeremy Sutherland, new card key system, and Mobile Blood Bank

7. Save, print (optional), and close the *MG_Minutes* document.

8. Show the Normal template styles to your instructor for verification and then delete the Major Headings, Minutes Title, and Names styles from the Normal template.

5. Creating a Letterhead AutoText Entry

You want to create a letterhead AutoText entry that you can use for letters, memos, and advertisements. You first create document text and then save it as an AutoText entry. In addition, you create AutoText entries for a commonly used phrase and for your name. Then, in a new document window, you insert a file and then insert the AutoText entries.

1. In a new document window, select the Justify horizontal alignment option and then type **Computer Training Solutions** in 28-point Times New Roman.

2. Select 12-point Times New Roman, press Shift+Enter to insert a line break, and type **6262 Technology Boulevard**.

3. Insert the computer symbol from the Wingdings font in the Symbol dialog box. It is the sixth symbol from the right on the second row.

4. Type **Nashua, NH 03063**, insert the computer symbol again, and then type **(603) 555-6262**.

5. Insert a space before and after each computer symbol.

6. Insert a line break and then a manual return after the second line. Choose the Left horizontal alignment option.

7. Select the two lines of text, including the paragraph mark, and set a box border using the eleventh border style. Apply the Gray 15% shading fill pattern.

8. Select the entire document, and create an AutoText entry named **\cts**. Close the document without saving it.

9. In a new document window, type **Please call me if you have any questions or if I can be of further assistance.** and then create an AutoText entry from it. Select only the sentence and period; do not select the paragraph mark. Name the entry **\pc**, and close the document without saving it.

10. Open *EW2_0310* and save it as `Request_Response`.
11. Insert the \cts AutoText entry at the top of the document.
12. Insert the \pc AutoText entry at the end of the last paragraph of the body of the letter.
13. Change the text *Your Name* to your name.
14. Save, print (optional), and close the *Request_Response* document.
15. Edit the \cts AutoText entry by adding Dark Blue font color to the text and Pale Blue shading with a Clear style pattern. Delete the blank line that contains shading. Change the text alignment for the paragraph inside the border to Center. After redefining the AutoText entry, close the document without saving it.
16. Open *EW2_0311* and save it as `Resume_Confirmation_Letter`.
17. Insert the \cts AutoText at the top of the document.
18. Delete + and then start typing today's date. Use AutoComplete to help you finish the date.
19. Delete ++ in the signature block, type `Your`, and accept the AutoComplete ScreenTip.
20. Save, print (optional), and close the *Resume_Confirmation_Letter* document.

DISCOVERY ZONE

Discovery Zone exercises require advanced knowledge of topics presented in the lessons or self-directed learning of new skills. You can work through one or more exercises in any order.

1. Using and Editing Styles from Another Document

You want to use the styles you created in the *September_Meeting_Minutes* document in Challenge exercise 3 to format minutes from a special meeting. You know, however, that copying the styles to the Normal template will not work because the secretary already typed the new minutes. Use Help and refer to the To Extend Your Knowledge section at the end of Lesson 7 to learn how to copy styles from one document to another (instead of copying styles to the Normal template).

Open *EW2_0312* and then save it as `January_Minutes`. Access the Organizer, and close the existing files listed. Select the *September_Meeting_Minutes* document on one side. If you did not complete Challenge exercise 4, select the *EW2_0313* document. Select the *January_Minutes* document on the other side of the dialog box. Change the file type to *All Word Documents* to make sure you can find the .doc files. Copy all styles from the September Minutes document (or the EW2_0313 document) to the January Minutes document.

Apply the styles to the *January_Minutes* document based on the way you applied styles to the *September_Meeting_Minutes* document. Apply the Names character style to a name in the second paragraph. Modify the Minutes Title style by changing the font color to Yellow and adding Blue shading color with no border lines. Modify the Major Headings style by changing the font color to Blue and then choosing no shading color. Modify the Body Text style by adding Justified horizontal alignment.

Save, print (optional), and close the *January_Minutes* document.

2. Creating a Newspaper Columns Template

You need to create a template for a monthly newsletter that you distribute throughout your company. The newsletter contains tips and tricks of software applications. The newsletter should have a standard masthead, continuous section break, newspaper columns, and a paragraph style for the article titles.

In a new document window, set 1" left and right margins and create the masthead shown in Figure 3.36.

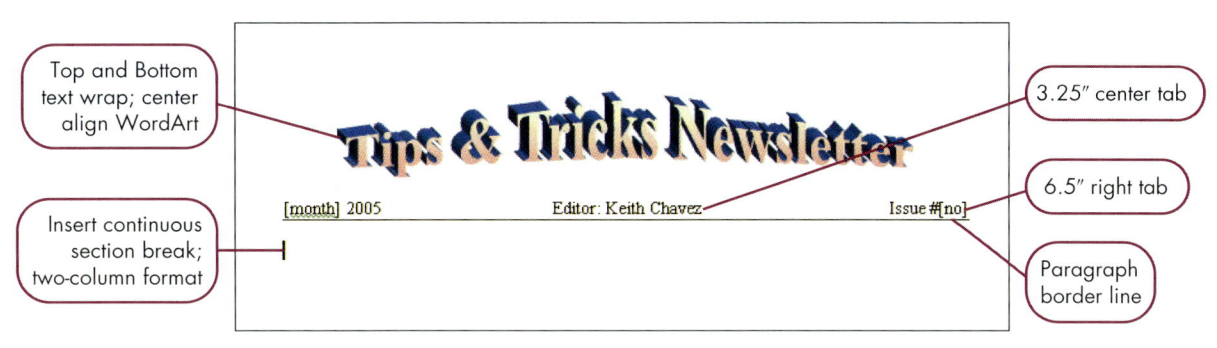

Callouts on Figure 3.36:
- Top and Bottom text wrap; center align WordArt
- Insert continuous section break; two-column format
- 3.25" center tab
- 6.5" right tab
- Paragraph border line

Masthead text: **Tips & Tricks Newsletter** — [month] 2005   Editor: Keith Chavez   Issue #[no]

FIGURE 3.36

Create a paragraph style called **Article Title** with these formats: 12-point Arial font, bold, Orange font color, Center horizontal alignment, 8-point spacing after paragraph. Use Help to learn how to save the contents of a document window as a template, and then save the document window contents as a template named **Tips_Masthead**. Print (optional) and close the template.

Choose the template you just created through the Templates dialog box. Change the placeholder *[month]* to **April** and change *[no]* to **4**. Insert *EW2_0314* after the continuous section break. The file should be formatted into two columns. Save the document as **April_Newsletter**. Apply the paragraph style to the headings. Make sure the document is formatted by 1" left and right margins. Insert a column break at the beginning of the *Other Ctrl Keyboard Shortcuts* heading.

Save, print (optional), and close the *April_Newsletter* document.

3. Creating a Table Style and a Table AutoText

You work for a local bookstore named Open Book Store. You send personalized letters to special customers to let them know about books on sale that are of particular interest to each of them. You want to create a table style that specifies overall formatting like a Table AutoFormat style. In addition, you want to create an AutoText entry that creates a table structure and sets table formats so you do not have to create the table from scratch each time you need it.

In a new window, create a table style called **Book Table**, change the *Apply formatting to* option to Header row, and set these formats for the header row: center vertical and horizontal alignment, Lavender shading, Violet font color, 12-point Arial Narrow, bold. Set all borders for the entire table. Save the style in the Normal template from within the New Style dialog box. Use Help if you need assistance in creating a table style. After creating the table style, close the current document without saving it.

In another new window, create a table with three columns and four rows. For the first row only, set a 0.35" row height. Set these column widths: 3", first column; 1.5", second column; and 1", third column. Type the following text in the first row:

Title of Book   **Author**   **Cost**

Center the table between the margins and then choose <u>N</u>one text wrapping. Select the second and third columns, and choose Center horizontal alignment. Select the table, and save the AutoText entry as **\tob**. Close the document without saving the changes.

Open *EW2_0315* and save it as **Hart_Letter**. Use the Organizer to copy the *\tob* style from the Normal template to the *Hart_Letter* document. Insert the AutoText table between the second and third paragraphs within the *Hart_Letter* document and then type the following data into the table:

Exquisite Gardens	McDougal	$15.99
I'll Promise You a Rose Garden	Vanderbelt	$24.99
Know Your Flowers and Their Needs	Patterson	$19.95

Make sure you have the same space above and below the table. Center the table between the left and right margins, if needed. Save, print (optional), and close the *Hart_Letter* document.

Open *EW2_0316* and save it as **Willison_Letter**. Use the Organizer to copy the *\tob* style from the Normal template to the *Willison_Letter* document. Insert the AutoText table between the second and third paragraphs within the *Willison_Letter* document and then type the following data into the table:

Famous Murder Mysteries	Frances	$29.99
Vanishing Passengers in Cabs	Davis	$32.99
Beware: Stranger in Town	Worthington	$17.95

Make sure you have the same space above and below the table. Center the table between the left and right margins, if needed. Save, print (optional), and close the *Willison_Letter* document.

4. Deleting Templates and Styles

After your instructor has verified the template and styles you created in this project, use Windows Explorer to copy your templates (*.dot) from the hard drive to a Zip disk or data disk; then use the Templates dialog box to delete the custom templates you created. Do not delete original Word templates, however. Delete any custom styles you added to the Normal template.

PROJECT 4

LEVEL 2

COLLABORATING WITH OTHERS

OBJECTIVES

In this project, you learn how to

- Insert, view, and edit comments
- Track changes
- Customize Track Changes options
- Review changes by type and reviewer
- Save versions and accept and reject changes
- E-mail a document as an attachment for review
- Compare and merge documents

WHY WOULD I DO THIS?

In today's organizational environment, teams of people with diverse backgrounds, skills, and knowledge prepare documentation. Team members work together while planning, developing, writing, and editing important documents. Various individuals submit ideas, provide feedback, review progress, and rewrite material. For example, the *Essentials* series consists of a team of authors, series editors, technical editors, production managers, designers, and so forth, who all contribute to producing high-quality textbooks.

Team members use Word's collaboration tools, such as comments and the Track Changes feature to indicate suggestions for improvement, clarification, and corrections to the manuscript pages before the documents are converted into actual book pages. You, too, can use Word's collaboration tools to track changes made by team members, date different versions of a document, and provide a method of communication within documents.

Finally, you might want to send a document to other people. You can e-mail a document as an attachment for others to review and edit, or you can e-mail a document as an attachment for the recipients to read without editing the document.

VISUAL SUMMARY

Recently, you and your team members conducted research to learn more about the Tablet PC. The **Tablet PC** looks like a laptop computer but contains additional functionality that enables people to use a tablet pen to write directly on the screen. Users can write annotations, just as they do on printed documents, or they can write on the writing pad and let the computer transcribe the written text into typed text. You and your team members prepared a preliminary report to distribute to managers within your organization. Because this report is a collaborative effort, you use collaboration tools to insert comments to each other and to edit the document. Figure 4.1 shows comments and edits made with the collaboration tools.

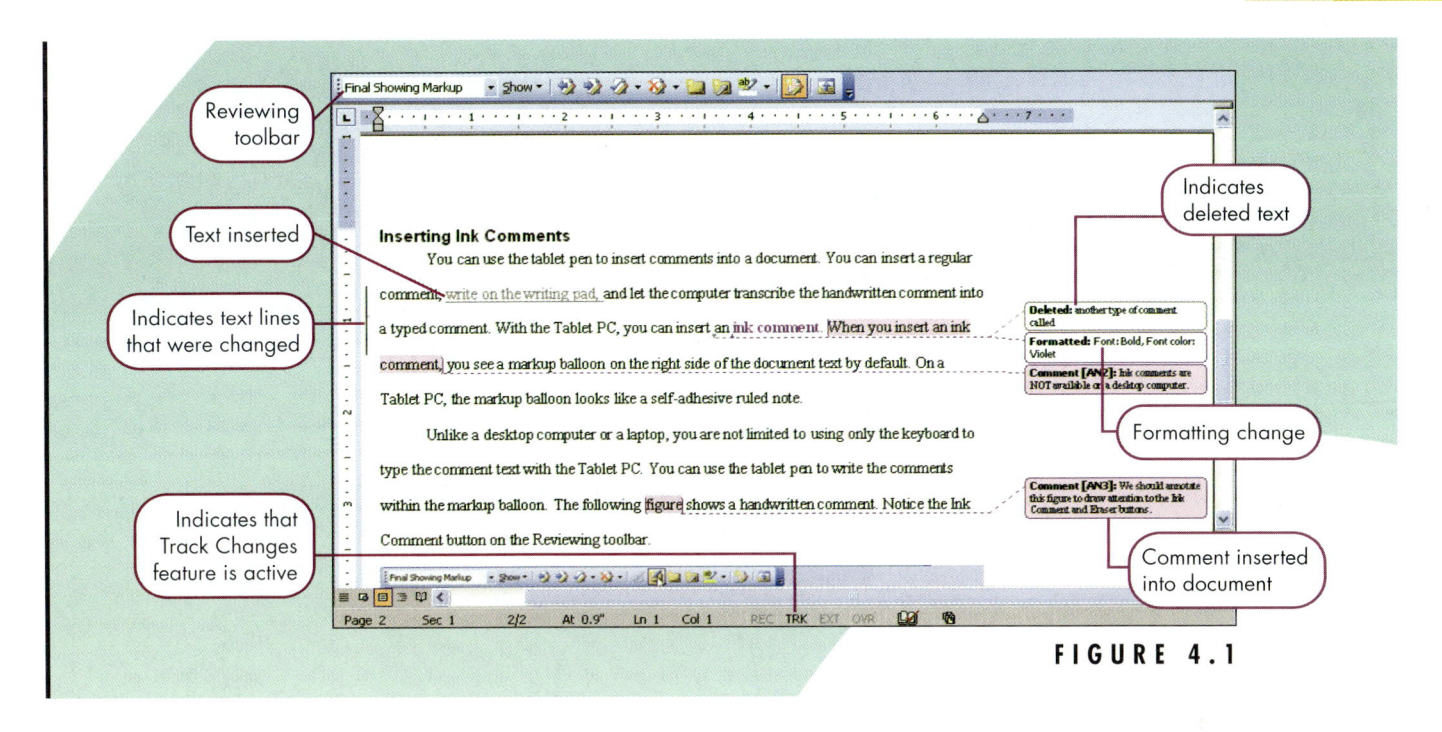

Lesson 1   Inserting, Viewing, and Editing Comments   **121**   LEVEL **2**

FIGURE 4.1

LESSON 1: Inserting, Viewing, and Editing Comments

You can make suggestions to another author or team member by inserting comments into a document. A ***comment*** is a note or annotation to ask a question or provide a suggestion to another person about the content of a document. Comments appear in markup balloons in Print Layout, Web Layout, and Reading Layout views. ***Markup balloons*** are colored circles that contain comments, insertions, and deletions in the right or left margin with a line drawn to where the insertion point was in the document prior to inserting the comment or editing the document. In Normal view, comments appear in the ***Reviewing Pane,*** a horizontal window at the bottom of the screen that shows all comments and editorial changes made to the main document when Track Changes was on.

In this lesson, you complete two sets of hands-on steps. In the first set, you change the User Information preferences so that Word uses your name to identify comments you insert and edits you make in this project. In the second set, you insert, view, and edit two comments into the *Tablet_PC* document.

To Change User Information

1 **In a new document window, choose Tools, Options.**
The Options dialog box opens. This dialog box enables you to specify default settings for using Microsoft Word.

2 **Click the User Information tab.**
The User Information tab provides a place for you to type your name and initials (see Figure 4.2). Word uses this information as the default name for the document summary when you create new documents. It also uses this information to indicate the name of the person who uses collaboration tools, such as comments.

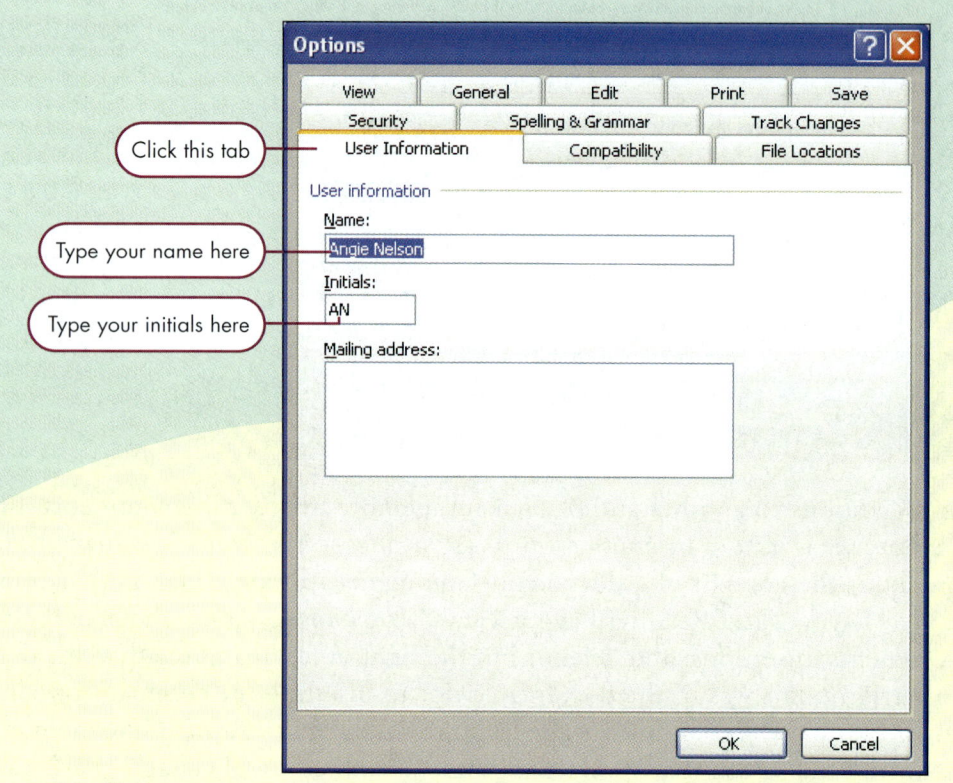

FIGURE 4.2

3 **Type your name in the *Name* box.**

4 **Type your first and last initials in the *Initials* box and click OK.**

You are now ready to insert comments into the *Tablet_PC* document. Your first comment poses a question, and your second comment makes a recommendation. After you insert the comments, you view the reviewer information and edit one comment.

Lesson 1 Inserting, Viewing, and Editing Comments   123   LEVEL 2

To Insert, View, and Edit Comments

1 Open *EW2_0401* and save it as `Tablet_PC`.

2 Change the zoom to Text Width and display the Reviewing toolbar.
The Reviewing toolbar contains buttons for using collaborative tools, such as inserting comments.

3 Scroll to the top of the second page, and select *When you insert an ink comment,* in the first paragraph.
Selecting text helps the reader see exactly what text you are commenting on.

4 Click Insert Comment on the Reviewing toolbar.
Word highlights the text you selected, displays a markup balloon in the right margin, and displays a colored line from the markup balloon to the text you selected (see Figure 4.3). The line and markup balloon might be a different color on your screen from the color shown in this textbook.

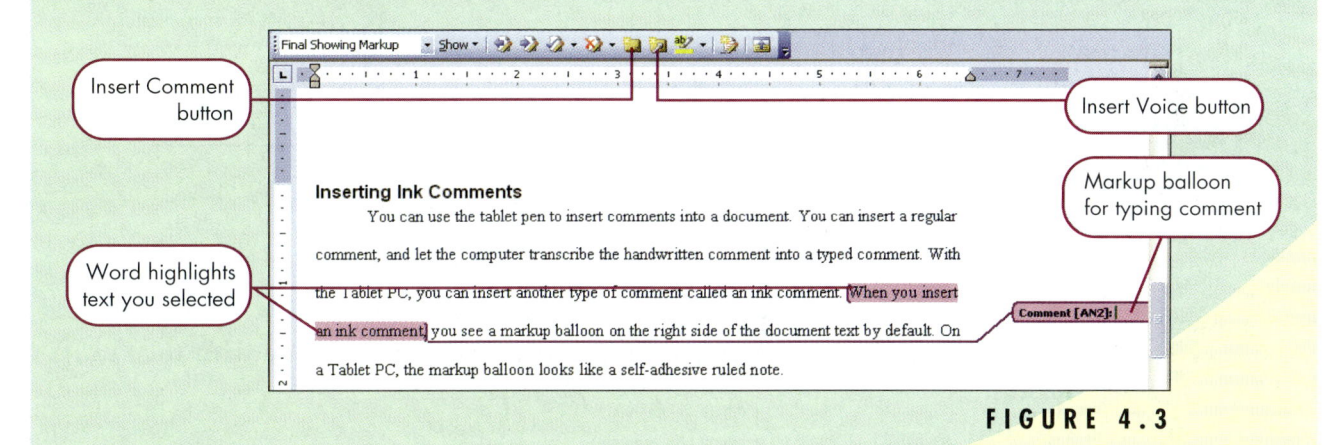

- Insert Comment button
- Insert Voice button
- Markup balloon for typing comment
- Word highlights text you selected

Inserting Ink Comments
You can use the tablet pen to insert comments into a document. You can insert a regular comment, and let the computer transcribe the handwritten comment into a typed comment. With the Tablet PC, you can insert another type of comment called an ink comment. [When you insert an ink comment,] you see a markup balloon on the right side of the document text by default. On a Tablet PC, the markup balloon looks like a self-adhesive ruled note.

FIGURE 4.3

If you have problems . . .

If you do not see the entire markup balloon, click the scroll button on the right side of the horizontal scrollbar or select the Page Width zoom. Although Page Width zoom displays the full width of the document, the figures in this book reflect Text Width zoom so that the document text is larger, making it easier for you to read.

5 Type `Can we create ink comments on a desktop computer?` in the markup balloon.
Now you want to comment on the last figure within the document.

6 Position the insertion point to the right of the words *following figure* in the last paragraph, and click Insert Comment on the Reviewing toolbar.
If you do not select anything prior to clicking Insert Comment, Word selects the word or object to the left of the insertion point for the comment reference. In this situation, Word displays colored parentheses around the word *figure*.

7 In the second markup balloon, type `We should annotate this figure to draw attention to the Ink Comment and Eraser buttons.`

8 Click inside the first markup balloon you created.
You see an insertion point inside the markup balloon, indicating that you can edit it.

9 Edit the comment text to read `Ink comments are NOT available on a desktop computer.`

10 Position the mouse pointer over the first markup balloon.
When you position the mouse pointer over a markup balloon, Word displays a ScreenTip that tells you who created the comment and when (see Figure 4.4).

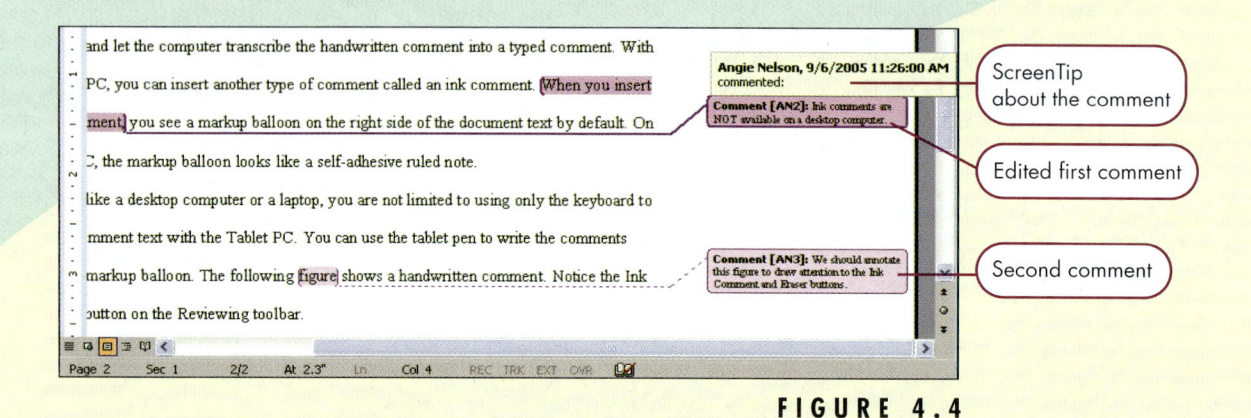

FIGURE 4.4

11 Save the *Tablet_PC* document, and keep it onscreen to continue with the next lesson.

TO EXTEND YOUR KNOWLEDGE...

INSERTING A COMMENT
Choosing Insert, Comment is another way to create a new comment.

INSERTING AN INK COMMENT ON A TABLET PC
If you have a Tablet PC, you can create regular comments or ink comments. An *ink comment* is a special comment you insert on a Tablet PC that enables you to use a tablet pen to write directly within the markup balloon on the screen. To create an ink comment, tap Ink Comment on the Reviewing toolbar and handwrite your comment with the tablet pen. The Ink Comment functionality is available only on a Tablet PC; it is not available on a desktop or regular laptop computer.

INSERTING VOICE COMMENTS
You can record voice comments if your computer contains a sound card and a microphone. To create a sound comment, position the insertion point where you want to insert the sound comment, and click Insert Voice on the Reviewing toolbar (refer to Figure 4.3 in the previous set of steps).

Click Record in the Sound Object dialog box, record your voice, and click Stop. Click Rewind to rewind the sound clip, and click Play to hear what you said. Use Help in the Sound Object dialog box to learn more about recording sounds. Then close the Sound Object dialog box. People can listen to the voice comment by double-clicking the sound icon within the document.

You can add the Insert Voice button to the Reviewing toolbar, if needed. Choose <u>T</u>ools, <u>C</u>ustomize, click the <u>C</u>ommands tab, choose *Insert* from the *Categories* list box, scroll down in the *Comman<u>d</u>s* list box, click and drag *Insert Voice* to the Reviewing toolbar, and then close the Customize dialog box.

INSERTING COMMENTS IN NORMAL VIEW

If you create comments in Normal view, you see the Reviewing Pane at the bottom of the screen instead of markup balloons (see Figure 4.5).

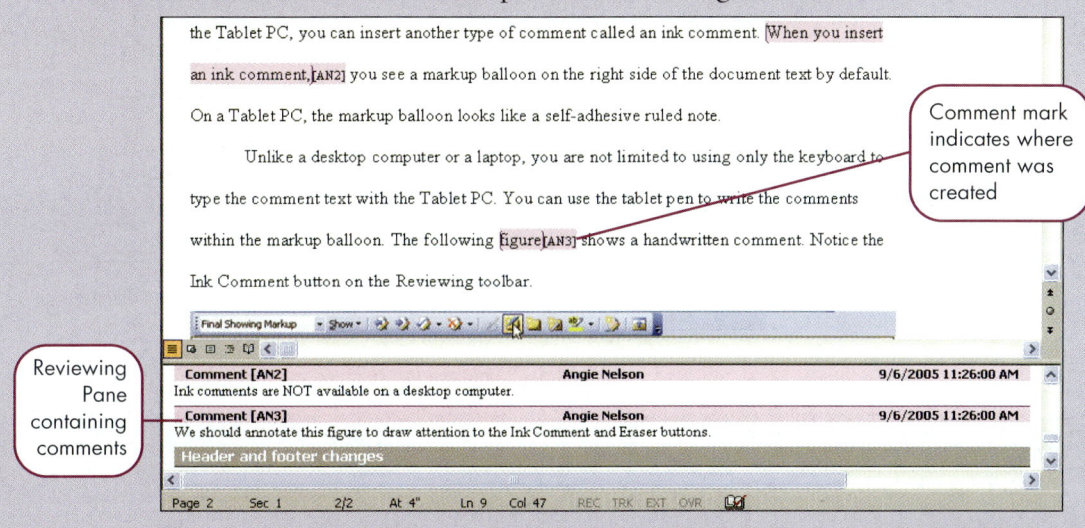

FIGURE 4.5

To display (or hide) the Reviewing Pane, click Reviewing Pane on the Reviewing toolbar. You can display the Reviewing Pane in all views *except* Reading Layout view.

DELETING COMMENTS

After reading, acting on, or printing comments, you can delete the comments either from within the markup balloon or in the Reviewing Pane. To delete a comment, right-click the comment markup balloon and choose Delete Co<u>m</u>ment from the shortcut menu, or click inside the comment markup balloon and click Reject Change/Delete Comment on the Reviewing toolbar.

LESSON 2: Tracking Changes

You can track changes to help you monitor document revisions. When you **track changes,** Word tracks all additions, deletions, and formatting changes you make by applying noticeable formatting called ***revision marks.*** Word includes markup tools, some of which allow you to accept or reject changes indicated by revision marks. The first page of the *Tablet_PC* document contains tracked changes for three reviewers.

When the Track Changes feature is active, Word underscores inserted text in another color. In Print Layout view, Word removes deleted text and displays a markup balloon that shows the deleted text. In Normal view, Word applies strikethrough to deleted text. Word uses colors for different reviewers who edit the document. You can position the mouse pointer over revision marks or markup balloons to see who made the change and on what date and time. Figure 4.6 shows the existing changes tracked by other reviewers; the reviewers' colors might differ on your screen.

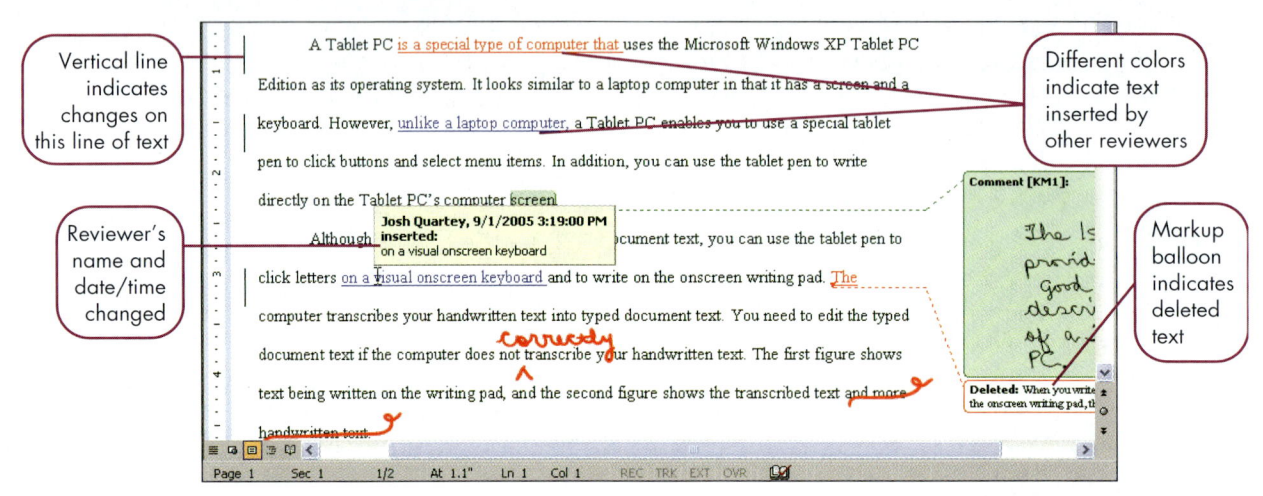

FIGURE 4.6

In this lesson, you activate the Track Changes feature to edit the *Tablet_PC* document.

To Track Changes

1 In the *Tablet_PC* document, click Track Changes on the Reviewing toolbar, or double-click the TRK indicator on the status bar.
The Track Changes feature is activated, as indicated by the orange background of the Track Changes button on the Reviewing toolbar, as well as by the active TRK toggle button on the status bar.

If you have problems . . .

If you close a document containing comments and/or tracked changes and open it later, the reviewers' colors might change. Do not worry about the different colors; just notice which color is yours.

2 Position the insertion point to the immediate left of the word *and* within the phrase *and let the computer* on the second line of the first paragraph on the second page.

3 Type `write on the writing pad,` and press Spacebar.
Word displays the inserted text in a different color and underscores it. A vertical black line, called a **changed line,** appears in the left margin, indicating the lines where changes have been made (see Figure 4.7).

Lesson 2 Tracking Changes 127

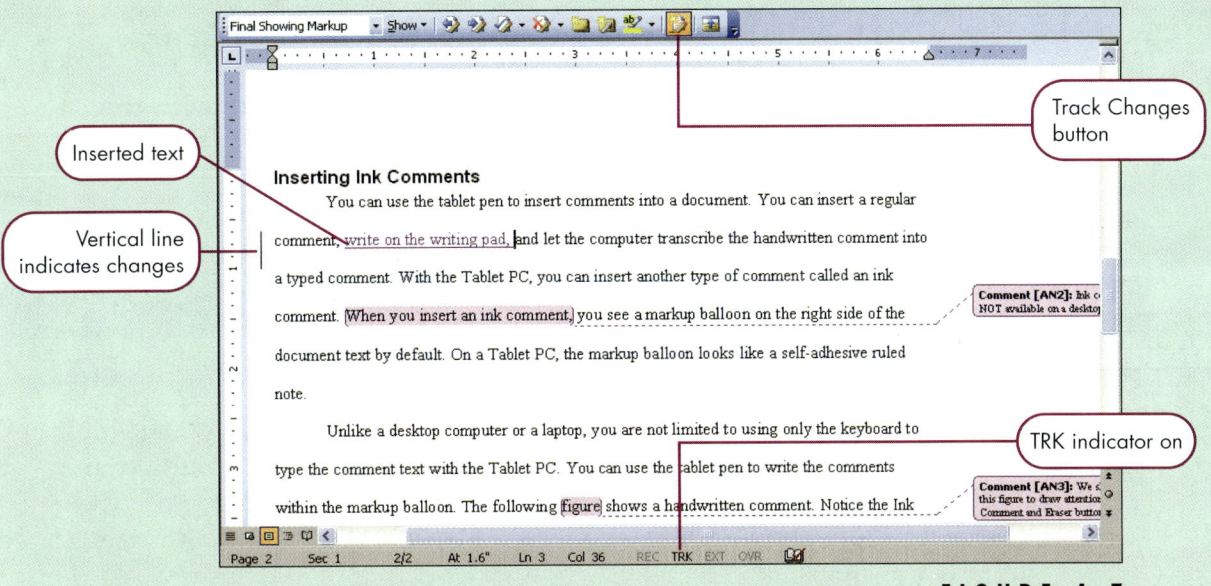

FIGURE 4.7

If you have problems...

If you do not see the changed line in the left margin, choose Tools, Options, click the Track Changes tab, and make sure the *Changed lines* setting is anything other than *(none)*, and click OK.

---

4 Select the phrase *another type of comment called* in the first paragraph on the second page, and press Del.
Word removes the deleted text and displays a markup balloon containing the deleted text.

5 Select the words *ink comment* at the end of the third sentence in the first paragraph on the second page.

6 Apply bold and Violet font color to the selected text; click inside the formatted text *ink comment*.
The changed line appears on the left side of the line you formatted, and a markup balloon indicates the formatting change you made (see Figure 4.8).

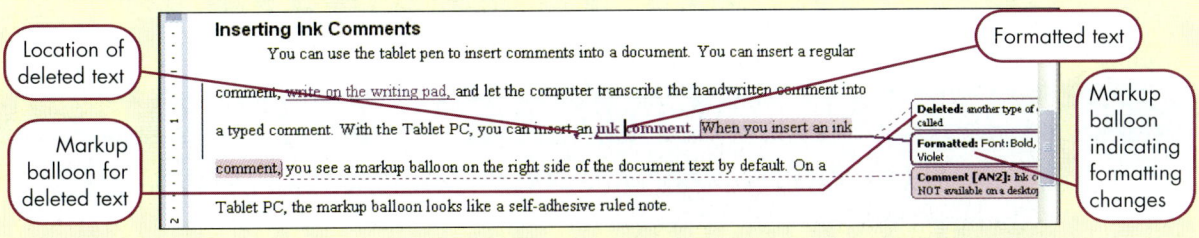

FIGURE 4.8

Project 4   Collaborating with Others

7 Click Track Changes on the Reviewing toolbar to turn off this feature.

8 Save the *Tablet_PC* document, and keep it onscreen to continue with the next lesson.

TO EXTEND YOUR KNOWLEDGE...

PRINTING COMMENTS AND TRACKED CHANGES
By default, the markup balloons appear when you print a document containing comments. When you display the Print dialog box, the *Print what* option is *Document showing markup*. If you do not want to print comments and tracked changes, click the *Print what* drop-down arrow and choose *Document*. If you want to print comments and tracked changes only, click the *Print what* drop-down arrow and choose *List of markup*.

LESSON 3: Customizing Track Changes Options

You can customize the Track Changes feature. By default, Word assigns a different color to each reviewer. However, the Track Changes tab of the Options dialog box enables you to specify the same color for all reviewers' insertions, deletions, and formatting. In addition, the Track Changes tab enables you to specify balloon options, such as the location and width of the markup balloons.

Reviewers who use a Tablet PC can make ***ink annotations***—electronic document markups made with a tablet pen, similar to using a regular pen, to mark up printed documents. The first page of the *Tablet_PC* document contains ink annotations. A reviewer used the tablet pen to draw proofreaders' marks to delete text and to insert text. In addition, the reviewer used the ink annotations tool to circle items on the images, draw a line, and write notes. Although you may not have a Tablet PC, you can change the color of the ink annotations on a regular desktop or laptop computer.

In this lesson, you change markup balloon settings and change ink annotation colors.

To Change Balloon Options and Change Ink Colors

1 In the *Tablet_PC* document, choose <u>T</u>ools, <u>O</u>ptions, and click the Track Changes tab.
The Track Changes tab contains options for customizing markup settings, such as changing colors for all insertions, deletions, and formatting changes. In addition, you can set options for the markup balloons (see Figure 4.9).

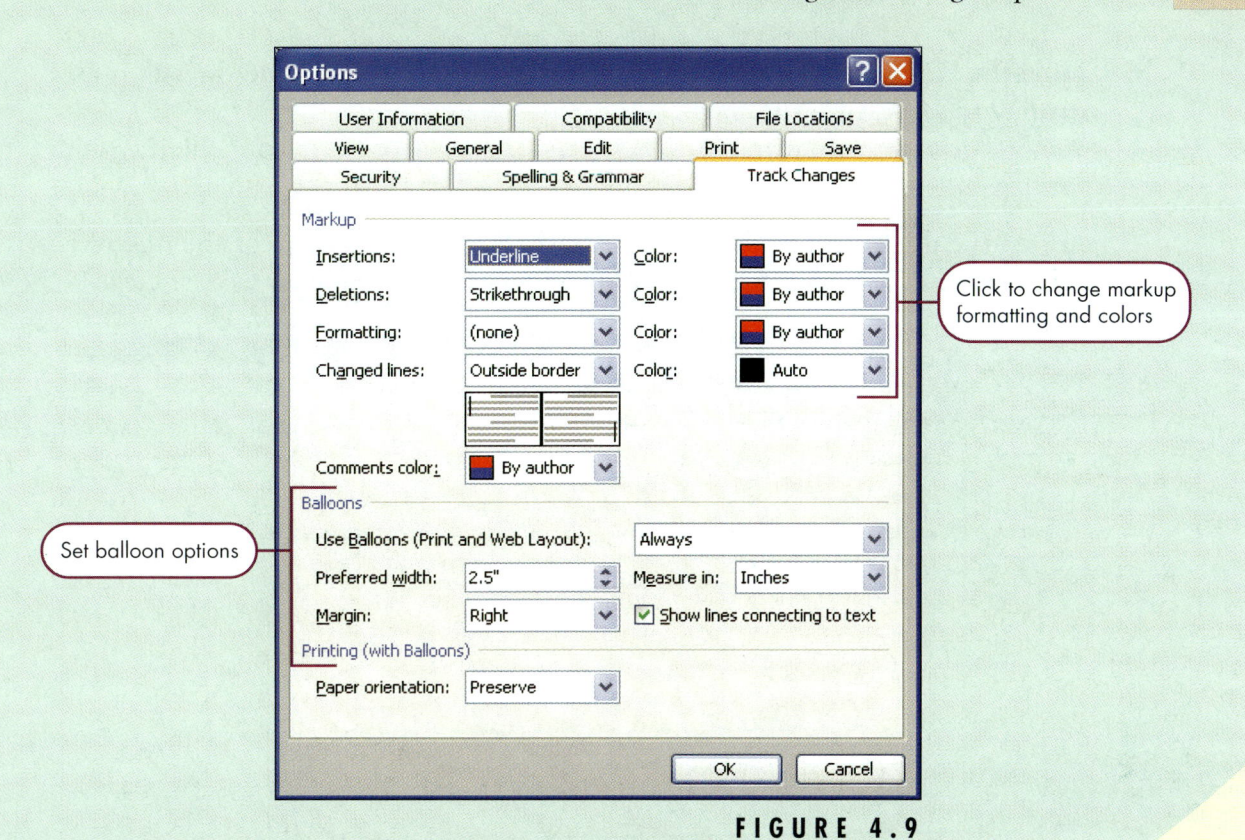

Lesson 3   Customizing Track Changes Options   **129**

FIGURE 4.9

2   In the *Balloons* section, change the *Preferred width* setting to **1.85"**.

3   Click the *Margin* drop-down arrow, choose *Left,* click OK, and click the ⬅ on the left side of the horizontal scrollbar.
The 1.85" wide markup balloons appear in the left margin (see Figure 4.10).

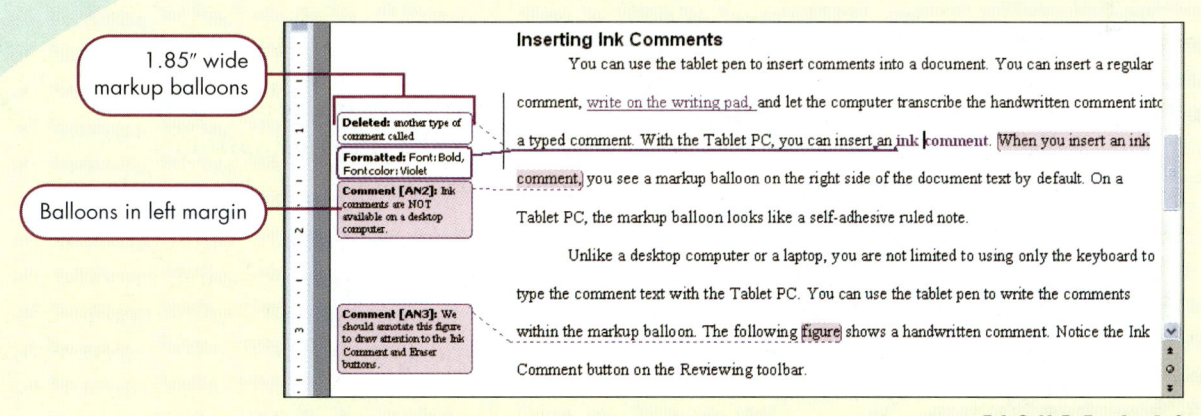

FIGURE 4.10

4   Use the above process to change the balloon width back to **2.5"** and to set balloons in the right margin.

5 **Hide the Standard, Formatting, and Reviewing toolbars; hide the ruler; and display the Drawing toolbar.**
You hide several screen components to be able to see all of the ink annotations on the first page.

6 **Adjust the document to see the bottom half of the first page of the document.**
A reviewer used a Tablet PC to insert ink annotations on this page (see Figure 4.11).

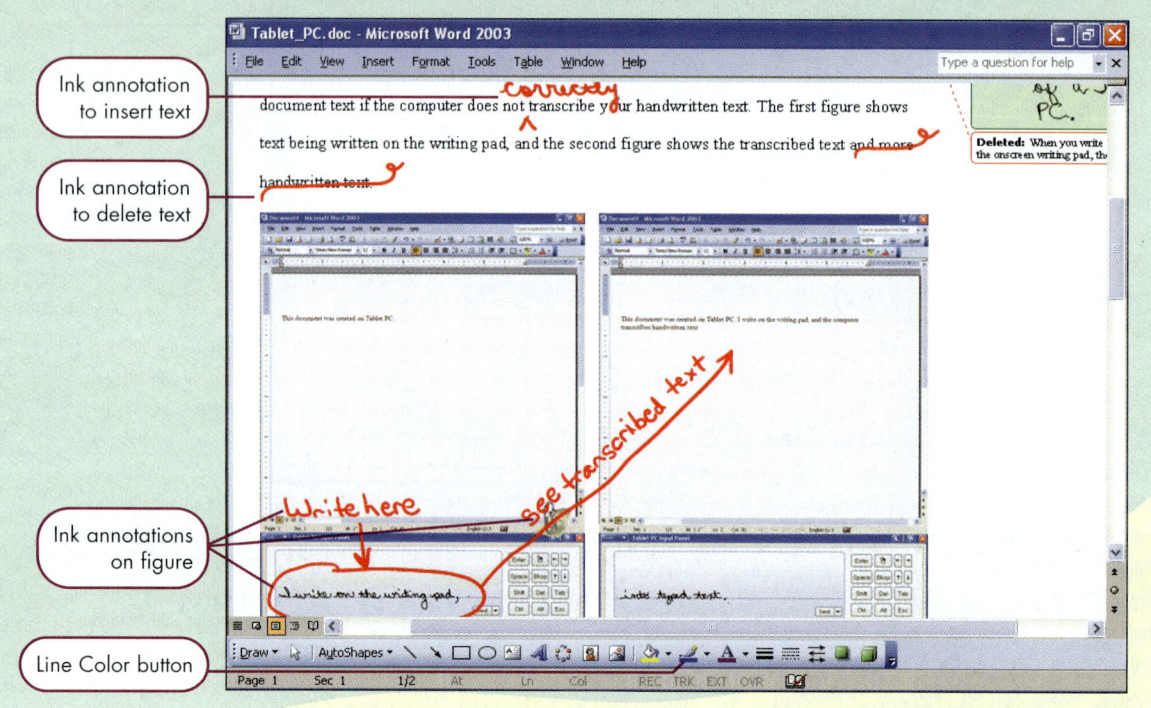

FIGURE 4.11

7 **Click the *Write here* ink annotation to select it.**

8 **Click the Line Color drop-down arrow on the Drawing toolbar, choose Violet on the Line Color palette, and deselect the ink annotation.**
Word changes the ink annotation color from Red to Violet.

You now want to change the color of the *see transcribed text* ink annotation that appears on the image within the document. Because the words are stored in two separate ink annotations—*see transcribed* in one ink annotation and *text* in another ink annotation, you must select the two ink annotations separately like you select two objects or images.

9 **Click the *see transcribed* ink annotation; then press and hold down Ctrl while you click the *text* ink annotation to select both ink annotations.**

10 **Click the Line Color drop-down arrow on the Drawing toolbar, choose Blue, and deselect the ink annotations.**
Figure 4.12 shows the color changes you made to a reviewer's ink annotations.

Lesson 3 Customizing Track Changes Options   **131**   LEVEL **2**

Violet ink annotation color

Blue ink annotation color

Original ink annotation color

FIGURE 4.12

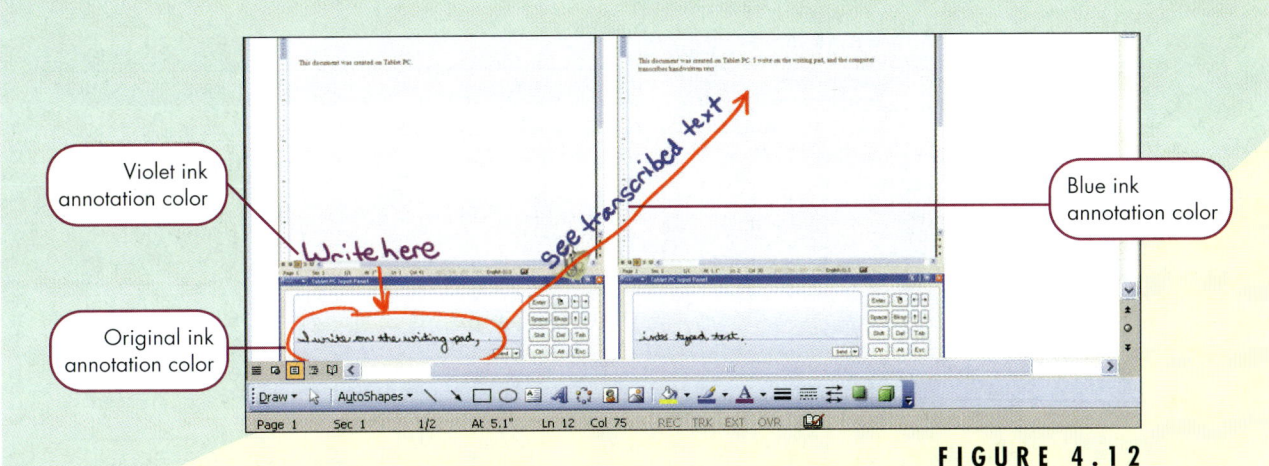

11 Display the Standard, Formatting, and Reviewing toolbars; display the ruler; and hide the Drawing toolbar.

12 Save the *Tablet_PC* document and keep it onscreen to continue with the next lesson.

TO EXTEND YOUR KNOWLEDGE...

INSERTING, CUSTOMIZING, AND ERASING INK ANNOTATIONS ON A TABLET PC

To insert an ink annotation on a Tablet PC, tap Insert Ink Annotations on the Reviewing toolbar with the tablet pen, and use the tablet pen to write directly on the computer screen.

If you display the Ink Annotations toolbar (see Figure 4.13), you can tap the Ink Annotations drop-down arrow with the tablet pen and choose from a variety of ballpoint pens, felt tip pens, and highlighter colors. After annotating the document, tap the Stop Inking button on the right side of the Ink Annotations toolbar. (Note: Figure 4.13 does not show the Stop Inking or Stop Erasing button in the current mode; these buttons only appear when you start creating an ink annotation or when the Eraser mode is active, respectively.)

Project 4 Collaborating with Others

FIGURE 4.13

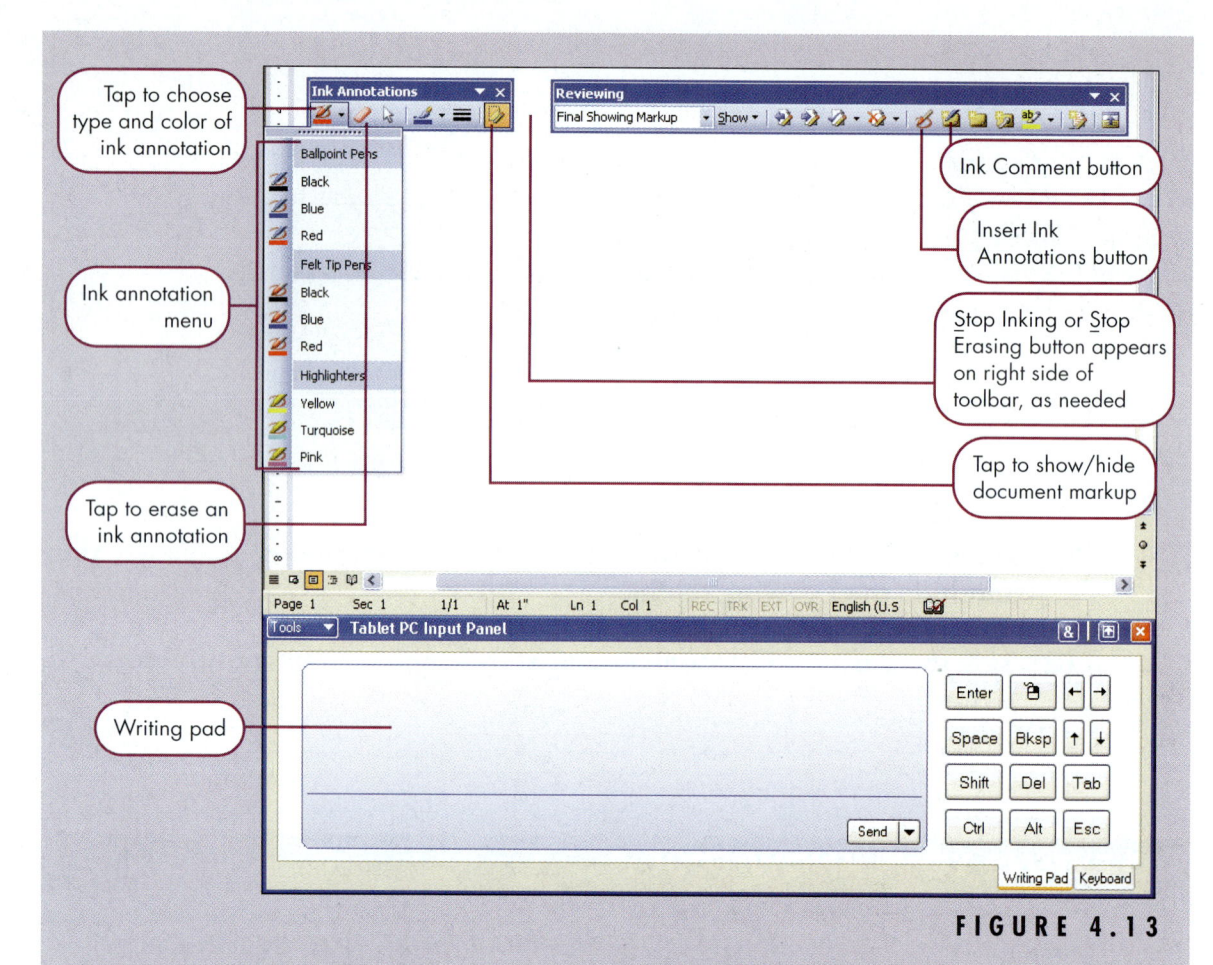

You can change the ink annotation color on a Tablet PC by tapping the ink annotation with the tablet pen to select it, tapping the Line Color drop-down arrow on the Ink Annotations toolbar, and tapping the desired color on the palette.

You can erase all or part of an ink annotation by tapping Eraser on the Ink Annotations toolbar and moving the tip of the tablet pen over the part of the ink annotation you want to erase. When you are done erasing, tap the Stop Erasing button that appears on the right side of the toolbar. If you want to erase the entire ink annotation, tap the ink annotation to select it and then press Del.

LESSON 4: Reviewing Changes by Type and Reviewer

After you and your team members finish editing a document, the document contains all the changes for your review. The *Display for Review* drop-down menu on the Reviewing toolbar enables you to display the document and changes from different perspectives. The default option, *Final Showing Markup*, shows the document with the revision marks and markup balloons. *Final* shows how the document looks if you accept and incorporate all tracked changes. *Original Showing Markup* shows deleted text with strikethrough but displays inserted text as

Lesson 4 Reviewing Changes by Type and Reviewer   133   LEVEL 2

markup balloons. *Original* shows the document prior to using the Track Changes feature. You can also choose <u>V</u>iew, M<u>a</u>rkup to toggle between *Final* and *Final Showing Markup*.

You can also specify which types of changes you want to review by using the <u>S</u>how drop-down menu on the Reviewing toolbar. You can review comments, ink annotations, insertions and deletions, formatting changes, or any combination of the four types. Also, you can click the <u>S</u>how drop-down menu and then click <u>R</u>eviewers. A list of reviewers opens from which you can choose which reviewer's markup changes you want to review. You can even decide what types of balloons to show, such as <u>O</u>nly for Comments/Formatting.

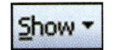

In this lesson, you see how the document looks if you accept all changes and then show changes by different reviewers.

To Change Display for Review and Show Changes by Type and Reviewer

1 With the *Tablet_PC* document onscreen, click the *Display for Review* drop-down arrow on the Reviewing toolbar.
By default, Word displays the document in *Final Showing Markup* so that you can see the tracked changes.

2 Choose *Final* from the drop-down menu.
Word now shows how the document will look if you accept all changes (see Figure 4.14). Comment balloons indicating deletions and formatting marks are hidden, and inserted text is inserted without showing revision marks.

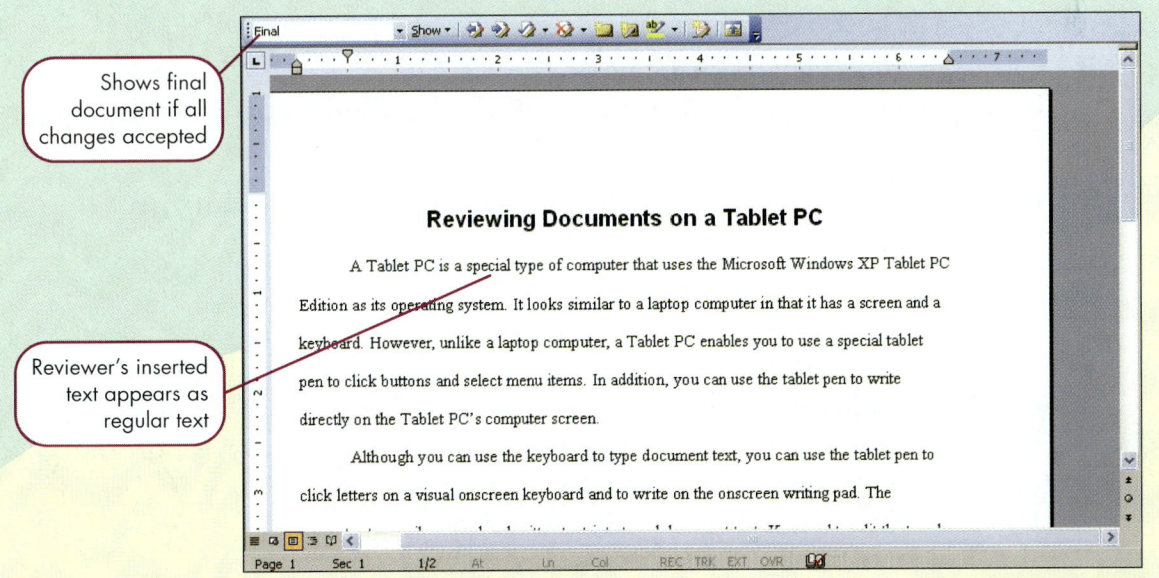

FIGURE 4.14

3 Click the *Display for Review* drop-down arrow and choose *Final Showing Markup*.

4 **Click Show on the Reviewing toolbar.**
The Show drop-down menu displays to allow you to specify which types of changes you want to review. By default, *Comments, Ink Annotations, Insertions and Deletions,* and *Formatting* are all selected as indicated by the check marks.

5 **Choose *Comments* on the drop-down menu.**
Word hides the comment and ink comment markup balloons. However, markup balloons for deleted text and formatted text remain onscreen.

6 **Repeat steps 4 and 5 to display comments again.**

7 **Click Show on the Reviewing toolbar and choose *Reviewers*.**
In addition to a check box for *All Reviewers,* you see a check box displaying your reviewing name and three other reviewers' names (see Figure 4.15).

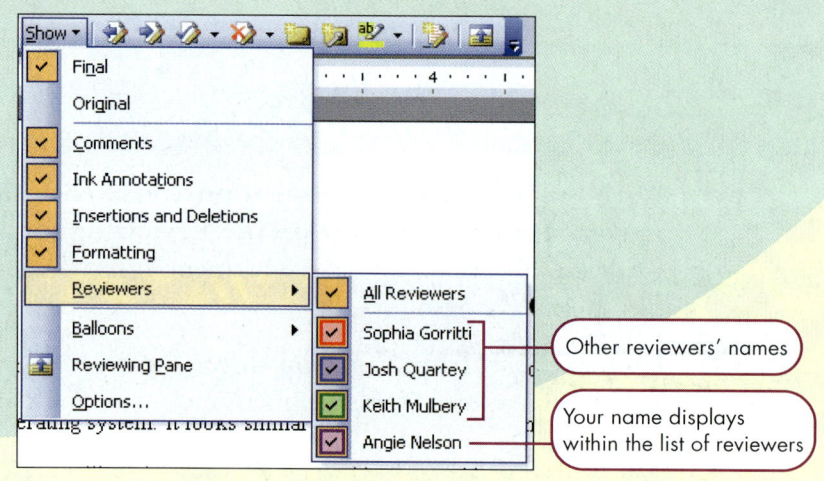

FIGURE 4.15

8 **Click the *All Reviewers* check box to deselect it.**
Because you deselected the *All Reviewers* check box, Word hides the tracked changes for all reviewers.

9 **Click Show, Reviewers, and click the check box for Sophia Gorritti.**
Figure 4.16 shows tracked changes by Sophia.

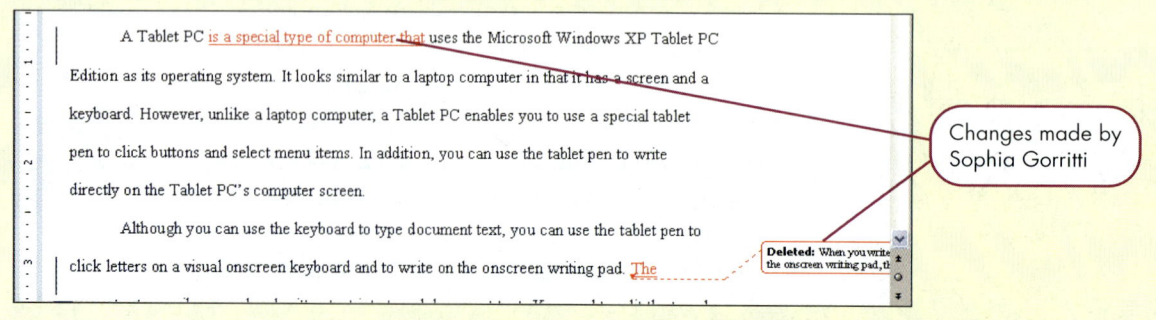

FIGURE 4.16

Lesson 5 Saving Versions and Accepting and Rejecting Changes 135 LEVEL 2

10 Click **S**how, **R**eviewers, **A**ll Reviewers.
Word displays all reviewers' changes again.

11 Save the *Tablet_PC* document and keep it onscreen to continue with the next lesson.

TO EXTEND YOUR KNOWLEDGE . . .

WORKING WITH CHANGES IN THE REVIEWING PANE

The Reviewing Pane lets you view a list of changes outside of the document text. Click Reviewing Pane on the Reviewing toolbar to display the pane below the horizontal scrollbar (refer to Figure 4.5 at the end of Lesson 1).

The Reviewing Pane shows changes made to different sections of the document. You can view and modify main document changes, comments, header and footer changes, text box changes, footnote changes, and endnote changes. If no changes have been made to a section, Word displays *(none)*.

UNDERSTANDING INK ANNOTATIONS

Word creates ink annotations as graphical objects. Therefore, ink annotations do not identify the reviewers who inserted them. Because ink annotations are not linked to a particular reviewer, they do not disappear when you deselect *All Reviewers,* as in step 8 in the previous set of steps.

LESSON 5: Saving Versions and Accepting and Rejecting Changes

While viewing changes submitted by reviewers, you can accept or reject the changes for the final document. If you agree with a reviewer's change, use the ***Accept Change*** option to remove the revision mark and incorporate the change into the regular document text. If you do not want to incorporate a reviewer's change, use the ***Reject Change*** option to remove the revision mark and the tracked change, thus restoring that part of the document to its previous state.

In Lesson 4, you used the *Display for Review* option to compare the differences in *Final Showing Markup* and *Final* document display. However, after you accept and reject changes, you can no longer display the document with the tracked changes. Therefore, you might want to save a version of the document before accepting and rejecting changes. A ***version*** is a "snapshot" of the document that is marked with the name of the person who saves it, as well as the date and time the version was saved. Using the Versions feature helps you keep copies of the original version, the version edited by reviewers, and the version that incorporates the reviewers' changes.

Saving versions is different from using the Save As command. With the Save As command, you create two or more totally separate documents. With the Versions command, you save each version with the original document. The Versions command saves disk space; only the differences between versions are saved with the document, not a separate copy of the document using a separate filename.

In this lesson, you complete three sets of hands-on steps. In the first set of steps, you save a version of the document with the tracked changes. In the second set of steps, you accept and reject reviewers' changes. In the third set of steps, you save another version of the document and open the first document version.

To Save a Version of the Document

1 **With the *Tablet_PC* document onscreen, choose File, Versions.**
The Versions in Tablet_PC.doc dialog box opens. Because this is the first version you create for this document, the dialog box is empty (see Figure 4.17).

FIGURE 4.17

2 **Click Save Now in the top-left corner of the dialog box.**
The Save Version dialog box opens so that you can add comments about the current version of the document (see Figure 4.18).

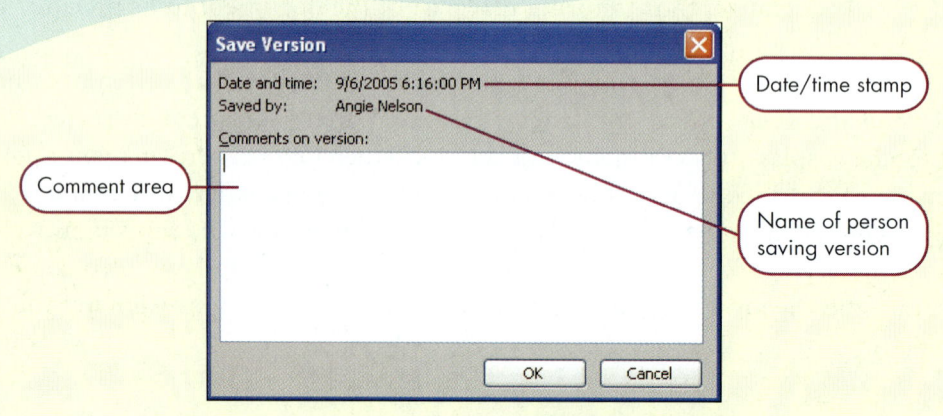

FIGURE 4.18

Lesson 5   Saving Versions and Accepting and Rejecting Changes   **137**   LEVEL 2

3 In the *Comments on version* box, type `This version shows the reviewers' suggestions as tracked changes.` Then click **OK**.
Word saves the version of the document and keeps the document open. If you continue editing the open document, the changes you make are not included in the version you just saved. Word also displays a Versions icon on the status bar, indicating that the document contains one or more versions. You can double-click it to open the Versions in Tablet_PC dialog box.

4 Save the *Tablet_PC* document and keep it onscreen to continue with the next set of steps.

Now that you have saved a version of the document with the tracked changes, you are ready to accept and reject tracked changes. After you accept and reject changes, you save another version of the document so that you can compare versions later if needed.

To Accept and Reject Changes

1 In the *Tablet_PC* document, press Ctrl+Home to position the insertion point at the beginning of the document.

2 Click **Next** on the Reviewing toolbar to highlight the first change, and position the mouse pointer over the tracked change.
When you position the mouse pointer on the revision mark, a ScreenTip appears that tells you who made the change, and the date and time the change was made (see Figure 4.19).

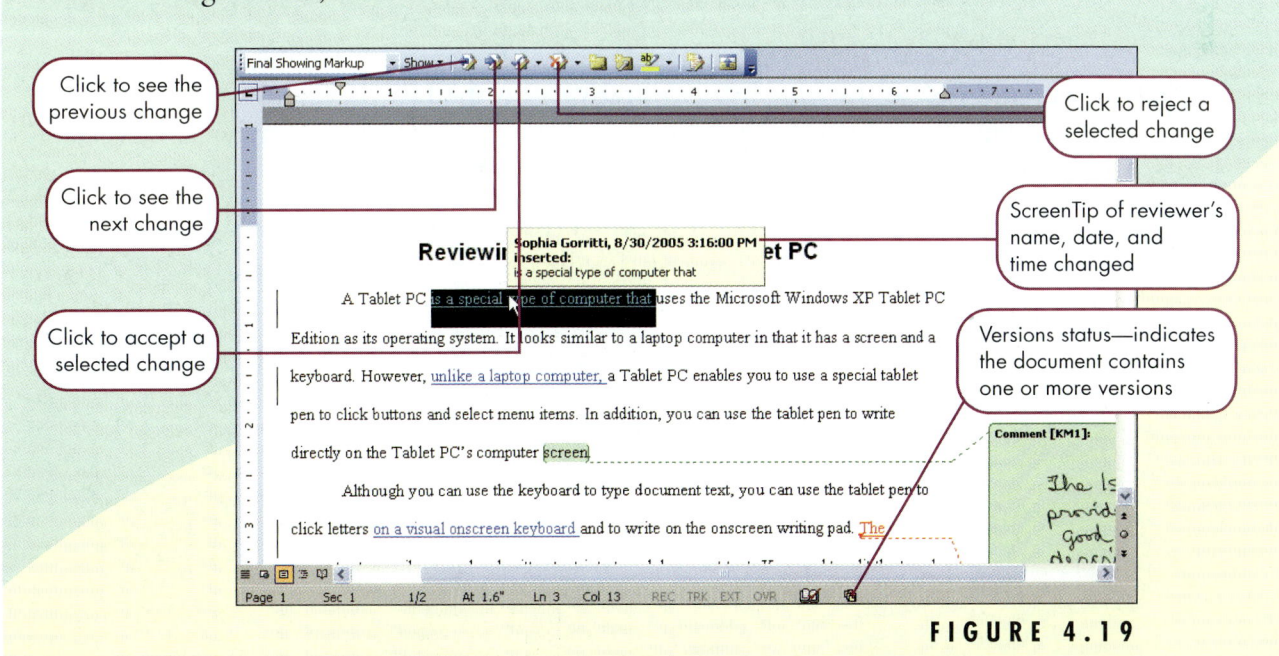

Click to see the previous change

Click to see the next change

Click to accept a selected change

Click to reject a selected change

ScreenTip of reviewer's name, date, and time changed

Versions status—indicates the document contains one or more versions

FIGURE 4.19

3 **Click Accept Change on the Reviewing toolbar.**
When you accept the inserted text change, Word removes the revision mark (the color and underscore) and converts the text to regular text.

4 **Click Next on the Reviewing toolbar.**
Word selects *unlike a laptop computer,*—the text that Josh inserted. Because you do not want that text, you reject the change.

5 **Click Reject Change/Delete Comment on the Reviewing toolbar.**
When you reject an inserted text change, Word removes it from the document. The next two changes are the ink comments.

6 **Click Next three times to skip the ink comments and select the next inserted text change,** *on a visual onscreen keyboard.*
When you click Next the first time, Word selects the first ink comment. When you click Next the second time, you do not see the ink comment unless you scroll down in the document.

7 **Click Reject Change/Delete Comment to reject the inserted text change.**
Word removes the text from the document.

8 **Click Next and click Accept Change to accept the change to delete text.**
Word officially deletes the text *When you write directly on the onscreen writing pad, the.* Because you accept the deleted text change, you need to accept the next change, which is to insert the word *The* with a capital *T* to start the next sentence.

9 **Click Next and click Accept Change to accept the change to insert the word** *The.*
The ink annotations change locations after you accept and reject previous changes because the document was not displayed in Reading Layout view before the ink annotations were inserted.

10 **Select and delete the four ink annotations on the last paragraph.**
The image on the left is farther down than the image on the right. Therefore, you need to move it up now.

11 **Click the image on the left and press ↑ three times.**
Figure 4.20 shows the first page of the document after accepting and rejecting changes, deleting four ink annotations, and moving the left image up.

Lesson 5 Saving Versions and Accepting and Rejecting Changes 139

Callouts on Figure 4.20:
- Inserted text accepted
- No vertical changed lines
- Inserted text change rejected and removed from the document
- Image moved up to align with top of second image
- Ink annotations deleted from paragraph
- Deleted text change and inserted word *The* accepted

FIGURE 4.20

12 Save the *Tablet_PC* document, and keep it onscreen to continue with the next set of steps.

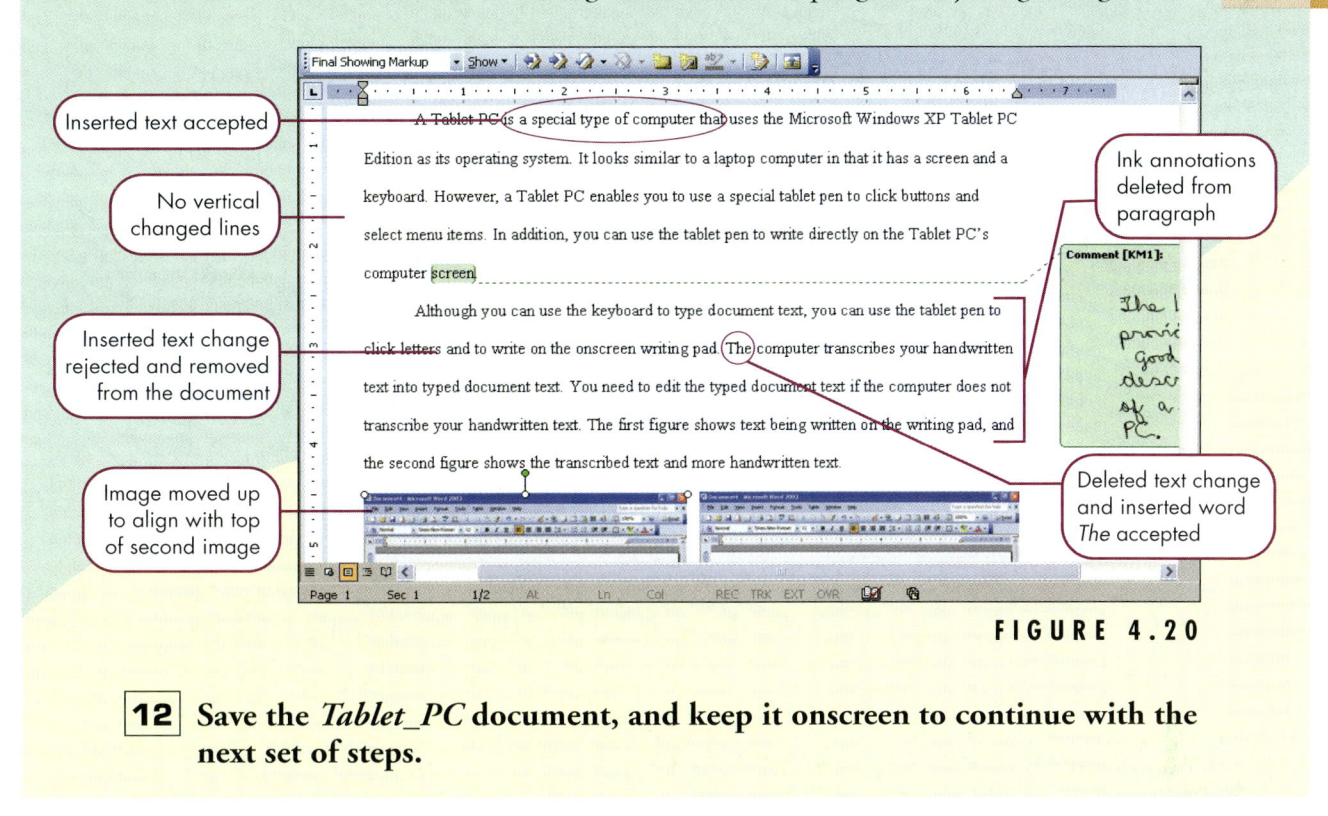

You want to save another version of the document in case you want to review different versions and make changes later. After saving a version, you open the first version to compare it with the newest version.

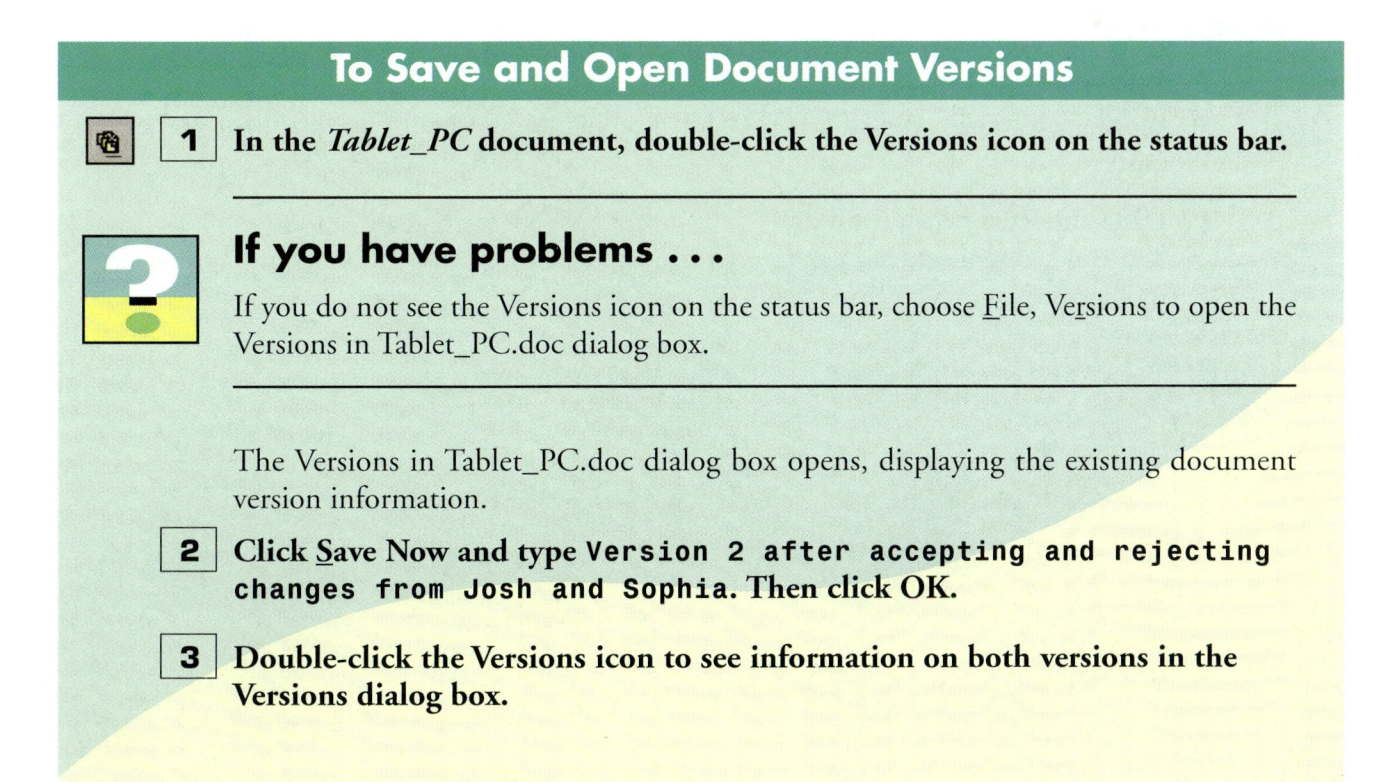

To Save and Open Document Versions

1 In the *Tablet_PC* document, double-click the Versions icon on the status bar.

If you have problems . . .

If you do not see the Versions icon on the status bar, choose File, Versions to open the Versions in Tablet_PC.doc dialog box.

The Versions in Tablet_PC.doc dialog box opens, displaying the existing document version information.

2 Click Save Now and type `Version 2 after accepting and rejecting changes from Josh and Sophia`. Then click OK.

3 Double-click the Versions icon to see information on both versions in the Versions dialog box.

4 Select the older version (indicated by the date/time), and click View Comments.

Figure 4.21 shows the Versions in Tablet_PC.doc and the View Comments dialog boxes.

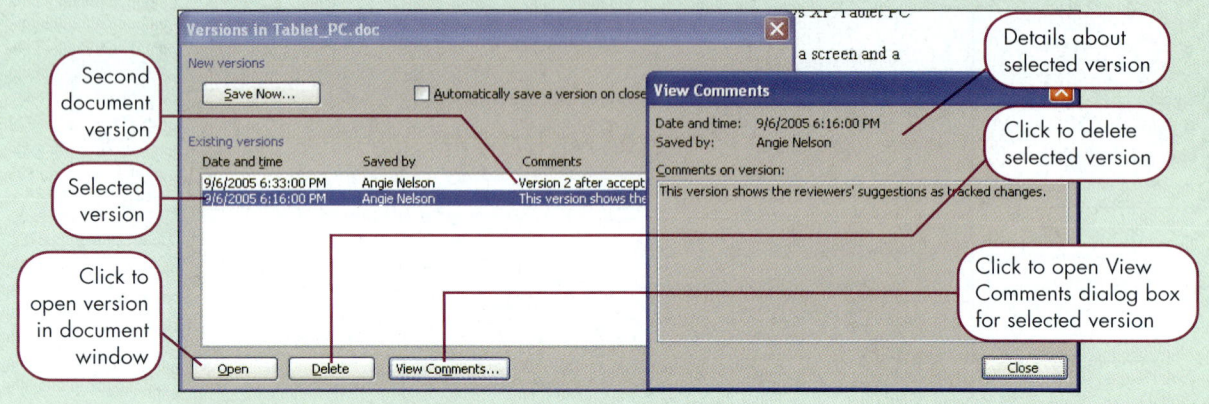

FIGURE 4.21

If you have problems . . .

If you do not see both dialog boxes side by side, you can close the top dialog box, move the Versions in Tablet_PC.doc dialog box to the left, click View Comments, and then click and drag the View Comments dialog box to the right.

5 Click Close in the View Comments dialog box.

6 With the older version still selected, click Open in the Versions in Tablet_PC.doc dialog box.

Word opens the document version while keeping the most current document version onscreen.

7 Hide the Reviewing toolbar.

You can see more document text within each window after hiding the Reviewing toolbar (see Figure 4.22).

Lesson 5   Saving Versions and Accepting and Rejecting Changes   **141**   LEVEL 2

Current version after accepting and rejecting changes

First version that contains tracked changes for Josh and Sophia

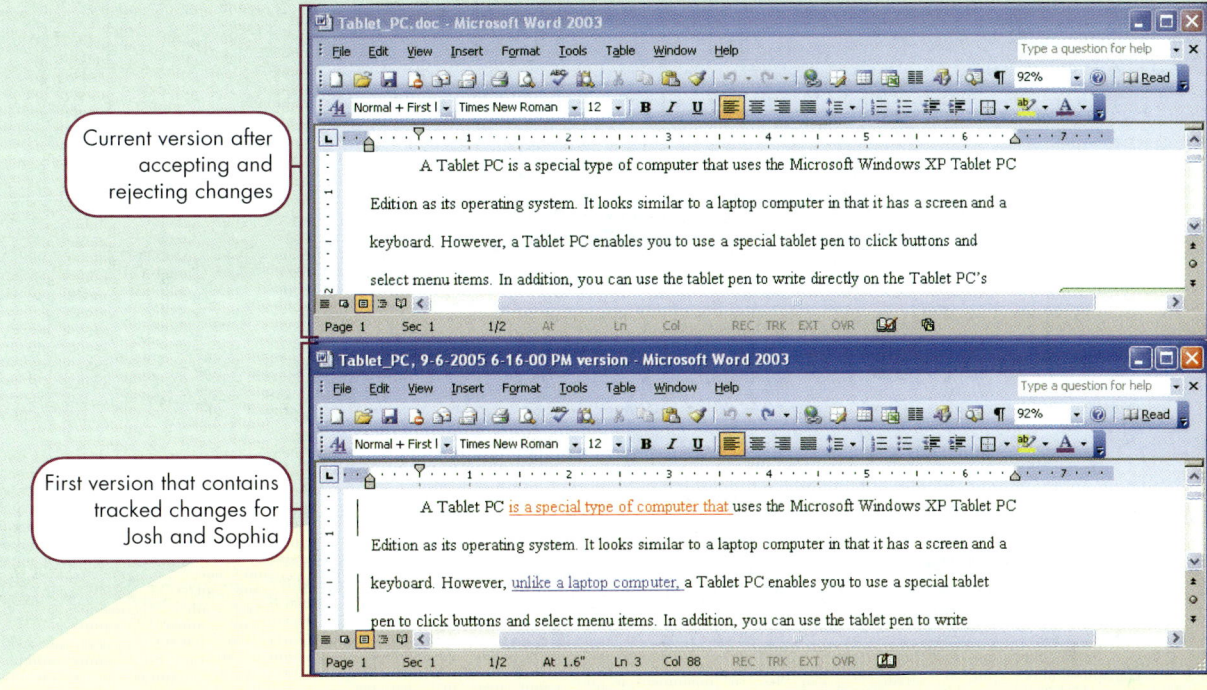

FIGURE 4.22

8 Close the document window containing the first version, and maximize the document window containing the second version (after accepting and rejecting changes).

9 Save the *Tablet_PC* document, and keep it onscreen to continue with the next lesson.

TO EXTEND YOUR KNOWLEDGE...

DELETING VERSIONS
If you no longer need a version, open the Versions dialog box, click the version you wish to delete, click Delete at the bottom of the dialog box, and click Yes to confirm the deletion.

USING THE SHORTCUT MENU
You can right-click within a tracked change to display a shortcut menu. When the menu is displayed, you can accept or reject the current tracked change.

ACCEPTING OR REJECTING ALL CHANGES
To accept all changes in a document at once, click the Accept Change drop-down arrow on the Reviewing toolbar and choose *Accept All Changes in Document* (see Figure 4.23). To delete all changes in a document at once, click the Reject

Change/Delete Comment drop-down arrow on the Reviewing toolbar and then choose *Reject All Changes in Document* (see Figure 4.24).

FIGURE 4.23

FIGURE 4.24

LESSON 6: E-Mailing a Document as an Attachment for Review

You can e-mail a Word document from within Word instead of taking the time to launch your e-mail program. Word has the capability to become an e-mail editing program with a toolbar specific for customizing e-mail. You can send a document for review, or simply as an attachment to be read but not edited. When you choose *Mail Recipient (for Review),* Word sends the current document as an attachment with the Track Changes feature active to track the recipient's changes. It sends the e-mail with a red flag to indicate to the recipient that a follow-up is requested. When you choose *Mail Recipient (as Attachment),* Word sends the document as an attachment without activating the Track Changes feature and without flagging the e-mail to the recipient.

In this lesson, you complete two sets of hands-on steps. In the first set, you e-mail the *Tablet_PC* document to another team member to review. In the second set, you e-mail a copy of the document to your supervisor as an attachment.

For the following set of steps to work correctly, Outlook must be the default e-mail program on your computer. If Outlook is not your default program, another e-mail program may open instead of the Word e-mail editor window, but you may be able to adapt the steps to complete the exercises (see If You Have Problems after step 2 in the next set of steps). With some e-mail programs, however, the process does not work. Even if you cannot complete the set of hands-on steps in this lesson, you should read the steps for understanding of the process.

To E-Mail a Document for Review

1 In the *Tablet_PC* document, choose File, Send To.
The Send To menu displays options where you can send the currently opened document (see Figure 4.25).

Lesson 6 E-Mailing a Document as an Attachment for Review   143   LEVEL 2

Callouts (Figure 4.25):
- E-mail the current document for review with Track Changes active → Mail Recipient (for Review)...
- Create a new e-mail message in Word → Mail Recipient
- E-mail the current document as an attachment → Mail Recipient (as Attachment)...

Menu items shown:
- Mail Recipient
- Mail Recipient (for Review)...
- Mail Recipient (as Attachment)...
- Routing Recipient...
- Exchange Folder...
- Online Meeting Participant
- Recipient using a Fax Modem...
- Recipient using Internet Fax Service...
- Microsoft Office PowerPoint

FIGURE 4.25

2 **Choose Mail Recipient (for Review).**
Word becomes an e-mail editor by displaying a special E-mail toolbar with buttons to send e-mail, insert (attach) a file, set priorities, and set options (see Figure 4.26). In addition, it displays *Review* above the e-mail heading boxes to indicate that you are sending a document to be reviewed by the recipient. The default subject line refers to the document you are sending, and the filename appears as an attachment.

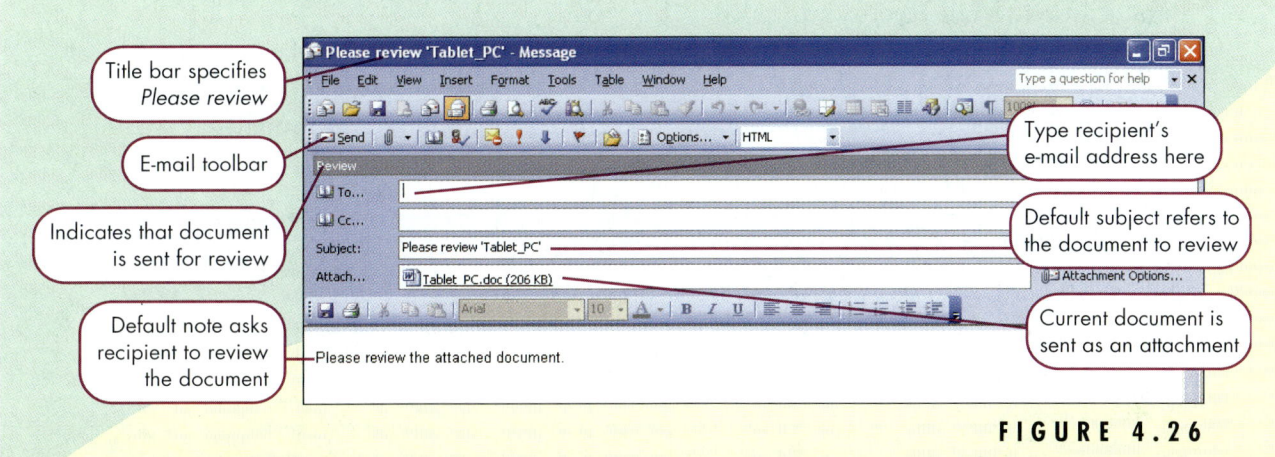

Callouts (Figure 4.26):
- Title bar specifies *Please review*
- E-mail toolbar
- Indicates that document is sent for review
- Default note asks recipient to review the document — Please review the attached document.
- Type recipient's e-mail address here
- Default subject refers to the document to review — Please review 'Tablet_PC'
- Current document is sent as an attachment — Tablet_PC.doc (206 KB)

FIGURE 4.26

If you have problems . . .

Depending on your computer setup, your default e-mail program, such as Novell GroupWise, might appear instead of the Word e-mail editor window. If so, you can continue with the rest of the steps. If you receive an error message, Microsoft Outlook may not be set up. You may have to start Outlook and set up your regular e-mail account through Outlook. Use Outlook Help to learn how to do this. If you do not wish to set up Outlook as your default e-mail program, continue to read through the remaining steps, even if you do not complete the exercises.

3 Type a classmate's or friend's e-mail address in the *To* box, and type your e-mail address in the *Cc* box.

4 Click *S*end to send the e-mail with the attached document to the recipient with a copy to your e-mail account.

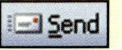

5 Close all document windows, open your e-mail program, open the e-mail you sent to yourself, and open the attached Word document.
Word activated the Track Changes feature when it attached the document, as you can see by the TRK indicator on the status bar.

6 Close all document windows.

While you are waiting for the recipients to review the document that you e-mailed to them, your supervisor contacted you to see the current draft of the *Tablet_PC* document. In the next set of steps you send the document to your supervisor as an attachment instead of for review, since she does not want to edit the document.

To Send a Document as an E-Mail Attachment

1 Open *Tablet_PC*, and choose <u>F</u>ile, Sen<u>d</u> To.

2 Choose M<u>a</u>il Recipient (as Attachment).
Word becomes an e-mail editor. The title bar and subject line display the name of the file, but do not display the request *Please review*. The message box does not display *Please review the attached document*. The current document is automatically included as an attachment, as indicated by the *Attach* box (see Figure 4.27).

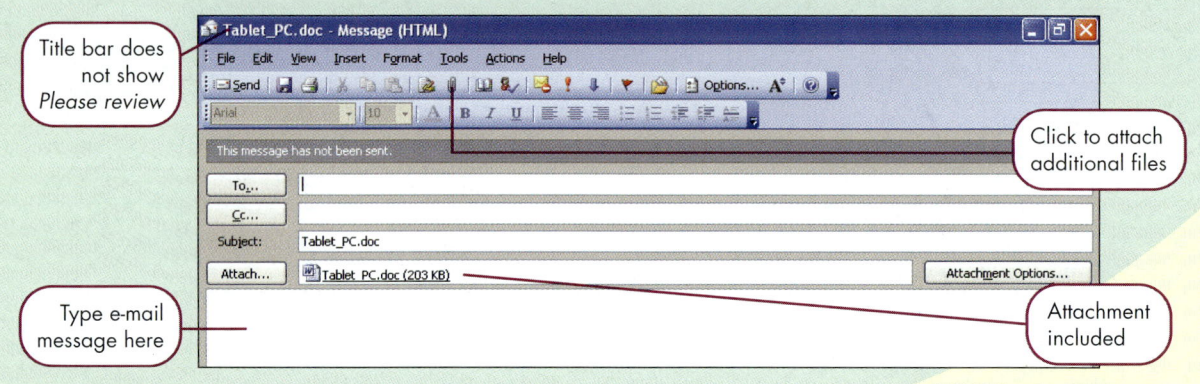

- Title bar does not show *Please review*
- Click to attach additional files
- Type e-mail message here
- Attachment included

FIGURE 4.27

3 In the *To* box, type your instructor's e-mail address.

4 In the *Subject* box, type `Second Version of the Tablet PC Document`.

5 In the message window, type Penny, press ←Enter twice, and type `Here is the latest version of the document. As soon as I receive feedback from the rest of the team members, I will finalize the document. We are excited to demonstrate the Tablet PC at our division meeting next week.`

6 Click <u>S</u>end on the toolbar to send the e-mail message to your instructor.

7 Close the e-mail window without saving it, and keep the *Tablet_PC* document open to continue with the next lesson.

TO EXTEND YOUR KNOWLEDGE...

USING THE E-MAIL TOOLBAR BUTTONS
Table 4.1 lists and describes the buttons on the E-mail toolbar.

TABLE 4.1

BUTTON	BUTTON NAME	DESCRIPTION
Send	Send	Sends the e-mail and attachments to the recipient(s).
	Insert File	Lets you select a document to attach to the e-mail. The recipient can save and open the attachment in the source program, such as Word.
	Address Book	Displays the Address Book so that you can select e-mail addresses. You can specify recipients, copy recipients, and blind copy recipients. A *blind copy* is a copy of the e-mail message sent to another person, but the primary recipient does not know that someone else received the e-mail.
	Check Names	Checks the recipient's e-mail address in Outlook to make sure it has a recognized e-mail address format.
	Permission (Unrestricted Access)	Helps ensure that documents are not forwarded or edited by unauthorized people. You must download and install the Windows Rights Management client in order to specify permission settings.
	Importance: High	Designates the e-mail as a high-priority message by displaying a red exclamation mark in the recipient's In Box if the recipient uses Outlook.
	Importance: Low	Designates the e-mail as a low-priority message by displaying a down-pointing arrow in the recipient's In Box if the recipient uses Outlook.
	Message Flag	Includes a "flagged" message that the recipient needs to take action based on the message. It is included automatically when you send a document for review.
	Create Rule	Specifies actions to be taken based on specific conditions for incoming messages. For example, sending automatic confirmation responses for incoming messages with a particular subject line.
Options...	Options	Opens a dialog box so that you can choose other options, such as delivery dates, for sending an e-mail message.

ENDING A REVIEW
The Reviewing toolbar contains an E_nd Review button after you open a document that was sent for review. You can click this button to end the review cycle. Use Help to learn more about ending a review process.

ROUTING A DOCUMENT TO MULTIPLE RECIPIENTS
If you need to send a document to more than one person, you can specify whether you want to send it to all reviewers simultaneously or one at a time in a specific order. Word includes a *routing slip,* which is list of recipients and your instructions on whether to send it in sequence or at the same time.

To attach a routing slip, choose F_ile, Send To, Routing Recipient. The Routing Slip dialog box opens (see Figure 4.28). Click A_ddress to display your e-mail system's address book and then choose the name of each reviewer. Click the option *One after another* to send the document to each reviewer in the order in which they are listed in the T_o list box, or click *All at once* to simultaneously send a copy of the document to each person listed in the T_o box.

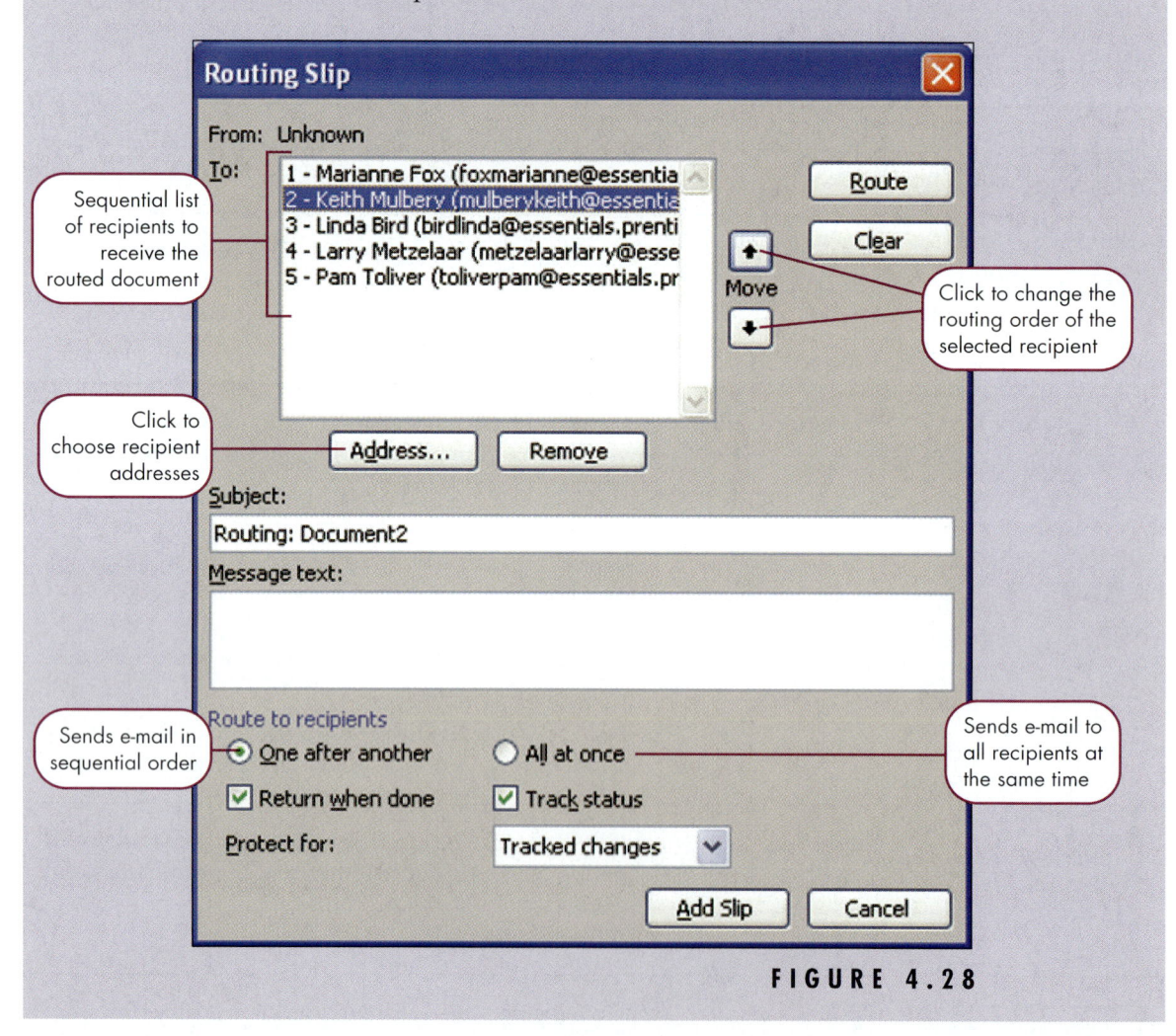

FIGURE 4.28

When you route a document, the first reviewer receives the e-mail with a subject line such as *Routing Reviewing Documents on a Tablet_PC*. The automatic message is *The attached document has a routing slip*. When you are done reviewing this document, choose Next Routing Recipient from the Microsoft Word Send To menu on the File menu to continue the routing.

CREATING A NEW E-MAIL DOCUMENT

You can create an e-mail message within Word if Outlook is the default e-mail program. To do this, start a new document and click E-mail on the Standard toolbar. Word becomes an e-mail editor so that you can use the document window to type the content of the e-mail message. The editing window looks similar to the e-mail editor you saw when you completed the previous two sets of hands-on steps. The toolbar enables you to insert a file as an attachment, display an address book, specify the importance level, and set options.

If a document is open when you click E-mail on the Standard toolbar, Word displays the e-mail editor window with the current document contents as the main e-mail message.

LESSON 7: Comparing and Merging Documents

Ideally, you want to route the same document to various team members so that all tracked changes are located in one document. However, sometimes it is necessary to have several people editing their own copy of the document simultaneously. When this occurs, you have several similar documents but with individual changes. Instead of comparing printed copies of the document to determine the differences, you can use the Compare and Merge feature to compare two or more documents.

When you *compare and merge documents,* Word displays markup balloons in the margins of a document window as it does when you make changes and the Track Changes feature is activated.

In this lesson, you compare the *Tablet_PC* document with *EW2_0402,* a document edited by another team member who did not activate the Track Changes feature.

To Compare and Merge Documents

1. In the *Tablet_PC* document, choose **T**ools, Compare and Merge **D**ocuments. The Compare and Merge Documents dialog box opens. It looks similar to the Open and Save As dialog boxes.

2. Find and select *EW2_0402.*

If you have problems...

If you double-click the filename, Word opens *EW2_0402* and automatically compares and merges the *Tablet_PC* document within the *EW2_0402*. Because you might not want to alter *EW2_0402*, you should not automatically double-click the filename or click the Merge button. If this happens, close the document (without saving changes) and complete steps 1 and 2 again.

3 Click the Merge drop-down arrow in the bottom-right corner of the dialog box.

You can choose from three options for comparing and merging two documents. Table 4.2 in the To Extend Your Knowledge section at the end of this lesson describes these three options.

4 Choose *Merge into current document*, and position the insertion point over the first tracked change.

Word compares differences between the open document, *Tablet_PC*, with *EW2_0402* and merges the differences into *Tablet_PC* as tracked changes by the author, Iris Ray. The text she added to her *EW2_0402* document appears as inserted text in your document, and text she deleted from *EW2_0402* is removed from its location (see Figure 4.29).

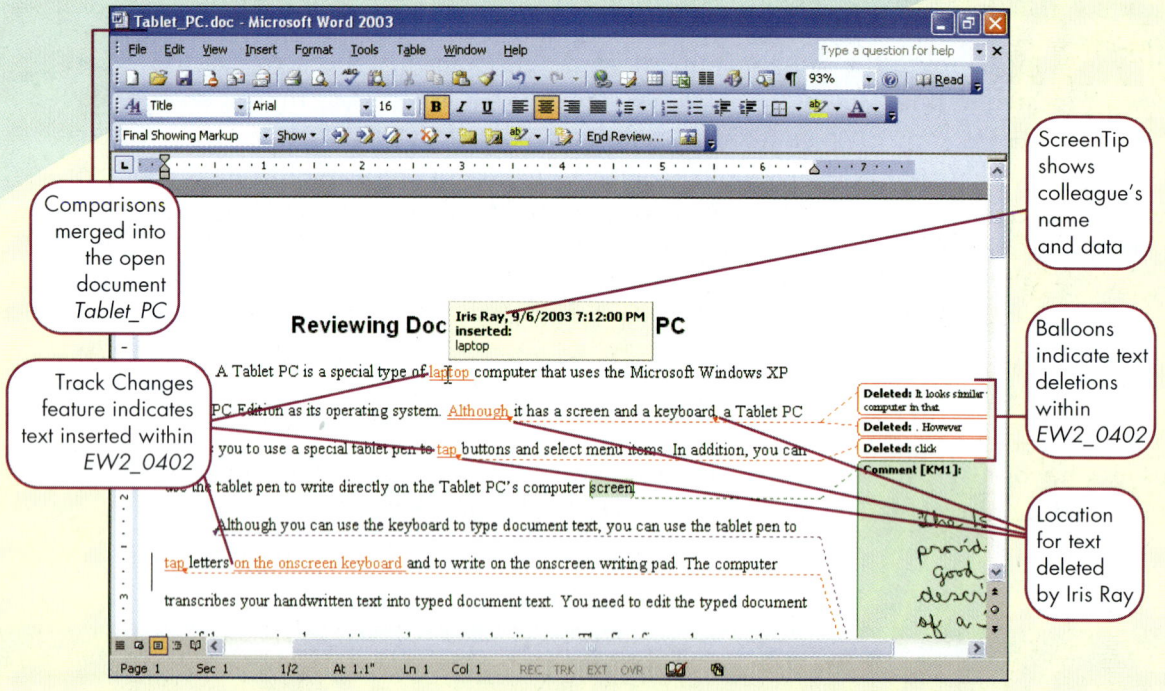

FIGURE 4.29

Although you would accept and reject changes to finalize the document, let's leave the tracked changes intact in this particular document.

5 Save, print (optional), and close the *Tablet_PC* document.

TO EXTEND YOUR KNOWLEDGE...

CHOOSING A MERGE OPTION

When you click the Merge drop-down arrow in the Compare and Merge Documents dialog box, you have a choice of three options. Table 4.2 lists and describes those options.

TABLE 4.2

MERGE OPTION	DESCRIPTION
Merge	Compares the open document with the one you select in the Compare and Merge Documents dialog box. Displays results in the document you select.
Merge into current document	Compares the open document with the one you select in the dialog box. Displays results in the open document.
Merge into new document	Compares the open document with the one you select in the dialog box. Displays results in a new document window.

SUMMARY

In this project, you used several collaboration features to work with a team to prepare and edit a document. You inserted, viewed, and edited comments to annotate the document with comments and questions. Next, you used the Track Changes feature to mark the edits you made—inserted text, deleted text, and formatting applied—so other team members know what edits you suggested. You also customized Track Changes options by changing the balloon options and applying a different ink color to ink annotations, and you reviewed changes by type and reviewer. After reviewing changes, you located successive changes by using the Next button on the Reviewing toolbar, and you accepted or rejected each change.

You sent the document to another team member for review and to your supervisor as an attachment. You saved two versions of the document to be able to review a previous version in the event you want to reinstate previous edits. Finally, you compared and merged the changes made in the *Tablet_PC* document into a file edited by another reviewer.

You can extend your learning by reviewing concepts and terms, and by practicing variations of skills presented in the lessons. Use the following table as a guide to the numbered questions and exercises in the end-of-project learning opportunities.

Project 4 Collaborating with Others

LESSON	MULTIPLE CHOICE	DISCUSSION	SKILL DRILL	CHALLENGE	DISCOVERY ZONE
Inserting, Viewing, and Editing Comments	1, 3, 5	3	1	1, 3, 5	1, 2
Tracking Changes	6	3	2	1, 3, 4	2
Customizing Track Changes Options	7		3	5	2
Reviewing Changes by Type and Reviewer	4, 10		3	2, 3	
Saving Versions and Accepting and Rejecting Changes	9	2	2, 3, 5	2, 3, 4, 5	
E-Mailing a Document as an Attachment for Review	8	1	4	1, 4	1
Comparing and Merging Documents	2		5	3, 4	

KEY TERMS

Accept Change
blind copy
changed line
comment
compare and merge documents

ink annotations
ink comment
markup balloons
Reject Change
Reviewing pane

revision marks
routing slip
Tablet PC
track changes
version

CHECKING CONCEPTS AND TERMS

MULTIPLE CHOICE

Circle the letter of the correct answer for each of the following.

1. Which of the following statements about comments is false? [L1]
   a. Comment balloons appear on the right side in Print Layout view by default.
   b. A ScreenTip showing the reviewer's name and date/time of comment creation appears when the mouse pointer is over a markup balloon.
   c. You can display the Reviewing Pane even if the Print Layout view is active.
   d. By default, comments do not print with the rest of the document.

2. What happens when you click the Merge button in the Compare and Merge Documents dialog box? [L7]
   a. The comparisons are displayed in a new document window.
   b. The comparison markings appear in the document you select from the Compare and Merge Documents dialog box.
   c. You are prompted for the second document to compare.
   d. The two documents to compare are displayed in tiled window panes.

3. What Options dialog box tab contains options for you to enter the name of the person using the computer so that that person's name appears in ScreenTips for tracked changes and markup balloons? [L1]
   a. View
   b. Track Changes
   c. Edit
   d. User Information

4. What option enables you to see how a document looks if you accept all tracked changes? [L4]
   a. Final Showing Markup
   b. Final
   c. Original
   d. Original Showing Markup

5. Which toolbar contains buttons for collaborating on documents? [L1]
   a. Standard
   b. Outlining
   c. Reviewing
   d. E-mail

6. By default, what does Word insert into the left margin to identify a tracked change? [L2]
   a. Underline
   b. Vertical line
   c. Asterisk
   d. Plus sign

7. What collaboration feature is available on a Tablet PC but not on a regular desktop or laptop computer? [L3]
   a. Ink Annotation
   b. Comment
   c. Track Changes
   d. Compare and Merge

8. To send a document to a recipient so that the document automatically activates the Tracked Changes feature, what option should you choose? [L6]
   a. Mail Recipient
   b. Mail Recipient (as Attachment)
   c. Mail Recipient (for Review)
   d. Any of the above

9. What should you do if you want to keep copies of different editions of a document within the same filename? [L5]
   a. Use the Save As command to provide a name for the edition.
   b. Activate the Track Changes feature.
   c. Save the document; you can always use Undo to display different editions.
   d. Save each edition as a version.

10. Which of the following is *not* a default Show option for Tracked Changes? [L4]
    a. Only the changes you make with Track Changes active are displayed.
    b. Comments are displayed.
    c. Any ink annotations inserted from a Tablet PC are displayed, even on a desktop computer.
    d. Inserted text, deleted text, and formatting changes are all displayed.

DISCUSSION

1. Compare and contrast sending a document to a recipient for review and sending a document as an attachment. [L6]
2. What advantages does the Versions feature have versus the Save As feature when you are revising a document? [L5]
3. When reviewing a document for a colleague, under what situation would you insert comments instead of tracking changes? [L1, L2]

SKILL DRILL

Skill Drill exercises reinforce project skills. Each skill reinforced is the same, or nearly the same, as a skill presented in the project. Detailed instructions are provided in a step-by-step format.

Work through the exercises in sequential order. Be sure to save your changes and close the document if you need more than one work session to complete the desired exercises. Continue working on *Sidewalk_Cafe* instead of starting over in the original *EW2_0403* file. After you complete all of the exercises, print a copy of the document (optional).

1. Inserting, Editing, and Deleting Comments

Your friend Janice Dumais just purchased the Sidewalk Cafe restaurant. She prepared an information sheet to distribute to several office buildings within the neighborhood. As you review the information sheet, you annotate the document with comments. After you review your comments, you edit one comment and delete another comment.

1. Open *EW2_0403* and save it as **Sidewalk_Cafe**.
2. Position the insertion point at the end of the subtitle.
3. Display the Reviewing toolbar, click Insert Comment, and type `Placing the italicized slogan below the restaurant name is a good idea.`
4. Position the insertion point after *Turkey Club,* click Insert Comment, and type `Adding some photos of lunch items will enhance the information sheet.`
5. In the fourth paragraph after the list, select *Sunday brunch,* click Insert Comment, and type `What's on this menu?`
6. Position the mouse pointer over the first comment markup balloon to see the comment with your name as the reviewer.
7. Click inside the second comment markup balloon and edit the comment by adding `full-color` between *some* and *photos*.
8. Click inside the third comment markup balloon and click Reject Change/Delete Comment on the Reviewing toolbar.

    You just deleted the third comment.

9. Save the *Sidewalk_Cafe* document.

2. Tracking Changes and Saving a Version

As you continue to review the information sheet, you decide to edit it. However, you want Janice to know what changes you make. So, you activate the Track Changes feature before editing the document. Because you will continue making changes to the document, you decide to save a version of it after you track your changes.

1. In the *Sidewalk_Cafe* document, click Track Changes on the Reviewing toolbar.
2. Select *diverse and eclectic* on the second line of the first main paragraph, and press `Del`.
3. Type **wide** and then press `Spacebar` where you left off from deleting text.
4. In the next paragraph, click before the word *lunch,* type **daily**, and press `Spacebar`.
5. Delete *on a daily basis,* including the space before *on,* but do not delete the colon at the end of that line.
6. Delete *displayed* in the paragraph below the bulleted list.
7. Delete *daily* before specials in the paragraph about the chef.
8. Select *11:30* and type **11:00**.
9. Italicize *Janice Dumais* and *Sam Dumais.*
10. Choose File, Versions.
11. Click Save Now, and type **Version 1 includes tracked changes.** Then click OK.
12. Save the *Sidewalk_Cafe* document.

3. Customizing and Reviewing Tracked Changes

You think that the changed line in the left margin is not enough to identify formatting changes; therefore, you customize the Track Changes feature to display double underlining for formatting changes. In addition, you want to see the final version of the document if you accept all tracked changes. Furthermore, you want to see the tracked changes of only one reviewer. Finally, Janice asks you to go ahead and accept or reject the changes as you see fit.

1. In the *Sidewalk_Cafe* document, choose Tools, Options, and click the Track Changes tab.
2. Click the Formatting drop-down arrow, choose *Double underline,* and click OK.

    The text you italicized now appears with a double underline to help you see exactly what was formatted with the Track Changes feature on.

3. Click the *Display for Review* drop-down arrow on the Reviewing toolbar and choose *Final* so that you can review what the document would look like if all changes were accepted.
4. Click the *Display for Review* drop-down arrow and choose *Final Showing Markup.*
5. Click Show on the Reviewing toolbar, choose Reviewers, and deselect *All Reviewers.*
6. Click Show, choose Reviewers, and select Marc Silver.

    Now only Marc's tracked changes are displayed onscreen.

7. Click the Accept Change drop-down arrow and choose *Accept All Changes Shown.*

   Because you displayed only Marc's tracked changes, you can accept all of his changes without accepting all other reviewers' changes.

8. Click Show on the Reviewing toolbar, choose Reviewers, and select *All Reviewers.*

9. Position the insertion point at the beginning of the document. Click Next twice on the Reviewing toolbar to select the deleted text *diverse and eclectic,* and click Accept Change on the toolbar.

10. Click Next and then click Accept Change to accept inserting the word *wide.*

11. Click Next and then click Accept Change to accept inserting the word *daily.*

12. Click Next and then click Accept Change to accept deleting the words *on a daily basis.*

13. Click Next twice and then click Reject Change/Delete Comment to reject the change to delete the word *displayed.*

14. Continue accepting changes, except reject the changes to delete *11:30* and to insert *11:00.*

15. Double-click TRK on the status bar to turn off the Track Changes feature.

16. Double-click the Versions icon on the status bar, click Save Now, and then type `Version 2 reflects the document after accepting and rejecting changes.` Then click OK.

17. Save the *Sidewalk_Cafe* document.

4. E-Mailing a Document for Review and Tracking Changes

You are ready to leave the office for the day and want to continue editing the document at home. Instead of saving the document to a disk, you decide to e-mail the document to yourself for review. This way, you won't forget to activate the Track Changes feature when you edit the document later tonight. After editing the document at home, you e-mail it back to yourself as an attachment that you will open at work the next day.

1. In the *Sidewalk_Cafe* document, choose File, Send To.

2. Choose Mail Recipient (for Review).

3. Type your e-mail address in the *To* box, click Send on the toolbar, and close the *Sidewalk_Cafe* document.

   You just finished making some personal calls at home and now want to check your e-mail and finish editing the document.

4. Open your e-mail program, read the incoming e-mail from yourself that contains the *Sidewalk_Cafe* document, and open the attached file.

   The Track Changes feature is activated in the document that was attached to the e-mail.

5. Select *those in the know come to* in the last paragraph, and type `trendy-conscious people`.

6. Turn off the Track Changes feature, and save the *Sidewalk_Cafe* document.

7. Choose File, Send To, Mail Recipient (as Attachment).

8. Type your e-mail address in the *To* box, click <u>S</u>end, and close the *Sidewalk_Cafe* document.

   The next morning you are back at your office and ready to open your e-mail.

9. Open your e-mail account, open the e-mail from yourself, and open the attached file.

   Notice that the Track Changes feature is not active this time.

10. Save the *Sidewalk_Cafe* document.

5. Comparing and Merging Documents

Janice reviewed a copy of the document on the computer at the restaurant last night while you edited your copy at home. She sent you a copy of the document containing her changes. Because changes have been made to two different documents, you need to use the Compare and Merge Documents feature to display tracked changes in one document to review. Finally, you save the final changes as a third document version.

1. In the *Sidewalk_Cafe* document, choose <u>T</u>ools, Compare and Merge <u>D</u>ocuments.
2. Select the *EW2_0404* document.
3. Click the <u>M</u>erge drop-down arrow and choose *Merge into <u>c</u>urrent document*.
4. Read the content of the markup balloons to see what Janice deleted, and read the text she inserted.
5. Select the last six items in the bulleted list, and click Reject Change/Delete Comment.
6. Click the Accept Changes drop-down arrow, and choose *Accept All C<u>h</u>anges in Document*.
7. Right-click each comment markup balloon, and choose *Delete Co<u>m</u>ment*.
8. Double-click the Versions icon, click <u>S</u>ave Now, and then type `Version 3 is the final version of the document.` Then click OK.
9. Double-click the Versions icon, select the first version, and click <u>O</u>pen.

   The third and first versions display in separate document windows onscreen.

10. Close the first version and maximize the window for the third version.
11. Save, print (optional), and close the *Sidewalk_Cafe* document.

CHALLENGE

Challenge exercises expand on or are somewhat related to skills presented in the lessons. Each exercise provides a brief narrative introduction, followed by instructions in a numbered-step format that are not as detailed as those in the Skill Drill exercises. You can work through one or more exercises in any order.

Before starting each exercise, make sure the Track Changes settings in the Options dialog box are set to the default settings: <u>I</u>nsertions Underline and By author, <u>D</u>eletions Strikethrough and By author, <u>F</u>ormatting (none) and By author, C<u>h</u>anged lines Outside border, *Balloons Preferred <u>w</u>idth* 2.5", and <u>M</u>argin Right. Also make sure the User Information tab of the Options dialog box displays your name and initials.

1. Inserting Comments and Tracking Changes in a Water Conservation Document

As a member of the city council, you are developing plans for water conservation this summer. Another council member drafted an information sheet that will be included in city residents' May water statement. You need to review the document before tonight's meeting; therefore, you insert comments and track changes you make.

1. Open *EW2_0405* and save it as `Water_Conservation_Plan`.
2. At the beginning of the first paragraph, insert the comment `We need to enhance the overall appearance of this document to entice residents to read it.`
3. Select the first two items in the second bulleted list and insert the comment `What about Monday, Thursday, and Saturday? Should we divide the city into thirds to avoid straining the water system on only four days of the week?`
4. Activate the Track Changes feature and make the following changes:
    a. Apply 14-point Arial font, Center horizontal alignment, bold, and Blue font color to the title.
    b. Insert the word `severe` between the words *experienced* and *drought* in the first paragraph.
    c. Select *using larger loads* at the end of the first bulleted item and type `washing less frequently with larger loads instead of frequent, small loads`.
    d. Insert another bulleted item at the end of the first bulleted list with this text: `Install water-saving shower heads.`
    e. In the next paragraph, select *$50* and type `$75`.
    f. Select *Lawns should be watered only between* and type `Lawn-watering is restricted to` in the third item in the second bulleted list.
    g. Delete *rest of the* in the last paragraph.
5. Add the following sentence after the existing text in the first comment: `We can use a more inviting font, add some color, and insert some clip art.`
6. Turn off the Track Changes feature, and save the *Water_Conservation_Plan* document.
7. Send the document to your instructor as an e-mail attachment.
8. Save, print (optional), and close the *Water_Conservation_Plan* document.

2. Reviewing Reviewer Changes for an Agenda

Your company is planning a national retreat in a couple of weeks. Your manager prepared an agenda and solicited feedback from three individuals who used the Track Changes feature. You've been asked to review the changes and accept and reject changes. Because someone might want to see a previous iteration of the agenda, you decide to save two versions of the document—the current version with the tracked changes and a final version after accepting and rejecting changes.

1. Open *EW2_0406* and save it as `Retreat_Agenda`.
2. Save a version with the following comment: `First draft includes tracked changes from the Project Manager, The District Manager, and an Executive Assistant.`
3. Display the final document for review to see how the document would look if you accept all changes (but do not accept changes now), and then change the display back to *Final Showing Markup.*
4. Display only the changes made by the Project Manager, and then accept only those changes.
5. Save a version with the following comment: `Second draft incorporates the Project Manager's changes.`
6. Show all other reviewers' changes.
7. Display the document in Normal view.
8. Display the shortcut menu for the following and reject the changes:

    Buffet insertion

    7 a.m. Light Breakfast insertion

    : Handle your time more efficiently deletion

    , lunch, and ski time insertion
9. Accept the rest of the tracked changes.
10. Save a version with the following comment: `Final document after accepting and rejecting changes.`
11. Display the first version with the last version to see the differences.
12. Close the first version window, and maximize the Retreat_Agenda document window.
13. Save, print (optional), and close the final version of the *Retreat_Agenda* document.

3. Reviewing a Letter About a Proposed Development Project

As a community leader, you need to inform residents about a proposed development project. Another member of the committee composed a letter to send to the residents and asked you to review it. After reviewing it, you receive a document from another committee member who did not use Track Changes; therefore, you have to compare and merge the documents to see the changes.

1. Open *EW2_0407* and save it as `Project_Development_Letter`.
2. On the right side of the date, insert the comment `Set a larger top margin to accommodate the letterhead.`
3. Select the recipient's name and address and insert the comment `This is just a prototype letter. We will use the Mail Merge feature to insert names and addresses.`
4. Activate the Track Changes feature and do the following:

a. Select the comma in the greeting and type a colon.
b. Insert the word **proposed** between the words *the* and *development* in the first paragraph.
c. Insert the words **residents in** between the words *from* and *the* in the first paragraph.
d. Select the three bolded headings and apply Green font color.
e. Delete *, as well as tourists* within the second paragraph.
f. Insert the words **at this site** at the end of the last sentence in the second paragraph.

5. Save the *Project_Development_Letter* document.
6. Compare the *Project_Development_Letter* document with the *EW2_0408* document. Merge the changes into a new document window.
7. Save the new document as **Project_Development_Letter2**, and display the new document in Normal view.
8. Display only the changes made by Betty Wilson and make the following changes:
   a. Accept the inserted text *to be completed on the site.*
   b. Reject the deleted text *on the main floor.*
   c. Accept the remaining changes shown.
9. Display all reviewers' changes, display the document in Print Layout view, and do the following by using the Next, Accept, and Reject buttons on the Reviewing toolbar:
   a. Ignore your own comments.
   b. Accept changing the comma to a colon in the greeting.
   c. Accept the inserted text *proposed.*
   d. Reject the inserted text *residents in.*
   e. Accept the formatting change (applying Green font color) in all three occurrences.
   f. Accept the deleted text *, as well as tourists.*
   g. Reject the text *at this site.*
10. Save, print (optional), and close the *Project_Development_Letter2* document. Close all open documents.

4. Tracking Changes and Comparing Halloween Invitation Documents

You and one of your college friends want to host a Halloween party at your house. You each prepared an invitation flyer. You want to track the changes you make to a copy of the flyer and then compare your edited document to the one your friend edited.

1. Open *EW2_0409* and save it as **Halloween_Invitation_1**.
2. Activate the Track Changes feature.
3. Make at least two insertions, two deletions, and one formatting change.
4. Save and print (optional) the *Halloween_Invitation_1* document. Send it as an e-mail attachment to one of your classmates. Have your classmate send you his or her edited Halloween document as an e-mail attachment. When you download the

attachment, save it as **Halloween_Invitation_2** to distinguish it from your document.

5. Compare the *Halloween_Invitation_1* document with the *Halloween_Invitation_2* document. Merge the changes into the *Halloween_Invitation_2* document. (Refer to the To Extend Your Knowledge section at the end of Lesson 7 to choose the correct option.)

6. Save the merged document as **Halloween_Invitation_3**.

7. Accept and reject changes as you see fit. Adjust line and paragraph spacing as needed.

8. Save, print (optional), and close the *Halloween_Invitation_3* document; also close the *Halloween_Invitation_1* document.

5. Reviewing the Description for an Auction Item

You want to create an interesting description for a Fiesta Lilac coffee server that you want to sell through an online auction service. You sent a draft of the description to a friend to edit and just received her edits. She inserted ink comments and ink annotations in the document. You want to change ink annotation colors and save that version of the document. You then remove the annotations and comments.

1. Open *EW2_0410* and save it as **Fiesta_Lilac_Coffee_Server**.

2. Save a version with the comment **Includes ink annotations and ink comments**.

3. Navigate through the tracked changes and do the following:
   a. Accept the formatting for the title.
   b. Accept the inserted text , *and the value keeps increasing.*
   c. Reject the deleted text , *which is unusual for this color.*

4. Click and drag the ink annotation of the proofreaders' mark for inserting text—the caret and the comma—so that it is positioned between *scratches or.*

5. Delete the ink annotation of the proofreaders' marks for deleting text and closing up space.

6. Change the ink annotation color of the insert symbol and *Fiesta Lilac* to Lavender.

7. Change the ink annotation color of the insert symbol and the comma to Violet.

8. Delete the space within *Pay Pal.*

9. Select the first comment markup balloon, and insert a comment to reply to the reviewer's comment. Type **Fiesta buyers know what pinpoints are.**

10. Select the second comment markup balloon, and insert a comment to reply to the reviewer's comment. Type **I think you are right.**

11. Save a version with the comment **Most of the edits are incorporated into this version.**

12. Save, print (optional), and close the *Fiesta_Lilac_Coffee_Server* document.

DISCOVERY ZONE

Discovery Zone exercises require advanced knowledge of topics presented in the lessons or self-directed learning of new skills. You can work through one or more exercises in any order.

Before starting each exercise, make sure the User Information tab of the Options dialog box displays your name and initials.

1. Inserting Audio Comments into a Document

You want to insert a couple of audio comments into a document. Open *EW2_0411* and save it as `Apartment_Newsletter_October`. If you have audio capabilities, record the comments listed below. If not, insert traditional comments.

- after *November 1:* "Should we recommend disconnecting hoses by the middle of October?"
- after *November 20:* "Let's start winter laundry hours on November 1."

Save the *Apartment_Newsletter_October* document and send it to your instructor as an e-mail attachment so that he or she can listen to your audio comments.

2. Inserting Ink Comments and Ink Annotations on a Tablet PC

If you have access to a Tablet PC, you can complete this exercise. If not, you can still use Help to learn about Tablet PCs, ink annotations, and ink comments. In addition, you might want to visit a computer store to see models of Tablet PCs and ask a sales representative for a demonstration.

Open *EW2_0407* on a Tablet PC and save it as `Project_Development_Letter3`. Use Help to learn about Tablet PCs, ink comments, and ink annotations within Word. Use the tablet pen to insert ink comments and ink annotations shown in Figure 4.30. Notice that two different ink annotation colors are used.

Discovery Zone   **161**   LEVEL **2**

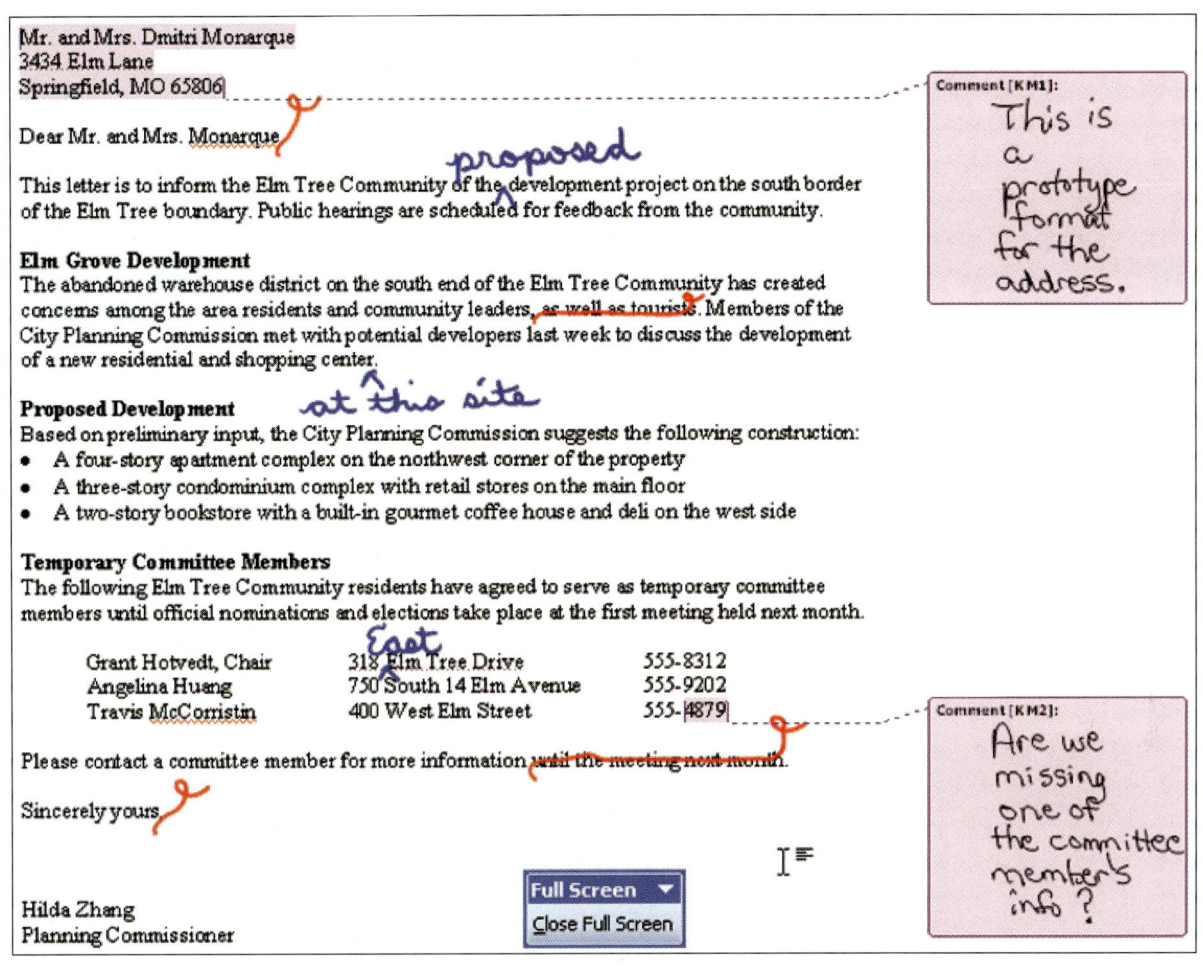

> Mr. and Mrs. Dmitri Monarque
> 3434 Elm Lane
> Springfield, MO 65806
>
> Dear Mr. and Mrs. Monarque
>
> This letter is to inform the Elm Tree Community of the ^proposed development project on the south border of the Elm Tree boundary. Public hearings are scheduled for feedback from the community.
>
> **Elm Grove Development**
> The abandoned warehouse district on the south end of the Elm Tree Community has created concerns among the area residents and community leaders, ~~as well as tourists~~. Members of the City Planning Commission met with potential developers last week to discuss the development of a new residential and shopping center.
>
> **Proposed Development** ^at this site
> Based on preliminary input, the City Planning Commission suggests the following construction:
> - A four-story apartment complex on the northwest corner of the property
> - A three-story condominium complex with retail stores on the main floor
> - A two-story bookstore with a built-in gourmet coffee house and deli on the west side
>
> **Temporary Committee Members**
> The following Elm Tree Community residents have agreed to serve as temporary committee members until official nominations and elections take place at the first meeting held next month.
>
> | | | |
> |---|---|---|
> | Grant Hotvedt, Chair | 318 ^East Elm Tree Drive | 555-8312 |
> | Angelina Huang | 750 South 14 Elm Avenue | 555-9202 |
> | Travis McCorristin | 400 West Elm Street | 555-4879 |
>
> Please contact a committee member for more information ~~until the meeting next month~~.
>
> Sincerely yours,
>
> Hilda Zhang
> Planning Commissioner

Comment [KM1]: This is a prototype format for the address.

Comment [KM2]: Are we missing one of the committee member's info?

FIGURE 4.30

If you make a mistake as you draw the ink annotations, you can stop inking and use the Eraser tool to erase your mistakes. Use Help to learn about the Eraser. If you have a hard time drawing the deletion proofreaders' marks, you can use the Format Picture option to adjust its height and width. Furthermore, you can tap Ctrl and tap an arrow on the onscreen keypad to move an ink annotation object left, right, up, or down a little.

Save, print (optional), and close the *Project_Development_Letter3* document.

PROJECT 5
LEVEL 2

PERFORMING MAIL MERGE

OBJECTIVES

In this project, you learn how to

- Start the mail merge process
- Create a recipient list
- Sort records in a data source
- Create a main document
- Merge the main document and the data source
- Create mailing labels

Project 5   Performing Mail Merge

WHY WOULD I DO THIS?

At some point in your personal or professional life, you will most likely need to send the same message to a number of people. For example, you might need to send a letter to all of your customers to inform them of a special discount, or you might want to send a holiday greeting to family and friends. You can use Microsoft Word's Mail Merge feature to generate these types of documents easily and efficiently.

Two types of files are needed to perform a mail merge: a main document and a data source. A *main document* (also known as a *form file*) contains the information that stays the same for all recipients. A *data source* contains a record of information for each recipient, such as names and addresses. The process of bringing the main document and data source together is called a *mail merge*.

VISUAL SUMMARY

In this project, you assume the role of an executive assistant for a training conference. You need to send registered participants a letter that acknowledges their registration and provides a few basic details. Because each registered participant needs the same information, you need to perform a mail merge to produce a letter for each participant. The first step is to create a data source that contains the names and addresses of the conference participants (see Figure 5.1).

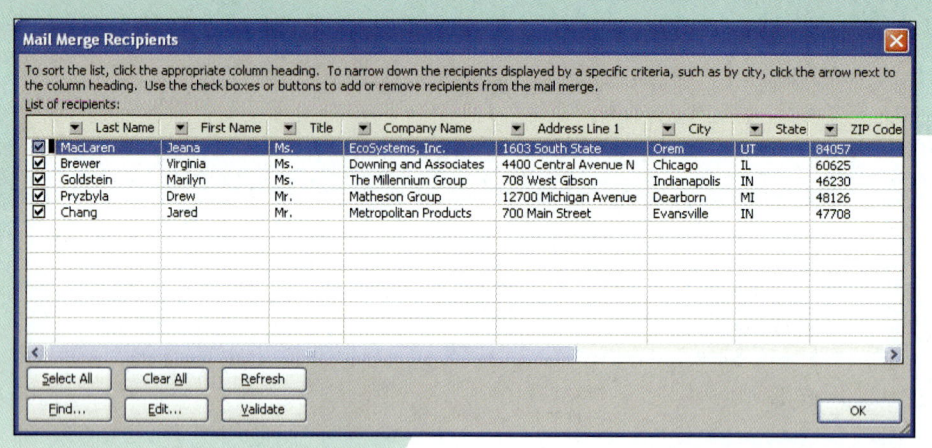

FIGURE 5.1

You must also create a main document that contains the standard message as well as codes indicating where the personalized data from the data source will appear. Figure 5.2 shows the main document.

Visual Summary **165** LEVEL 2

August 15, 2005

Merge fields where data from data source will appear → «AddressBlock»

«GreetingLine»

Your registration for the Technology Training Conference is confirmed. The fifth annual training conference is being held from October 13–17 at the Mountaintop Resort Conference Center in Park City, Utah.

Standard paragraph → The enclosed map includes driving instructions from the Salt Lake City International Airport. Shuttle information is provided on the back of the map.

Here is the agenda for each daily session:

Continental Breakfast	8:30 a.m.
Session Starts	9:00 a.m.
Morning Refreshment Break	10:30 a.m.
Lunch	12:00 p.m.
Session Resumes	1:00 p.m.
Afternoon Refreshment Break	2:30 p.m.
Session Ends	4:30 p.m.

Thank you for registering in advance. I look forward to seeing you at the conference!

Sincerely,

Mitch Lebaron
Conference Coordinator

Enclosure

FIGURE 5.2

After creating the data source and the main document, you merge the two together to produce individual letters for the conference participants. Figure 5.3 shows one of the final letters after performing the mail merge. Notice that the merge fields are replaced with the data from the data source.

August 15, 2005

Data from data source creates address ⟶ Ms. Virginia Brewer
Downing and Associates
4400 Central Avenue N
Chicago, IL 60625

Data from data source creates greeting ⟶ Dear Ms. Brewer:

Your registration for the Technology Training Conference is confirmed. The fifth annual training conference is being held from October 13–17 at the Mountaintop Resort Conference Center in Park City, Utah.

The enclosed map includes driving instructions from the Salt Lake City International Airport. Shuttle information is provided on the back of the map.

Here is the agenda for each daily session:

        Continental Breakfast............................8:30 a.m.
        Session Starts ....9:00 a.m.
        Morning Refreshment Break...............10:30 a.m.
        Lunch ....12:00 p.m.
        Session Resumes....................................1:00 p.m.
        Afternoon Refreshment Break ....2:30 p.m.
        Session Ends ....4:30 p.m.

Thank you for registering in advance. I look forward to seeing you at the conference!

Sincerely,

Mitch Lebaron
Conference Coordinator

Enclosure

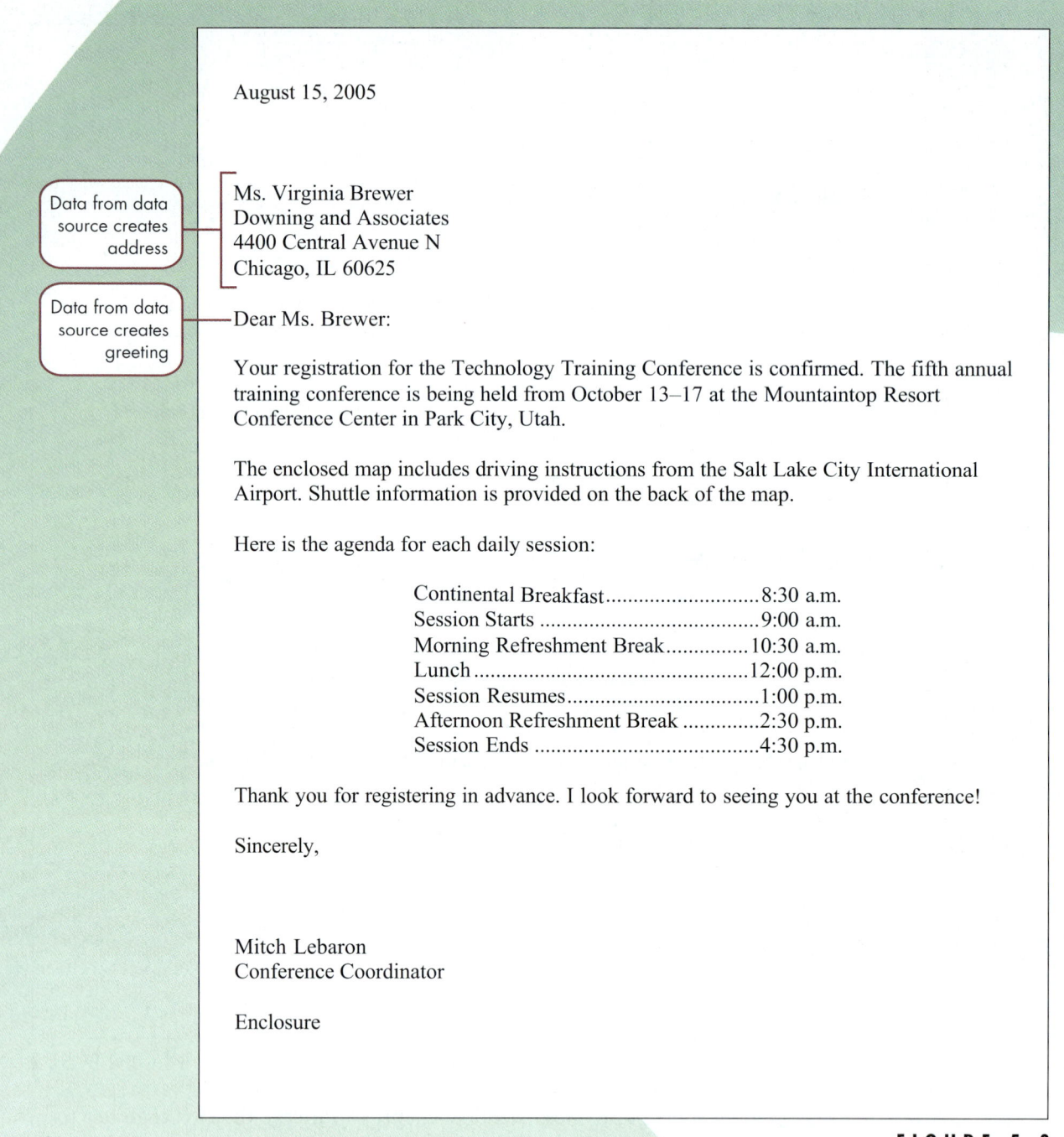

FIGURE 5.3

LESSON 1: Starting the Mail Merge Process

You can use either the Mail Merge task pane or the Mail Merge toolbar to perform a mail merge. The ***Mail Merge task pane*** provides six numbered steps that guide you through the process of completing a mail merge. You complete the following six steps as you work through the lessons in this project:

1. Specify the document type that you want to create. ***Document type*** refers to the end result you want to generate in a mail merge, such as a letter or an envelope.

Lesson 1   Starting the Mail Merge Process   **167**

2. Choose the ***starting document***—the source that provides the standard content to be included in all mail merge results. You can specify the current document, a template, or an existing main document.
3. Select or create a data source that lists the recipients of your document.
4. Create the content of the main document.
5. Preview the mail merge and make any necessary changes.
6. Perform the merge and print the documents.

In this lesson, you complete the first two steps of the Mail Merge process: You specify that you want to create a letter, and you identify an existing document that contains the paragraphs you want in the form letters.

To Specify the Document Type and Starting Document

1 Open *EW2_0501* and save it as `Conference_Form_Letter`.
This document contains the standard information that you want to send to all people who registered for the conference.

2 Choose **T**ools, **L**etters and Mailings, **M**ail Merge.
The Mail Merge task pane opens. *Step 1 of 6* displays near the bottom of the pane (see Figure 5.4). You use this pane to choose the type of document you want to create. The default document type is *Letters*.

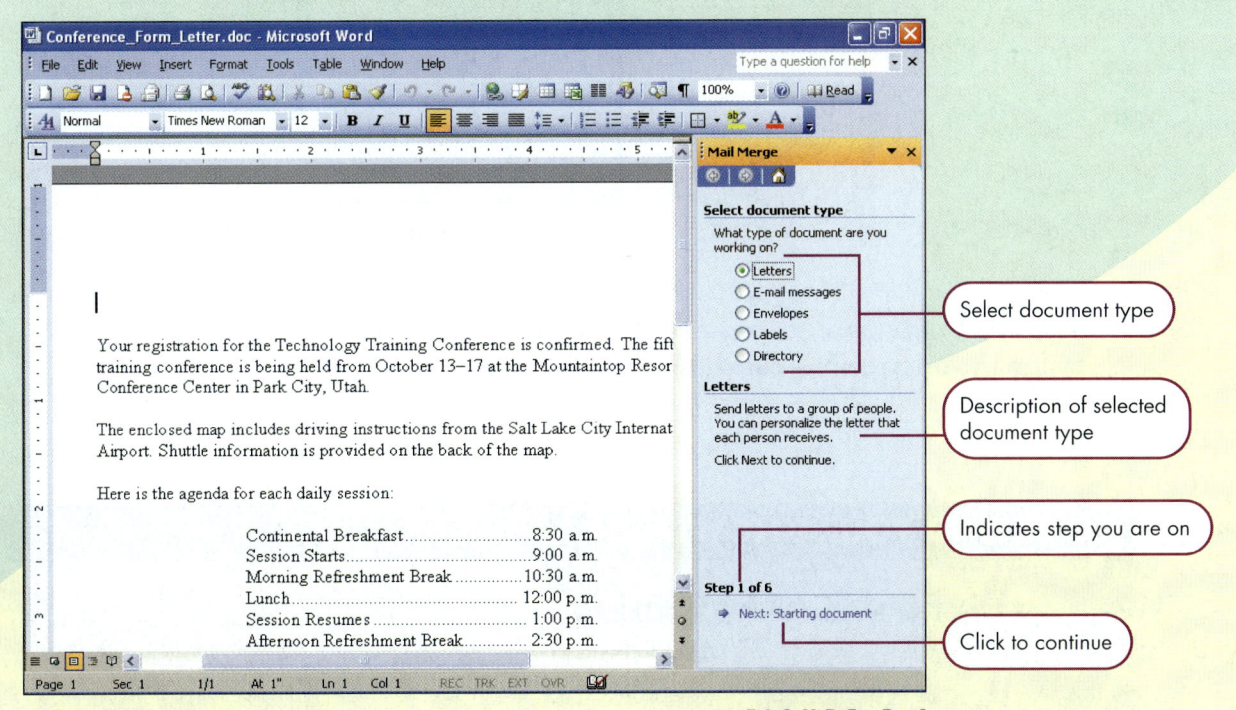

FIGURE 5.4

If you have problems . . .

If the zoom percentage decreases when you display the Mail Merge task pane, click the Zoom drop-down arrow and change it back to 100%.

The *Letters* option lets you send personalized letters to each receiver of a standardized letter. Although you do not complete the letter at this time, you must select the document type first.

3 Click *Next: Starting document* at the bottom of the Mail Merge task pane.

Figure 5.5 shows the second step: selecting the starting document. The figures depicting the task pane are shorter than what you see on your screen to save space in this book.

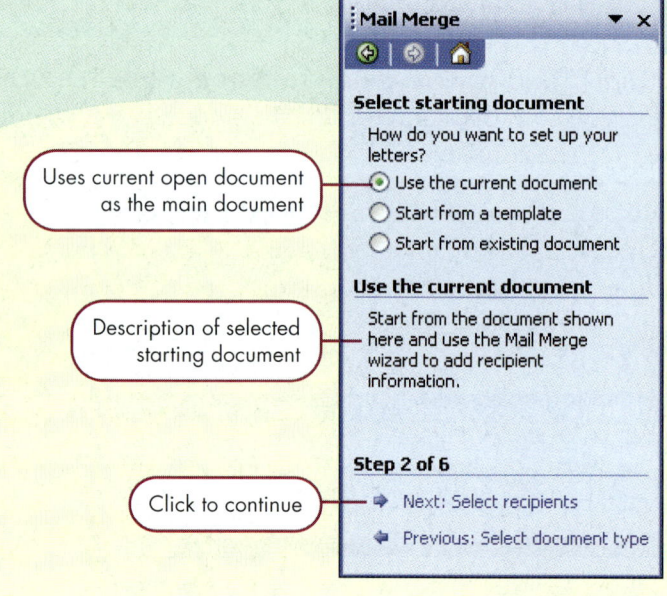

FIGURE 5.5

4 Save the *Conference_Form_Letter* document and keep it and the Mail Merge task pane onscreen to continue with the next lesson.

TO EXTEND YOUR KNOWLEDGE . . .

USING THE MAIL MERGE TOOLBAR

Choose View, Toolbars, Mail Merge to display the Mail Merge toolbar if you want to perform a mail merge on your own without using the Mail Merge task pane. Table 5.1 lists and describes the toolbar buttons.

Lesson 1 Starting the Mail Merge Process   169   LEVEL 2

TABLE 5.1

BUTTON	BUTTON NAME	DESCRIPTION
	Main Document Setup	Opens the Main Document Type dialog box. Lets you choose the type of main document, such as letters or envelopes, to create.
	Open Data Source	Opens the Select Data Source dialog box. Lets you select the data source file that you want to open and use with the main document.
	Mail Merge Recipients	Opens the Mail Merge Recipients dialog box. Lets you sort or select records to include in a merge. Also lets you add, edit, and delete the data source records.
	Insert Address Block	Opens the Insert Address Block dialog box. Lets you choose the formats for the inside address.
	Insert Greeting Line	Opens the Greeting Line dialog box. Lets you choose the level of formality for the salutation.
	Insert Merge Fields	Opens the Insert Merge Field dialog box. Lets you select and insert fields in the main document.
Insert Word Field ▼	Insert Word Field	Displays a list of Word data fields.
	View Merged Data	Displays the data from the data source into the respective fields in the main document so that you can verify correct placement.
	Highlight Merge Fields	Highlights in gray the fields contained in the main document.
	Match Fields	Opens the Match Fields dialog box. Lets you specify fields from another data source, such as an Access database table, with required fields in Word.
	Propagate Labels	Copies the merge fields from the first label to the other labels.
	First Record	Displays the first merged record. Works with the View Merged Data button.

TABLE 5.1 (continued)

BUTTON	BUTTON NAME	DESCRIPTION
	Previous Record	Displays the previous merged record. Works with the View Merged Data button.
1	Go to Record	Lets you enter the number of a specific record to go to.
	Next Record	Displays the next merged record. Works with the View Merged Data button.
	Last Record	Displays the last merged record. Works with the View Merged Data button.
	Find Entry	Opens the Find Entry dialog box. Lets you find data in a particular field or in all fields.
	Check for Errors	Helps you check for errors and report those errors during the merge process.
	Merge to New Document	Merges the data source with the main document and displays the merged document in a new document window.
	Merge to Printer	Opens the Merge to Printer dialog box so that you can specify which records to merge and print. The merged document is immediately printed.
	Merge to E-mail	Opens the Merge to E-mail dialog box so that you can select e-mail options. The merged document is e-mailed to those recipients.
	Merge to Fax	Merges the data source and main document. The merged document is sent to fax machines.

LESSON 2: Creating a Recipient List

The third step of using the Mail Merge task pane is to select the recipients. You can use an existing data source file or database, select recipients from your Outlook contacts folder, or type a new list of recipients. Once you create a recipient list file, you can use it over and over for other main documents.

A recipient list, or a data source, contains individual components of data known as *fields.* Common fields in a data source include first name, last name, address, city, state, and ZIP

Lesson 2   Creating a Recipient List   **171**   LEVEL 2

code. You can also include fields for phone numbers and e-mail addresses. A group of fields for a particular person or thing is called a ***record.***

In this lesson, you type a new recipient list of people who registered to attend the technology conference.

To Create a Recipient List

1 Make sure that the *Conference_Form_Letter* document is open and the Mail Merge task pane displays *Step 2 of 6.*

If you have problems . . .

If you closed the document at the end of Lesson 1, open *Conference_Form_Letter,* and then choose <u>T</u>ools, <u>L</u>etters and Mailings, <u>M</u>ail Merge to display the Mail Merge task pane. Click the *Next: Starting document* option and then continue with step 2.

2 Click *Next: Select recipients* at the bottom of the task pane.
Figure 5.6 shows the options for selecting recipients. Choose *Use an existing list* if you want to use a previously created data source; choose *Select from Outlook contacts* if your Outlook e-mail program contains data you want to use; or choose *Type a new list* if you do not have a data source and need to create one.

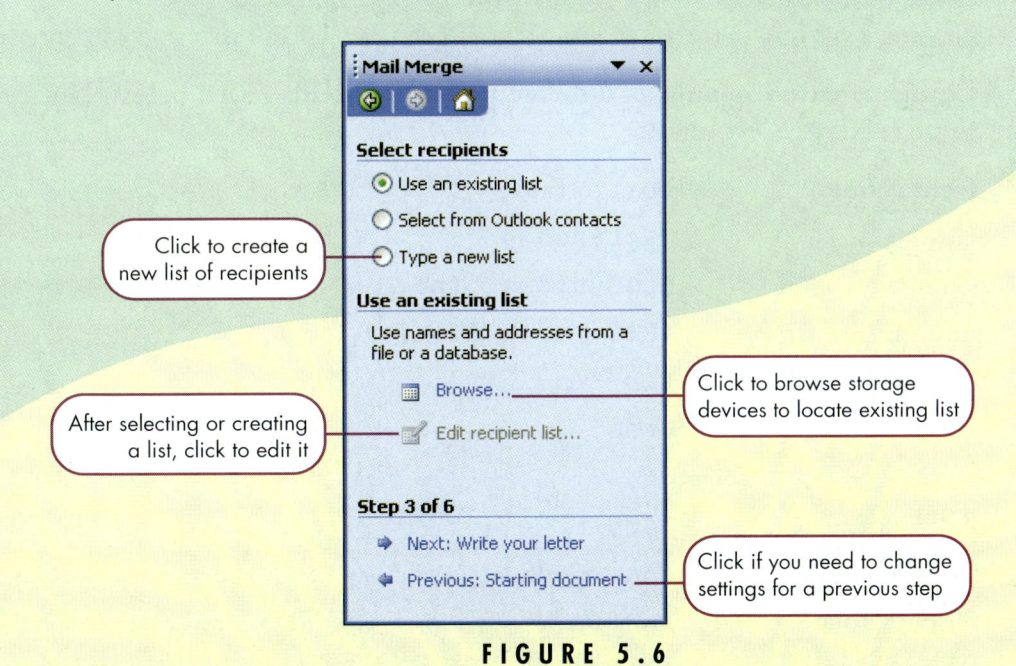

FIGURE 5.6

If you want to use an existing list, you must click *Browse* to locate the data source.

3 Click the *Type a new list* option in the *Select recipients* section on the task pane.
You see the description for typing a new list, along with an option for creating a new list.

4 Click the *Create* option in the *Type a new list* section on the task pane.

The New Address List dialog box opens so that you can enter data into existing fields (see Figure 5.7).

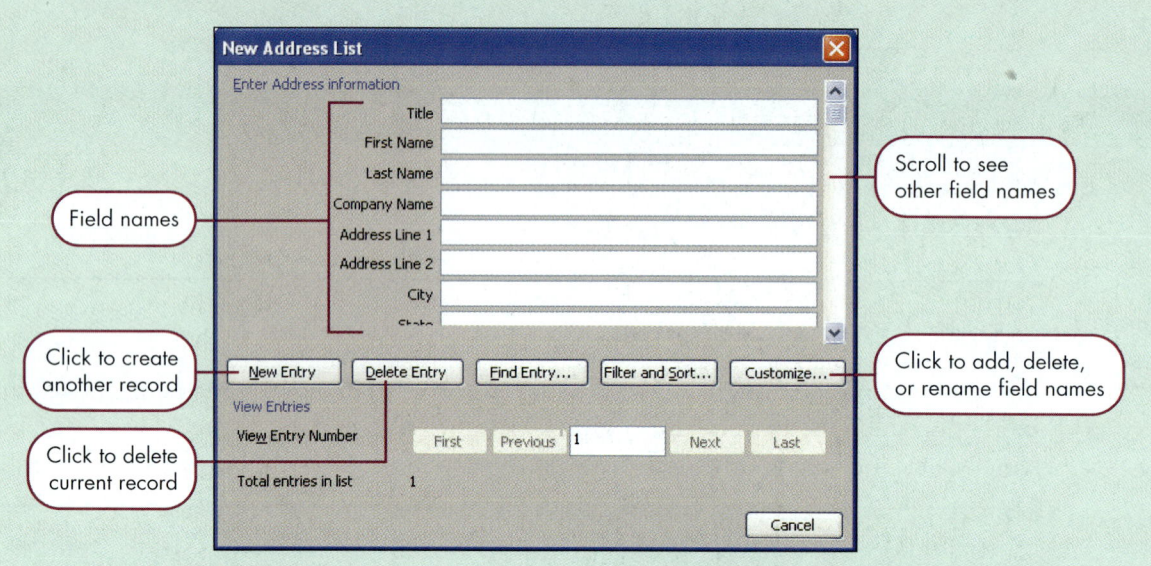

FIGURE 5.7

5 Type `Ms.` in the *Title* box.

6 Press Tab and then type `Jeana` in the *First Name* box.

Pressing Tab moves the insertion point to the next field so that you can enter data.

7 Continue entering data as indicated, into the fields listed below. Notice that some fields are left blank.

Field Names	Data to Enter
Last Name	MacLaren
Company Name	EcoSystems, Inc.
Address Line 1	1603 South State
Address Line 2	*[leave blank]*
City	Orem
State	UT
ZIP Code	84057
Country	*[leave blank]*
Home Phone	*[leave blank]*
Work Phone	*[leave blank]*
E-mail Address	*[leave blank]*

If you have problems...

If you need to correct mistakes, click in the field's text box or press ⇧Shift+Tab⇆ to move up to the field that contains the error.

8 Click <u>N</u>ew Entry at the bottom of the New Address List dialog box.
After typing the data for one record, you can click <u>N</u>ew Entry to enter data for another record.

9 Using the same process, enter the records listed below into the New Address List dialog box, making sure you enter the correct data into each field. Do *not* type the comma after the city and do not insert spaces after the last character in each field.

```
Ms. Virginia Brewer
Downing and Associates
4400 Central Avenue N
Chicago, IL 60625

Ms. Marilyn Goldstein
The Millennium Group
708 West Gibson
Indianapolis, IN 46230

Mr. Drew Pryzbyla
Matheson Group
12700 Michigan Avenue
Dearborn, MI 48126

Mr. Jared Chang
Metropolitan Products
700 Main Street
Evansville, IN 47708
```

10 Click Close at the bottom of the New Address List dialog box.
The Save Address List dialog box opens.

11 Specify a storage device and folder in which to save the file, type `Conference_Participants` in the *File <u>n</u>ame* box, and click <u>S</u>ave.
The Mail Merge Recipients dialog box opens. You use this dialog box to sort, select, or edit the data (see Figure 5.8).

Project 5 Performing Mail Merge

Instructions for sorting or selecting records

Second row is second record

Field names

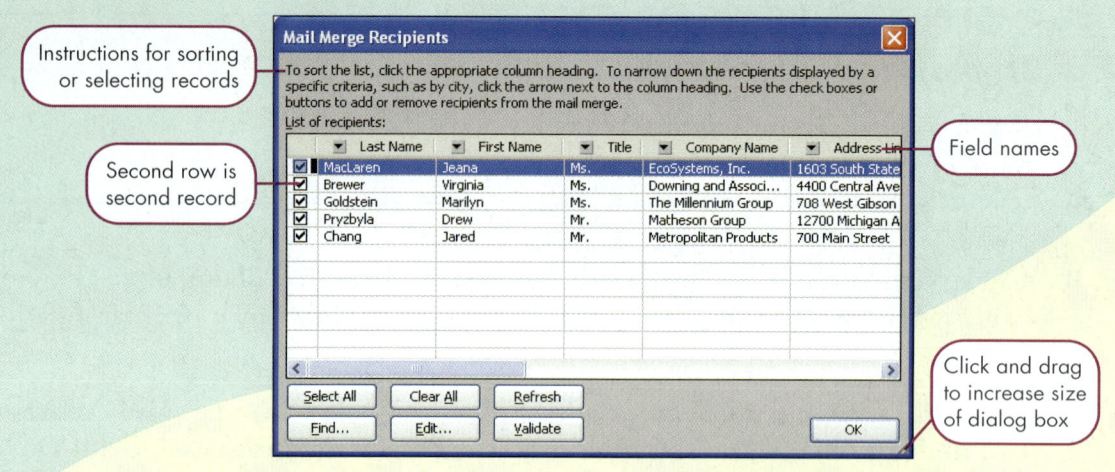

Click and drag to increase size of dialog box

FIGURE 5.8

12 Click OK to close the Mail Merge Recipients dialog box.

13 Save the *Conference_Form_Letter* document and keep it and the Mail Merge task pane onscreen to continue with the next lesson.

TO EXTEND YOUR KNOWLEDGE...

CUSTOMIZING THE FIELDS IN A RECIPIENT LIST

If you want to add, delete, move, or rearrange field names, click Customize in the New Address List dialog box (refer to Figure 5.7 in the previous set of steps). The Customize Address List dialog box opens so that you can change the field names (see Figure 5.9).

FIGURE 5.9

OPENING A DATA SOURCE

Word saves the data source in Microsoft Office Address List format with the .mdb extension. You cannot open that file like a regular *.doc* file; you must open it by clicking the *Edit recipient list* option on the Mail Merge task pane or by clicking Open Data Source on the Mail Merge toolbar.

If you open the data source from the task pane, the Mail Merge Recipients dialog box opens (see Figure 5.8 in the previous set of steps). When you click Open Data Source on the toolbar, the Select Data Source dialog box opens so that you can select and open a data source file. After opening a data source, click Mail Merge Recipients on the toolbar to open the Mail Merge Recipients dialog box.

ADDING NEW RECORDS

If you want to add new records, you can click Edit from the Mail Merge Recipients dialog box; then click New Entry within the next dialog box that opens. You can then add new entries, using the same process that you used earlier in this lesson.

USING A WORD TABLE AS A DATA SOURCE

You can use a regular Word table as a data source. To ensure the mail merge will work correctly, save the table by itself in a separate file with no blank lines above the table. The first row of the table must contain field names. To use your table as a recipient list, choose the *Use an existing list* option from the Mail Merge task pane, click the *Browse* option, select the file, and click Open.

Figure 5.10 shows a Word table, and Figure 5.11 shows the Mail Merge Recipients dialog box that opens after selecting the filename in Step 3 of the Mail Merge task pane. The dialog box reverses the order of the FirstName and LastName fields.

FirstName	LastName	Phone	Office
Rose	Komoroskpi	555-8357	BUS 351
Kendall	Schuster	555-8371	BUS 353
Austin	Ouyang	555-8325	SC 412
Mindi	Stauffer	555-8234	SC 444
Thomas	Hoffmann	555-7323	SC 445

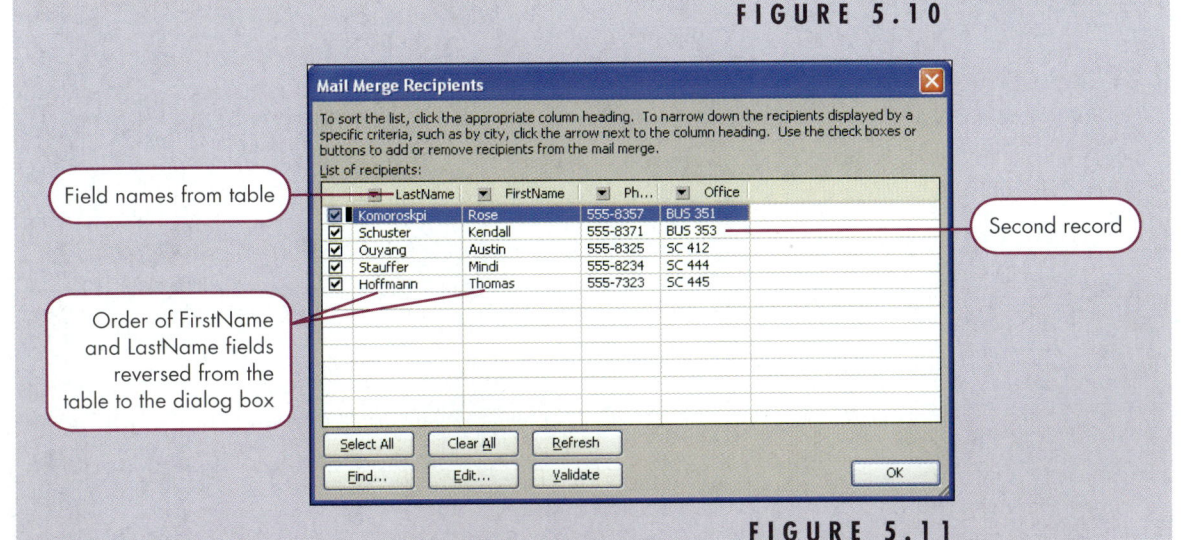

FIGURE 5.10

FIGURE 5.11

LESSON 3: Sorting Records in a Data Source

Before merging the data source with the main document, you might want to rearrange the records in the data source. For example, you might want to sort the data source in alphabetical order by last name, or in descending order by sales, if included. If you have a large number of form letters to send, you can receive a discount at the post office if you follow certain procedures. One procedure is to sort the letters by ZIP code. You can save a lot of work hours if you sort the data source *before* merging instead of after merging and printing.

In this lesson, you sort the data source in alphabetical order by last name.

To Sort the Data Source Records

1 Make sure that the *Conference_Form_Letter* document is open and that the Mail Merge task pane is displayed.

If you have problems . . .

If you closed the document at the end of Lesson 2, open Conference_Form_Letter. Word displays the message *Opening this document will run the following SQL command: SELECT * FROM 'Office Address List.' Data from your database will be placed in the document. Do you want to continue?* Click Yes to continue opening the main document with its associated data source. Then choose Tools, Letters and Mailings, Mail Merge to display the Mail Merge task pane, showing Step 3 of 6.

---

2 Click the *Edit recipient list* option in the *Use an existing list* section on the Mail Merge task pane.
The Mail Merge Recipients dialog box opens. You can sort records by a particular field, select recipients, or click Edit to edit a record, add more records, or perform multilevel sorts.

3 Click the *Last Name* field name.
The records are sorted in alphabetical order by last name (see Figure 5.12).

Lesson 3   Sorting Records in a Data Source

Click to sort by last name

Brewer listed first

FIGURE 5.12

4   Click OK to close the Mail Merge Recipients dialog box.

5   Save the *Conference_Form_Letter* document and keep it and the Mail Merge task pane onscreen to continue with the next lesson.

TO EXTEND YOUR KNOWLEDGE . . .

FILTERING OR PERFORMING MULTIPLE SORTS

The Filter and Sort dialog box enables you to perform more complex sorts. With the Mail Merge Recipients dialog box open, click Edit to see an individual record; then click Filter and Sort to specify filter or sort settings.

The Filter Records tab lets you *filter*, or specify criteria for including records that meet certain conditions during the merge process. The Sort Records tab enables you to specify up to three levels for sorting records. For example, you can first sort by state, further sort by city within state, and finally sort by last name within city (see Figure 5.13).

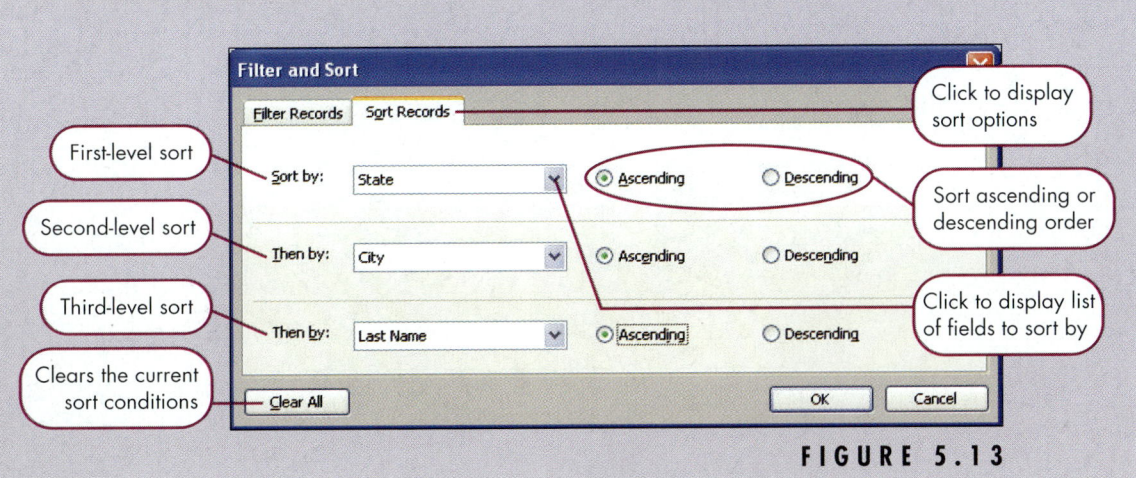

First-level sort

Second-level sort

Third-level sort

Clears the current sort conditions

Click to display sort options

Sort ascending or descending order

Click to display list of fields to sort by

FIGURE 5.13

LESSON 4: Creating a Main Document

You are now ready to insert the merge fields within your main document. *Merge fields* are placeholders of field names stored in the data source. These merge fields specify where data will be inserted from the data source when you complete the mail merge. In this case, you need fields that produce the inside address and salutation. Instead of inserting each field yourself, you can use the options in Word that simplify creating the inside address and salutation. You insert the ***AddressBlock field,*** a single merge field that produces the inside address, and the ***GreetingLine field,*** a single merge field that produces the salutation.

In this lesson, you type the date and then insert fields to complete the main document.

To Create the Main Document

1 With the *Conference_Form_Letter* document open and the Mail Merge task pane displayed, click the *Next: Write your letter* option at the bottom of the task pane.

If you have problems . . .

If you closed the document at the end of Lesson 3, open *Conference_Form_Letter,* click Yes when you see the message *Opening this document will run the following SQL command: SELECT * FROM 'Office Address List' ORDER BY 'Last Name' ASC. Data from your database will be placed in the document. Do you want to continue?* Click Yes, and then choose Tools, Letters and Mailings, Mail Merge to display the Mail Merge task pane. If needed, click the *Next: Write your letter* option.

If you click No when prompted with the above message, you must complete the set of steps in Lesson 3 to sort the data source again.

Figure 5.14 shows the fourth step in the Mail Merge task pane.

Lesson 4　Creating a Main Document　179

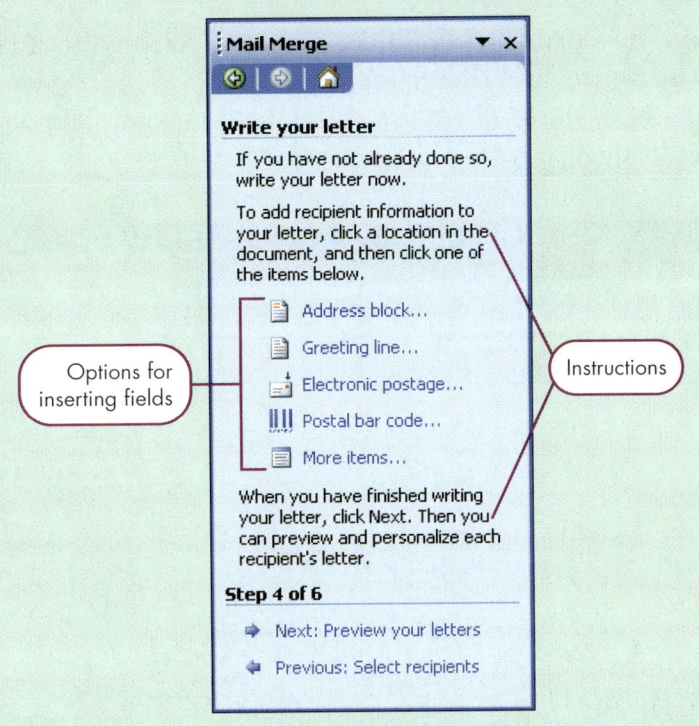

Mail Merge task pane callouts: Options for inserting fields; Instructions

FIGURE 5.14

2 Type today's date at the top of the current document, and press ⏎Enter four times.

3 Click the *Address block* option on the task pane.
The Insert Address Block dialog box opens so that you can specify the format for the inside address (see Figure 5.15).

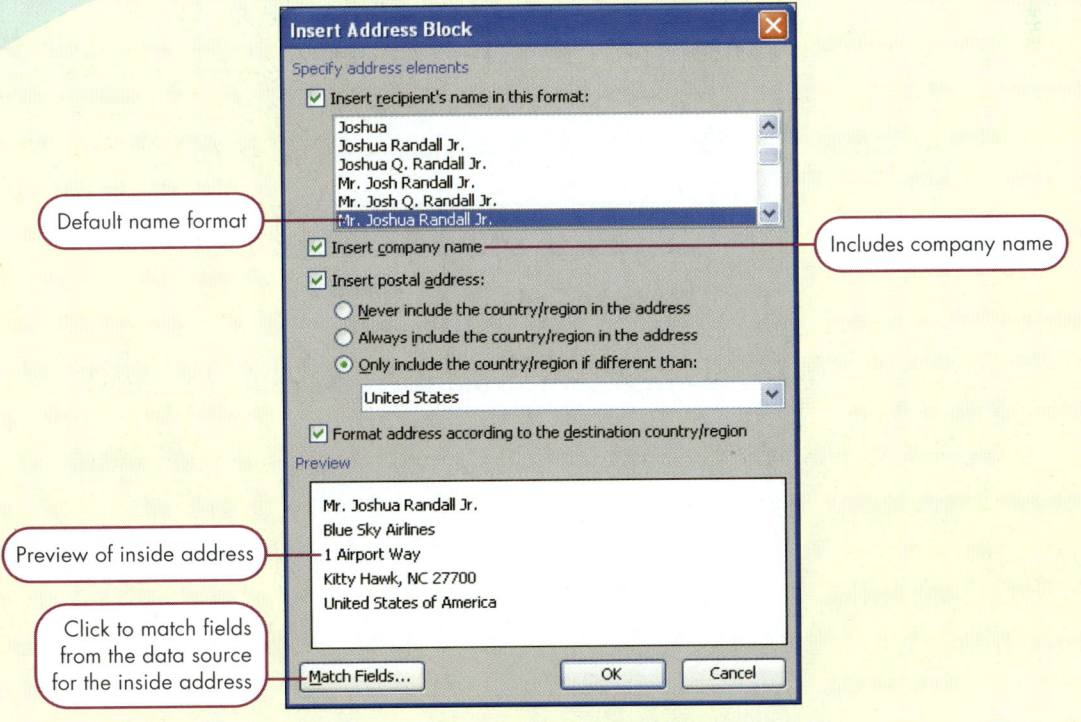

Insert Address Block dialog callouts: Default name format; Includes company name; Preview of inside address; Click to match fields from the data source for the inside address

FIGURE 5.15

Project 5   Performing Mail Merge

4 **Make sure your dialog box options are selected to match the selected options in the figure, and then click OK.**

Figure 5.16 shows the AddressBlock field in your main document; you do not need to individually insert fields to create the address block.

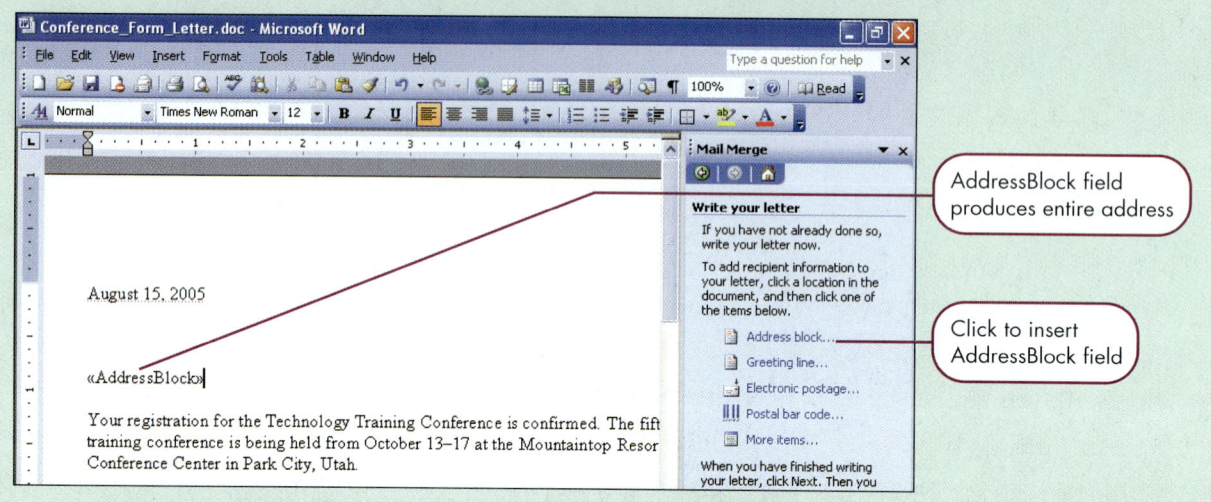

FIGURE 5.16

5 **Press ↵Enter twice.**

6 **Click the *Greeting line* option on the task pane.**

The Greeting Line dialog box opens so that you can choose the greeting line format and punctuation (see Figure 5.17).

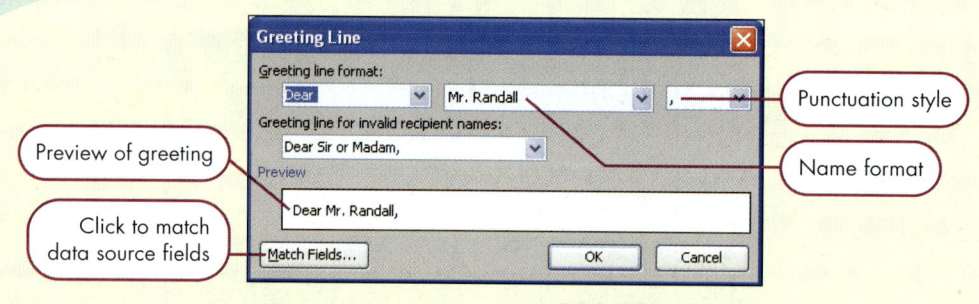

FIGURE 5.17

7 **Click the punctuation drop-down arrow, select the colon (:), and then click OK.**

Figure 5.18 shows the GreetingLine field inserted into the main document.

Lesson 4 Creating a Main Document   **181**   LEVEL 2

Blank line after AddressBlock field

GreetingLine field

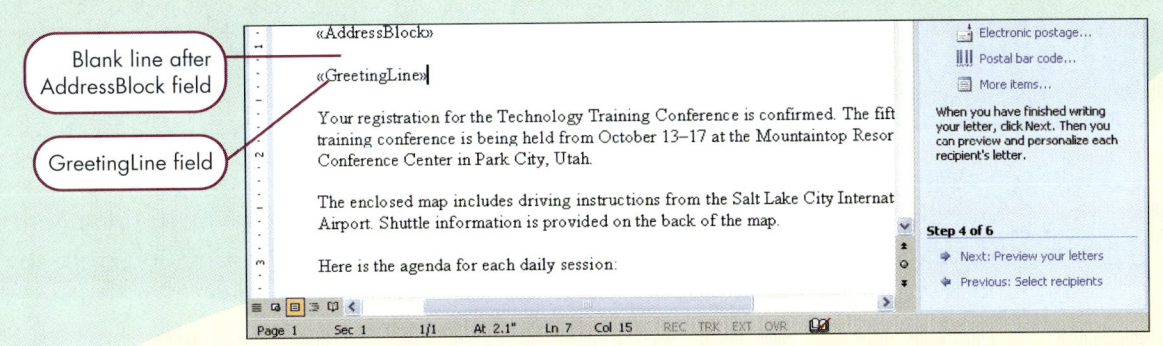

FIGURE 5.18

8 Save the *Conference_Form_Letter* document, and keep it and the Mail Merge task pane onscreen to continue with the next lesson.

TO EXTEND YOUR KNOWLEDGE . . .

MATCHING DATA SOURCE FIELDS

Because you can use other data sources, such as an Access database table, the data source field names may not match the officially recognized field names in Word. Therefore, you must match the data source fields to official Word fields. When you click the *Address block* or *Greeting line* options to display their respective dialog boxes, click the Match Fields button to open the Match Fields dialog box (see Figure 5.19).

Official Word field names

Click to select data source field names that match official Word field names

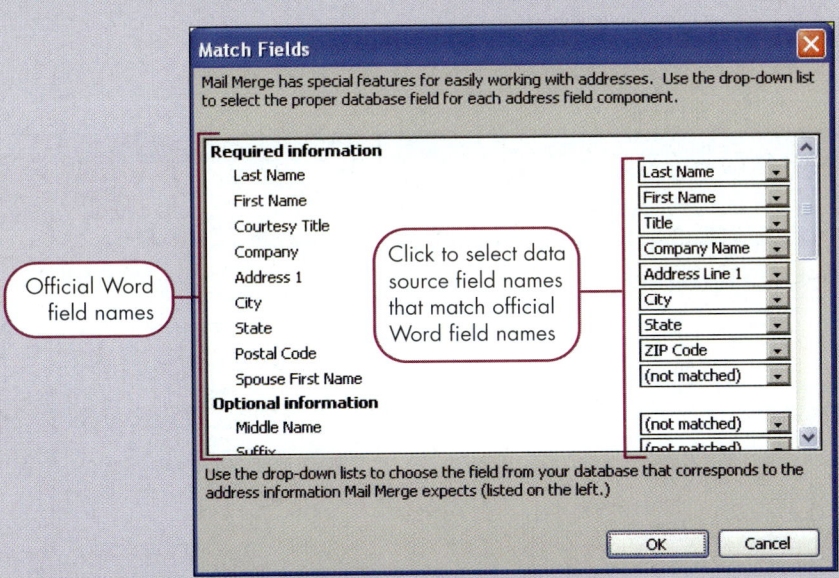

FIGURE 5.19

CHOOSING GREETING AND ADDRESS FORMAT

Word 2003 correctly formats mail merge addresses based on the recipient's geographical region. Furthermore, if the default language is not English (U.S.), Word uses the recipient's gender to choose the appropriate greeting format. Use Help to learn more about how Word customizes options based on the default language selected.

LESSON 5: Merging the Main Document and the Data Source

After you create the data source and main document, you are ready to merge them. When you merge these documents, Word matches the merge field codes in the main document with those in the data source. When a match is found, Word pulls the information from the data source and inserts it into the main document, replacing the merge fields. Word creates a new copy of the main document for each record in the data source.

In this lesson, you merge your data source with the main document.

To Merge the Documents

1 In the *Conference_Form_Letter* document, click the *Next: Preview your letters* option on the Mail Merge task pane.

If you have problems . . .

If you closed the document at the end of Lesson 4, open *Conference_Form_Letter*, click Yes when you see the message *Opening this document will run the following SQL command*, and then choose Tools, Letters and Mailings, Mail Merge to display the Mail Merge task pane. Click the *Next: Preview your letters* option.

Figure 5.20 shows a preview of the first merged letter for *Ms. Virginia Brewer*.

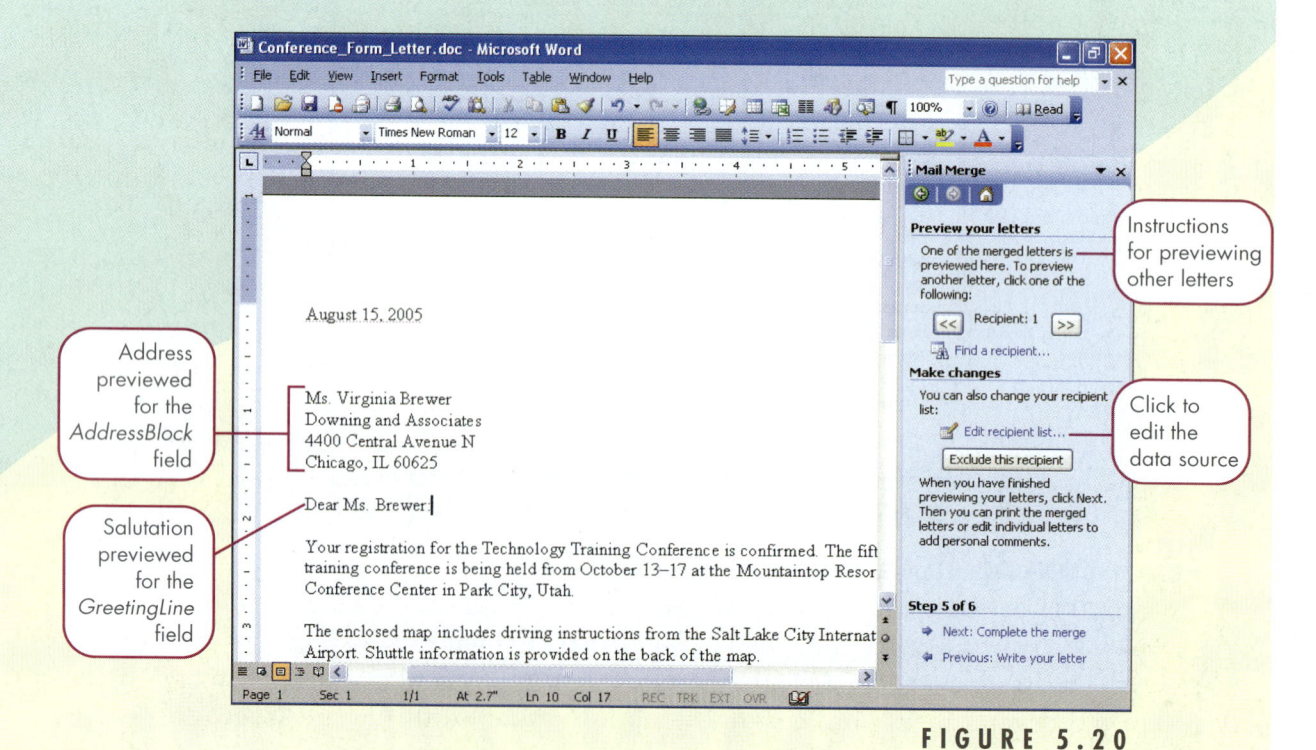

FIGURE 5.20

Lesson 5 Merging the Main Document and the Data Source   183   LEVEL 2

2 **Click the *Next: Complete the merge* option on the task pane.**
You can click the *Print* option to specify which merged records to print, or you can click the *Edit individual letters* option to merge to a new document.

3 **Click the *Edit individual letters* option.**
The Merge to New Document dialog box opens (see Figure 5.21) so that you can specify which records to merge.

FIGURE 5.21

4 **Click OK to merge all records.**
The records are merged into a new document window (see Figure 5.22). The new document window contains letters for all records, with each letter on a separate page separated by section page breaks.

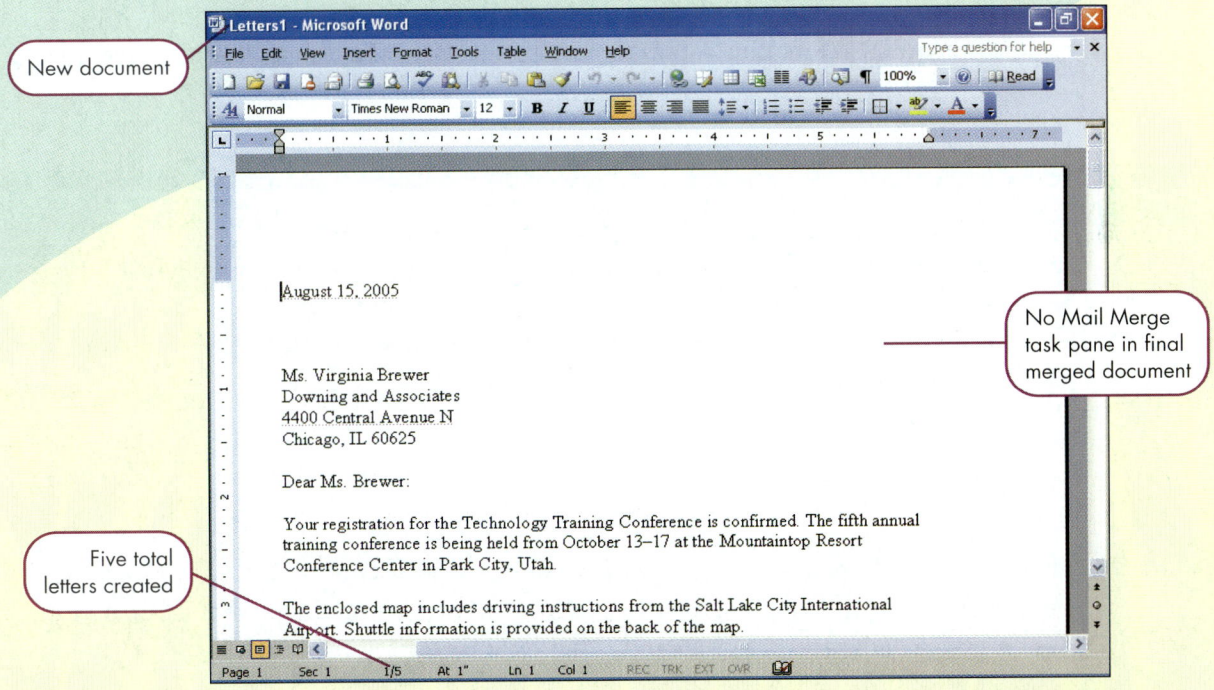

FIGURE 5.22

If you have problems . . .

If the addresses do not look correct, go back and edit your data source. You might have data in the wrong fields. For example, if you enter a city name in the Address 2 field, the city will be separated from the state and ZIP code.

5 Save the merged document as `Conference_Merged_Letters` and then close it.

You now need to close the main document and the Mail Merge task pane.

6 Save the *Conference_Form_Letter* main document and then close it.

LESSON 6: Creating Mailing Labels

After creating the merged form letters, you need to create mailing labels to attach to envelopes, or print the addresses directly on envelopes. Some printers do not have envelope trays, so you have to feed one envelope at a time through the printer. You might find printing addresses on labels more efficient because you can print about 30 labels on a typical sheet.

In this lesson, you create mailing labels to correspond with the letters you just merged.

To Create a Label Main Document

1 In a new document window, choose <u>T</u>ools, L<u>e</u>tters and Mailings, <u>M</u>ail Merge.

The first step is to choose the *Labels* document type on the Mail Merge task pane.

2 Click the *Labels* document type option on the Mail Merge task pane, and then click *Next: Starting document.*

Choose *Change document layout* if you need to choose label options, or *Start from existing document* if you previously created a label format.

3 Make sure *Change document layout* is selected and then click *Label options.*

The Label Options dialog box opens so that you can choose the printer information, label product name and number, and other details (see Figure 5.23).

Lesson 6 Creating Mailing Labels

FIGURE 5.23

[Label Options dialog box with callouts: "Click to choose paper tray", "Select label brand name", "Description of selected label", "Choose from list of label product numbers"]

4 Make sure *Avery standard* is the selected *Label products* option.

5 Scroll through the *Product number* list box, choose *5160 - Address,* and click OK.
The horizontal and vertical rulers indicate the heights and widths of the labels.

6 Click the *Next: Select recipients* option at the bottom of the task pane.
Instead of creating a new list, you will use the data source you created in Lesson 2.

7 Make sure that *Use an existing list* is selected and then click the *Browse* option.
The Select Data Source dialog box opens so that you can select the existing data source file.

8 Display the folder that contains files for this project, select *Conference_Participants.mdb,* and then click **Open**.
The Mail Merge Recipients dialog box opens, but it lists the records in the original order, not the way you sorted the records in Lesson 3. To make sure the labels print in the same sequence as the envelopes, you need to sort the records.

9 Click the Last Name field name to sort the records alphabetically by last name and then click OK.
You see Next Record fields in the document window. The fields indicate where each label will appear.

10 Click the *Next: Arrange your labels* option at the bottom of the task pane.

11 Click the *Address block* option and then click OK to accept the settings in the Insert Address Block dialog box.
The AddressBlock field appears for only the first label. The *Replicate labels* section tells you how to copy the first label's layout to the other labels (see Figure 5.24).

FIGURE 5.24

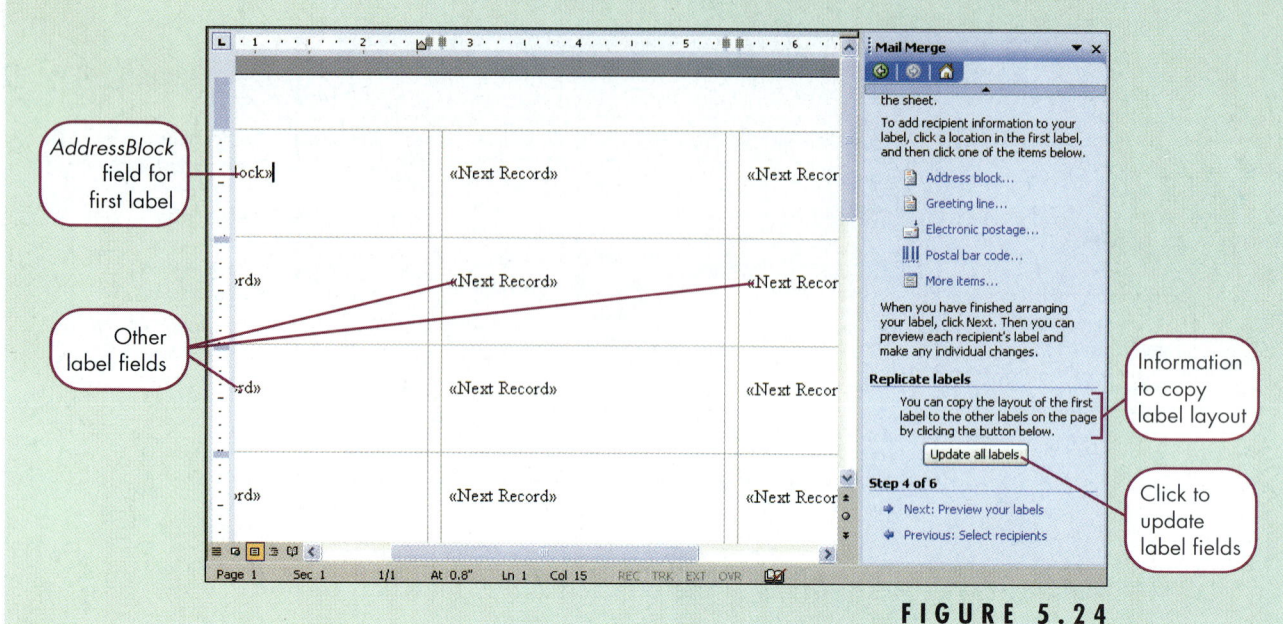

12 Click *Update all labels.*
Figure 5.25 shows the fields in the document window.

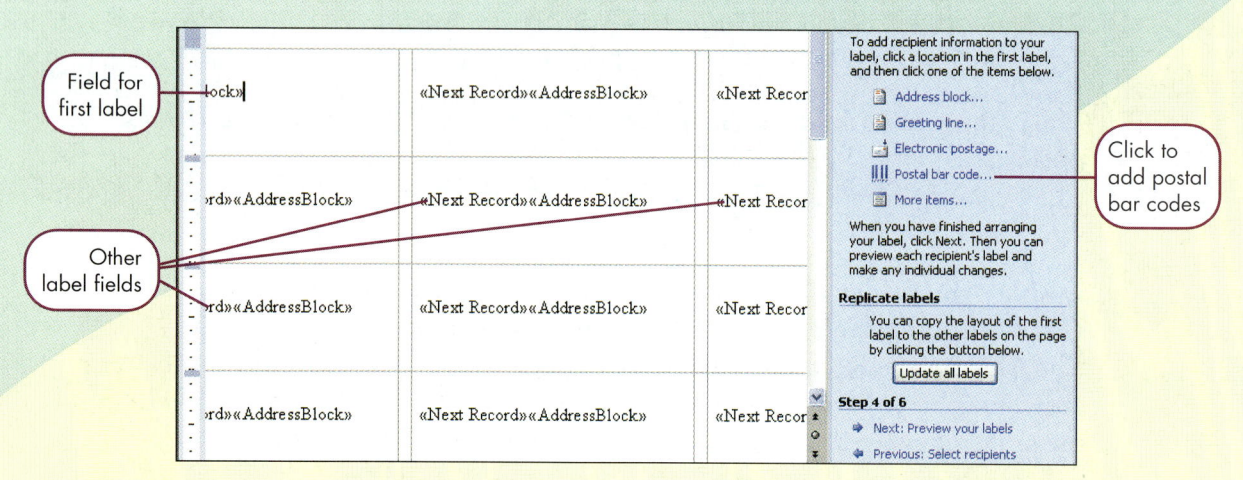

FIGURE 5.25

13 Click *Next: Preview your labels* on the task pane.
You see a preview of how the merged labels will appear.

14 Click the *Next: Complete the merge* option on the task pane.

15 Click the *Edit individual labels* option on the task pane and then click OK in the Merge to New Document dialog box to merge all labels in a new document window.
Figure 5.26 shows the merged sheet of labels. You may or may not see the nonprinting gridlines. The labels are arranged in alphabetical order by last name going across the first row and then continuing to the next row.

Summary 187 LEVEL 2

First label alphabetized by last name

Nonprinting gridlines show label boundaries

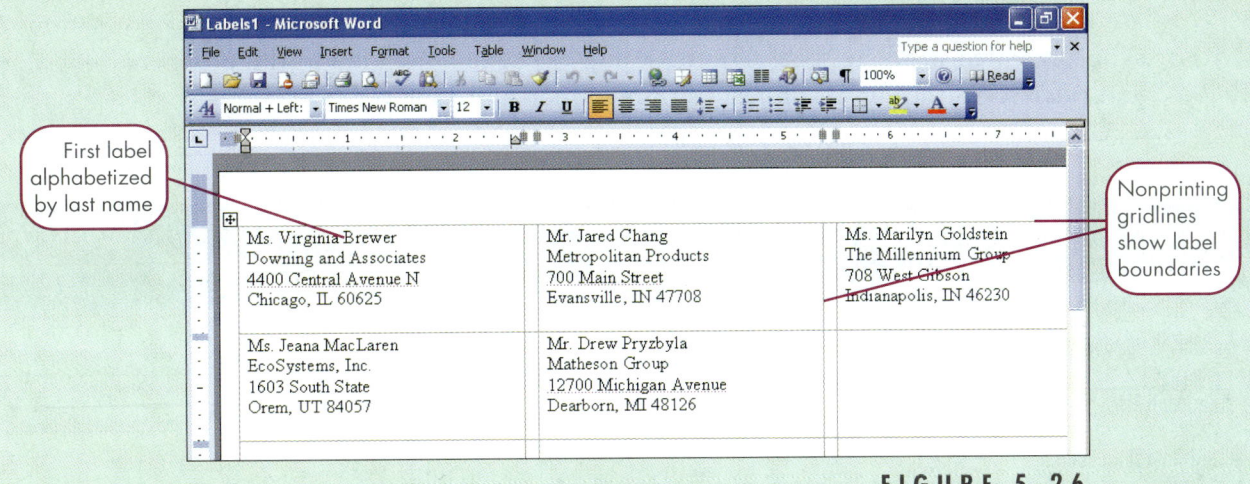

FIGURE 5.26

16 Save the merged document as `Conference_Merged_Labels`, and close the document.

The label main document window is maximized. You can save the label format as the main document to use in the future.

17 Save the label format as `Conference_Form_Labels`, and close it.

TO EXTEND YOUR KNOWLEDGE . . .

PROPAGATING LABELS
If you create labels by using the Mail Merge toolbar instead of the task pane, you need to click Propagate Labels after inserting the AddressBlock field in the first mailing label. When you *propagate labels,* you instruct Microsoft Word to copy or reproduce the AddressBlock field to the other labels.

INSERTING A BAR CODE
You can insert the postal bar code field to generate bar codes for the labels. Bar codes help the post office sort the mail faster. Click the *Postal bar code* option on the task pane and then select options in the Insert Postal Bar Code dialog box.

SUMMARY

In this project, you used the Mail Merge task pane to produce form letters and mailing labels. You used the Mail Merge task pane to specify a letter as the document type and to specify the current document as the starting document for creating a main document. Next, you created a data source and sorted it alphabetically by last name. You then finished the main document by inserting the AddressBlock and GreetingLine fields to generate the inside address and salutation. After finalizing the main document, you merged it with the data source to produce the merged document. Finally, you created labels through the mail merge process.

You can extend your learning by reviewing concepts and terms and by practicing variations of skills presented in the lessons. Use the following table as a guide to the numbered questions and exercises in the end-of-project learning opportunities.

LESSON	MULTIPLE CHOICE	DISCUSSION	SKILL DRILL	CHALLENGE	DISCOVERY ZONE
Starting the Mail Merge Process	1, 4	1	1	1, 2, 3, 4	1, 2
Creating a Recipient List	3, 5, 7	2	2	1, 2, 3, 4	1, 2
Sorting Records in a Data Source	2, 8		2	1, 2, 3, 4	1, 2
Creating a Main Document	6		3	1, 2, 3, 4	1, 2
Merging the Main Document and the Data Source	9	3	4	1, 2, 3, 4	1, 2
Creating Mailing Labels	10		5	4	

KEY TERMS

AddressBlock field
data source
document type
fields
filter

form file
GreetingLine field
mail merge
Mail Merge task pane
main document

merge fields
propagate labels
record
starting document

CHECKING CONCEPTS AND TERMS

MULTIPLE CHOICE

Circle the letter of the correct answer for each of the following.

1. Which of the following is *not* a valid document type option for creating a mail merge? [L1]

    a. Letters
    b. Envelopes
    c. Labels
    d. Reports

2. From which dialog box can you directly sort the contents of a data source by one field? [L3]

    a. New Address List
    b. Mail Merge Recipients
    c. Insert Address Block
    d. Select Data Source

3. When you save a data source file during the mail merge process, what filename extension does Word assign to the file? [L2]
   a. .doc
   b. .dat
   c. .mdb
   d. .xls

4. After specifying the document type in the Mail Merge task pane, what is the next step? [L1]
   a. Selecting a start document
   b. Selecting recipients
   c. Writing the letter
   d. Inserting merge fields

5. What term refers to a group of data for one person? [L2]
   a. Field
   b. Record
   c. Main document
   d. Data source

6. What merge field creates the inside address for form letters? [L4]
   a. InsideAddress
   b. GreetingLine
   c. AddressBlock
   d. MergeField

7. What term refers to an individual piece of data? [L2]
   a. Field
   b. Record
   c. Recipient list
   d. Propagate

8. You can _____ a data source to restrict the mail merge process to specific criteria, such as a particular city. [L3]
   a. sort
   b. propagate
   c. delete
   d. filter

9. When you click *Edit individual letters* on the Mail Merge task pane and then click OK, the merged document _____. [L5]
   a. overwrites the main document
   b. is automatically printed
   c. is saved to a new document file
   d. appears in a new document window

10. What option do you select to copy the address field from the first label to the rest of the labels before performing the merge? [L6]
    a. Copy and paste
    b. Update all labels
    c. Edit recipient list
    d. Sort and filter

DISCUSSION

1. Visit with some businesses and find out what types of documents they mass-produce as form documents. Make a list and provide any details for clarification. [L1]
2. How can you recognize a data source that you created in Word by looking at a file list? How can you open a data source? [L2]
3. What is the purpose of the preview step in the Mail Merge task pane? Why would you want to complete that step if it looks similar to the final merged document? [L5]

SKILL DRILL

Skill Drill exercises reinforce project skills. Each skill reinforced is the same, or nearly the same, as a skill presented in the project. Detailed instructions are provided in a step-by-step format.

Work through all exercises in this section in sequential order. Be sure to save your changes and close the document if you need more than one work session to complete the desired exercises. Continue working on *Holiday_Form_Letter* instead of starting over in the original *EW2_0502* file. After you complete all of the exercises, print a copy of the merged document (optional). Figure 5.27 shows a side-by-side comparison of the first and second merged letters, sorted in alphabetical order by city.

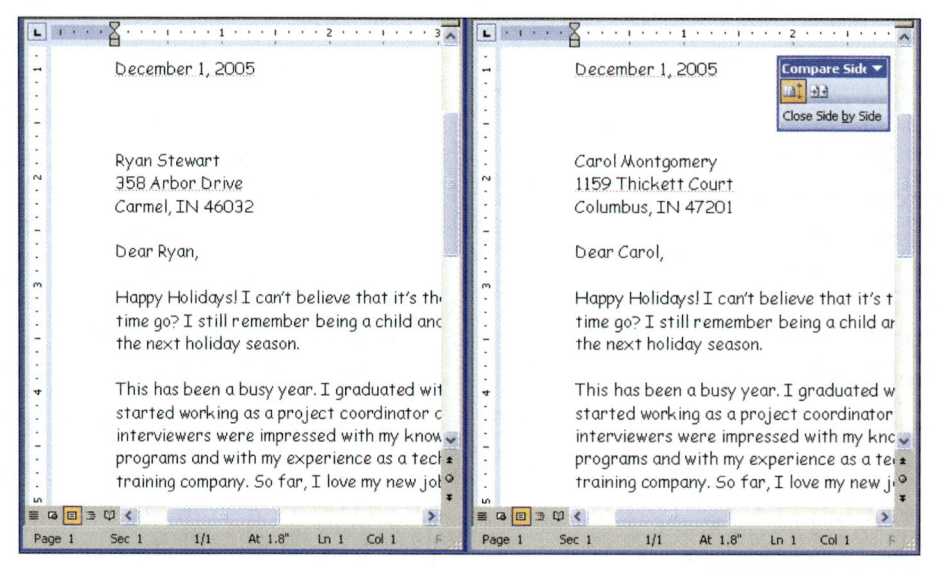

FIGURE 5.27

1. Specifying a Document Type and Starting Document

You are writing a holiday letter to send to your close friends from college. Although you are sending a form letter, you want to personalize the letter by including each recipient's name and address on his or her respective printed letter. Your first step is to specify the document type, which is a letter, and the starting document, which is a Word document you created recently.

1. Open *EW2_0502* and save it as **Holiday_Form_Letter**.
2. Choose Tools, Letters and Mailings, Mail Merge.
3. Make sure the *Letters* option is selected.
4. Click *Next: Starting document* at the bottom of the Mail Merge task pane.
5. Make sure the *Use the current document* option is selected.
6. Save the *Holiday_Form_Letter* document and keep it and the Mail Merge task pane onscreen to continue with the next exercise.

2. Creating and Sorting a Recipient List

As you complete the mail merge process, you realize that you do not have an existing recipient list to use. Therefore, you need to create a data source to store the recipient information, such as people's names and addresses. After entering records into the data source, you want to sort the records by city.

1. With the *Holiday_Form_Letter* document and the Mail Merge task pane onscreen, click *Next: Select recipients* at the bottom of the task pane.

2. Click the *Type a new list* option and then click the *Create* option.

3. Press Tab, and type **Ryan** in the First Name field.

4. Press Tab, and type **Stewart** in the Last Name field.

5. Enter the following text in their respective fields:

Address Line 1	`358 Arbor Drive`
City	`Carmel`
State	`IN`
ZIP Code	`46032`
Home Phone	`(317) 555-6249`

6. Click <u>N</u>ew Entry to create another record.

7. Enter the data for the following records:

Record 2	**Record 3**	**Record 4**
`Alice`	`Carol`	`Seth`
`Lorenzana`	`Montgomery`	`Higton`
`1571 Locust Street`	`1159 Thickett Court`	`230 Sycamore`
`Elkhart`	`Columbus`	`Silver Lake`
`IN`	`IN`	`IN`
`46514`	`47201`	`46982`
`(219) 555-7947`	`(812) 555-4163`	`(219) 555-5026`

8. Click Close.

9. Specify a storage device and folder to store the file, and save the data source as `Holiday_Recipient_List` with the default *.mdb* file extension.

10. With the Mail Merge Recipients dialog box open, click the scroll right arrow until you see the City field.

11. Click the City field name to sort the records alphabetically by the city name and then click OK.

12. Save the *Holiday_Form_Letter* document and keep it and the Mail Merge task pane onscreen to continue with the next exercise.

3. Inserting Merge Fields into the Main Document

You are now ready to finish creating the main document. You need to insert the AddressBlock and GreetingLine field names in the appropriate location to correctly format the letter.

1. With the *Holiday_Form_Letter* document and the Mail Merge task pane onscreen, click *Next: Write your letter* at the bottom of the task pane.

2. Delete the asterisk placeholder (*) below the date, but do not delete any paragraph marks.

3. Click the *Address block* option in the task pane and then click OK to accept the settings in the Insert Address Block dialog box.

4. Press `Enter` twice.

5. Click the *Greeting line* option on the task pane.

6. Click the name drop-down arrow, scroll down through the list, and choose the *Joshua* name format.

7. Leave the comma punctuation mark because this is a personal letter; then click OK.

8. Save the *Holiday_Form_Letter* document and keep it and the Mail Merge task pane onscreen to continue with the next exercise.

4. Previewing and Merging the Documents

Your main document contains the merge fields, and your data source is complete. You are now ready to preview the merge and then perform the merge.

1. With the *Holiday_Form_Letter* document and the Mail Merge task pane onscreen, click *Next: Preview your letters* at the bottom of the task pane.

2. Click the >> button on the task pane to preview the next merged letter.

3. Click *Next: Complete the merge* at the bottom of the task pane.

4. Click the *Edit individual letters* option on the task pane.

5. Make sure the *All* option is selected in the Merge to New Document dialog box and then click OK.

6. Scroll through the letters to make sure the addresses and greetings look correct.

7. Save the merged document as **Holiday_Merged_Letters**, print (optional), and close it.

8. With the *Holiday_Form_Letter* document onscreen, choose View, Toolbars, Mail Merge if the Mail Merge toolbar is not already onscreen.

9. Click View Merged Data on the Mail Merge toolbar to change from preview to field names.

10. Save, print (optional), and close the *Holiday_Form_Letter* document.

5. Creating Mailing Labels

You purchased holiday envelopes that match your holiday stationery. You do not want to feed each envelope into the printer, so you purchased some Avery labels on which you can print the addresses and then attach to the envelopes.

1. Click New Blank Document on the Standard toolbar and save it as **Holiday_Form_Labels**.

2. Choose Tools, Letters and Mailings, Mail Merge.

3. Click *Labels* on the task pane and then click *Next: Starting document* at the bottom of the task pane.

4. Click *Label options* on the task pane to open the Label Options dialog box, select *5160 - Address* in the *Product number* list box, and click OK.

5. Click *Next: Select recipients* on the task pane, click *Browse* to open the Select Data Source dialog box, select *Holiday_Recipient_List.mdb,* and then click <u>O</u>pen.

6. With the Mail Merge Recipients dialog box displayed, click the City field name to sort alphabetically by city name, and click OK.

7. Click *Next: Arrange your labels* at the bottom of the task pane.

8. Click *Address block* and then click OK in the Insert Address Block dialog box.

9. Choose <u>V</u>iew, <u>T</u>oolbars, Mail Merge if the Mail Merge toolbar is not already onscreen.

10. Click the Propagate Labels button on the Mail Merge toolbar to copy the label format to the other labels.

11. Click *Next: Preview your labels* at the bottom of the task pane.

12. Click Merge to New Document on the Mail Merge toolbar; then click OK in the Merge to New Document dialog box that opens.

13. Save the merged labels as *Holiday_Merged_Labels.* Print (optional) and close the document.

14. Click View Merged Data on the Mail Merge toolbar to view the field names again.

15. Save, print (optional), and close the *Holiday_Form_Labels* document.

CHALLENGE

Challenge exercises expand on or are somewhat related to skills presented in the lessons. Each exercise provides a brief narrative introduction, followed by instructions in a numbered-step format that are not as detailed as those in the Skill Drill exercises. You can work through one or more exercises in any order.

1. Creating Cover Letters to Apply for Jobs

You are applying for jobs that you recently found through an Internet source. You created the body of the main letter. Now, you need to create the data source, sort the data source by company name, insert fields in the main document to generate the address block and greeting, and then merge the documents.

1. Open *EW2_0503* and save it as **Application_Form_Letter**.

2. Use the Mail Merge task pane to select the document type and starting document.

3. Create a data source named **Application_Recipients**. Use the following data to create the data source records.

Record 1	Record 2	Record 3	Record 4
Mr.	Ms.	Mr.	Ms.
Craig	Rona	Trevor	Lilian
Hogue	Boutelle	Kirkland	Trevino
Livingston Corporation	Canyon & Sons	Solis, Inc.	Horizon Products
5399 New Haven Avenue	2010 E.2nd Street	1200 Shiloh Square	31 Imperial Palace
Fort Wayne	Bloomington	Evansville	Lafayette
IN	IN	IN	IN
46803	47401	47714	47905

 4. Edit the records by changing *Solis, Inc.* to **Solis Corporation.**

 5. Sort the data source by company name.

 6. Delete the asterisk placeholder and then complete the main document by inserting appropriate fields to generate the address block and greeting. Use business format—last name in the greeting and a colon as the punctuation mark.

 7. Change *Student's Name* to your name in the signature block.

 8. Vertically center the document.

 9. Save the *Application_Form_Letter* document.

 10. Perform the merge to a new document window, and save the merged document as **Application_Merged_Letters**.

 11. Print (optional) the merged letters and close the document.

 12. View the merge fields in the *Application_Form_Letter* document; save and close it.

2. Creating and Merging Envelopes for the Cover Letters

You purchased high-quality envelopes that match the stationery on which you printed your application letters. You need to use the Mail Merge task pane to create envelopes using the data source that you created in Challenge exercise 1. If you did not complete Challenge exercise 1, you create the data source in this exercise.

 1. Start a new blank document, save the document as **Application_Form_Envelope**, and display the Mail Merge task pane.

 2. Choose the *Envelopes* data type and then select the *Size 10* envelope size.

 3. Type your name and address in the return address part of the envelope.

 4. Use *Application_Recipients.mdb* as the data source, and sort the data source by company name. If you did not complete Challenge exercise 1, create the data source as specified in steps 3–5 in Challenge exercise 1 before continuing with this exercise.

 5. Click in the middle of the document window. You should see *Envelope Address* in the Style box, and a border should display to indicate the address area. Insert the AddressBlock field in this area.

 6. Perform the merge to a new document window, save the merged envelopes as **Application_Merged_Envelopes**, print (optional) the envelopes on plain paper, and close the document.

 7. Display the Mail Merge toolbar, if needed, and view the merge fields.

 8. Save and close the *Application_Form_Envelope* document.

3. Preparing More Conference Confirmations

After merging a data source with the conference form letter that you created earlier in this project and mailing the letter to the original list of participants, you received additional registrations. You now want to add those records to a copy of your existing data source, and selectively merge the documents.

1. Use Windows Explorer to copy *EW2_0504.mdb* and then rename the copied file as `Conference_Participants2.mdb`. Then close Windows Explorer.

2. In a new document window, use the Mail Merge task pane to specify the *Letters* document type.

3. Specify the starting document as an existing document, and then select the appropriate task pane option to browse and open *EW2_0505*. (Do not open the document as you typically open documents; use the Mail Merge task pane.)

   When you do this, the document contents open onscreen, but the title bar displays a document number, such as *Document1*.

4. Save the document contents as `Conference_Form_Letter2`.

5. Select *Conference_Participants2.mdb* as the data source, and edit the records.

6. Add the following three new records to the data source.

Record 6	Record 7	Record 8
Mr.	Ms.	Mr.
Pierre	Melody	Marc
Schneider	Kaiser	Zarbock
Winston Company	Interloop, Inc.	Wyman Enterprises
319 North Main	900 West Locust	3812 Lincoln Avenue
Hinton	Canadian	Lexington
OK	TX	KY
73047	49014	40517

7. Sort the records by state, in alphabetical order.

8. Clear check boxes for all records and then select the three new records that you just added.

9. Insert the appropriate fields to produce the inside address and greeting. Use appropriate spacing.

10. Vertically center the document.

11. Merge the selected records to a new document window.

12. Save the merged document as `Conference_Merged_Letters2`. Print (optional) and close the merged document.

13. In the *Conference_Form_Letter2* document, display the Mail Merge toolbar (if needed) and click View Merged Data to see the merge fields instead of a preview of the merged data.

14. Save, print (optional), and close the *Conference_Form_Letter2* document.

4. Using a Word Table as a Data Source

As Dean of Students at a state college, you need to create a form letter that congratulates students whose grade-point averages (GPAs) during the last semester reflected outstanding academic performance. You are also awarding scholarships to these students. Before composing the letter, however, you started a table to store student names, addresses, GPAs, and scholarship amounts. Now you need to add two more names to the table and add the field names.

You then compose the content of the main letter. Using the table document as the data source, you need to insert the AddressBlock and GreetingLine fields. In addition, you want the letters to be personalized by specifying the respective student's GPA and scholarship amount.

1. Open *EW2_0506* and save it as **Scholarship_Recipients**.
2. Format the document in landscape page orientation.
3. Insert a new row at the top of the table and then type the following field names in boldface:

   First Name, Last Name, Address Line 1, City, State, ZIP Code, GPA, Scholarship

4. Add two rows at the end of the table and then enter the following records:

   Tyler, Dahl, 491 Grove Drive, Alpine, UT, 84004, 3.95, $2,000

   Arlene, Mullenix, 650 N. Roosevelt, Chicago, IL, 60614, 4.00, $3,000

5. Adjust the column widths in the table to avoid word-wrapping data.
6. Save, print (optional), and close the *Scholarship_Recipients* data source document.
7. In a new document window, create the standard text for the main document using these specifications:

   a. Type a two-paragraph letter that provides congratulations based on GPA and mentions the scholarship. Do not type specific GPAs or scholarship amounts in the main document because these numbers differ for each student. Type placeholders now, which you will replace with merge fields later.

   b. Type a signature block with a complimentary closing, your name, and your job title. Do not type punctuation after the complimentary closing (e.g., *Sincerely*) because you are using open punctuation style. Refer to an office reference manual, a business communication text, or the Research tool in Word, if necessary, to learn about open punctuation style.

   c. Set appropriate margins and center the document vertically.

   d. Save the main document as **Scholarship_Form_Letter**.

8. Use the Mail Merge task pane to use the current document as the main document.
9. Select the *Scholarship_Recipients.doc* data source. Sort the records by scholarship.
10. Complete the main document by doing the following:

    a. Type today's date at the top of the document, and press ⏎Enter four times.

    b. Insert the AddressBlock and the GreetingLine merge fields in the appropriate locations. Use the students' first names in the greeting and do not use punctuation in the greeting field.

c. Insert the GPA and Scholarship fields in the appropriate locations within the paragraphs.

d. Save the *Scholarship_Form_Letter* document.

11. Perform the merge to a new document window and save it as **Scholarship_Merged_Letters**. Print (optional) and close the merged document.

12. Display the merge fields in the *Scholarship_Form_Letter.*

13. Save, print (optional), and close the *Scholarship_Form_Letter* document.

14. Create labels for the letters by doing the following:

    a. In a new document window, create a label main document named **Scholarship_Form_Labels** and use the Avery 5260 address label product number.

    b. Select the *Scholarship_Recipients.doc* document as the data source. Make sure the records are sorted by scholarship.

    c. Insert the AddressBlock field in the labels and propagate the labels.

    d. Perform the merge to a new document window.

    e. Save the merged label document as **Scholarship_Merged_Labels**, print (optional), and close the document.

    f. Display the merge fields, save, print (optional), and close the *Scholarship_Form_Labels* document.

DISCOVERY ZONE

Discovery Zone exercises require advanced knowledge of topics presented in the lessons or self-directed learning of new skills. You can work through one or both of these exercises in any order.

1. Creating a Bonus Memo from Scratch

You need to send out memos to individuals who are receiving a bonus this month. First, you compose a short memo and designate it as the main document. You then create a data source and perform the merge.

After using the Mail Merge task pane several times, you are ready to try performing a merge with the Mail Merge toolbar instead. You believe you might be able to save time. First, study Table 5.1 in this project, and use Help to learn more about the Mail Merge toolbar buttons. Do *not* use the Mail Merge task pane in this exercise; complete all merge tasks by using the Mail Merge toolbar instead.

Create a new blank document and set up the main document as *Letters*. Type the memo shown in Figure 5.28, omitting the merge fields indicated by << >>. You insert merge fields after creating the data source.

TO: «FirstName» «LastName», «Department» Department

FROM: District Manager

DATE: July 1, 2005

SUBJECT: Special Bonus

Congratulations! Your high evaluation score has earned you a special summer bonus. Because of your rating, I'm enclosing a check for $«Bonus».

This is our way of saying "thanks for doing a good job."

Enclosure

FIGURE 5.28

Set a 2" top margin, save the memo main document as **Bonus_Form_Memo**, and keep this document onscreen.

Create a new blank document, and create the table shown in Figure 5.29.

FirstName	LastName	Department	Extension	Bonus
Mike	Chadworth	Administration	610	350
Monica	Farnsworth	Human Resources	501	450
Tim	Foster	Public Relations	783	415
Kalen	Nelson	Sales	900	360
Kim	Nettles	Human Resources	560	350
Amanda	Peterson	Manufacturing	103	425
Mark	Sabey	Manufacturing	101	275
Patty	Stinson	Marketing	688	300
Belinda	Wilson	Sales	716	415
Jon	Zaugg	Marketing	605	400

FIGURE 5.29

Save the table document as **Bonus_Data_Source**. Use Help to learn how to sort a Word table, and then sort the table by department and then by last name. Save, print (optional), and close the *Bonus_Data_Source* document.

With the *Bonus_Form_Memo* document onscreen, open the data source from the Mail Merge toolbar. Insert the merge fields as shown in Figure 5.28. Save and print (optional) the *Bonus_Form_Memo* main document.

Merge the documents to a new document window, and save the merged document as **Bonus_Merged_Memos**. Print (optional) and close the merged document. Save and close the main document.

2. Creating a Directory of Employee Information

You want to create a reference list of each employee's emergency contact and phone number. Use Help to learn how to create a directory using the Mail Merge Wizard.

In a new document window, create a directory document through the Mail Merge task pane or the Mail Merge toolbar. Use the Excel worksheet *EW2_0507.xls* as the data source. Hint: Use the *More items* option on the task pane or the Insert Merge Fields button on the toolbar to insert these field names separated by tabs: **LastName**, **FirstName**, **EmergencyContactName**, **EmergencyContactPhone**, and **EmergencyContactRelation**. Do not worry about the field names word-wrapping. Press Shift+Enter after inserting the last field name. Save the main document as **Emergency_Form_Directory**.

Perform the merge to a new document window. Set tabs for all fields, including the first one. Press Tab to indent the first column. Make sure the columns are evenly spaced. Go to the top of the document, and insert four hard returns before the first line. Save the directory document as **Emergency_Merged_Directory**.

Type the title **Emergency Contact Information** at the top of the document and format it with the built-in Title style. On the blank line immediately above the first line of the records, type these column headings in boldface: **Last Name**, **First Name**, **Contact Name**, **Phone No.**, and **Relation**. The headings should have the same tabs as the directory list. Select and double-space the column headings as well as the rest of the document.

Save, print (optional), and close the *Emergency_Merged_Directory* document. Save, print (optional), and close the *Emergency_Form_Directory* document.

PROJECT **6** LEVEL **2**

USING DRAWING TOOLS AND SPECIAL EFFECTS

OBJECTIVES

In this project, you learn how to

- Draw and size shapes
- Draw lines
- Insert text with a text effect
- Position shapes
- Format shapes and lines
- Layer and group shapes

Project 6   Using Drawing Tools and Special Effects

WHY WOULD I DO THIS?

Graphical elements—such as lines, arrows, stars, and other shapes—help enhance your documents by adding excitement and visual interest. Microsoft Word enables you to combine shapes and lines to produce one-of-a-kind drawings. For example, you can create shapes that represent balloons on strings and format the shapes by applying different fill colors. You can also position, size, and overlap shapes to achieve the visual effect you desire.

In addition to using the Drawing toolbar to create and customize shapes, you can apply text effects to draw attention to onscreen text. For example, you can animate text to blink, sparkle, or shimmer.

VISUAL SUMMARY

In this project, you use Word's drawing tools, drawing canvas, and text effects to create and format shapes to use in an advertising flyer for the 10th anniversary sale at a toy store called Kids' Playground. Figure 6.1 shows the completed flyer, which contains various shapes.

Visual Summary 203 LEVEL 2

Kids' Playground 10th Anniversary Sale

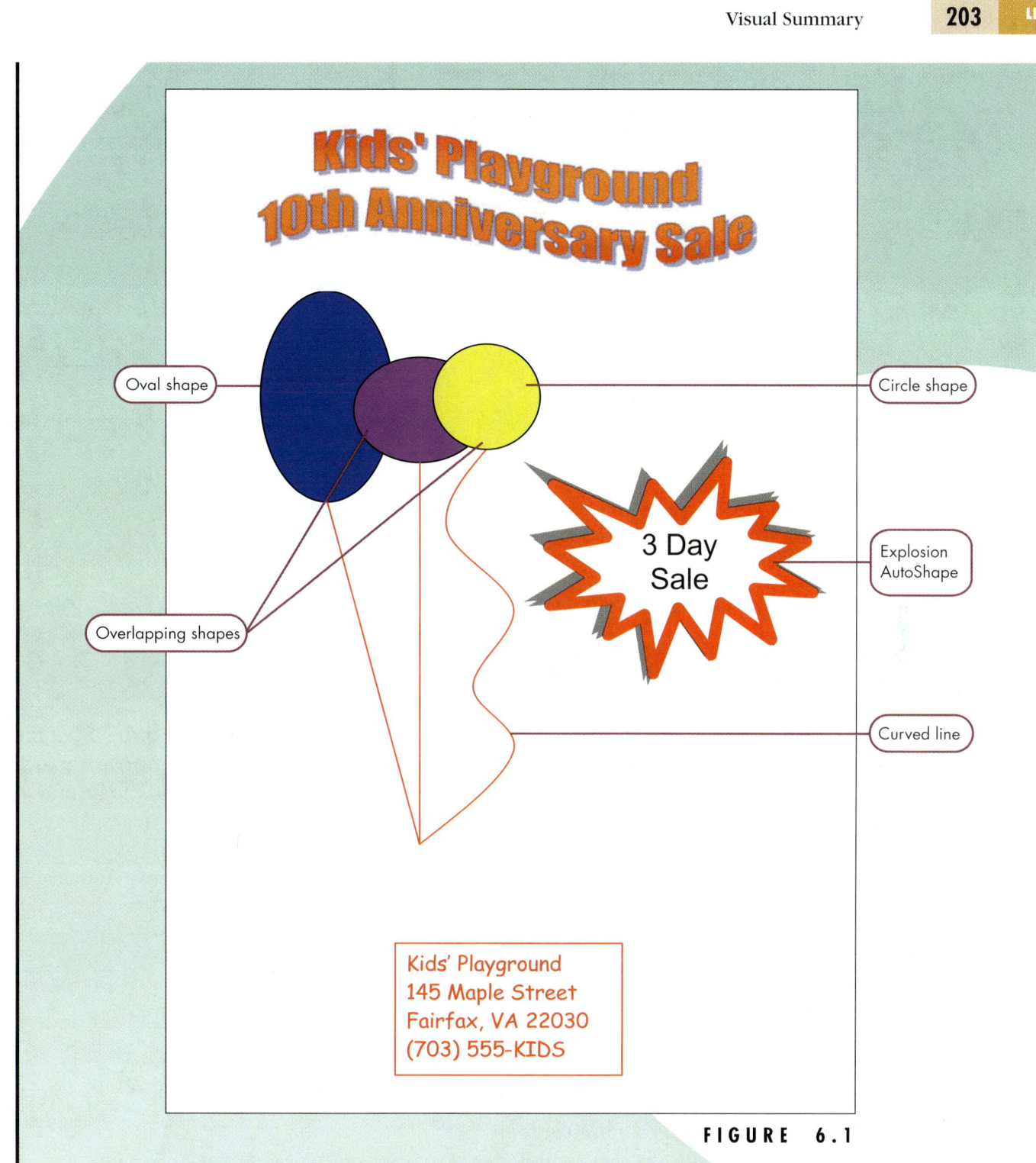

- Oval shape
- Circle shape
- Overlapping shapes
- Explosion AutoShape — 3 Day Sale
- Curved line

Kids' Playground
145 Maple Street
Fairfax, VA 22030
(703) 555-KIDS

FIGURE 6.1

Figure 6.2 shows the onscreen drawing canvas that displays when you create drawings. The drawing canvas keeps your objects together and adjusts to any size.

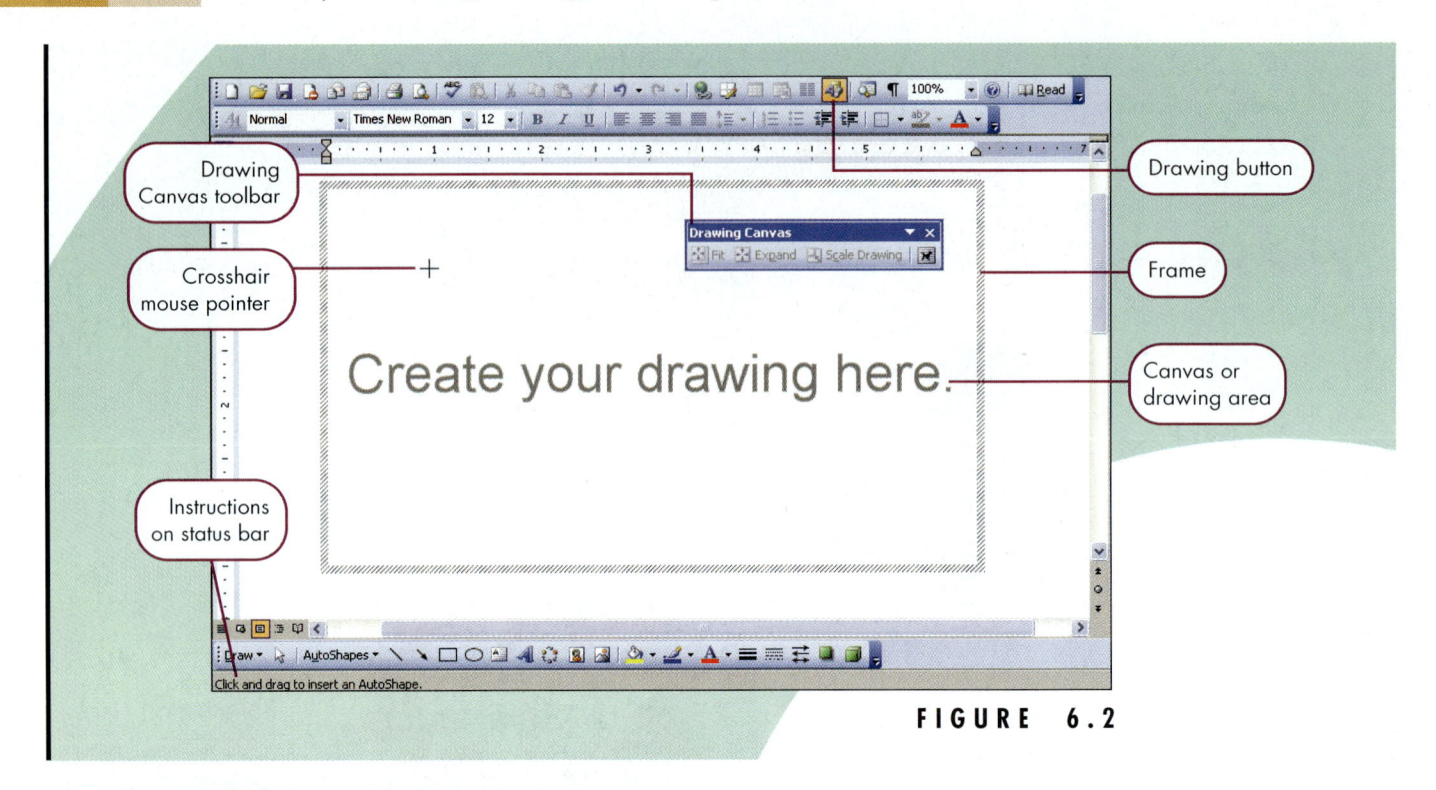

Project 6 Using Drawing Tools and Special Effects

(Screenshot of Word drawing canvas with callouts: Drawing Canvas toolbar, Crosshair mouse pointer, Instructions on status bar, Drawing button, Frame, Canvas or drawing area)

FIGURE 6.2

LESSON 1: Drawing and Sizing Shapes

You add ***AutoShapes,*** which are predefined shapes such as circles and banners, by using the ***Drawing toolbar,*** a collection of drawing tools and options, and the ***drawing canvas,*** an area upon which you create objects. Shapes are placed within the drawing canvas and can be moved and resized easily.

In this lesson, you draw and size three closed shapes: an oval, a circle, and an explosion AutoShape.

To Draw and Size Closed Shapes

1 Open *EW2_0601,* and save it as `Playground_Sale`.

2 Click Drawing on the Standard toolbar.
The Drawing toolbar appears above the status bar at the bottom of the screen.

3 Click Oval on the Drawing toolbar.
The drawing canvas displays, outlining the area for creating a drawing. The mouse pointer looks like a crosshair, indicating that you are ready to drag to create an oval.

If you have problems . . .

If the drawing canvas does not appear, choose Tools, Options, click the General tab, click the *Automatically create drawing canvas when inserting AutoShapes* check box, and click OK.

Lesson 1   Drawing and Sizing Shapes

4 **Click and hold the mouse button below the WordArt object, near the left edge of the drawing canvas frame, and drag down and to the right approximately 1½". Release the mouse button.**

Use Figure 6.3 as a guide and example. Do not worry about exact positions of the shapes; you learn how to position shapes in Lesson 4. The place you start clicking and dragging is the object's *anchor*—the location that the object is attached to.

FIGURE 6.3

5 **Click Oval on the Drawing toolbar, position the mouse pointer approximately 1" to right of the existing oval, and click.**

When you click Oval or Rectangle on the Drawing toolbar and then click within the drawing canvas, Word creates a perfect 1" circle or square, respectively. Figure 6.4 shows the shapes you created to represent balloons.

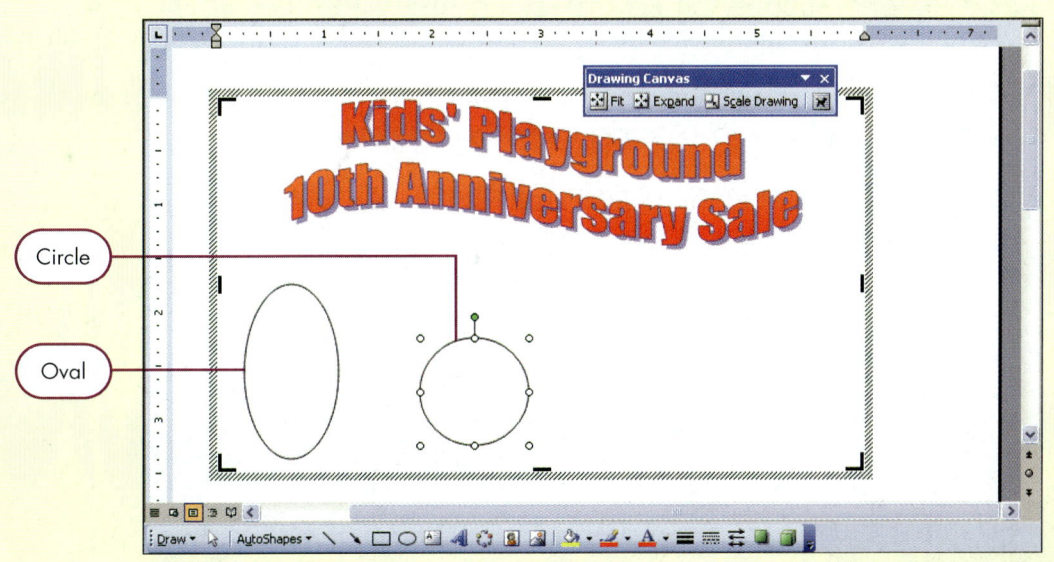

FIGURE 6.4

Project 6 Using Drawing Tools and Special Effects

? If you have problems . . .
To add an object to an existing drawing canvas, you must select the drawing canvas before clicking the object button on the Drawing toolbar. If you do not select the canvas first, Word creates a new drawing canvas for the object.

---

6 **Click AutoShapes on the Drawing toolbar, choose Stars and Banners, and position the mouse pointer on the top-left shape on the palette.**

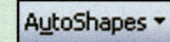

Figure 6.5 shows a palette that contains a list of stars and banners. When you place the mouse pointer over any shape in a palette or any button on the Drawing toolbar, you see a ScreenTip that displays the name of the feature.

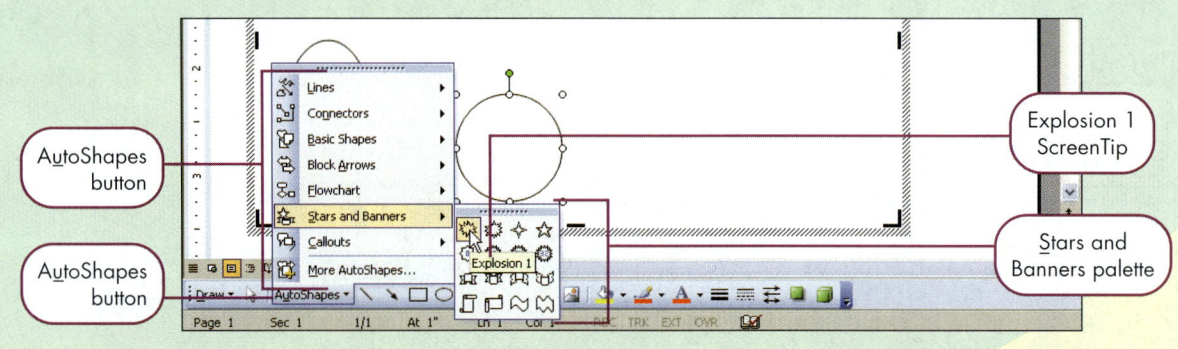

FIGURE 6.5

7 **Click the Explosion 1 shape on the Stars and Banners palette.**
Your mouse pointer becomes a crosshair when you move it onto the screen.

8 **Click and hold the mouse pointer to the right of the circle; drag down about 2" and to the right about 2". Release the mouse button.**
Word inserts the explosion shape. Now you need to set specific sizes for the shapes.

9 **Right-click the star shape, choose Format AutoShape, click the Size tab, set 2" for the height and 2.5" for the width, and click OK.**

10 **For the oval, set 2" as the height and 1.25" as the width.**
Your document should look similar to Figure 6.6.

Lesson 1 Drawing and Sizing Shapes 207

FIGURE 6.6

11 Save the *Playground_Sale* document, and keep it onscreen to continue with the next lesson.

TO EXTEND YOUR KNOWLEDGE . . .

USING THE DRAWING TOOLBAR BUTTONS
Table 6.1 identifies and describes the buttons on the Drawing toolbar.

TABLE 6.1

BUTTON	BUTTON NAME	DESCRIPTION
Draw ▾	Draw	Displays menu of drawing options, such as Group and Order
	Select Objects	Selects one or more objects
AutoShapes ▾	AutoShapes	Displays a menu of predefined shapes, such as lines, arrows, and callouts
	Line	Draws a straight line
	Arrow	Draws a line with an arrowhead at the end
	Rectangle	Draws a rectangle or square

TABLE 6.1 (continued)

BUTTON	BUTTON NAME	DESCRIPTION
	Oval	Draws an oval or circle
	Text Box	Creates a box in which you type and format text
	Insert WordArt	Displays the WordArt Gallery
	Insert Diagram or Organization Chart	Displays the Diagram Gallery
	Insert Clip Art	Opens the Clip Art task pane
	Insert Picture	Opens the Insert Picture dialog box
	Fill Color	Applies a fill color or fill effect to an object
	Line Color	Applies a color or pattern to a line
	Font Color	Changes the color of selected text
	Line Style	Applies a line thickness or style to a selected line or border
	Dash Style	Applies a dashed-line style to a selected line or border
	Arrow Style	Applies an arrow style or direction to a selected line
	Shadow Style	Applies a shadow to a selected object
	3-D Style	Applies a three-dimensional setting to the selected objects

REMOVING THE DRAWING CANVAS

You might find it easier to remove the drawing canvas if you are inserting an arrow or a single shape in your document. Click the shape button you want on the Drawing toolbar. When the drawing canvas appears, press the Esc key to remove it. You can then drag to create the shape without the drawing canvas.

If you do not want the drawing canvas to appear automatically for new drawings, you can change the default setting. To do this, choose Tools, Options, click the General tab, deselect the *Automatically create drawing canvas when inserting AutoShapes* check box, and click OK.

RESIZING SHAPES

To resize a shape, click to select it. Place your mouse pointer on a handle so that it becomes a double arrow; then click and drag. Use corner handles and press ⇧Shift to proportionately resize the shape, use top and bottom centered handles to change the height, and use left and right centered handles to change the width.

DRAWING PERFECT CIRCLES OR SQUARES

You can draw a perfect circle or square by clicking the Oval button or Rectangle button, respectively. Then hold down ⇧Shift while dragging the shape.

LESSON 2: Drawing Lines

You can also draw a variety of lines in your document. When you choose Lines from the AutoShapes menu, you can draw straight lines, curved lines, freeform shapes, or arrowhead lines. After drawing a line, you can change the *arrow style* by applying arrowheads, circles, or diamonds at the ends of the lines by clicking Arrow Style on the Drawing toolbar and choosing the style from the palette. The basic technique for drawing lines is to click to position the anchor point of the line and then drag the mouse pointer to draw the line.

The line tools even include a *scribble line* tool that enables you to draw as if with a pencil. Word displays a pencil image next to the mouse pointer while you press your mouse button and draw the shape or text you want, such as your signature. Double-click the mouse button to end the line.

In this lesson, you use AutoShape lines to draw strings for the balloons.

To Draw Lines

1 **In the *Playground_Sale* document, position your mouse pointer over the bottom-center sizing handle on the drawing canvas.**
You need to expand the drawing canvas to allow room for the balloon strings. The mouse pointer changes shape when positioned over a drawing canvas sizing handle.

2 **Drag the bottom-center sizing handle down to align with the 7½″ indicator on the vertical ruler.**
Figure 6.7 shows the bottom location of the drawing canvas.

Project 6 Using Drawing Tools and Special Effects

Shapes located here

Drag middle framing handle down to 7½"

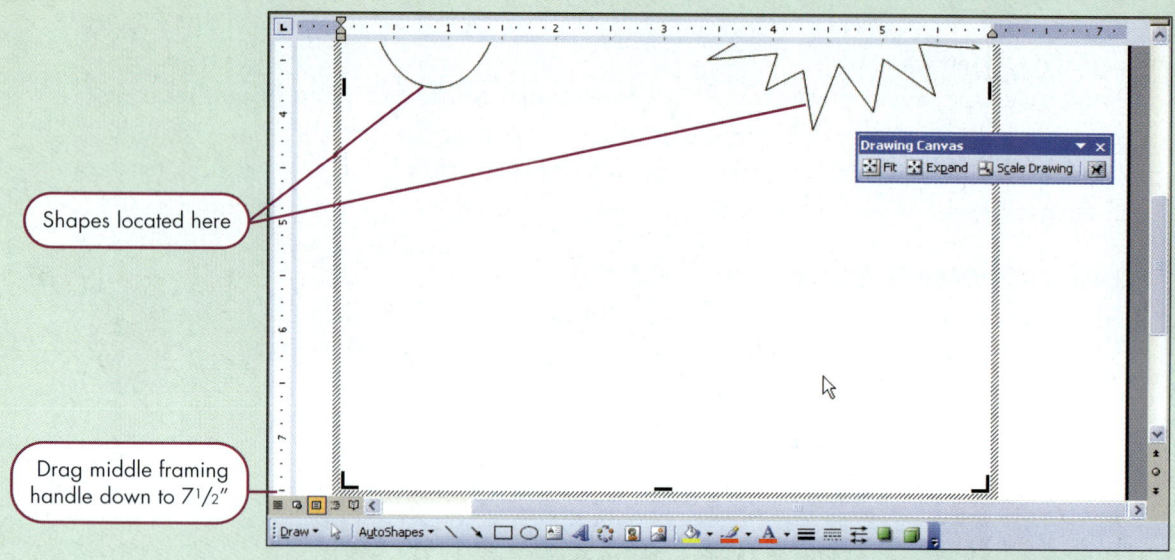

FIGURE 6.7

3 **Click Line on the Drawing toolbar.**
The mouse pointer becomes a crosshair when you move it onto the document screen.

4 **Click and hold the mouse pointer on the bottom of the oval and drag it down about 3" and slightly to the right. Release the mouse button to end the line.**
The line becomes the string for the balloon (see Figure 6.8).

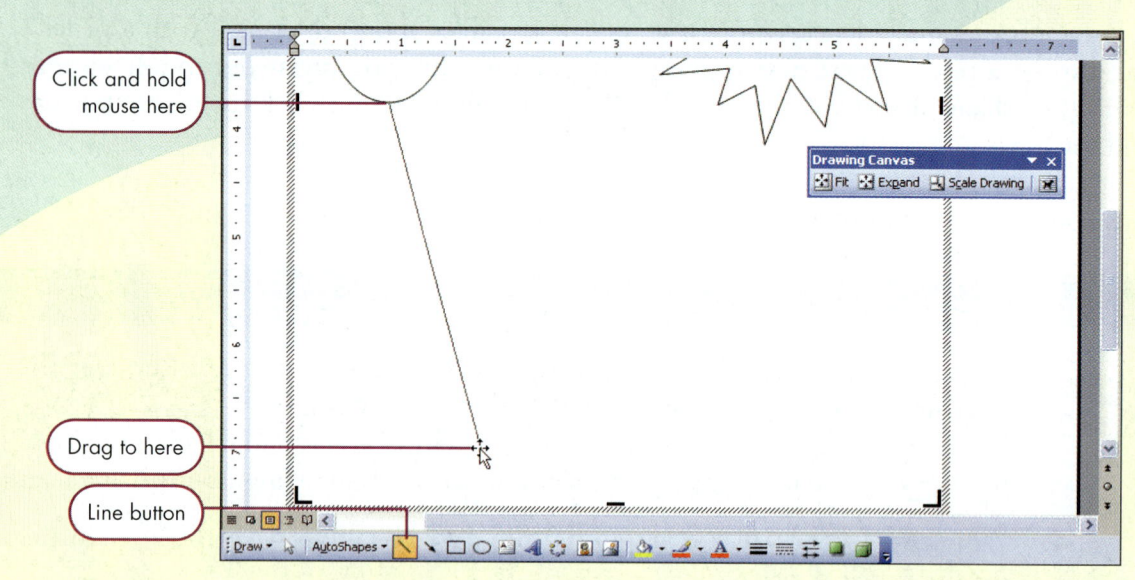

Click and hold mouse here

Drag to here

Line button

FIGURE 6.8

5 **Click AutoShapes, select Lines, and select the Curve tool.**
The mouse pointer becomes a crosshair. You will draw a *curved line,* which is a line that contains smooth curves wherever you change directions. Click the mouse button to anchor it. Double-click where you want to end the line.

6 **Click the mouse button once on the bottom of the circle.**
When you move the mouse pointer, a line is attached to it. Use Figure 6.9 as a guide when you complete the next three steps.

Lesson 2   Drawing Lines   **211**   LEVEL **2**

Click here to begin the line

Click here to set an anchor point

Click here to set another anchor point

Double-click here

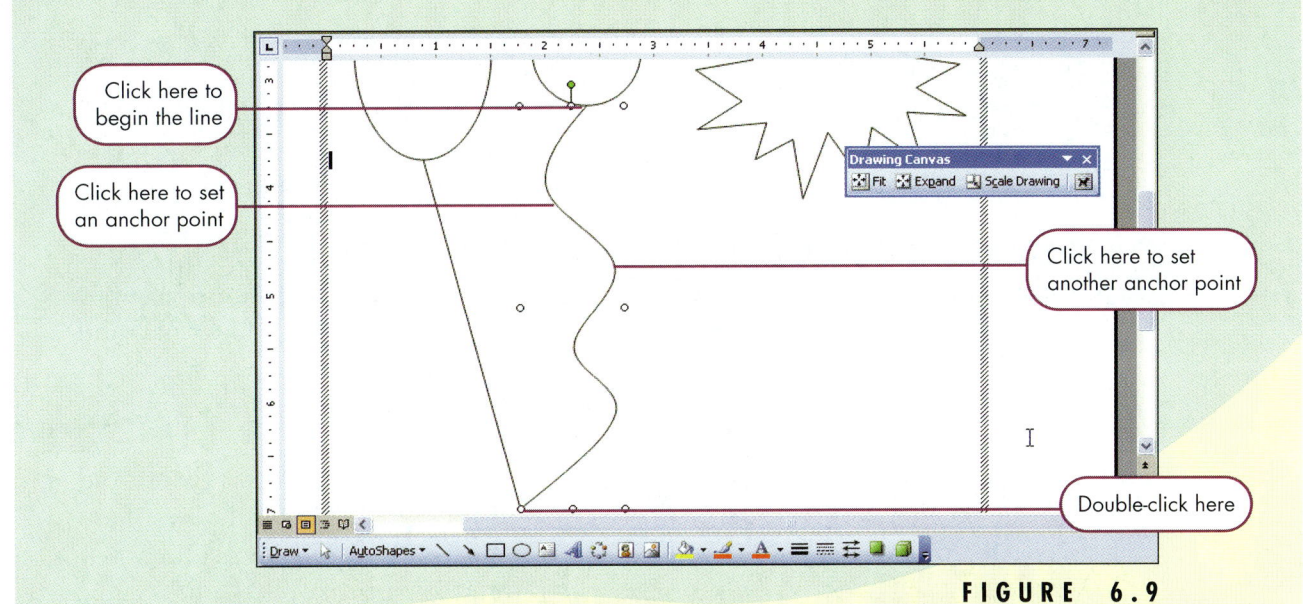

FIGURE 6.9

7 Drag the mouse pointer down and to the left about ½", and click.
This creates and anchors a point for the first curve.

8 Move the mouse pointer down and to the right about ½", and click again.
This creates the curve around the first anchor point and creates a second anchor point.

9 Repeat the previous two steps until the curved line meets the straight line from the other balloon. Double-click the mouse, or click the mouse and then press Esc to end the curved line.
Word inserts the curved line into the document and selects it, as shown in Figure 6.9.

10 Save the *Playground_Sale* document, and keep it onscreen to continue with the next lesson.

TO EXTEND YOUR KNOWLEDGE . . .

RESIZING THE DRAWING CANVAS
To shrink the drawing canvas to fit your objects, click Fit Drawing To Contents on the Drawing Canvas toolbar. To expand the drawing canvas in even increments, click Expand Drawing on the Drawing Canvas toolbar.

RESIZING LINES
To resize a line, click the line shape to select it. Place your mouse pointer on an object handle so it becomes a double arrow; then click and drag to the desired length.

DRAWING STRAIGHT LINES

To draw a straight line, click Line on the Drawing toolbar and hold down ⇧Shift; then click and drag the mouse pointer in the document. Also, pressing ⇧Shift as you draw the line changes the angle of the line in 15-degree increments.

DRAWING CONNECTOR LINES FOR FLOWCHART SHAPES

A *flowchart* is a visual representation of shapes that illustrate a process. To draw flowchart shapes, click AutoShapes on the Drawing toolbar, choose Flowchart and click a flowchart shape from the palette, and then draw the shape in the document. Continue selecting and drawing flowchart shapes as needed.

Flowcharts usually include **connector lines,** special lines that join two shapes and indicate the flow from one process or decision to another. To draw connector lines between flowchart shapes, click AutoShapes on the Drawing toolbar, choose Connectors and click a connector line shape from the palette, click the first shape you want to attach the connector line to, and then click the second shape you want to attach to the connector line. When you attach a connector line to two shapes, Word anchors both ends of the connector lines to the shapes. Therefore, if you move one shape, the line remains attached to it and expands or decreases as needed.

LESSON 3: Inserting Text with a Text Effect

Some shapes, such as stars or banners, are designed to display text. You can add and format text to these shapes—for instance, by applying Center horizontal alignment, bold, and Red font color. In addition to inserting text within a shape, you can apply a text effect. A ***text effect*** is an animation setting that draws attention to a document onscreen (although the text effect does not appear on the printed document). This format can be very effective in a document that you e-mail to a friend or customer.

In this lesson you insert and format text within the star shape. In addition, you apply the Sparkle Text effect.

To Insert Text with a Text Effect

1 In the *Playground_Sale* document, select the Explosion 1 AutoShape.

2 Right-click the Explosion 1 AutoShape and choose *Add Text* from the shortcut menu.

A text box with an insertion point inside appears around the shape. A thick frame appears around the text box (see Figure 6.10).

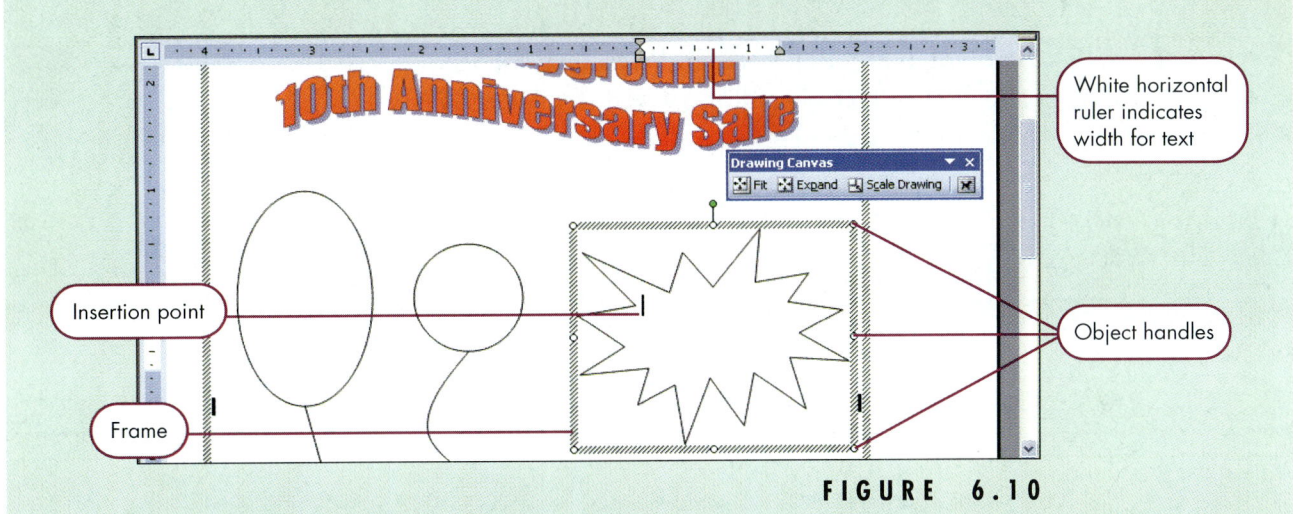

Lesson 3 Inserting Text with a Text Effect   213   LEVEL 2

Callouts on Figure 6.10: Insertion point; Frame; White horizontal ruler indicates width for text; Object handles

FIGURE 6.10

3 **Apply Arial font, 20-point font size, and Center horizontal alignment.**
You applied formats so that the text will stand out.

4 **Type 3 Day Sale within the text box.**
The word *Sale* wraps to the next line due to the size of the text box frame.

5 **Select *3 Day Sale* within the text box, open the Font dialog box, and click the Te*x*t Effects tab.**
The Text Effects tab of the Font dialog box contains animation options (see Figure 6.11).

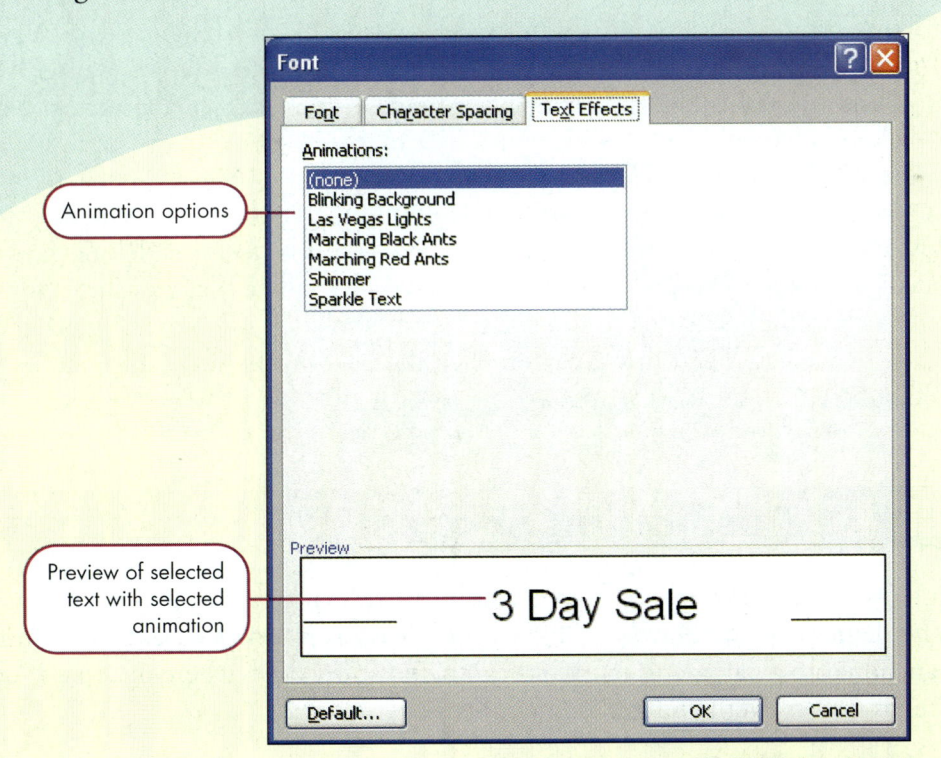

Callouts on Figure 6.11: Animation options; Preview of selected text with selected animation

FIGURE 6.11

6 Click *Sparkle Text,* click OK, and deselect the text.
The Sparkle Text effect is visible onscreen (see Figure 6.12).

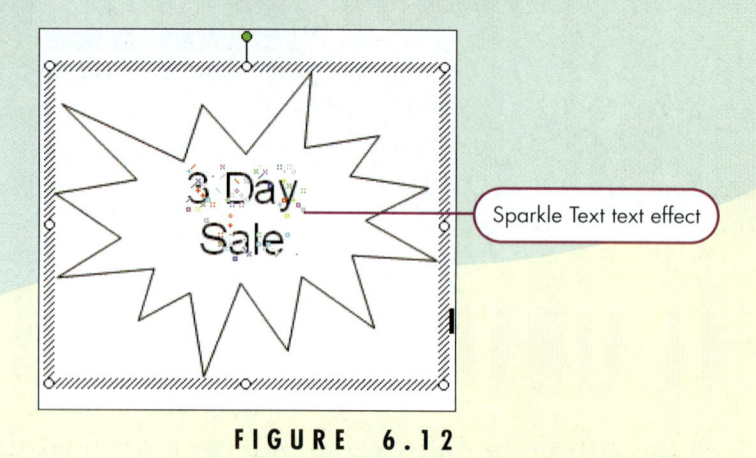

Sparkle Text text effect

FIGURE 6.12

7 Save the *Playground_Sale* document, and keep it onscreen to continue with the next lesson.

TO EXTEND YOUR KNOWLEDGE...

CREATING A TEXT BOX

You can create a *text box,* a free-standing shape specifically designed to display text. To create a text box, click Text Box on the Drawing toolbar or choose Insert, Text Box, and then click and drag within the drawing canvas to create the text box.

ROTATING THE TEXT IN TEXT BOXES

In addition to the typical horizontal alignment (Left, Centered, Right, and Justify), you can rotate the text in a text box—so it is positioned "sideways"—by clicking Change Text Direction on the Text Box toolbar. The first time you click the button, the text turns to the right. When you click the button again, the text turns to the left. The third time you click the button, the text returns to its original position.

LESSON 4: Positioning Shapes

By default, Word inserts drawing shapes within the drawing canvas so you can easily control them. The shapes and the drawing canvas are inserted as **floating objects,** which means they are not anchored to a paragraph mark but can be positioned anywhere on a page, overlapping each other as well as overlapping document text.

You can easily move the drawing canvas by dragging it to a new location. All shapes contained within the drawing canvas are moved with it. You can also move a shape that is not contained within a drawing canvas.

In this lesson, you adjust the position of the shapes.

Lesson 4 Positioning Shapes   215   LEVEL 2

To Position Shapes

1 In the *Playground_Sale* document, select the frame for the star shape.
The insertion point disappears, and the star shape is selected.

2 **Click and drag the star shape down so that the top of the star shape's frame is aligned with the top of the curved line that connects to the round balloon.**
You may need to adjust the position of the other objects. Do this by clicking and dragging the objects where you want them. Use Figure 6.13 as a guide for adjusting the positions of the shapes.

FIGURE 6.13

3 **Click an object and drag it into place, if necessary.**
Sometimes clicking and dragging moves an object too far from where you want it, so in those instances you need to use the arrow keys on the keyboard to position the shapes.

4 **Click an object and press ←, →, ↑, or ↓ to adjust its position, if necessary.**
If using the arrow keys still does not perfectly adjust the position of an object, you can use Ctrl with the arrow keys to micro-position the shapes.

5 **Click an object and press Ctrl while pressing an arrow key to micro-position the object, if needed.**
Because the text became part of the shape when it was created, it moves with the explosion object. Keep repositioning objects until your document looks similar to Figure 6.13.

6 **Save the *Playground_Sale* document, and keep it onscreen to continue with the next lesson.**

TO EXTEND YOUR KNOWLEDGE...

ROTATING AND FLIPPING SHAPES

You can easily rotate or flip shapes automatically. Select a shape, click Draw on the Drawing toolbar, and then choose *Rotate or Flip*. Click the desired menu option to reposition the shape.

To manually rotate a shape, you use the Free Rotate tool. The **Free Rotate tool** is a green-filled circle above the center handle of each shape you create (see Figure 6.14). When you position the mouse pointer over the green circle, it changes to a circular arrow. The mouse pointer changes to four circular arrows as you click the shape. Drag the pointer to rotate the shape.

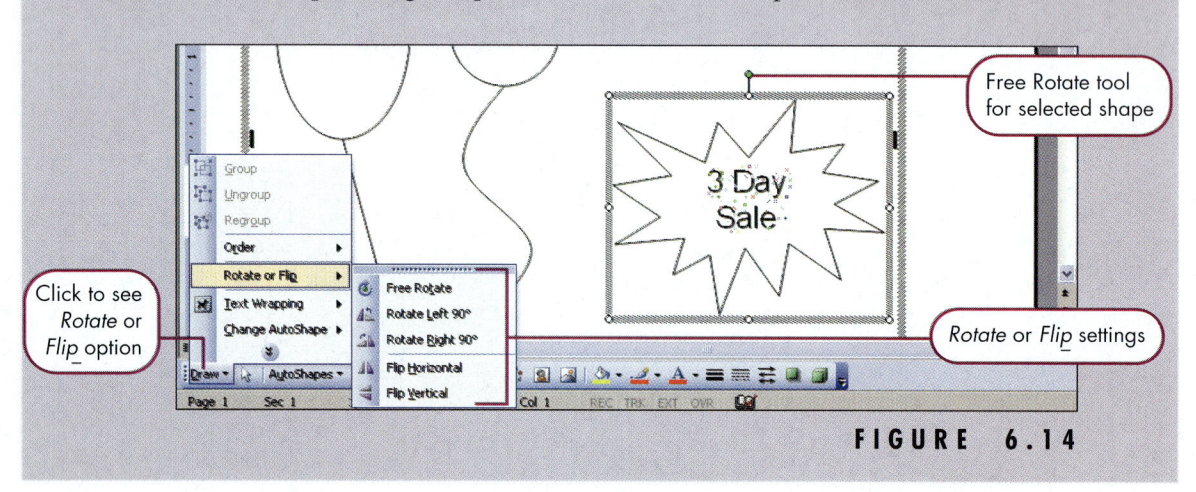

FIGURE 6.14

LESSON 5: Formatting Shapes and Lines

You can enhance the appearance of shapes by using the formatting tools on the Drawing toolbar. You can add color or fill effects as well as change the line style, dash style, and arrow style. You can even apply a three-dimensional effect or a shadow. Drawing shapes have two main components that can contain color: the line or border and the fill (the interior space of the object). Although lines obviously do not contain an interior area for applying a fill color, you can change the color of the line itself.

In this lesson, you format shapes within your advertising flyer.

Lesson 5 Formatting Shapes and Lines   217   LEVEL 2

To Format Shapes and Lines

1 In the *Playground_Sale* document, click the oval balloon shape to select it.

2 Click the Fill Color drop-down arrow on the Drawing toolbar and then click Blue on the Fill Color palette.
The interior of the balloon shape is filled with the Blue fill color.

3 Select the round balloon shape in the *Playground_Sale* document, click the Fill Color drop-down arrow, and choose Yellow on the color palette.
The interior of the round balloon shape is filled with the Yellow fill color.

4 Select the two line shapes connected to the balloons, click the Line Color drop-down arrow on the Drawing toolbar, and choose Red on the Line Color palette.
Both the straight line and the curved line shapes are red.

5 Click the explosion shape to select it, click Line Style on the Drawing toolbar, and choose the solid *6 pt* option on the menu.
Word increases the width of the line used to draw the explosion shape.

6 Click Line Color on the Drawing toolbar.
Because you selected Red line color in step 4, Red is the default line color. This is why you could just click the Line Color button here without displaying the palette. Word changes the explosion border line to red.

7 With the explosion object still selected, click Shadow Style on the Drawing toolbar.
The Shadow Style palette appears (see Figure 6.15).

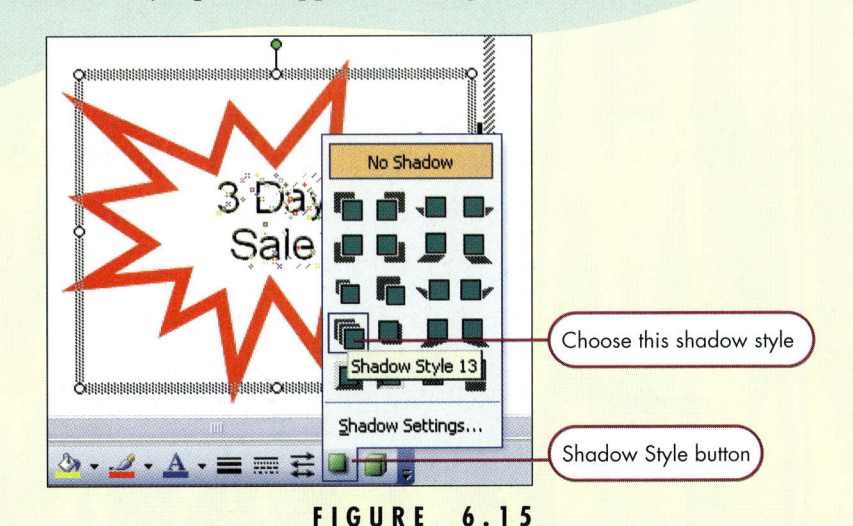

FIGURE 6.15

8 Choose Shadow Style 13 on the palette.
Word adds the Shadow Style 13 style to the explosion shape. You can apply either a shadow or a 3-D effect to a shape, but you cannot apply both.

9 Save the *Playground_Sale* document, and keep it onscreen to continue with the next lesson.

TO EXTEND YOUR KNOWLEDGE...

APPLYING COLORS AND EFFECTS

In addition to applying color, you can also apply fill effects to your shapes. Select a shape, click the Fill Color drop-down arrow, and select Fill Effects. Select one of the tabs in the Fill Effects dialog box, such as Gradient, Texture, Pattern, or Picture. Choose the fill effect options and click OK.

LESSON 6: Layering and Grouping Shapes

When you create shapes, clip art, images, or other objects that overlap existing shapes, Word places one shape on top of an existing shape through a process called *layering.* This process is similar to working on a project on a desk: You pick up a piece of paper and place it on top of another piece. At any time, you can rearrange the order of the papers or add to the stack of papers on your desk.

As you work with shapes in Word, you can bring a shape to the front by one layer, push a shape back by one layer, move a shape to the front of all layers, or push a shape to the back of all layers.

When you work with several shapes, you might need to group them. *Grouping* is the process of treating selected objects as a single object, which means you can move and format them as one group.

In this lesson, you change the layering of the balloons and group the balloon and string shapes.

To Layer and Group Shapes

1. In the *Playground_Sale* document, select the drawing canvas.

2. Draw another oval balloon shape (wider than it is tall) between the existing two balloon shapes. Apply the Violet fill color to the shape. Create a straight line red string shape.
   The new balloon shape is drawn on the top layer, in front of the existing balloon shapes, as shown in Figure 6.16.

Lesson 6 Layering and Grouping Shapes   219   LEVEL 2

FIGURE 6.16

3 **Click the yellow balloon shape to select it.**
Depending on the size of the balloon shapes, two or three sizing handles appear inside the violet balloon, indicating that an object (the yellow balloon) is located behind it.

4 **Click Draw on the Drawing toolbar and choose Order.**
Figure 6.17 shows the Order menu, which lists the methods for layering the current object.

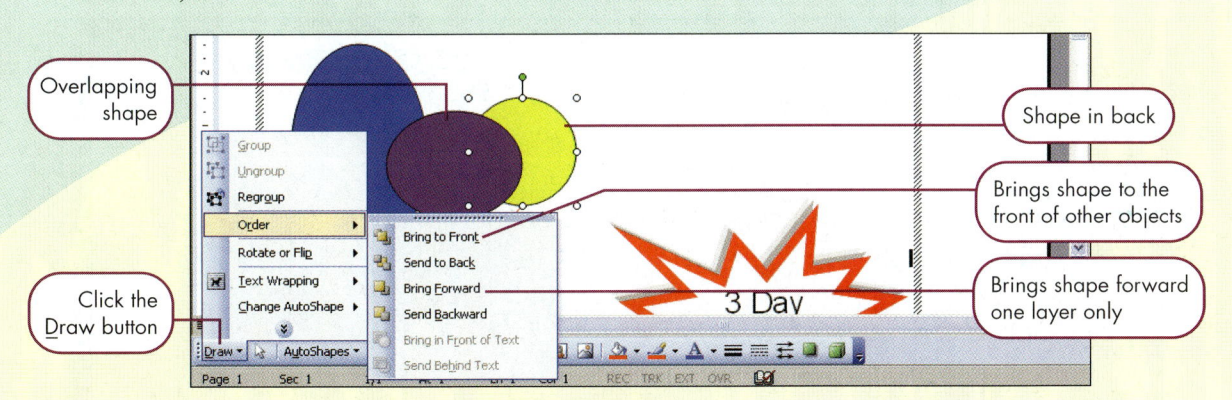

FIGURE 6.17

5 **Choose *Bring to Front*.**
Word brings the yellow balloon to the front of the violet balloon.

6 **With the yellow balloon still selected, hold down ⇧Shift and click the other two balloon shapes and each balloon line string, one at a time.**
Holding down ⇧Shift as you click the shapes selects them, with each one surrounded by its own object handles (see Figure 6.18).

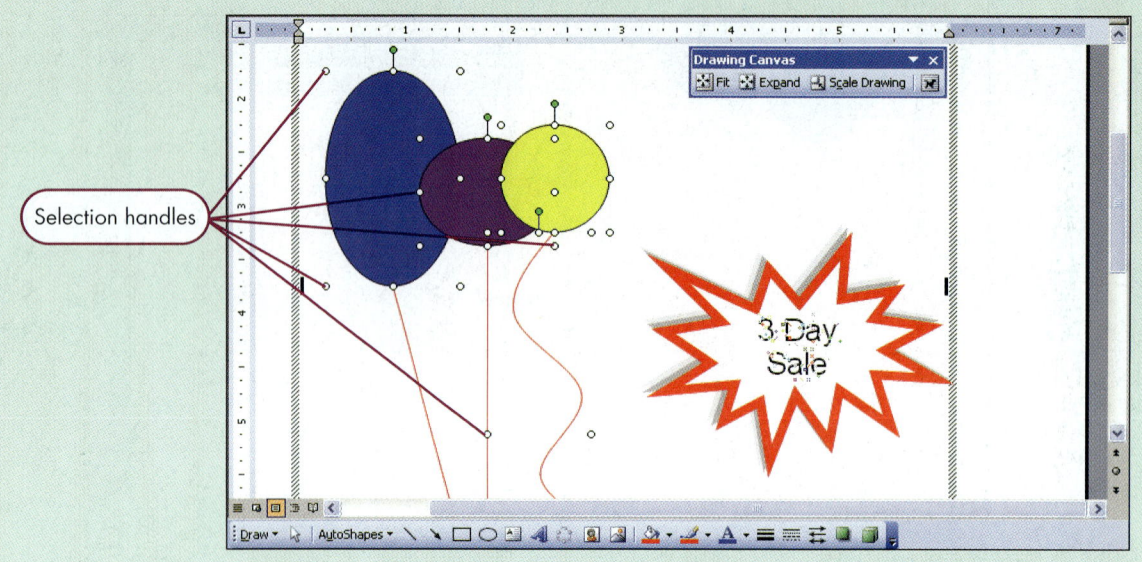

Project 6 Using Drawing Tools and Special Effects

FIGURE 6.18

7 **Click Draw on the Drawing toolbar and then choose Group from the menu.**
Word groups the objects together, making it possible to format or move all of the shapes as a single shape. Notice that there is now only one set of selection handles.

8 **Click the Fill Color drop-down arrow, and select Red on the color palette.**
Word applies the fill color to all objects, including the surface area of the curved line (see Figure 6.19).

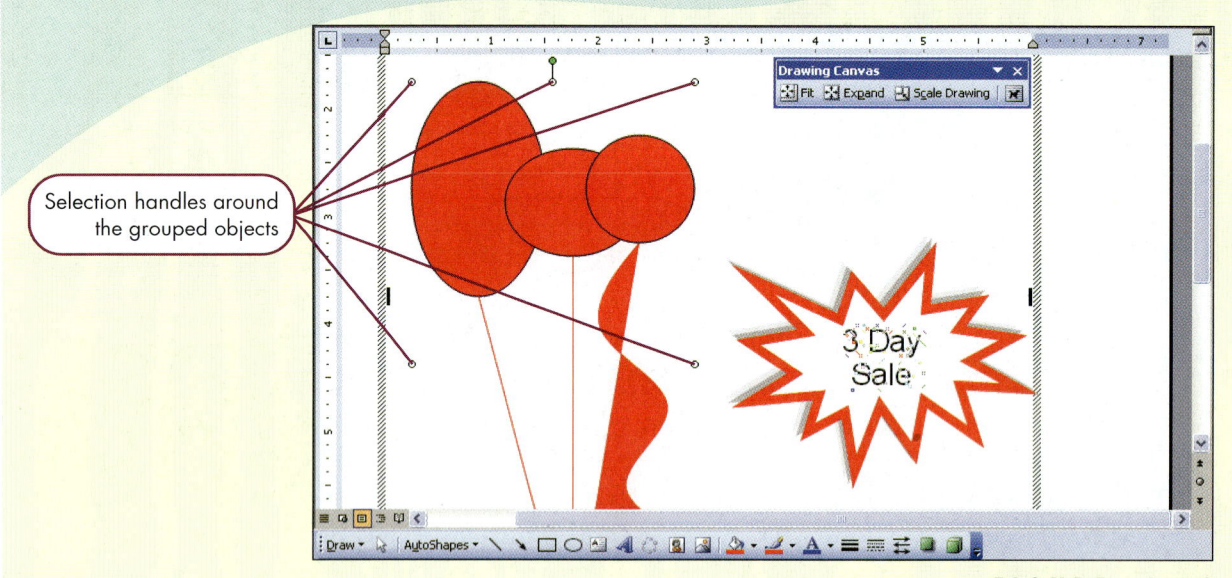

FIGURE 6.19

9 **Click Undo on the Standard toolbar.**
Word changes the shapes back to their original colors.

10 **Click and drag the grouped object to the right about ½".**

11 **Save, print (optional), and close the *Playground_Sale* document.**

TO EXTEND YOUR KNOWLEDGE...

SELECTING OBJECTS

When you want to select multiple objects, you should select the interior objects first. You can then press ⇧Shift to select the outer objects. If you select the outer object first, you might find selecting the interior object to be impossible.

Another method for selecting multiple objects is to click Select Objects on the Drawing toolbar, and drag a selection rectangle around the objects you want to select.

UNGROUPING AND REGROUPING OBJECTS

You can separate grouped objects by *ungrouping* them. If you need to ungroup objects to format one object, click the grouped objects, click Draw, and choose Ungroup.

Word remembers how you grouped the objects. To group the objects back again, select one of the objects that was originally grouped, click Draw, and choose Regroup. *Regrouping* is the process of grouping objects back together again.

SUMMARY

In this project, you learned how to enhance your documents with visual elements. You learned to draw shapes and format their color and style. You learned to insert text in AutoShapes and apply a text effect, such as Sparkle Text. You positioned the shapes by dragging them to a particular location and by using the arrow keys on the keyboard. Furthermore, you learned how to layer objects by bringing one shape in front of the other. Finally, you grouped several shapes together to treat them as a single object in order to format it.

You can extend your learning by reviewing concepts and terms, and by practicing variations of skills presented in the lessons. Use the following table as a guide to the numbered questions and exercises in the end-of-project learning opportunities.

LESSON	MULTIPLE CHOICE	DISCUSSION	SKILL DRILL	CHALLENGE	DISCOVERY ZONE
Drawing and Sizing Shapes	1, 4, 5, 10	1, 2	1	1, 2, 3, 4, 5	1, 2
Drawing Lines	8		2	2, 4, 5	
Inserting Text with a Text Effect	6, 9		3	1, 3, 5	2
Positioning Shapes	3		5	1, 2, 3, 5	1, 2
Formatting Shapes and Lines	5, 10		4	1, 2, 3, 4, 5	1, 2
Layering and Grouping Shapes	2, 7	3	5	1, 3, 4	1, 2

KEY TERMS

anchor	Drawing toolbar	layering
arrow style	floating objects	regrouping
AutoShapes	flowchart	scribble line
connector lines	Free Rotate tool	text effect
curved line	grouping	ungrouping
drawing canvas		

CHECKING CONCEPTS AND TERMS

MULTIPLE CHOICE

Circle the letter of the correct answer for each of the following.

1. Which term refers to the place you click and start dragging to create an object? [L1]
   a. Object handle
   b. Resizing handle
   c. Attachment point
   d. Anchor

2. To work with several shapes or objects as one object, you must _____ them. [L6]
   a. position
   b. group
   c. anchor
   d. layer

3. To reposition a selected shape by the smallest possible distance to the right, you need to _____. [L4]
   a. click and drag the shape where you want it
   b. press →
   c. cut the shape, move the insertion point, and paste the shape
   d. press Ctrl+→

4. Which of the following methods does not resize the drawing canvas? [L1]
   a. Drag a resize handle on the drawing canvas frame.
   b. Select the drawing canvas and press Esc.
   c. Click the Fit Drawing To Contents button on the Drawing Canvas toolbar.
   d. Click the Expand Drawing button on the Drawing Canvas toolbar.

5. Click _____ to apply a color to the inside of an oval or rectangular shape. [L1, L5]
   a.
   b.
   c.
   d.

6. Which of the following is a text effect animation? [L3]
   a. Highlight
   b. Layering
   c. Blinking Background
   d. 3-D Style 14

7. What term refers to placing objects in a certain order on top of each other? [L6]
   a. Rotating
   b. Layering
   c. Grouping
   d. Ungrouping

8. After drawing a curved line shape, how do you end it? [L2]
   a. Press [Break]
   b. Single-click
   c. Click the Line button on the Drawing toolbar
   d. Click and then press [Esc]

9. You can right-click all of the following shapes except _____, and choose Add Text. [L3]
   a. a curved line
   b. an oval
   c. a circle
   d. a star AutoShape

10. All of the following are buttons that help you format a line, except which one? [L1, L5]
    a.
    b.
    c.
    d.

DISCUSSION

1. What are the advantages of placing drawing objects on the drawing canvas? [L1]
2. Explore the AutoShapes menu palettes and describe when you would use at least three different types of shapes. [L1]
3. What is the purpose of grouping objects together? [L6]

SKILL DRILL

Skill Drill exercises reinforce project skills. Each skill reinforced is the same, or nearly the same, as a skill presented in the project. Detailed instructions are provided in a step-by-step format.

Work through the exercises in sequential order. Be sure to save your changes and close the document if you need more than one work session to complete the desired exercises. Continue working on *Ergonomics_Flyer* instead of starting over in the original *EW2_0602* file. After you complete all of the exercises, print a copy of the document (optional). Figure 6.20 shows the completed document.

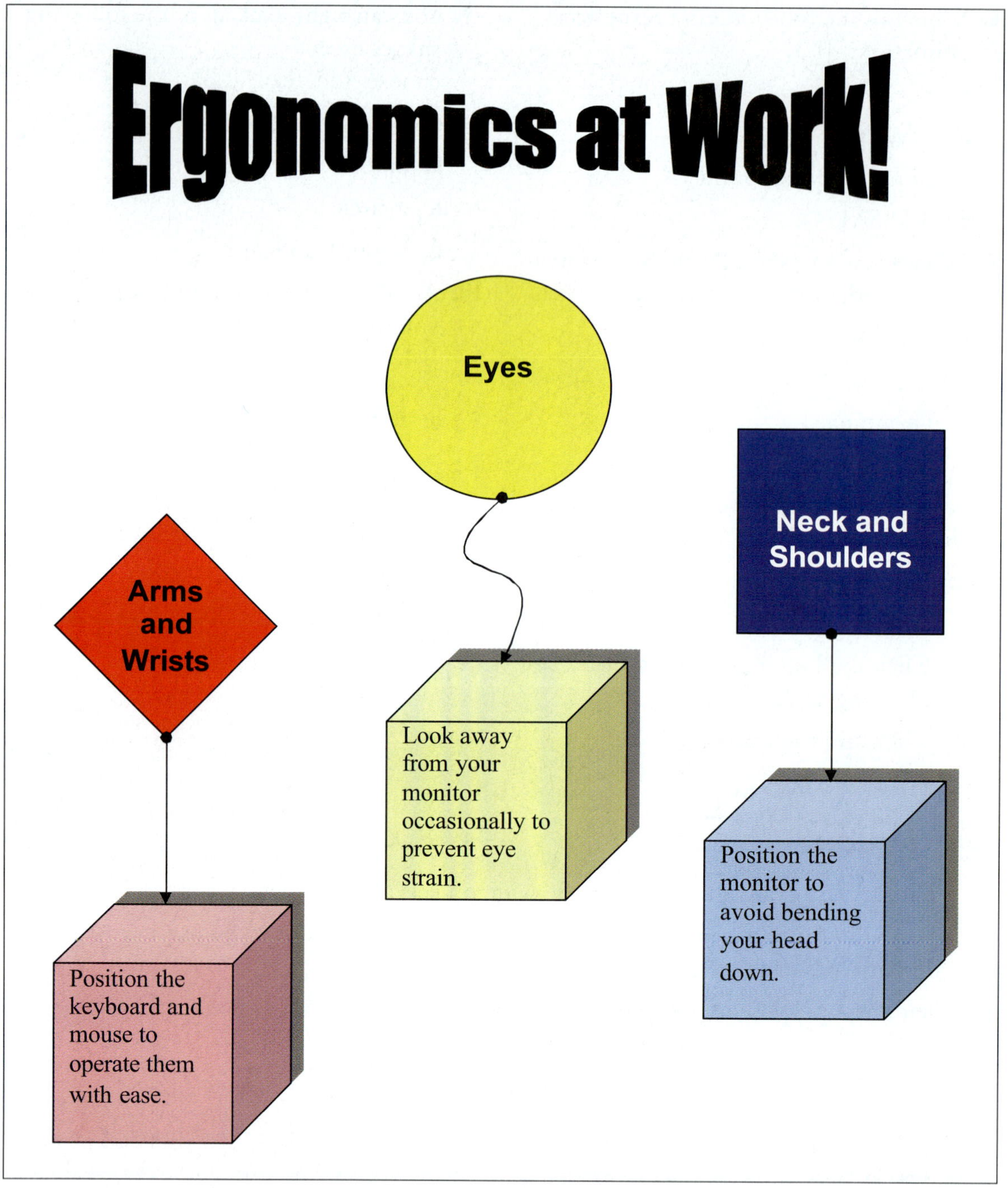

Ergonomics at Work!

Eyes

Arms and Wrists

Neck and Shoulders

Look away from your monitor occasionally to prevent eye strain.

Position the keyboard and mouse to operate them with ease.

Position the monitor to avoid bending your head down.

FIGURE 6.20

1. Drawing and Sizing Shapes

As a member of the Human Resources department at your company, you are involved in company health issues. You decide to create a flyer to educate employees about ergonomic issues. Your first task is to create diamond, circle, and square shapes.

1. Open *EW2_0602* and save it as `Ergonomics_Flyer`.
2. Display the Drawing toolbar, if necessary.

3. Draw a diamond by completing the following steps:
   a. Click AutoShapes, choose Basic Shapes, and then select the Diamond.
   b. Press and hold down [Shift].
   c. Starting below the WordArt object at the left inside edge of the drawing canvas, click and drag down and to the right about 1½" in each direction.
   d. Release [Shift].
4. Draw a circle by completing the following steps:
   a. Click Oval on the Drawing toolbar.
   b. Press and hold down [Shift].
   c. About ¾" to the right of the diamond, click and drag down and to the right about 1½" in each direction.
   d. Release [Shift].
5. Click Rectangle on the Drawing toolbar. Repeat steps 4b–4d to create a 1½" square to the right of the circle.
6. Adjust the size of each shape individually by doing the following:
   a. Right-click the shape and choose Format AutoShape.
   b. Click the Size tab.
   c. Set the height at 1.5", click the *Lock aspect ratio* check box, and click OK.
7. Click and drag the bottom of the drawing canvas frame down about 3".
8. Create a cube shape by completing the following steps:
   a. Click AutoShapes, choose Basic Shapes, and then select the Cube.
   b. Press and hold down [Shift].
   c. About 1" below the diamond, click and drag down and to the right about 1½".
   d. Release [Shift].
9. With the cube shape still selected, repeat steps 6a–6c, except set the height and width at 1.6" each.
10. With the cube shape still selected, press and hold down [Ctrl], and drag the cube to the right to copy it below the circle. Release the mouse button. Then copy another cube to the right below the square.
11. Save the *Ergonomics_Flyer* document.

2. Drawing Directional Lines

You want to insert line shapes between the first row of shapes and the cube shapes to guide the employees' eyes to further information. You decide to use straight line shapes to connect the diamond to the cube and to connect the square to the cube. You plan to draw a curved line to connect the circle to the middle cube.

1. In the *Ergonomics_Flyer* document, make sure the drawing canvas is selected.
2. Select the first cube to see the selection handles (circles).
3. Draw a line from the diamond to the cube by doing the following:

a. Click Line on the Drawing toolbar.

b. Click at the bottom point of the diamond.

c. Drag straight down to the top-middle selection handle (circle) on the left cube shape.

The line should connect the diamond and the cube; there should be no space between the line and the shapes. If so, open the Format AutoShapes dialog box for the line, and adjust its height, or click the cube and press `Ctrl`+`↑`.

4. Draw a line down from the square to the right cube by adapting steps 3a–3c as needed.

5. Draw a curved line from the circle to the middle cube by doing the following:

    a. Select the middle cube shape to display its selection handles (circles).

    b. Click AutoShapes on the Drawing toolbar.

    c. Choose Lines and select Curve on the palette.

    d. Starting at the bottom-center of the circle, click and drag down and to the left $1/3''$, and click to set an anchor.

    e. Click and drag to the right and down another $1/3''$ and click to set an anchor.

    f. Click and drag to the middle selection handle (circle) of the middle cube shape, and then press `Esc` to end the curved line.

    g. If necessary, use `Ctrl`+`↑` to move the cube up, or use the Format AutoShape dialog box to adjust the height of the curved line shape.

6. Save the *Ergonomics_Flyer* document.

3. Adding Text to AutoShapes

You need to identify the parts of the body that relate to ergonomics. To do this you need to insert text within the six AutoShapes.

1. In the *Ergonomics_Flyer* document, select the diamond shape.

2. Insert text into the diamond shape by doing the following:

    a. Right-click the diamond shape and choose Add Text from the shortcut menu.

    b. Apply Arial font, 14-point size, bold, and Center horizontal alignment.

    c. Type **Arms and Wrists**.

3. Insert text into the circle shape by doing the following:

    a. Right-click the circle shape and choose Add Text.

    b. Apply the same formats specified in step 2b, press `Enter`, and type **Eyes**.

4. Insert text into the square shape by doing the following:

    a. Right-click the square shape and choose Add Text.

    b. Apply the same formats specified in step 2b, press `Enter` twice, and type **Neck and Shoulders**.

5. Insert text into the first cube shape by doing the following:

    a. Right-click the first cube shape and choose Add Text.

    b. Type **Position the keyboard and mouse to operate them with ease.**

6. Insert the following text into the second cube shape: **Look away from your monitor occasionally to prevent eye strain.**

7. Insert the following text into the third cube shape: `Position the monitor to avoid bending your head down.`

8. Save the *Ergonomics_Flyer* document.

4. Formatting the Shapes within the Flyer

To call attention to the flyer and make it more attractive, you decide to apply vivid, primary fill colors for the AutoShapes. You also plan to use the formatting tools on the Drawing toolbar to format the line shapes.

1. In the *Ergonomics_Flyer* document, click outside any shape to deselect it, and then select the drawing canvas frame.
2. Select the diamond shape and format it by doing the following:
    a. Click the Fill Color drop-down arrow.
    b. Select Red from the palette.
3. Adapt steps 2a and 2b to do the following:
    a. Apply Yellow fill color to the circle shape.
    b. Apply Blue fill color to the square shape.
    c. Apply Rose fill color to the first cube shape.
    d. Apply Light Yellow fill color to the second cube shape.
    e. Apply Pale Blue fill color to the third cube shape.
4. Select the first line shape—the line below the diamond shape—then click Arrow Style on the Drawing toolbar, and choose Arrow Style 9.
5. Repeat step 4 to format the other two line shapes.
6. Using the Shift key, select the three cube shapes. Click Shadow Style on the Drawing toolbar, and choose Shadow Style 2.
7. Save the *Ergonomics_Flyer* document.

5. Grouping and Positioning Shapes

As you examine the flyer, you notice that it seems to have a boxy, symmetrical look. You decide to reposition the shapes so that the flyer conveys a more informal, asymmetrical look. You decide to stagger the three columns of shapes. Before you move any of the shapes, you want to group related shapes together to make sure they move as a group instead of as individual shapes.

1. In the *Ergonomics_Flyer* document, click outside the drawing canvas to deselect all shapes.
2. Select the drawing canvas and drag the bottom-middle selection handle down about 2".
3. Group the first column of shapes down by doing the following:
    a. Select the diamond shape.
    b. Hold down Shift.
    c. Click the line shape and then click the first cube shape.
    d. Release Shift.

You should have three shapes selected with handles surrounding each shape.

    e. Right-click the selected shapes and choose <u>G</u>rouping, and choose <u>G</u>roup.

4. Adapt steps 3a–3e to group the second column of shapes together.

5. Adapt steps 3a–3e to group the third column of shapes together.

6. Select the first column of grouped shapes, and drag the grouped shapes down approximately 2″ (see Figure 6.20 for positioning).

7. Select the third column of grouped shapes, and drag the grouped shapes down about 1″.

8. Save, print (optional), and close the *Ergonomics_Flyer* document.

CHALLENGE

Challenge exercises expand on or are somewhat related to skills presented in the lessons. Each exercise provides a brief narrative introduction, followed by instructions in a numbered-step format that are not as detailed as those in the Skill Drill exercises. You can work through one or more exercises in any order.

1. Creating a Back-to-School Flyer

You want to create a back-to-school flyer for a school. You plan to draw a banner shape with text, insert some academic clip art, and insert several WordArt objects. After inserting shapes and objects, you layer and group them. Figure 6.21 shows the completed flyer.

1. Open *EW2_0603* and save it as `School_Flyer`.

2. Without using the drawing canvas, insert an AutoShape at the top of the document with these specifications:

    a. Horizontal Scroll shape from the Stars and Banners palette

    b. 1.75″ height and 5.75″ width

    c. *In front of text* wrapping setting

    d. Center horizontal alignment

    e. Parchment texture fill effect

    f. `Back to School` text in Comic Sans font, 52-point size, Brown font color, and Center horizontal alignment

3. Insert the clip art image shown in Figure 6.21. Search for `school supplies` or `academics` to find the image. Set a 3.5″ width, Square text wrapping setting, and Center horizontal alignment.

4. Create the five WordArt objects with the text shown in Figure 6.21. Apply these WordArt formats:

    a. Square text wrapping style to all WordArt objects

    b. WordArt objects positioned in relation to the clip art image

    c. Shadow Style 5 to the *Reading* WordArt object

    d. Free rotation and Deflate shape for the *History* WordArt object

FIGURE 6.21

e. Layering settings to place *Reading, Math,* and *English* behind the clip art image
f. Layering settings to place *Spelling* and *History* in front of the clip art image
5. Group the clip art image and the five WordArt images.
6. Insert hard returns, as needed, to make sure the last line of text appears below the grouped objects. Make sure the flyer fits on only one page.
7. Save, print (optional), and close the *School_Flyer* document.

Project 6 Using Drawing Tools and Special Effects

2. Drawing a House

You need to draw a house to use as an illustration in a short story that your friend wrote. Listed below are guidelines for drawing the house. Use your imagination and any drawing tools to create the house. Remember to increase the magnification of your screen when working with small objects. Figure 6.22 shows a sample completed document. Your document may differ.

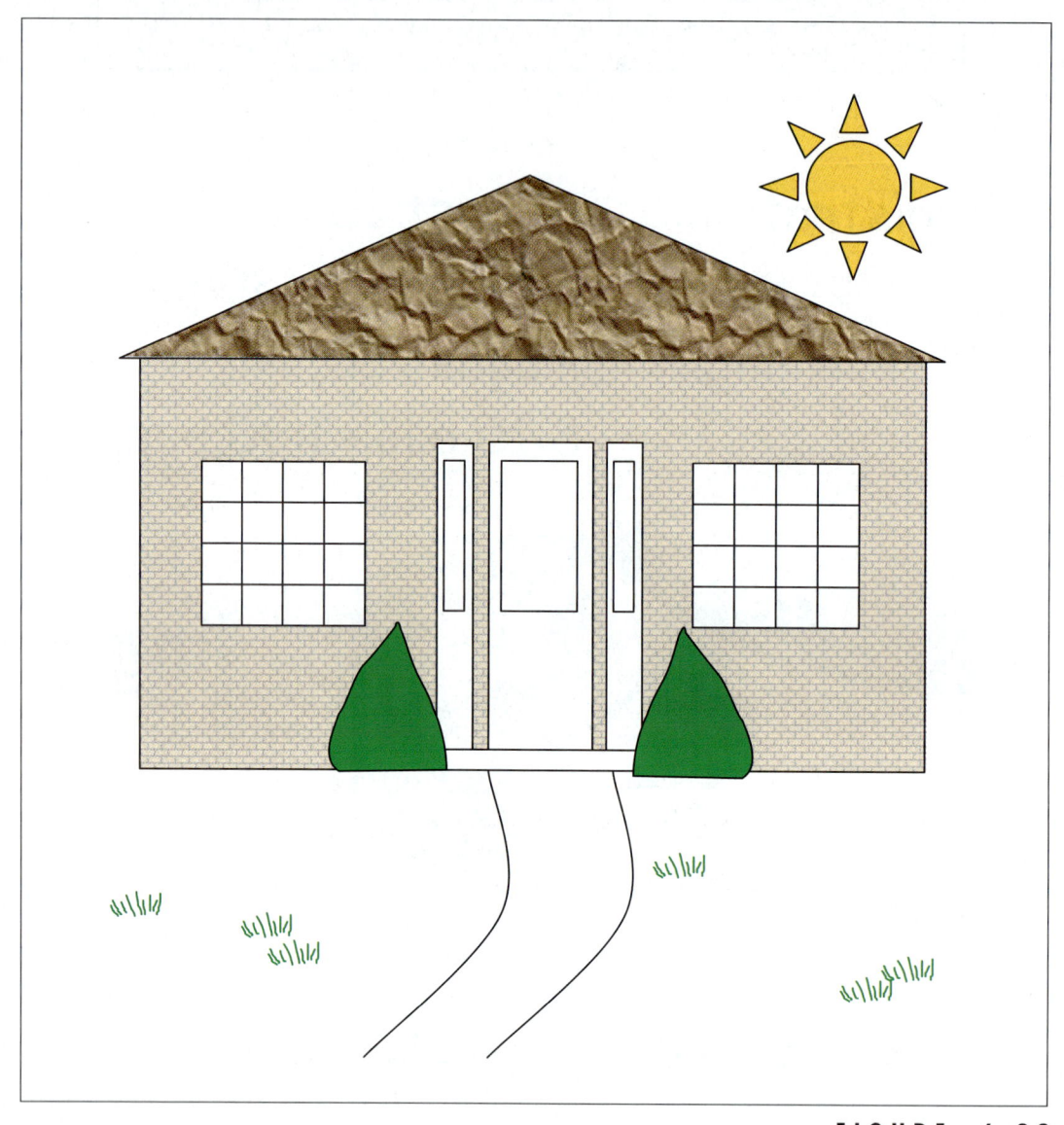

FIGURE 6.22

1. Open a new document and then save it as **House_Drawing**.
2. Create the house, front door, and windows by drawing rectangle and square shapes.
3. Use the Flowchart: Extract AutoShape for the roof.
4. Draw line shapes for windowpanes and sidewalks.
5. Use the Scribble line tool to draw grass around the house.
6. Use the Freeform line tool to add bushes or trees. (You can apply fill color to Freeform drawings.)

7. Draw a shape of the sun and position it in an appropriate location.
8. Apply appropriate fill colors to each shape.
9. Save, print (optional), and close the *House_Drawing* document.

3. Grouping Shapes and Inserting a Text Box

You need to finish a flyer to distribute at the Chamber of Commerce, advertising an Internet flower service. The flyer contains several shapes, but you need to layer, group, and reposition them. You also need to add a text box listing this month's specials.

1. Open *EW2_0604* and save the document as **Flower_Flyer**.
2. Change the order of the objects by bringing each flower shape in front of its stem shape.
3. Group each flower with its own stem.
4. Reposition the flowers so they appear to grow from the period in the WordArt title. They should appear as a bunch with the stems overlapping. You need to rotate them. Use Help, if needed, to learn how to rotate shapes. Move the dark flower shape between the other two shapes, and flip the shape horizontally.
5. Add a small ribbon to the bunched flowers, using the Up Ribbon AutoShape. Apply the Pink fill color to the ribbon.
6. Insert a text box above and to the left of the flowers, about 1³/₄" high and 4" wide, with these specifications:
    a. Type the heading **This Month's Specials** and then press ⏎Enter twice.
    b. On the next line, create a bulleted list with the default black round bullet symbol.
    c. Type **Dozen Roses for $16.99** and press ⏎Enter.
    d. Type **Dozen Tulips for $14.50**.
    e. Apply Arial font, 22-point size, bold, and Center horizontal alignment to the first line in the text box.
    f. Apply Arial font, 18-point size, and bold to the bulleted list.
    g. Apply Red font color to the word *Roses*, and apply Violet font color to the word *Tulips*.
    h. Apply the Blinking Background text effect to *$16.99*.
    i. Apply the Marching Red Ants text effect to *$14.50*.
    j. Adjust the height and width of the text box as needed.
7. Insert a WordArt object at the beginning of the document with these specifications:
    a. Use the same WordArt gallery style as the WordArt object style at the bottom of the document.
    b. Type **Beautiful Flowers** on two different lines.
    c. Apply Square text wrapping style and Center horizontal alignment.
    d. Set a **5.5"** width for the WordArt object.
8. Save, print (optional), and close the *Flower_Flyer* document.

4. Drawing and Formatting Boxes and Arrows

You and several friends want to open your own business. You have scheduled a meeting to discuss how to get started. You created an overhead transparency for the meeting that shows the first four phases of the business plan. It looks bland, however, and you want to add some boxes and arrows. After inserting the shapes, you need to change the layer to display text on top of the shapes.

1. Open *EW2_0605* and save the document as **Business_Plan**.
2. Use the Rectangle tool to draw boxes around each of the text items, except for the WordArt title. Because the text has already been created, you need to press Esc to eliminate the drawing canvas before you begin dragging the rectangles.
3. Apply these formats to all boxes:
    a. Change the order of the shapes to appear behind the text.
    b. Apply a 3-point double line style for the rectangle shapes.
4. Apply these formats to the respective rectangle shapes:
    a. Apply Yellow fill color and Light Yellow fill color, respectively, to the rectangle shapes on the first row.
    b. Apply Blue fill color and Pale Blue fill color, respectively, to the rectangle shapes on the second row.
    c. Apply Green fill color and Light Green fill color, respectively, to the rectangle shapes on the third row.
    d. Apply Violet fill color and Lavender fill color, respectively, to the rectangle shapes on the fourth row.
5. Draw an arrow from each phase box to the corresponding description, and apply these formats:
    a. Change the line style of each arrow to 1½ points.
    b. Apply Red line color to all of the line shapes.
6. Save, print (optional), and close the *Business_Plan* document.

5. Creating a Flowchart with Shapes

As a programming instructor at a college, you are preparing your lesson on IF statements. You want to use a common example of calculating weekly pay: If an employee works 40 or fewer hours, multiply the regular pay rate by the number of hours worked; otherwise, calculate the maximum weekly pay, determine the number of overtime hours, calculate the overtime pay rate, calculate the overtime pay, and calculate the gross pay. You decide to create a flowchart using shapes in Word. Figure 6.23 shows the final document.

1. In a new document window, use Help to learn about flowchart shapes and connector lines. Pay close attention to the Help window on attaching connector lines to shapes.
2. Set 0.75" top and bottom margins, select Legal paper size, and save the document as **Weekly_Pay_Flowchart**.
3. Type the text **Calculating Weekly Pay** and apply the Title style to the text.
4. Insert the first shape—Terminator—within the drawing canvas and add its text.

Challenge

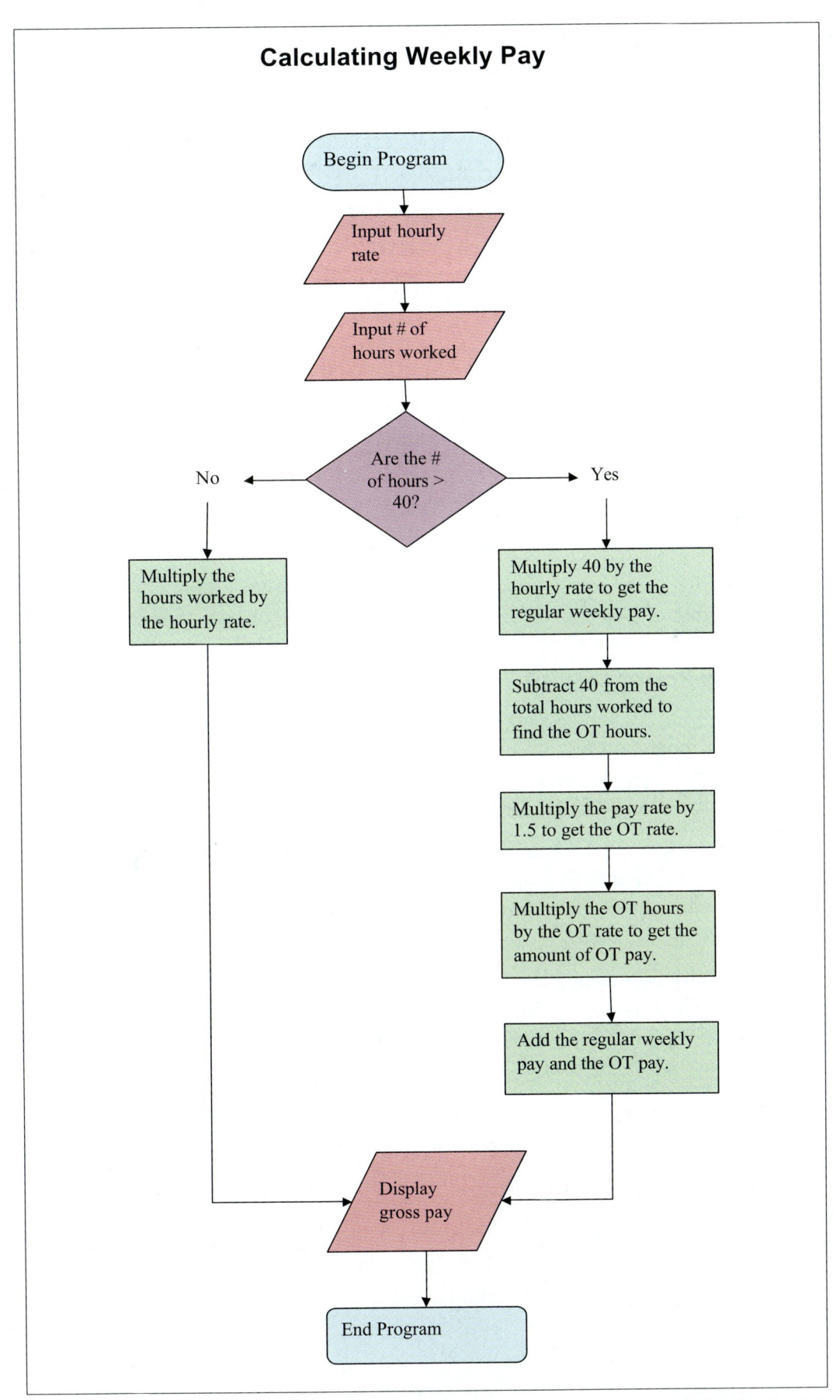

Calculating Weekly Pay

```
Begin Program
   ↓
Input hourly rate
   ↓
Input # of hours worked
   ↓
Are the # of hours > 40?
   ├── No ──→ Multiply the hours worked by the hourly rate. ──→ Display gross pay
   └── Yes ─→ Multiply 40 by the hourly rate to get the regular weekly pay.
              ↓
              Subtract 40 from the total hours worked to find the OT hours.
              ↓
              Multiply the pay rate by 1.5 to get the OT rate.
              ↓
              Multiply the OT hours by the OT rate to get the amount of OT pay.
              ↓
              Add the regular weekly pay and the OT pay.
              ↓
              Display gross pay
                 ↓
              End Program
```

FIGURE 6.23

Project 6   Using Drawing Tools and Special Effects

5. Increase the drawing canvas to the bottom of the page.
6. Insert the Data, Decision, and Process flowchart shapes, as well as the final Terminator shape; then add text, and position the shapes.
7. Insert connector lines between the flowchart shapes based on what you learned from the Help windows.
8. Adjust the shape positions and sizes as needed.
9. Apply these color schemes to the shapes:
   a. Light Turquoise for Terminator shapes
   b. Rose for Data shapes
   c. Lavender for the Decision shape
   d. Light Green for Process shapes
10. Save, print (optional), and close the *Weekly_Pay_Flowchart* document.

DISCOVERY ZONE

Discovery Zone exercises require advanced knowledge of topics presented in the lessons or self-directed learning of new skills. You can work through one or more exercises in any order.

1. Creating a Room Layout

You received a promotion and, as part of the benefits, you move from a cubicle to an individual office. Furthermore, you receive an allowance to furnish your new office. Before purchasing furniture, however, you want to experiment with different arrangements of furniture. Save a new blank document as **Office_Layout**.

You can use AutoShapes, More AutoShapes, to access additional drawing shapes that you can customize. When you choose this option, Word opens the Clip Art task pane that contains objects such as desks, chairs, computers, and folders. Using this option, create a room layout and apply appropriate fill colors.

If you have difficulty positioning the shapes exactly where you want them, use Help to learn about the grid and how to turn off the Snap Objects to Grid feature. Figure 6.24 shows a sample room layout. Save, print (optional), and close the *Office_Layout* document.

FIGURE 6.24

2. Creating a Workshop Flyer

You need to create a flyer advertising a workshop on conflict management sponsored by your organization. You want to insert a WordArt object, shapes, clip art, a bulleted list, and a paragraph border. Use Microsoft Help as a reference if you are unfamiliar with any of these features. Save a new document as **Conflict_Resolution**.

Create the flyer shown in Figure 6.25. Insert *Conflict Management* as a WordArt object, use any clip art image that represents *anger* or *fighting*, insert the Lightning Bolt shape, and group it to the clip art image. Use paragraph shading and font color to format the question. Type the bulleted list as shown in the figure. Insert a rectangle shape at the bottom of the document, add its text, apply a texture or gradient fill, and center the shape. Save, print (optional), and close the *Conflict_Resolution* document.

FIGURE 6.25

PROJECT 7
LEVEL 2

CREATING CHARTS AND DIAGRAMS

OBJECTIVES

IN THIS PROJECT, YOU LEARN HOW TO

- Create a chart
- Format a chart object
- Insert titles
- Format chart elements
- Import Excel data to create a chart in Word
- Create an organization chart
- Add positions to an organization chart
- Design diagrams

LEVEL 2   238   Project 7   Creating Charts and Diagrams

WHY WOULD I DO THIS?

Numerical data neatly arranged in a table or in tabular columns can be helpful for conveying values; however, numbers alone do not provide a great visual image. A *chart,* on the other hand, is a visual representation of numerical data that enhances the reader's understanding and comprehension of the values. People create charts to depict various numerical data, such as sales for a three-year period, number of passengers during different times of the day, departmental budgets, and so on.

In addition to creating charts, you can create diagrams. A *diagram* is a visual representation that illustrates relationships and processes. You can use Microsoft Word to create simple diagrams, such as an organization chart or a cycle diagram.

VISUAL SUMMARY

A chart consists of several different elements created from a table-like structure. Word converts the data from columns and rows into the visual chart. Figure 7.1 shows a chart depicting sales that you create in this project.

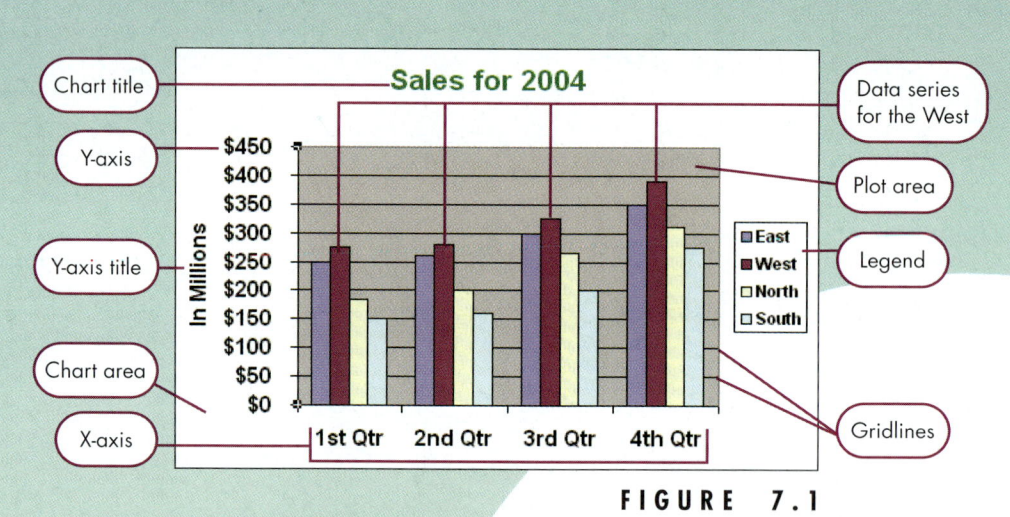

FIGURE 7.1

As you work through Lessons 1–5, you encounter a variety of chart-related terms. Table 7.1 lists and defines the components of a typical chart.

Visual Summary 239 LEVEL 2

TABLE 7.1

CHART ELEMENT	DESCRIPTION
Chart title	Brief description of contents of the chart.
Data series	A series of values depicting different components of a single category, such as the four quarterly sales values for the West in Figure 7.1.
Legend	A color-coded key that indicates what color represents a particular category. For example, dark blue represents the data series for the East in Figure 7.1.
Plot area	The area that contains (plots) the data points for all data series.
Chart area	The area that contains all chart elements.
X-axis	The horizontal axis located at the base of the chart. Typically displays categories such as time periods (months, quarters, decades) or locations (cities, states, nations).
Y-axis	The vertical axis along the left side of a two-dimensional chart. Typically displays values at consistent increments to help the reader determine relative values for the data series.
Y-axis title	A brief description of the Y-axis values.
Z-axis	The vertical axis along the left side of a three-dimensional chart. Similar purpose and appearance as the Y-axis.
Gridlines	Lines that guide the eye from the Y-axis values across the columns or bars to help the reader determine the relative value of each data marker.

In Lessons 6 and 7 you create and expand an organization chart. Figure 7.2 shows the results of your efforts—an organization chart illustrating, in a hierarchical structure, the three levels of management for an organization. In the last lesson in this project, you create a diagram.

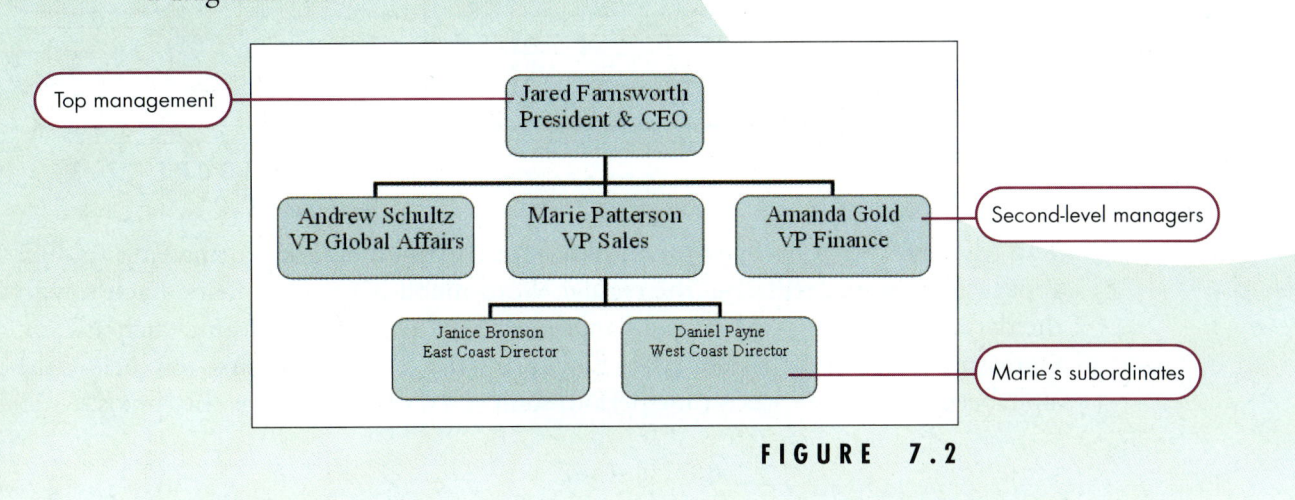

FIGURE 7.2

LEVEL 2 | **240** | Project 7 Creating Charts and Diagrams

LESSON 1: Creating a Chart

You can create a chart by using any of the following three methods: (1) entering data into the Microsoft Graph datasheet, (2) using an existing Word table, or (3) importing data from another program, such as Excel. *Microsoft Graph Chart,* an application that runs within Word, enables you to create and format a variety of charts, such as column charts or pie charts. You can create a Microsoft Graph chart by choosing Insert, Picture, Chart. Because a chart is an object within Word, you can also create a chart by choosing *Microsoft Graph Chart* from within the Create New tab of the Object dialog box.

In this lesson, you create a basic column chart with the Microsoft Graph Chart feature.

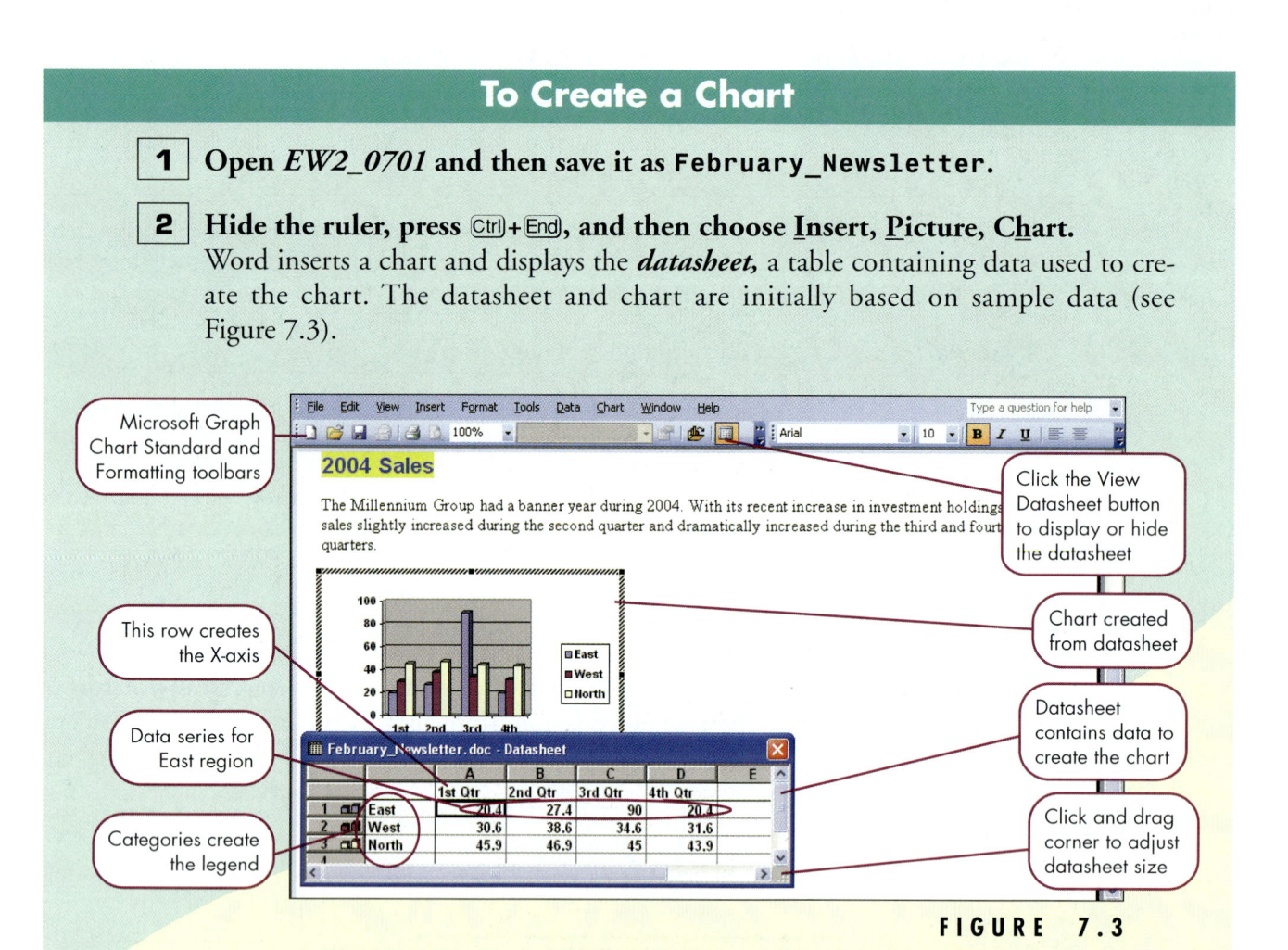

To Create a Chart

1 Open *EW2_0701* and then save it as `February_Newsletter`.

2 Hide the ruler, press Ctrl+End, and then choose Insert, Picture, Chart.
Word inserts a chart and displays the ***datasheet,*** a table containing data used to create the chart. The datasheet and chart are initially based on sample data (see Figure 7.3).

Callouts:
- Microsoft Graph Chart Standard and Formatting toolbars
- This row creates the X-axis
- Data series for East region
- Categories create the legend
- Click the View Datasheet button to display or hide the datasheet
- Chart created from datasheet
- Datasheet contains data to create the chart
- Click and drag corner to adjust datasheet size

FIGURE 7.3

The Microsoft Graph Chart menu bar, Standard toolbar, and Formatting toolbar appear, temporarily replacing the regular Word menu bar and toolbars. Each row in the datasheet, starting with 1, is a data series. Text in the first column, such as *East,* represents the name of a data series and forms the legend. The first row below the alphabetic letters indicates a time period, such as *1st Qtr,* and forms the X-axis.

Lesson 1 Creating a Chart   **241**   LEVEL 2

> **If you have problems . . .**
> If you cannot see all of the data in the datasheet, click and drag the bottom-right corner of the datasheet window to increase its size. Furthermore, if the datasheet blocks your view of the chart, click and drag the datasheet title bar to move the datasheet to another area of the screen.

3 **Click in the datasheet cell below *North*, type South, and press →.**
Entering data in the first column creates a new data series.

4 **Click and drag across the existing 12 values in the datasheet, and press Del.**
Before you start to enter your own values, you should clear the existing values. This way, you do not forget which values are yours and which values were sample values.

5 **Use Figure 7.4 to enter values into the rest of the datasheet.**

		A	B	C	D	E
		1st Qtr	2nd Qtr	3rd Qtr	4th Qtr	
1	East	250	260	300	350	
2	West	275	280	325	390	
3	North	185	200	265	310	
4	South	150	160	200	275	
5						

FIGURE 7.4

6 **Choose Chart, Chart Type.**
The Chart Type dialog box opens so that you can choose a chart type and a chart sub-type (see Figure 7.5).

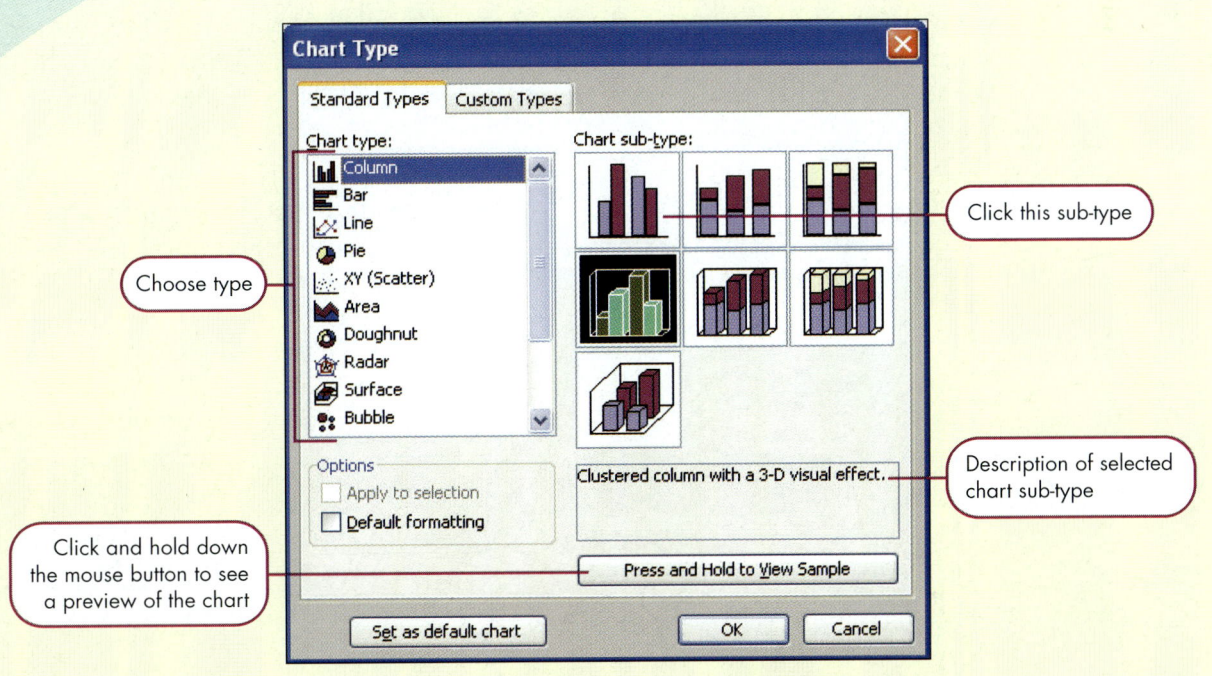

FIGURE 7.5

Project 7 Creating Charts and Diagrams

7 Make sure that *Column* is selected in the *Chart type* list, click the sub-type in the top-left corner of the *Chart sub-type* palette, and click OK.
The top-left sub-type is a clustered column chart.

8 Click in the space outside the chart to close Microsoft Graph Chart and the datasheet.
The regular Word Standard and Formatting toolbars appear, and the Microsoft Graph Chart toolbar disappears. Figure 7.6 shows the clustered column chart positioned at the left margin.

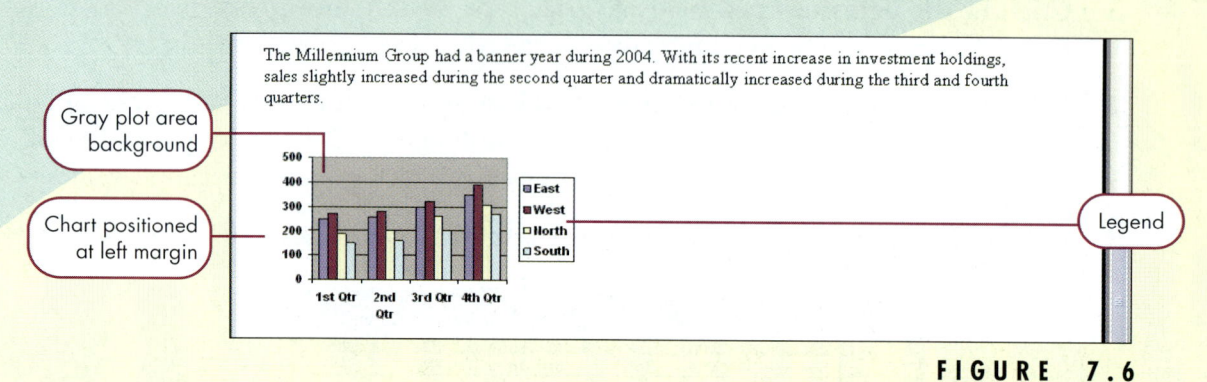

Gray plot area background

Chart positioned at left margin

Legend

The Millennium Group had a banner year during 2004. With its recent increase in investment holdings, sales slightly increased during the second quarter and dramatically increased during the third and fourth quarters.

FIGURE 7.6

9 Save the *February_Newsletter* document, and keep it onscreen to continue with the next lesson.

TO EXTEND YOUR KNOWLEDGE...

CHOOSING AN APPROPRIATE CHART TYPE

You can change the chart type for an active chart by clicking the Chart Type drop-down arrow on the Microsoft Graph Chart Standard toolbar. You can also right-click the chart and choose *Chart Type* to display the Chart Type dialog box from which to specify a chart type.

You should choose the chart type that is appropriate for depicting data from a particular perspective. Table 7.2 lists four major chart types and their purposes.

TABLE 7.2

CHART TYPE	DESCRIPTION AND PURPOSE
Column	Compares data series for the same time period by using vertical columns. For example, comparing profits for four regions for the second quarter of the year.
Bar	Compares data series by using horizontal bars. Looks like a column chart on its side. Helpful when you have long category descriptions instead of time periods.
Pie	Shows the proportions (percentages) of each component compared to the total by using a circle with "pie slices" for each component. For example, showing that the East contributed 35% to the total sales for the quarter.
Line	Shows trends over time. For example, showing population trends for major cities, such as Salt Lake City, over the past 25 years.

CREATING A NEW CHART OBJECT

You can display the Microsoft Graph Chart window by creating a chart object. To do this, choose Insert, Object and click the Create New tab; then scroll down the Object type list, select *Microsoft Graph Chart* (see Figure 7.7), and click OK.

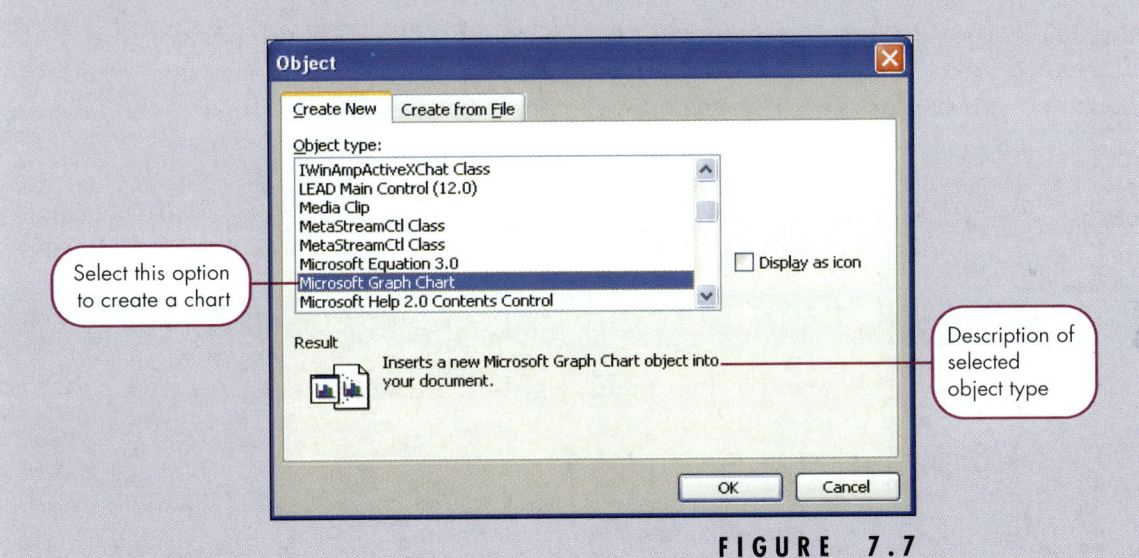

FIGURE 7.7

The Microsoft Graph Chart window looks the same regardless of whether you choose Insert, Picture, Chart or display the Object dialog box and choose Microsoft Graph Chart.

CLICKING VS. DOUBLE-CLICKING A CHART OBJECT

Note the difference between clicking and double-clicking the chart. When you click a chart object, selection handles appear so that you can format the chart object like an image. For example, you can display the Format Object dialog box to specify the chart's size, text wrapping option, horizontal position, and border.

When you double-click a chart object, on the other hand, you activate the chart. The datasheet and Microsoft Graph Chart toolbar appear, so you can edit values that produce the chart.

CREATING A CHART FROM A TABLE
If you want to create a chart from the data in a Word table, select the entire table or select the cells containing the data you want to chart; then choose Insert, Picture, Chart.

DISPLAYING OR HIDING THE LEGEND
With the datasheet displayed, click Legend on the Microsoft Graph Chart Standard toolbar to display or hide the legend within the chart area. By default, the legend is displayed. However, if you add labels to the chart, you might want to hide the legend.

LESSON 2: Formatting a Chart Object

The chart you created is too small for your needs. In addition, the chart is positioned at the left side, which leaves a lot of space on the right side. You can use the same format options for charts that you use for clip art images. You can apply borders, change the size, choose layout options, and so on.

In this lesson, you increase the chart's size, change the text wrap, and position the chart.

To Format a Chart Object

1 In the *February_Newsletter* document, right-click the chart.

2 Choose *Format Object*.
The Format Object dialog box opens (see Figure 7.8). It contains the same tabs and options as the Format Picture dialog box.

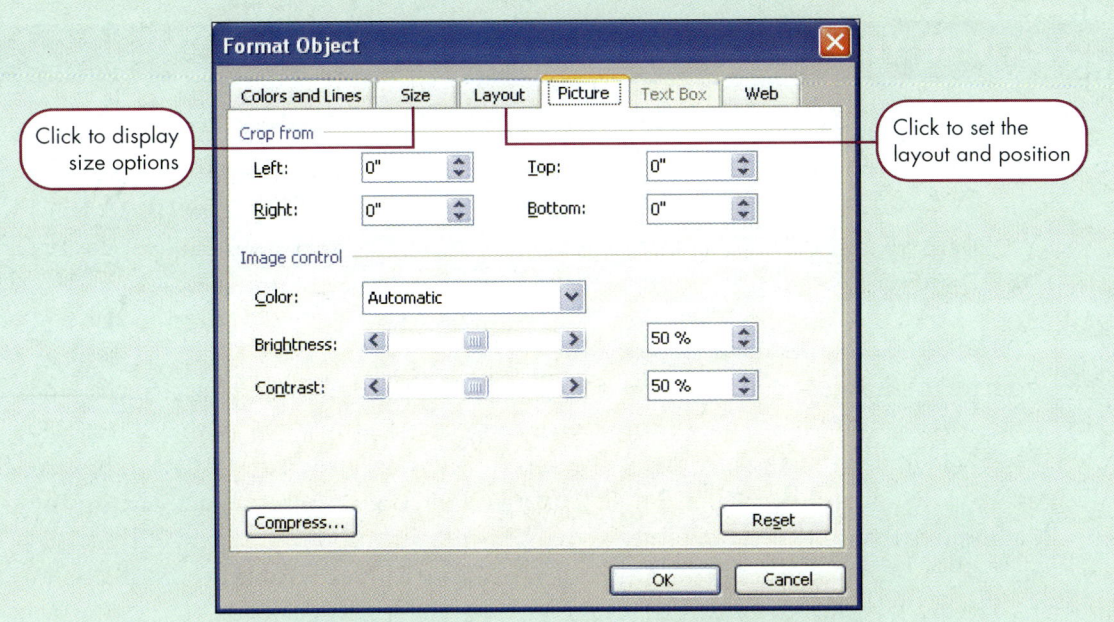

Lesson 2   Formatting a Chart Object   245   LEVEL 2

Click to display size options

Click to set the layout and position

FIGURE   7.8

3 **Click the Size tab, delete the existing width, and type 5.**
Increasing the width to 5″ makes the chart easier to see.

4 **Click the Layout tab.**
The Layout tab contains options for choosing the wrap style and position of the object.

5 **Click Advanced in the bottom-right corner of the dialog box, choose the *Top and bottom* wrapping style option, and click OK.**
The *Top and bottom* wrapping style positions a chart with text above and below it but not wrapping around on the left and right sides.

6 **Click the *Center* horizontal alignment option and click OK.**
Figure 7.9 shows the bigger chart that is centered between the left and right margins.

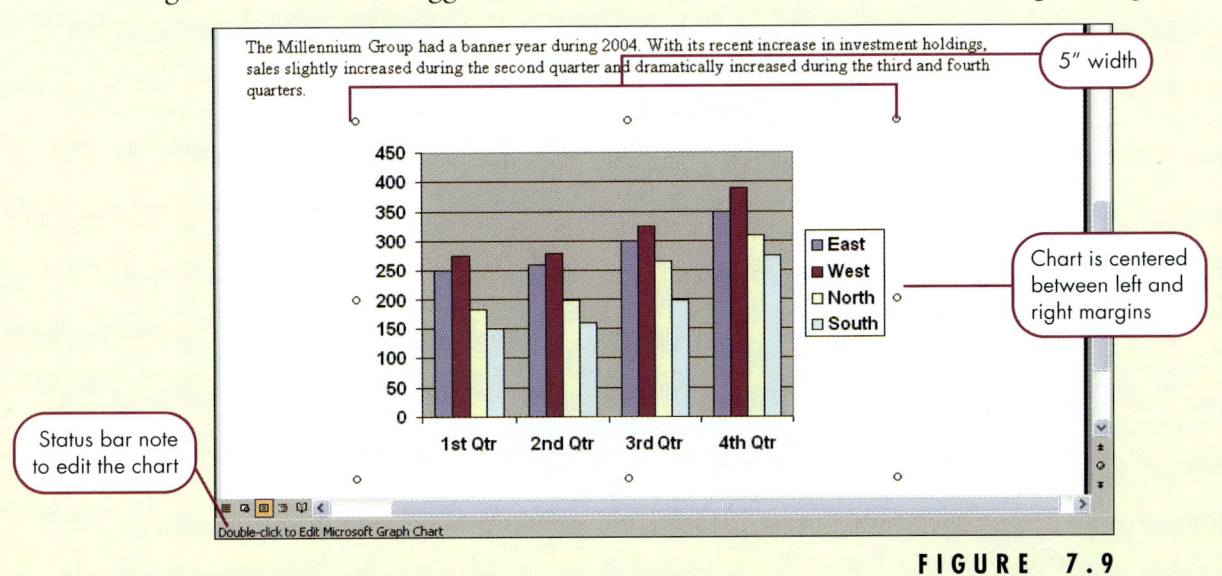

5″ width

Chart is centered between left and right margins

Status bar note to edit the chart

FIGURE   7.9

7 **Save the *February_Newsletter* document, and keep it onscreen to continue with the next lesson.**

TO EXTEND YOUR KNOWLEDGE...

ADDING A BORDER AROUND A CHART
You can apply a border around the edges of the chart. Right-click the object, and choose *Format Object*. Click the Colors and Lines tab, click the *Line Color* drop-down arrow, and then choose a line color. You can also select a line style, dashed style, and weight.

CHANGING THE ANGLE OF AXIS CONTENT
You are not limited to positioning the labels either parallel or perpendicular to the axes. To accommodate space limitations, or perhaps simply for aesthetic reasons, you can change the angle of the value axis numbers or the X-axis labels. Click an axis to select it and then click Angle Clockwise or Angle Counterclockwise on the right side of the Microsoft Graph Chart Formatting toolbar. If you do not see these two buttons, you need to display the Standard and Formatting toolbars on two rows.

LESSON 3: Inserting Titles

To help your readers understand a chart, you should include necessary descriptions and titles. You should typically create a brief chart title that describes the purpose of the chart or what it conveys. You might also need to include a Y-axis title that describes what types of quantities are depicted on the Y-axis.

In this lesson, you insert a chart title and a Y-axis title.

To Insert Titles

1 In the *February_Newsletter* document, double-click the chart to activate it.
You now see the chart, datasheet, and Microsoft Graph Chart toolbar buttons.

If you have problems...
If your toolbars display on a single row, click the Toolbar Options button on the right side of the toolbar, and then choose *Show Buttons on Two Rows* from the menu that appears.

2 Click View Datasheet on the Microsoft Graph Chart Standard toolbar to hide the datasheet.
By hiding the datasheet, you can see the entire chart. If you need to see the datasheet again, click View Datasheet again.

Lesson 3 Inserting Titles 247 LEVEL 2

3 **Choose Chart, Chart Options.**
The Chart Options dialog box opens (see Figure 7.10) so that you can add chart elements, such as titles, to your chart.

Type the title of chart here

Type the title for Y-axis here

Preview of chart with its options

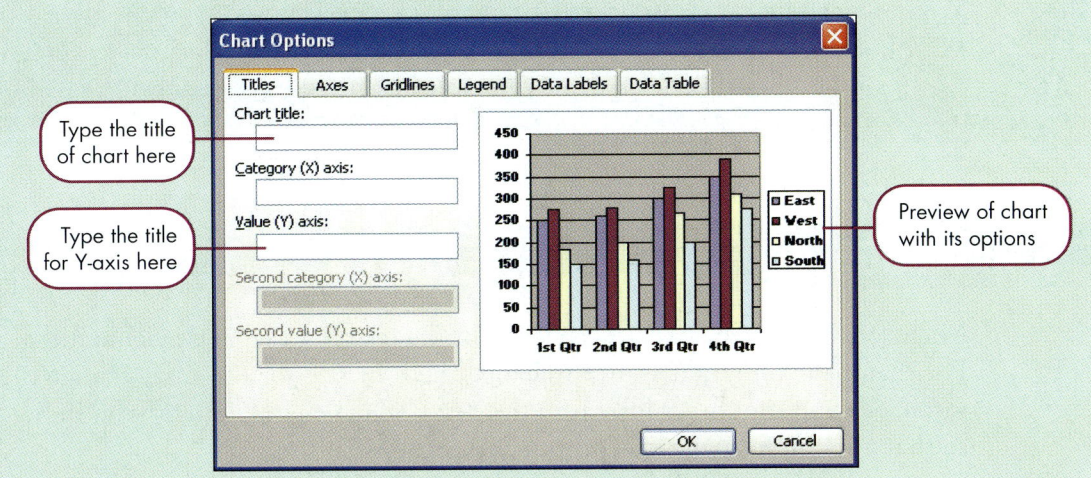

FIGURE 7.10

4 **Type `Sales for 2004` in the *Chart title* text box.**
Because the X-axis is self-explanatory as quarterly values, you do not need to type a category title for the X-axis. However, you need to type a Y-axis title to explain the unit of measurement for the Y-axis.

5 **Type `In Millions` in the *Value (Y) axis* text box and click OK.**
The value (Y) axis title is a heading that describes the values or quantities displayed on the Y-axis. This title clarifies whether the values are units, monetary values, and so on. Figure 7.11 shows the chart containing the titles.

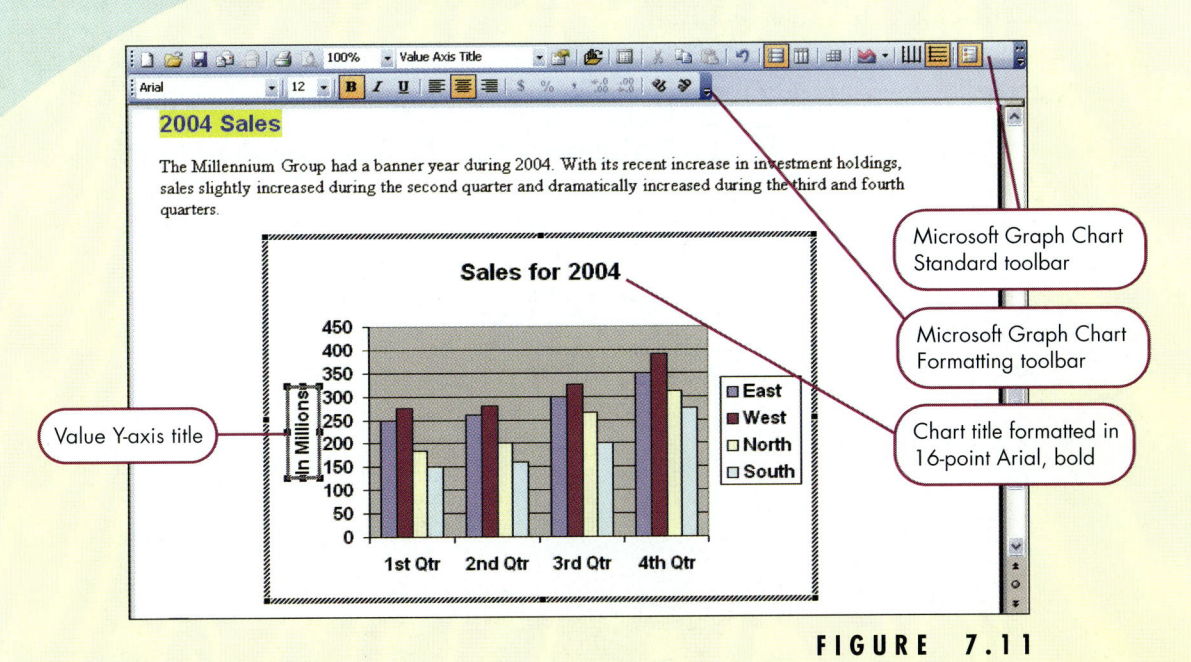

Value Y-axis title

Microsoft Graph Chart Standard toolbar

Microsoft Graph Chart Formatting toolbar

Chart title formatted in 16-point Arial, bold

FIGURE 7.11

6 **Save the *February_Newsletter* document, and keep it onscreen (with the chart activated) to continue with the next lesson.**

TO EXTEND YOUR KNOWLEDGE...

Y-AXIS AND Z-AXIS TITLES

Depending on the particular type of column chart, you might see a *Value (Z) axis* title option instead of the *Value (Y) axis* title option. Both titles describe the contents of the vertical axis. Unlike the Y-axis title, the Z-axis title is not rotated on its side.

LESSON 4: Formatting Chart Elements

Microsoft Graph Chart treats each part of the chart as a separate element that you can format. For example, you might want to change the font size for the title, change the color of a data series, or apply a number format to the Y-axis. Each chart element is an individual component so that you can format each component as you wish.

In this lesson, you change the format of the chart title, and add dollar signs to the Y-axis.

To Format Chart Elements

1 **In the *February_Newsletter* document, double-click the chart if it is not already activated with the Microsoft Graph Chart toolbars displayed.**
You need to view the chart within Microsoft Graph Chart to format individual chart elements. You need to select the chart element that you want to format.

2 **Click the chart title to select it.**
Selection handles—little black squares—and a selection box appear around the title. Always make sure you select the appropriate chart element before applying formatting.

3 **Click Format Chart Title on the Microsoft Graph Chart Standard toolbar.**
The Format Chart Title dialog box opens so that you can apply a background color, select font options, or specify alignment options (see Figure 7.12).

Lesson 4 Formatting Chart Elements 249

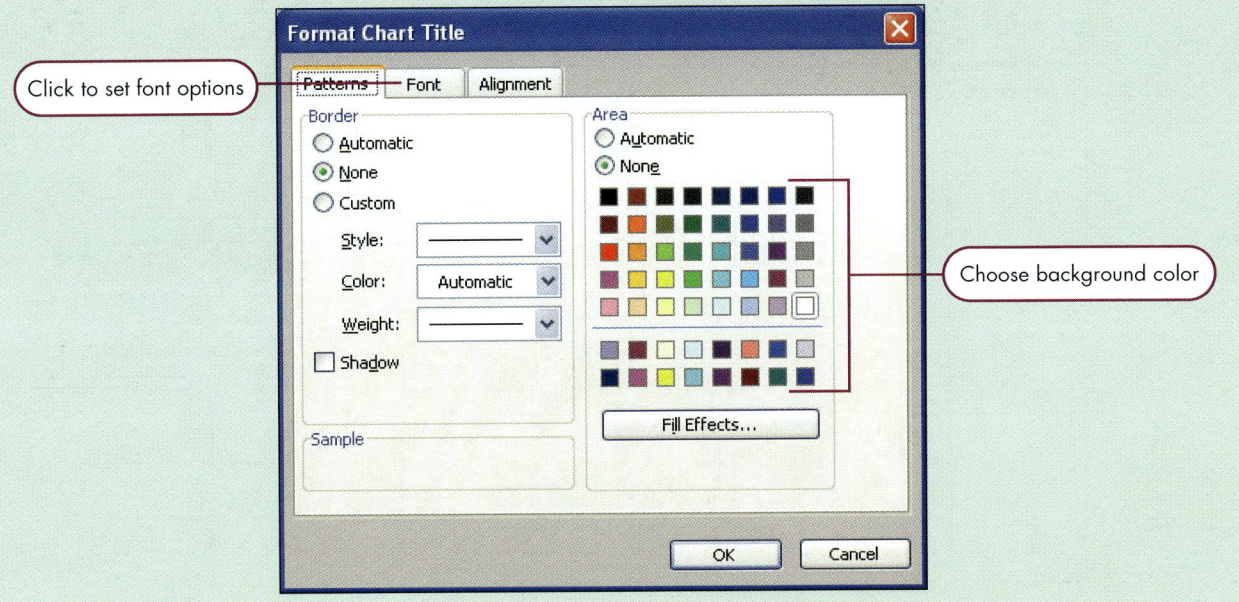

[Dialog box: Format Chart Title with Patterns, Font, Alignment tabs. Border section with Automatic/None/Custom options, Style, Color, Weight dropdowns, Shadow checkbox. Area section with color palette. Annotations: "Click to set font options" pointing to Patterns/Font tabs, "Choose background color" pointing to color palette.]

FIGURE 7.12

4 **Click the Font tab.**
The Font tab contains options that are similar to the Font dialog box. Although you can select the font face and font size from the toolbar, the dialog box offers more options.

5 **Click the *Color* drop-down arrow, choose *Green,* and click OK.**
The chart title appears in Green font color.

6 **Click the border line of the legend to select it.**
Although you could click Format Legend on the toolbar to set the font size for the legend, you can do so faster by using the Font Size button on the Formatting toolbar.

7 **Click the Font Size drop-down arrow on the Microsoft Graph Chart Formatting toolbar and choose *9.***
The legend's smaller font size is more appropriate compared with the other chart elements.

8 **Point to and click the Y-axis values when the ScreenTip displays *Value Axis.***
You do not see four sizing handles around the value axis like you saw when you selected the legend. You see sizing handles to the right of the first and last value on the axis to indicate that you selected the Y-axis.

9 **Click Currency Style on the Microsoft Graph Chart Formatting toolbar.**
The values on the Y-axis are formatted with dollar signs; however, the values now have a decimal point and trailing zeros, which are unnecessary.

10 **Click Decrease Decimal twice on the Microsoft Graph Chart Formatting toolbar.**
The Y-axis values appear as whole numbers now. Figure 7.13 shows the formatted chart.

Project 7 Creating Charts and Diagrams

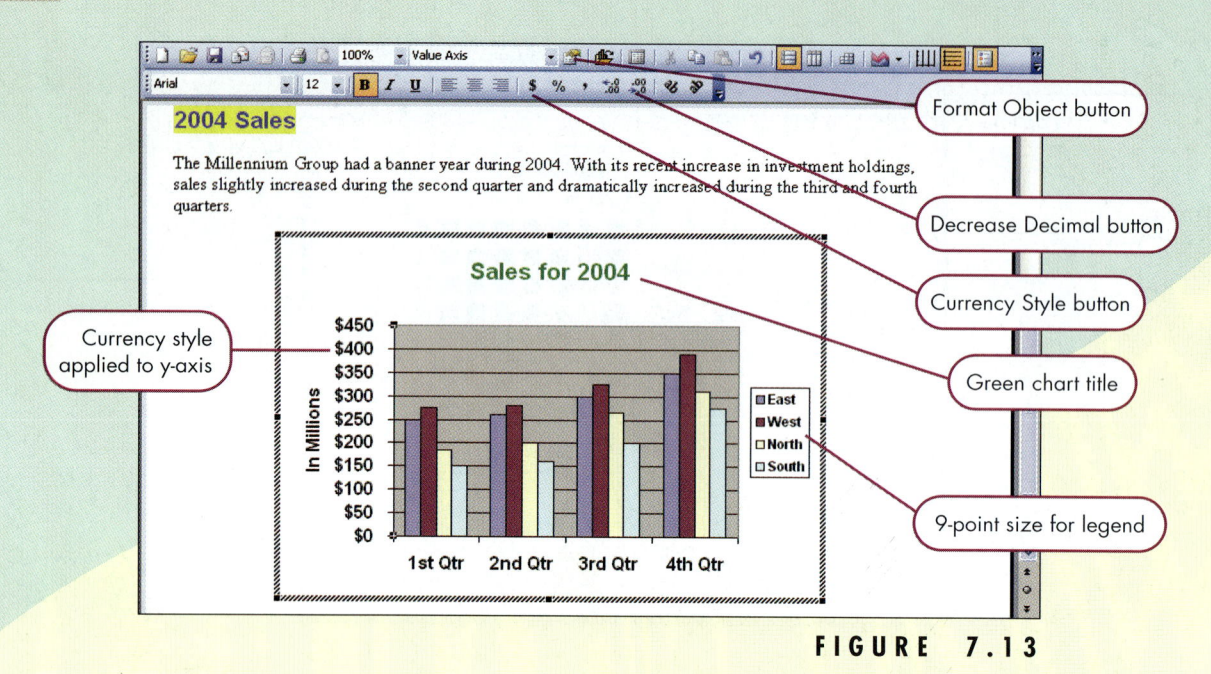

FIGURE 7.13

Callouts on figure: Format Object button; Decrease Decimal button; Currency Style button; Green chart title; 9-point size for legend; Currency style applied to y-axis.

11 Deselect the chart.

12 Save the *February_Newsletter* document, and keep it onscreen to continue with the next lesson.

TO EXTEND YOUR KNOWLEDGE . . .

USING THE FORMAT OBJECT BUTTON

The ScreenTip for the Format Object button changes based on what is selected. When the chart title is selected and you position the mouse pointer over the button, the ScreenTip displays *Format Chart Title*.

CHANGING THE BACKGROUND COLOR

The plot area (the area that displays the charted data series) is gray, and the chart area (the area containing all chart elements) is white by default. You can change the background color of the plot and chart areas. To do this, select the plot area or chart area and then click Format Plot Area or Format Chart Area, respectively, on the Microsoft Graph Chart Standard toolbar.

You can then choose the desired background color, or you can click the Fill Effects button to select gradients, textures, patterns, or an image. For example, you might want to use an image that relates to the content of the chart. To use an image as the background, click the Picture tab within the Fill Effects dialog box, click *Select Picture,* and then select an image.

Lesson 5 Importing Excel Data to Create a Chart in Word

FORMATTING THE DATA SERIES
You can format a data series by clicking a data series column and then clicking Format Data Series. You can change the color, add *data labels* (values above the data series), or change other data series options.

LESSON 5: Importing Excel Data to Create a Chart in Word

You might have an Excel workbook that contains data that you want to chart. An Excel file is called a *workbook*. Each workbook can contain several *worksheets,* or pages of data. You can create the chart in either Excel or Word. If you decide to create the chart in Word, you can import the Excel data. *Import* refers to the process of bringing in data from another source application, such as bringing Excel data into Word.

In this lesson, you import a part of an Excel worksheet into the Microsoft Graph Chart datasheet and create a chart there.

To Import Excel Data and Create a Chart

1. In the *February_Newsletter* document, position the insertion point on the blank line immediately above the heading *2004 Sales*.

2. Choose Insert, Picture, Chart.
   You need to import the Excel worksheet data into the datasheet.

3. Click in the blank datasheet cell above *East*.

4. Click Import File on the Microsoft Graph Chart Standard toolbar.
   Excel workbook filenames end with the .xls extension.

5. Select *EW2_0702.xls* and click Open.
   The Import Data Options dialog box opens (see Figure 7.14) so that you can choose the worksheet and range.

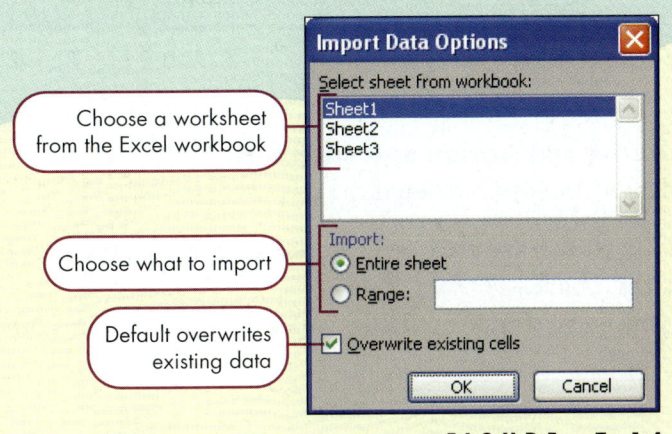

FIGURE 7.14

6 **Click the *Range* option, type A3:D6 in the box, and click OK.**
You do not want the entire worksheet page; you want a specific range or area within that sheet. The range address is A3 through D6. The colon separates the beginning and ending points of the range.

Word imports the Excel worksheet data into the Microsoft Graph Chart datasheet. The column headings import as a data series, however, instead of on the first row of the datasheet; therefore, you need to move the column heading data up one row to create the legend (see Figure 7.15).

First row headings treated as data series

Move column headings to this row

	A	B	C	D	E
1	Area	2002	2003	2004	
2	Hotels	$ 45,750	$ 55,000	$ 70,750	
3	Restauran	$ 38,450	$ 45,750	$ 52,750	
4	Retail	$ 85,000	$ 90,150	$100,000	
5					

February_Newsletter.doc - Datasheet

FIGURE 7.15

7 **Click and drag across *Area, 2002, 2003,* and *2004* to select these cells.**

8 **Click Cut, click in the first cell in the first row of the datasheet, and click Paste.**
The data are pasted on the first row; however, the datasheet now has an empty data series row that you need to delete.

9 **Click in the cell that displays *3-D Column* in gray.**

10 **Choose Edit, Delete.**
The Delete dialog box opens (see Figure 7.16).

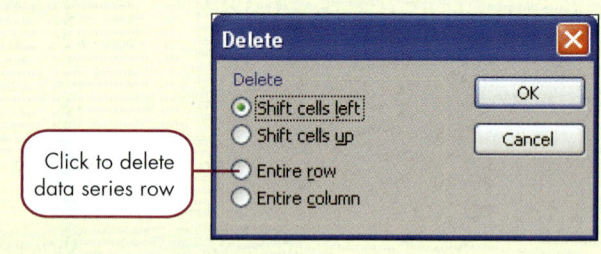

Click to delete data series row

Delete
- ● Shift cells left
- ○ Shift cells up
- ○ Entire row
- ○ Entire column

OK   Cancel

FIGURE 7.16

11 **Click the *Entire row* option and click OK.**
The extra data series row is deleted.

12 **Click outside the chart area, and make sure you have one blank line above and below the chart.**
The chart you created by importing Excel data appears in your document window (see Figure 7.17).

Lesson 6 Creating an Organization Chart 253 LEVEL 2

FIGURE 7.17

13 Save the *February_Newsletter* document, and keep it onscreen to continue with the next lesson.

TO EXTEND YOUR KNOWLEDGE...

FORMATTING THE CHART
You can format the chart by changing its size, position, and text wrapping, just as you did in Lesson 2.

LESSON 6: Creating an Organization Chart

An *organization chart* shows the hierarchy of positions within an organization. The chart shows who reports to whom and the different positions within a department or division by connecting rectangular shapes with lines. An organization chart typically displays people's names and their job titles.

In this lesson, you create an organization chart with a company president and three vice presidents.

To Create an Organization Chart

1 In the *February_Newsletter* document, position the insertion point on the blank line above the heading *Three Growth Areas*.
This is where you want the organization chart to appear.

2 Choose Insert, Diagram.
The Diagram Gallery dialog box opens (see Figure 7.18).

Project 7 Creating Charts and Diagrams

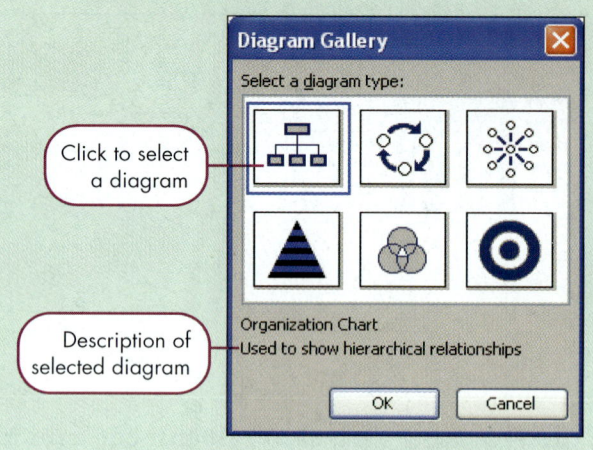

Click to select a diagram

Description of selected diagram

FIGURE 7.18

3 **Make sure the organization chart is selected, and click OK.**
The Organization Chart toolbar and an organization chart enclosed in a frame appear. The chart contains *placeholders*—text and space reserved for entering data (see Figure 7.19).

Type name of top executive

Organization Chart toolbar

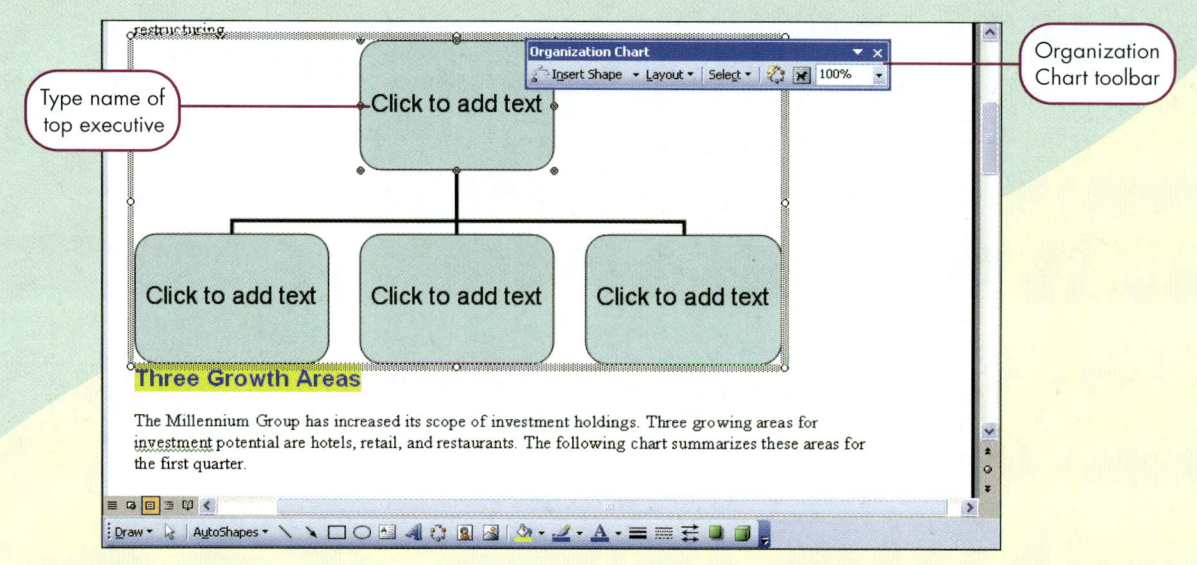

FIGURE 7.19

4 **Click in the first placeholder, type Jared Farnsworth, press ↵Enter, and type President & CEO.**

5 **Type the following names, titles, and divisions for the three positions below Jared's position:**

Andrew Schultz	Marie Patterson	Amanda Gold
VP Global Affairs	VP Sales	VP Finance

Because the text within the organization chart is small, you need to increase the font size.

6 **Press and hold down Ctrl as you click the edges of all four positions to select them. Then click the Font Size drop-down arrow and choose *16*.**
Figure 7.20 shows your organization chart.

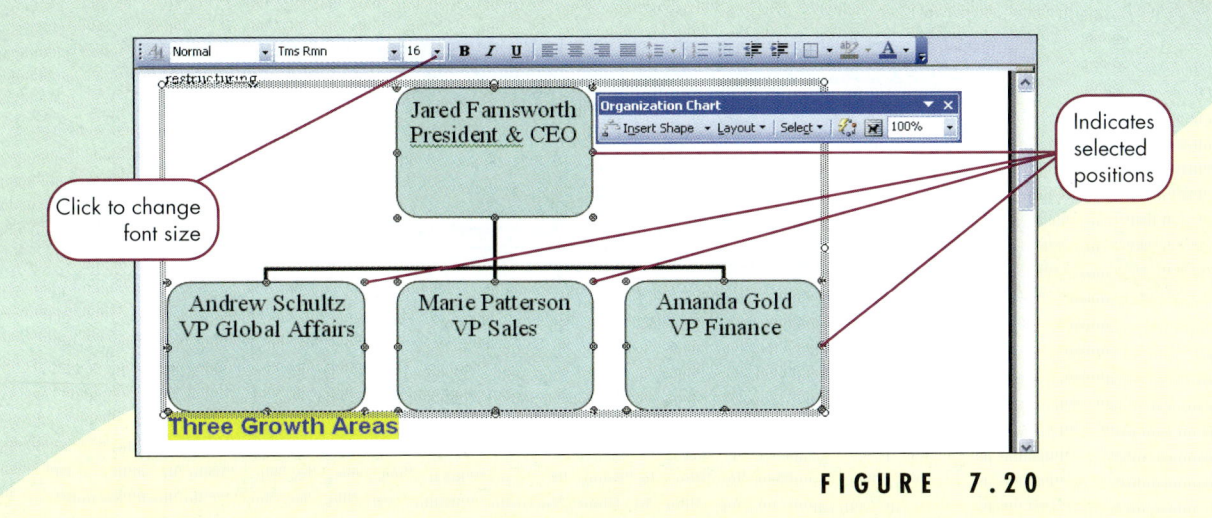

Lesson 7   Adding Positions to an Organization Chart   **255**   LEVEL 2

FIGURE 7.20

7 Save the *February_Newsletter* document, and keep it onscreen to continue with the next lesson.

TO EXTEND YOUR KNOWLEDGE . . .

ANOTHER OPTION TO CREATE AN ORGANIZATION CHART
You can also create an organization chart by choosing Insert, Picture, Organization Chart.

LESSON 7: Adding Positions to an Organization Chart

The default organization chart provides the main position and three subordinate positions; however, you can add subordinates, coworkers, managers, and assistants. In addition, you can change the layout of the organization chart.

In this lesson, you add two subordinate positions for Marie Patterson.

To Add Positions to an Organization Chart

1 In the *February_Newsletter* document, click the outside border of Marie's position.

2 Click the Insert Shape drop-down arrow on the Organization Chart toolbar.
A menu appears so that you can insert a position in relation to the selected position (see Figure 7.21).

Project 7   Creating Charts and Diagrams

Figure 7.21 shows an organization chart with Jared Farnsworth (President & CEO) at the top, and Andrew Schultz (VP Global Affairs), Marie Patterson (VP Sales), and Amanda Gold (VP Finance) below. Marie Patterson's box is the selected position box. The Organization Chart toolbar shows Insert Shape dropdown with options: Subordinate, Coworker, Assistant. Callouts point to "List of positions" and "Selected position box".

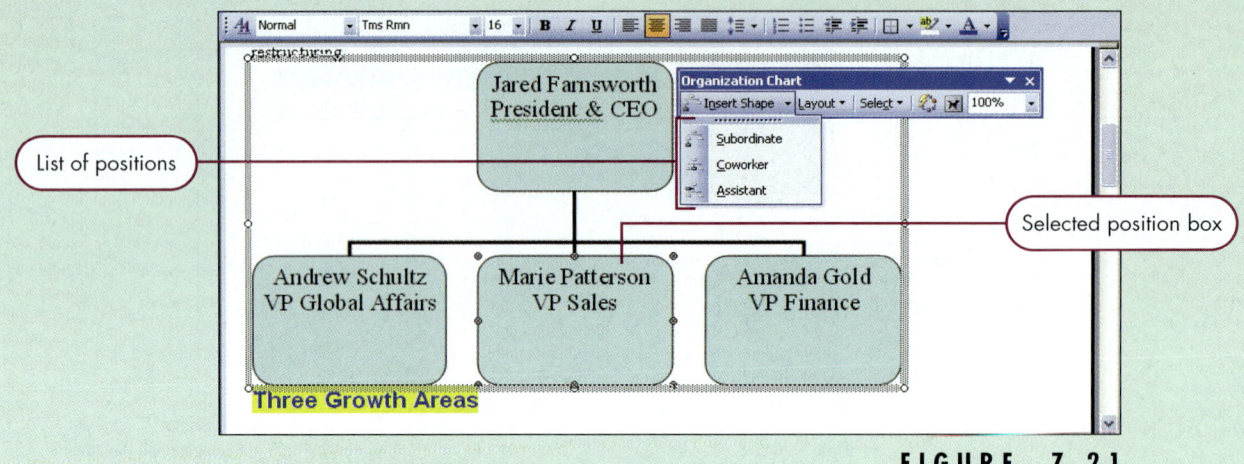

FIGURE 7.21

3 **Choose _Subordinate_.**
A placeholder appears below Marie's position.

If you have problems . . .

If you accidentally create the wrong position, press Del while the placeholder is selected to delete the placeholder so that you can try again.

4 **Click the new placeholder, type `Janice Bronson`, press ⏎Enter, and type `East Coast Director`.**
You need to add a coworker position for Janice. You want to place the coworker's data to the right of Janice's box.

5 **With Janice's position selected, click the I_n_sert Shape drop-down arrow, and choose _Coworker_.**
A placeholder appears to the right of Janice's position.

6 **Click the new placeholder, type `Daniel Payne`, press ⏎Enter, and type `West Coast Director`.**

7 **Click outside the organization chart.**
Figure 7.22 shows the completed organization chart.

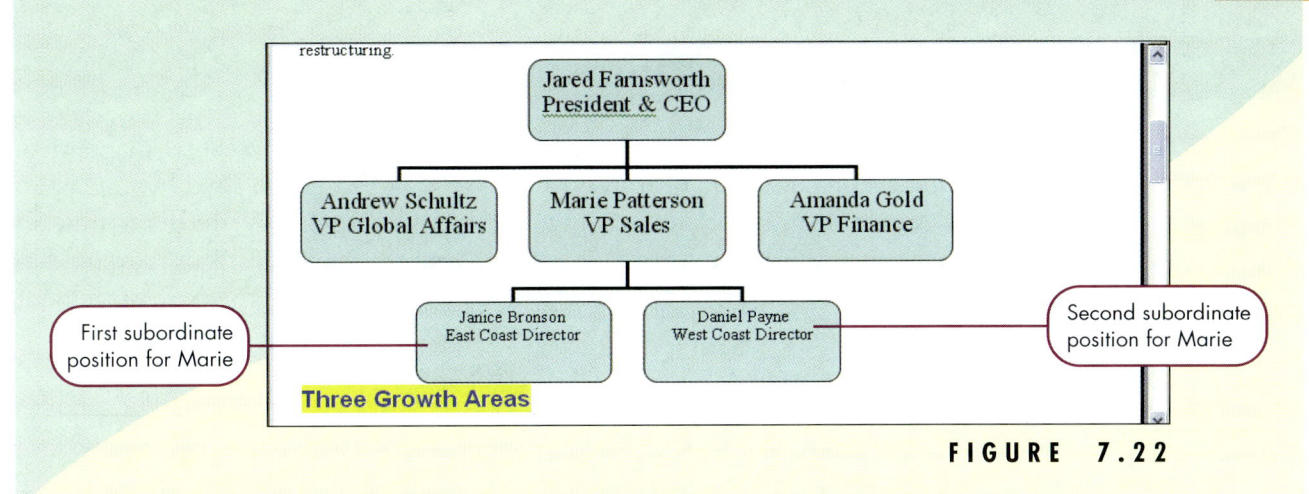

Lesson 7 Adding Positions to an Organization Chart   257   LEVEL 2

First subordinate position for Marie

Second subordinate position for Marie

Three Growth Areas

FIGURE 7.22

8 Save, print (optional), and close the *February_Newsletter* document.

TO EXTEND YOUR KNOWLEDGE...

CUSTOMIZING THE ORGANIZATION CHART
You used the Insert Shape drop-down menu on the Organization Chart toolbar to add subordinate positions to the chart. The toolbar also provides other menus and buttons to customize the chart.

The Layout drop-down menu enables you to select a specific layout. For example, you can choose a layout that displays all positions hanging down on only the left or right side of the top-level position.

The Select drop-down menu enables you to select positions of a certain level or type, or you can select all connecting lines. For example, if a second-level position is already selected, you can select all second-level positions by choosing Level from the Select drop-down menu.

When you click the AutoFormat button, the Organization Chart Style Gallery opens. It contains options for selecting a diagram style, such as Gradient or Primary Colors.

Finally, click the Text Wrapping button to specify how the text wraps around the diagram—similar to selecting text wrapping options for clip art and other drawing objects.

FORMATTING THE ORGANIZATION CHART OBJECT
You can add a border, adjust the size, choose a horizontal position, and select the text wrap option for an organization chart. To open the Format Organization Chart dialog box, double-click the chart or right-click the organization chart and choose *Format Organization Chart*.

LESSON 8: Designing Diagrams

As you create documents for various organizations, you might need to create a diagram to illustrate relationships or processes. You can use Microsoft Word to create six different types: organization chart, Cycle diagram, Radial diagram, Pyramid diagram, Venn diagram, and Target diagram. Each diagram has a specific purpose. For example, statisticians use a Venn diagram to show the probability that two events occur at the same time. Project management leaders, on the other hand, often use Cycle diagrams to show the ongoing process of developing a project.

In this lesson, you create a Venn diagram that shows the primary colors—red, yellow, and blue—and the new colors that result when they overlap.

To Design a Diagram

1. Start a new document window and save it as `Color_Diagram`.

2. Display the Drawing toolbar, if needed, and click *Insert Diagram or Organization Chart* on the Drawing toolbar.

If you have problems . . .
If the Drawing toolbar is not visible, you can display it and then click *Insert Diagram or Organization Chart,* or you can choose Insert, Diagram.

The Diagram Gallery dialog box opens. The Venn diagram is the second diagram type on the second row—the one with three overlapping circles.

3. Click the Venn diagram type and click OK. Then scroll down and change the zoom to Page Width, if needed, to see as much of the diagram as possible.
A drawing canvas appears with three overlapping circles and placeholders indicating *Click to add text* (see Figure 7.23).

Lesson 8 Designing Diagrams — 259 — LEVEL 2

Diagram toolbar

Venn diagram

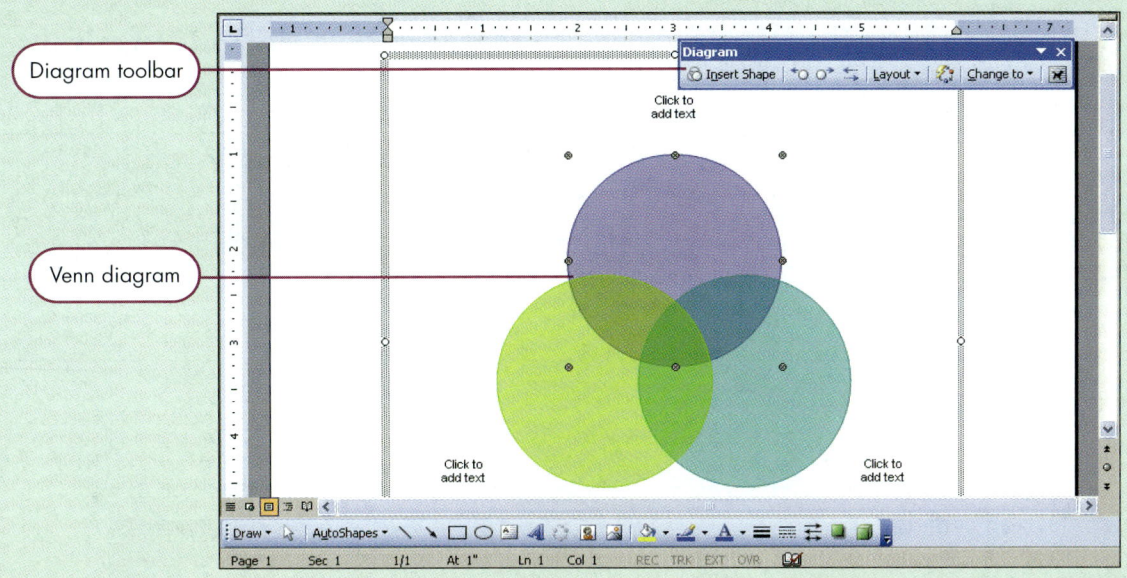

FIGURE 7.23

4 **Click AutoFormat on the Diagram toolbar.**
Figure 7.24 shows the Diagram Style Gallery dialog box, which enables you to choose a different style.

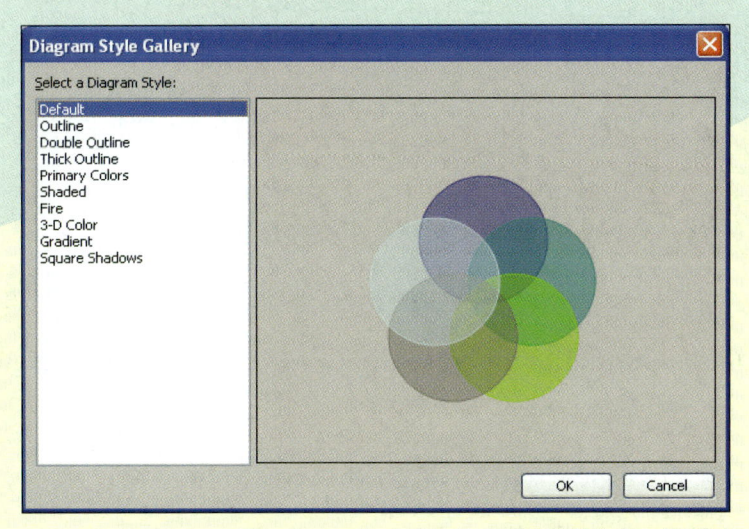

FIGURE 7.24

5 **Click the *Primary Colors* diagram style and click OK.**
The circles in the Venn diagram are blue, yellow, and red. You see green where the blue and yellow colors overlap.

6 **Click the placeholder above the top circle and type `Blue`.**

7 **Click the placeholder next to the bottom-left circle and type `Yellow`.**

8 **Click the placeholder next to the bottom-right circle and type `Red`.**

Project 7 Creating Charts and Diagrams

9 Select the word *Blue,* click Bold, and change the font size to *14.* Apply the same format to the words *Red* and *Yellow.*

If you have problems . . .

If the word *Yellow* word-wraps, you must abbreviate the text or use a smaller font size. Unfortunately, you cannot increase the size of the text AutoShapes. If needed, decrease the font size for *Yellow.*

Figure 7.25 shows the completed Venn diagram.

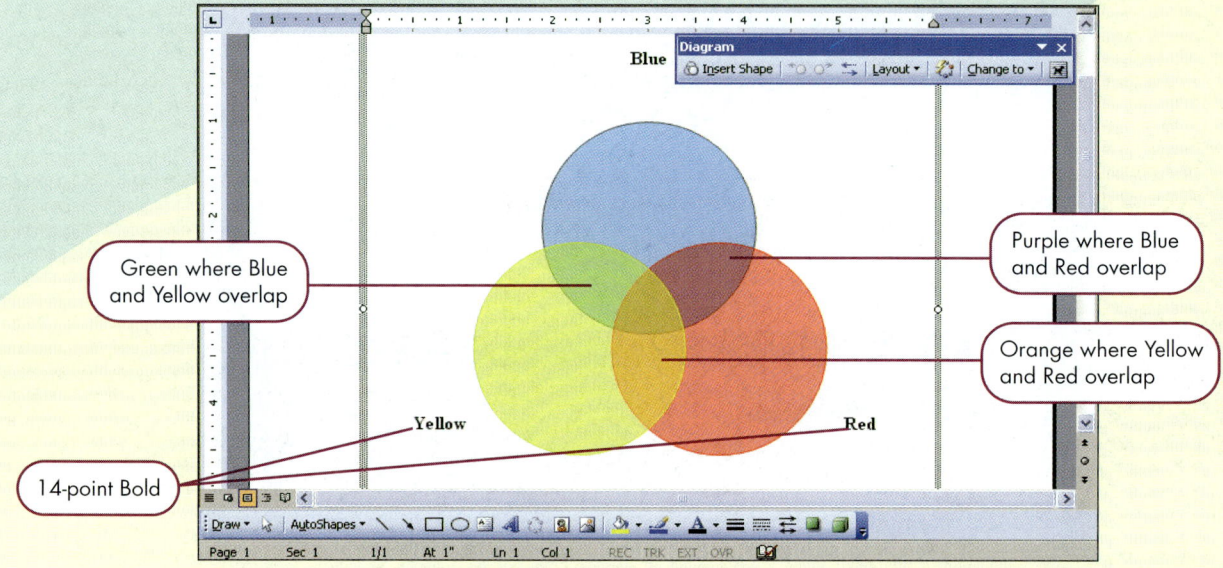

FIGURE 7.25

10 Save, print (optional), and close the *Color_Diagram* document.

Lesson 8 Designing Diagrams — 261

TO EXTEND YOUR KNOWLEDGE...

USING DIAGRAM TOOLBAR BUTTONS
Table 7.3 lists and describes the buttons on the Diagram toolbar.

TABLE 7.3

BUTTON	BUTTON NAME	DESCRIPTION
Insert Shape	Insert Shape	Adds another shape to the current diagram. For example, if you insert a shape within a Venn diagram, another overlapping circle appears.
	Move Shape Backward	Moves the selected shape back one layer.
	Move Shape Forward	Moves the selected shape up one layer.
	Reverse Diagram	Rearranges the selected object. For example, if selected object is on top, it is moved to the bottom.
Layout	Layout	Lets you reduce, expand, or scale the diagram contents.
	AutoFormat	Displays a dialog box to choose a format for the diagram.
Change to	Change to	Lets you change the current diagram to another type of diagram.
	Text Wrapping	Specifies how text wraps around the diagram object.

EXPERIMENTING WITH DIAGRAMS
Probably the best way to learn more about diagrams is to create each diagram and experiment with the Diagram toolbar buttons to see their effects. To learn more about each diagram's purpose, type **About diagrams** in the *Type a question for help* box and search the Help information. Definitions are provided for each diagram name.

CREATING FLOWCHARTS
You can create flowcharts that indicate a process of steps to follow and alternatives to choose from. Click AutoShapes on the Drawing toolbar

and then choose *Flowchart*. Select a flowchart shape to insert. Use the AutoShapes menu to also select connectors, basic shapes, and block arrows as needed to complete the flowchart.

For more information about creating flowcharts, type **flowcharts** in the *Type a question for help* box and select *Draw a flowchart* to display Help information.

SUMMARY

In this project, you created a chart by entering data into a datasheet, which builds the chart. You learned how to insert titles to describe the overall purpose of the chart and to insert Y-axis titles to describe the value axis. You formatted chart elements to improve the chart's appearance. Furthermore, you created an organization chart to show a company's hierarchy of top management. Finally, you created a diagram and changed one of its characteristics.

You can extend your learning by reviewing concepts and terms, and by practicing variations of skills presented in the lessons. Use the following table as a guide to the numbered questions and exercises in the end-of-project learning opportunities.

LESSON	MULTIPLE CHOICE	DISCUSSION	SKILL DRILL	CHALLENGE	DISCOVERY ZONE
Creating a Chart	1, 2	1	1	1, 2, 3	1, 2
Formatting a Chart Object	7	1	2	1, 2, 3	1, 2
Inserting Titles	3	1	3	1, 3	1, 2
Formatting Chart Elements	10	1	3	1, 2, 3	1, 2
Importing Excel Data to Create a Chart in Word	6	2		2	2
Creating an Organization Chart	5		4	4	
Adding Positions to an Organization Chart	9		5	4	
Designing Diagrams	8	3	6	5	3

KEY TERMS

chart	gridlines	plot area
chart area	import	workbook
chart title	legend	worksheets
data labels	Microsoft Graph Chart	X-axis
data series		Y-axis
datasheet	organization chart	Y-axis title
diagram	placeholders	Z-axis

CHECKING CONCEPTS AND TERMS

MULTIPLE CHOICE

Circle the letter of the correct answer for each of the following.

1. What type of chart shows the proportion to the whole? [L1]
   a. Column
   b. Line
   c. Pie
   d. Radar

2. Look at Figure 7.3 in Lesson 1. What datasheet content creates a data series within the chart? [L1]
   a. 1st Qtr, 2nd Qtr, 3rd Qtr, 4th Qtr
   b. 30.6, 38.6, 34.6, 31.6
   c. South
   d. North

3. Look at Figure 7.10 in Lesson 3. If you delete the *Qtr* labels, you should type **Quarter** as the _____ title. [L3]
   a. Chart
   b. Category (X) axis
   c. Value (Y) axis
   d. Legend

4. What term refers to the vertical axis on a column chart? [Visual Summary]
   a. X-axis
   b. Y-axis
   c. Plot area
   d. Legend

5. What type of visual aid shows the hierarchy of positions in a company? [L6]
   a. Organization chart
   b. Radar chart
   c. Venn diagram
   d. Pyramid diagram

6. Which of the following is *not* an option for importing data from an Excel workbook into a chart datasheet in Word? [L5]
   a. Overwriting existing data in the datasheet
   b. Selecting a worksheet within the workbook
   c. Importing either the entire sheet or a specific range
   d. Selecting which columns of a column chart to import

7. Which of the following chart formats is *not* available in the Format Object dialog box? [L2]
   a. X-axis angle
   b. Size
   c. Horizontal placement
   d. Border

8. What type of diagram should you create to illustrate the steps to achieving a goal? [L8]
   a. Organization chart
   b. Radial diagram
   c. Pyramid diagram
   d. Target diagram

9. Look at Figure 7.21 in Lesson 7. For which person can you *not* create a coworker position? [L7]
   a. Jared Farnsworth
   b. Andrew Schultz
   c. Marie Patterson
   d. Amanda Gold

10. Which chart element is the most likely to be formatted as currency? [L4]
    a. Title
    b. Y-axis
    c. Legend
    d. X-axis

DISCUSSION

1. Locate several charts in newspapers, corporate annual reports, and other publications. Evaluate each chart for effectiveness. Show the charts to your classmates and discuss your evaluations. [L1–L4]

2. Under what situations would you import Excel worksheet data into a Word datasheet instead of typing the data in the datasheet? [L5]

3. Find examples of diagrams in magazines. Bring copies to class to discuss the types of data displayed in the diagrams. [L8]

SKILL DRILL

Skill Drill exercises reinforce project skills. Each skill reinforced is the same, or nearly the same, as a skill presented in the project. Detailed instructions are provided in a step-by-step format.

You modify one document named *Enrollment_Chart* in the first three Skill Drill exercises. Work through exercises 1–3 in sequential order, and work exercises 4 and 5 in sequential order. Exercise 6 is independent of the others and can be worked at any time. Be sure to save your changes and close the document if you need more than one work session to complete the desired exercises. Continue working on modified documents instead of starting over. Figure 7.26 shows the completed *Enrollment_Chart* document.

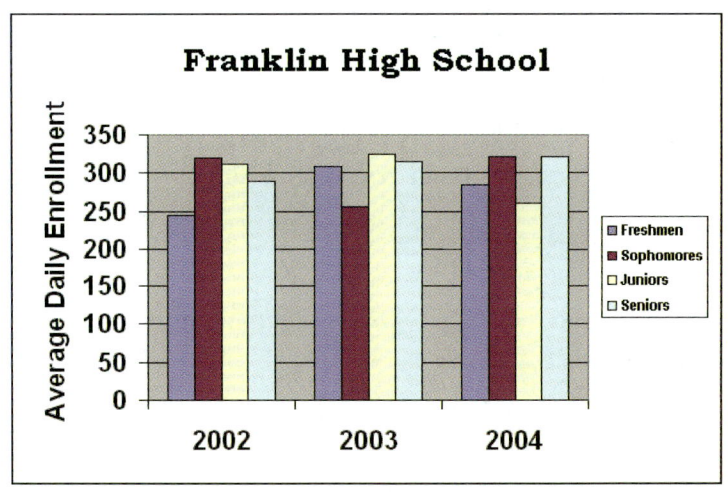

FIGURE 7.26

1. Creating a Chart

You are an assistant at a local high school, and your principal has asked you to create a chart depicting the number of students in each grade for the past three years. You decide to create a clustered column chart to depict the data.

1. In a new document window, choose Insert, Picture, Chart.
2. Click and drag across all the data in the datasheet and then press Del.
3. Type the following data in the datasheet, leaving the top-left cell empty:

	2002	2003	2004
Freshmen	245	308	284
Sophomores	320	255	321
Juniors	312	325	261
Seniors	289	315	322

4. Click the *Column D* heading.
5. Choose Edit, Delete to clear the column.
6. Choose Chart, Chart Type.
7. Click the *Clustered Column* chart sub-type and then click OK.
8. Click outside the chart area.
9. Save the document as **Enrollment_Chart**.

2. Formatting a Chart Object

Because the chart is the only item on the page, you want to balance the chart. In addition, you want to increase the size of the chart so that you can use a printout to make a transparency master.

1. In the *Enrollment_Chart* document, click the chart to select it.
2. Right-click the chart and then choose *Format Object.*
3. Click the Layout tab and then click the *Square* wrapping style.

4. Click the Size tab, type **4** in the *Height* box, and click OK.
5. Right-click the chart, and choose *Format Object.*
6. Click the Colors and Lines tab.
7. Click the *Line Color* drop-down arrow, click the *Black* color, and click OK.
8. Deselect the chart.
9. Choose *File, Page Setup.*
10. Click the Layout tab, click the *Vertical alignment* drop-down arrow, and choose *Center;* then click OK.
11. Save the *Enrollment_Chart* document.

3. Adding and Formatting Chart Elements

The chart does not look detailed enough; therefore, you decide to add a chart title and Y-axis title. In addition, you apply different fonts and font sizes to various chart elements.

1. In the *Enrollment_Chart* document, double-click the chart.
2. Choose *Chart, Chart Options.*
3. Type `Franklin High School` in the *Chart title* box.
4. Type `Average Daily Enrollment` in the *Value (Y) axis* box. Click OK.
5. If needed, select the *Average Daily Enrollment* text and apply a slightly smaller font size.
6. Format the legend by completing these steps:
   a. Click the legend to select it.
   b. Click the Font drop-down arrow, and choose *Arial Narrow.*
   c. Click the Font Size drop-down arrow, and choose *10.*
7. Format the chart title by completing these steps:
   a. Click the chart title.
   b. Click the Font drop-down arrow and choose *Bookman Old Style.*
8. Click outside the chart.
9. Save, print (optional), and close the *Enrollment_Chart* document.

4. Creating a School Organization Chart

You want to create a simple organization chart showing the superintendent, three principals, and the teacher-of-the-year. The printout will be used to create a transparency to display at the general faculty meeting at the beginning of the semester.

1. In a new document window, choose *File, Page Setup.*
2. Click the Margins tab, click the *Landscape* option, and click OK.
3. Save the document as `School_Chart`.
4. Choose *Insert, Picture, Organization* Chart.
5. Right-click the edge of the organization chart, and choose *Format Organization Chart.*

6. Click the Size tab, and type **8** in the *Wi<u>d</u>th* box.

7. Click the Layout tab, click the *Square* wrapping style option, and click the *<u>C</u>enter* horizontal alignment; then click OK.

8. Save the *School_Chart* document.

5. Completing the School Organization Chart

After setting up the main document formats and creating the initial organization chart, you are ready to enter names and titles into the placeholders. In addition, you need to insert a subordinate position for one of the school principals.

1. In the *School_Chart* document, click in the first placeholder.

2. Type `Ms. Kennison`, press ⏎Enter, and type `Superintendent`.

3. Click in the placeholder on the left side of the next row.

4. Type `Mr. Peters`, press ⏎Enter, and type `HS Principal`.

5. Click in the placeholder in the middle of the second row.

6. Type `Mr. Lee`, press ⏎Enter, and type `Jr. High Principal`.

7. Click in the placeholder on the right side of the second row.

8. Type `Mrs. Jayroe`, press ⏎Enter, and type `Elementary Principal`.

9. Click the box for *Mr. Peters,* click the I<u>n</u>sert Shape drop-down arrow on the toolbar, and choose *<u>S</u>ubordinate*.

10. Click in the new subordinate box.

11. Type `Ms. Partee`, press ⏎Enter, and type `Biology Teacher`.

12. Adjust font size for the principal positions by completing the following steps:
    a. Select Mr. Lee's position.
    b. Click the Sele<u>c</u>t drop-down arrow on the Organization Chart toolbar.
    c. Choose *<u>L</u>evel*.
    d. Apply 20-point font size to the selected positions.

13. Change the superintendent's position to 25-point font size.

14 Click outside the organization chart.

15. Set a 2.25" top margin.

16. Save, print (optional), and close the *School_Chart* document.

6. Designing a Diagram

As an assistant to a financial planning firm, you have been asked to prepare a chart that helps people reduce their credit card debt. Your supervisor typed a general information sheet and now wants an appropriate chart to accompany it. You decide to create a Target diagram with the information she wants.

1. Open *EW2_0703* and save it as `Debt_Reduction_Chart`.

2. Position the insertion point at the end of the document.

3. Click the *Insert Diagram or Organization Chart* button on the Drawing toolbar.

4. Click the *Target Diagram* option in the bottom-right corner of the palette and then click OK.

5. Click the third *Click to add text* placeholder and then type **Create a monthly budget**.

    The outside placeholder is the first step in achieving the goal.

6. Click in the second *Click to add text* placeholder and then type **Quit buying luxury items**.

    The middle placeholder is the second step in achieving the goal.

7. Press Ctrl+A to select the text within the second box.

8. Click the Font Size drop-down arrow, and choose *11*.

9. Click the first *Click to add text* placeholder, and type **Lower Total Balance**.

    The inside placeholder is the target or goal to accomplish.

10. Press Ctrl+A to select the text within the first placeholder, and click Bold.

11. Click *AutoFormat* on the Diagram toolbar.

12. Click the *Primary Colors* diagram style and then click OK.

13. Click outside the diagram.

14. Display the Page Setup dialog box, set a 0.5" bottom margin, and then click OK. (Hint: If the diagram still does not fit on one page, decrease the left and right margins slightly.)

15. Save, print (optional), and close the *Debt_Reduction_Chart* document.

CHALLENGE

Challenge exercises expand on or are somewhat related to skills presented in the lessons. Each exercise provides a brief narrative introduction, followed by instructions in a numbered-step format that are not as detailed as those in the Skill Drill exercises. You can work through one or more exercises in any order.

1. Creating a Stacked Column Chart

Brock, the manager of a regional video rental store, composed a memo to send to the shift managers. He wants you to prepare a chart that depicts rentals by category for the last month. You decide to create a stacked column chart to show all the data he provides to you.

1. Open *EW2_0704* and save it as **May_Rentals**.

2. Create a chart at the end of the document.

3. Delete the existing data in the datasheet, and enter the following data:

	Week 1	Week 2	Week 3	Week 4
Action	45	55	65	30
Children	15	18	22	25
Comedy	46	57	72	35
Drama	35	36	51	25
Horror	18	14	34	10
Other	10	10	20	5

4. Apply the *Stacked Column* chart type.
5. Enter the chart title **May Rentals**, and enter the value (Y) axis title **No. of Rentals**.
6. Apply the *Square* wrapping style, and center the chart object between the margins.
7. Set a 4.25" width for the chart object.
8. Apply a border around the chart object.
9. Apply 8-point size to the legend, 9-point size to the X-axis, 9-point size to the value Y-axis, and Dark Blue font color for the chart title.
10. Save, print (optional), and close the *May_Rentals* document.

2. Creating a Line Chart from Excel Data

As the executive assistant to a department chair at the local college, you need to create a line chart to accompany a memo to the dean. The line chart should compare salaries for four instructors from 1996 to 2004. The salary information is stored in an Excel worksheet.

1. In Word, open *EW2_0705* and save it as **Salaries_Memo**.
2. Create a line chart at the end of the document.
3. Delete the current datasheet data and then import *EW2_0706.xls* into the datasheet. Adjust the placement of the data in the datasheet.
4. Apply the *Square* wrapping style, center the chart object between the margins, and set a 3.5" height.
5. Set 10-point font size for the legend, the X-axis, and the Y-axis.
6. Format the Y-axis by setting these scale options:
    a. **35000** minimum
    b. **2000** major unit
7. Change Winegar's 2004 salary to **44000** in the datasheet.
8. Save, print (optional), and close the *Salaries_Memo* document.

3. Creating a Pie Chart from a Word Table

You are preparing a memo for the manager of a local music store. The memo contains a table that you want to chart.

1. Open *EW2_0707* and save it as `Music_Sales_Memo`.
2. Select the entire table and then create a chart; choose the *Pie Chart* sub-type.
3. Using the Microsoft Graph Chart Standard toolbar, make sure the chart is created by columns instead of by rows.
4. Create a title called `September Sales`.
5. Explore the Chart Options dialog box and display percentage data labels.
6. Click outside the chart, set a 4.5" width, *Square* wrap, and *Center* horizontal alignment.
7. Select 8-point size for the legend.
8. Remove the plot area border and fill color.
9. Click and drag the plot area within the chart area to increase its size. Reposition the plot area as needed.
10. Select 9-point size for the data labels. Select the 5% data label and move it a little to avoid overlapping the *September Sales* chart title, if necessary.
11. Save, print (optional), and close the *Music_Sales_Memo* document.

4. Creating Organization Charts

You need to create two organization charts showing the hierarchy of your school. The first chart should reflect the structure of your administration and the second should reflect a specific department within the school. For example, you might create an organization chart of the College of Business Administration. Then you can create a second organization chart for the Department of Information Systems.

1. In a new document window, set 1" top, bottom, left, and right margins.
2. Research the structure of your school hierarchy. Use the school's course catalog or browse the school's Web page, if it has one. Refer to Figure 7.27 for sample organizational charts. Sketch out the structure of your school before creating the charts.
3. Save the document as `College_Chart`.
4. Create a heading using the title of your top administration. Apply the Title style to the heading.
5. Refer to your sketch and create the organization chart with these specifications:
    a. Apply the Beveled Gradient style.
    b. Format the dean's position in 16-point Arial font.
    c. Increase the spacing before paragraphs within the dean's position to center the text vertically within the position.
    d. Apply the *Top and bottom* wrapping style and center the diagram.
6. Create a heading for the title of your department. Apply the Title style to the heading.
7. Create the departmental organization chart, using the Beveled Gradient diagram style. Apply the *Top and bottom* wrapping style and center the diagram.

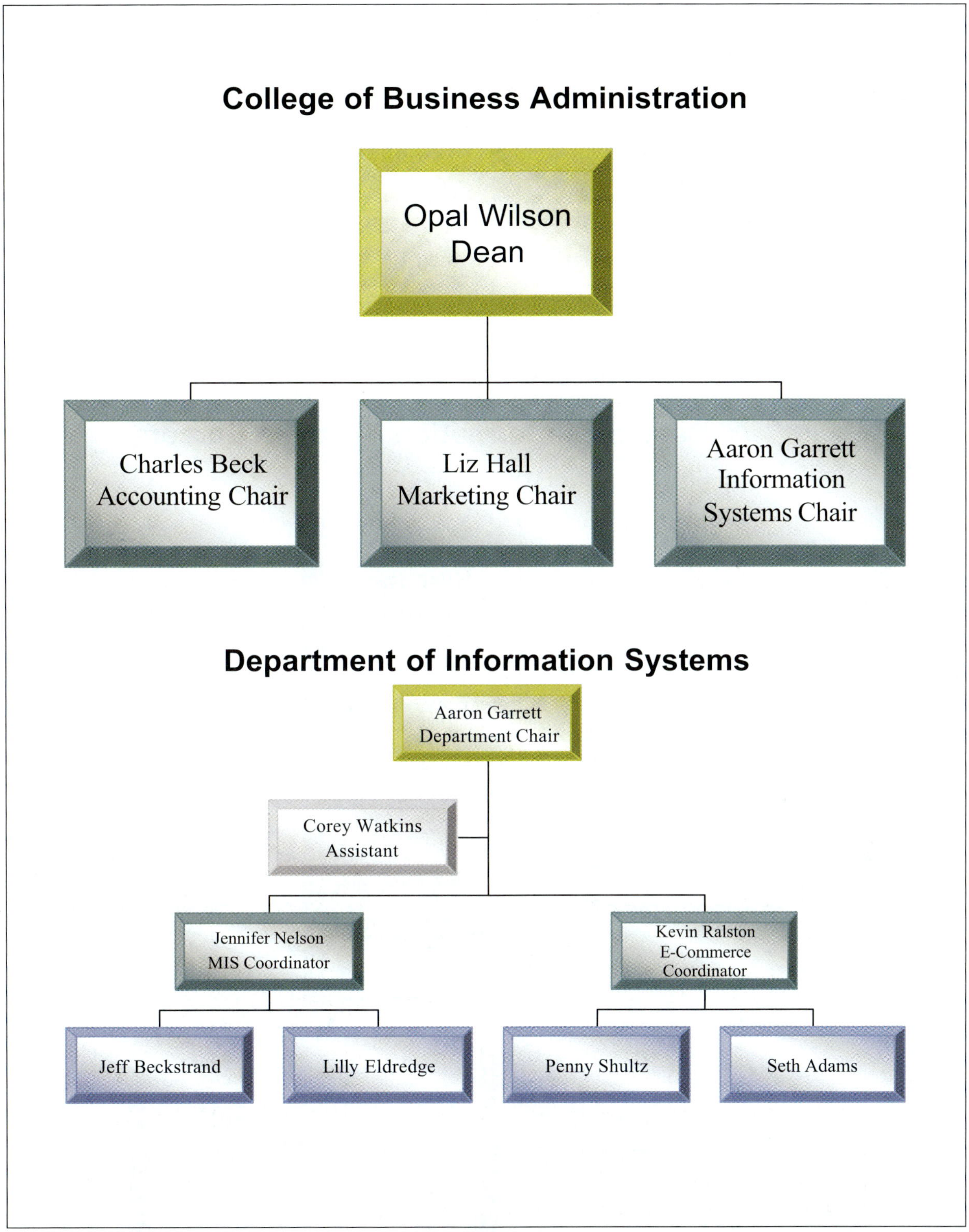

College of Business Administration

- Opal Wilson, Dean
  - Charles Beck, Accounting Chair
  - Liz Hall, Marketing Chair
  - Aaron Garrett, Information Systems Chair

Department of Information Systems

- Aaron Garrett, Department Chair
  - Corey Watkins, Assistant
    - Jennifer Nelson, MIS Coordinator
      - Jeff Beckstrand
      - Lilly Eldredge
    - Kevin Ralston, E-Commerce Coordinator
      - Penny Shultz
      - Seth Adams

FIGURE 7.27

8. Adjust spacing and font sizes as needed. Also increase the spacing before paragraphs on the first line of text for most positions to vertically center text within the positions.

9. Save, print (optional), and close the *College_Chart* document.

5. Designing a Radial Diagram

As an advisor for business information systems (BIS) students, you want to create a simple diagram that shows some of the careers available for BIS majors. You decide to create a radial diagram.

1. In a new document window, type **Business Information Systems Careers**.
2. Format the text by applying the Title style.
3. Create a radial diagram below the title.
4. Enter the data shown in Figure 7.28, and insert shapes as needed.

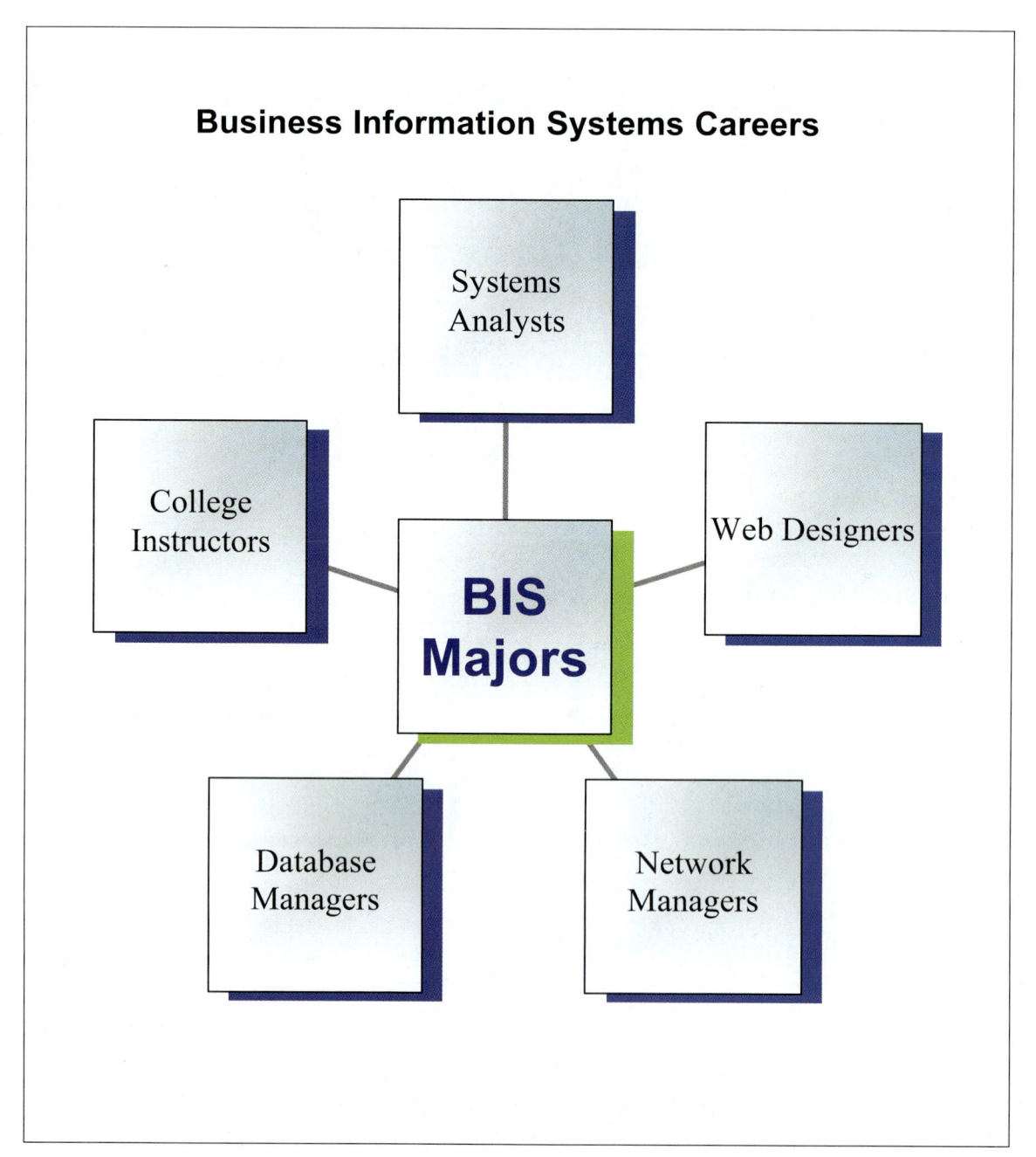

Business Information Systems Careers

- BIS Majors (center)
  - Systems Analysts
  - Web Designers
  - Network Managers
  - Database Managers
  - College Instructors

FIGURE 7.28

5. Save the document as **BIS_Careers_Diagram**.
6. Apply the Square Shadows diagram style.
7. Apply 16-point Times New Roman to the outer boxes of the diagram.
8. Apply 25-point Arial Bold Blue font to the *BIS Majors* box.
9. Center text vertically in each box by increasing the spacing before paragraphs on the first line of text within each box.
10. Center the diagram object between the left and right margins.
11. Center the document vertically on the page.
12. Save, print (optional), and close the *BIS_Careers_Diagram* document.

DISCOVERY ZONE

Discovery Zone exercises require advanced knowledge of topics presented in the lessons or self-directed learning of new skills. You can work through one or more exercises in any order.

1. Creating a Pie Chart with Data Labels

Your supervisor wants to try another approach to depicting the video rentals. This time, she wants a pie chart comparing the proportion of each category to all rentals. Open *EW2_0704* and save it as **May_Rentals_Pie**.

Create a pie chart at the end of the document. Enter the category names listed in Challenge exercise 1. Delete all sample values and data; then enter **Month** in the first cell in column A. Use the Windows calculator to find the total rentals for each category, such as *Action,* and enter those respective totals in the datasheet. Chart the data by column instead of by row.

Type **Categorical Rentals** for the chart title and display percentage data labels.

Set these chart object formats: square text wrap, center alignment, and 6" width. Make these adjustments to the chart: 11-point size for the legend, legend placed below the plot area, inside end position for the data labels, no plot border, white plot area, and white chart area. Increase the plot area within the chart area. Change the *Horror* data point color to Rose, and change the *Other* data point color to Light Green. Explode the *Drama* pie slice. Use Help to learn how to apply these formats, if necessary. Apply 14-point size for the data labels.

Save, print (optional), and close the *May_Rentals_Pie* document.

2. Creating a Horizontal Bar Chart from Imported Excel Data

Greg, one of your college friends, is applying for a short-term loan to help cover college expenses. He created a simple worksheet listing his major expenses. Greg asked you to create a bar chart depicting his expenses and insert it into a letter you helped him compose.

Open *EW2_0708* and save it as **Loan_Letter**. Create a bar chart between the last two one-sentence paragraphs, importing *EW2_0709.xls* into the datasheet. Enter the range address **A4:D9** to import the Excel data. Click the appropriate chart type to display the categories, such as *Rent,* along the Y-axis, quantities on the X-axis, and months in the legend. Delete extraneous columns or rows in the datasheet. Use the Help feature if you need assistance in setting the specifications required in this exercise.

Apply these chart object formats: center alignment, *Top and bottom* text wrapping, and 5" width. Include an appropriate title in Blue font color. Format the values on the X-axis for Currency with zero decimal places. Apply Yellow, Red, and Blue to the data series. Apply the White Marble textured fill for the chart area and Lavender fill for the plot area. Apply 11-point size to the legend, X-axis, and Y-axis. Adjust the width of the chart, if needed, to prevent the Y-axis labels from appearing at an angle.

Save, print (optional), and close the *Loan_Letter* letter.

3. Creating a Pyramid Diagram with Text Boxes and Lines

You want to create a food pyramid diagram developed by the Department of Health and Human Services (HHS) and based on the USDA's research. Use the Research feature to search the Internet to find information about this diagram and print a copy of it.

In a new document window, set 0.75" left and right margins, and type **Food Pyramid Guide** in 20-point Arial Bold. Save the document as **Food_Pyramid_Guide**.

Within Word, create a 7"-wide pyramid diagram using the Fire diagram style. Include the different components. For each level, list the category and the recommended servings. Because some components, such as fruits and vegetables, are shown on the same pyramid level, you will need to create and format see-through text boxes to separate components on the same level. Remove the text box borders, and set 100% transparency fill. Insert a 3-point white vertical line between the categories on the same level. (Hint: To get rid of the placeholder text, click inside the placeholder and press Spacebar.)

Use Help to learn how to create and format text boxes. Adjust font sizes and text placement. Save, print (optional), and close the *Food_Pyramid_Guide* document.

PROJECT 8 LEVEL 2

USING WORD WITH OTHER APPLICATIONS

OBJECTIVES

IN THIS PROJECT, YOU LEARN HOW TO

- Insert and modify hyperlinks
- Insert an Excel workbook as an object
- Embed Excel data into Word
- Modify embedded data
- Link Excel data into Word
- Save documents in different formats

Project 8 Using Word with Other Applications

WHY WOULD I DO THIS?

As you create and modify Word documents, you might want to enable another user or yourself to display a different location within the same document, to open another file, or to display a specific Web page that contains related information. In addition, you might want to use data that were created in another program. For example, you might want to include Excel data or an Excel chart in a Microsoft Word document. Depending on how you incorporate data from other programs into Word, you might need to format or modify the data.

In addition to jumping to other locations and inserting data from other programs, you might need to save a Word document in a different format so that another person can open it within a different word processing or text editing program.

VISUAL SUMMARY

In this project, you insert and modify a hyperlink that displays the contents of an Excel file. A *hyperlink* is an electronic code that jumps the insertion point to a different location within the current document, opens another file, or displays a particular Web page. Next, you insert a Microsoft Excel file as an object within a Word document. You also use the Paste Special dialog box to embed specific cells from an Excel workbook into Word so that you can edit the object within Word. In addition, you also insert an Excel chart into Word so that any changes made to the original Excel chart are reflected in your Word document. Finally, you save the document in another format so that you can use it with other text-editing programs. Figure 8.1 shows the hyperlink you create, the Microsoft Excel worksheet object you insert from a file, and the embedded data from a specific area of an Excel worksheet.

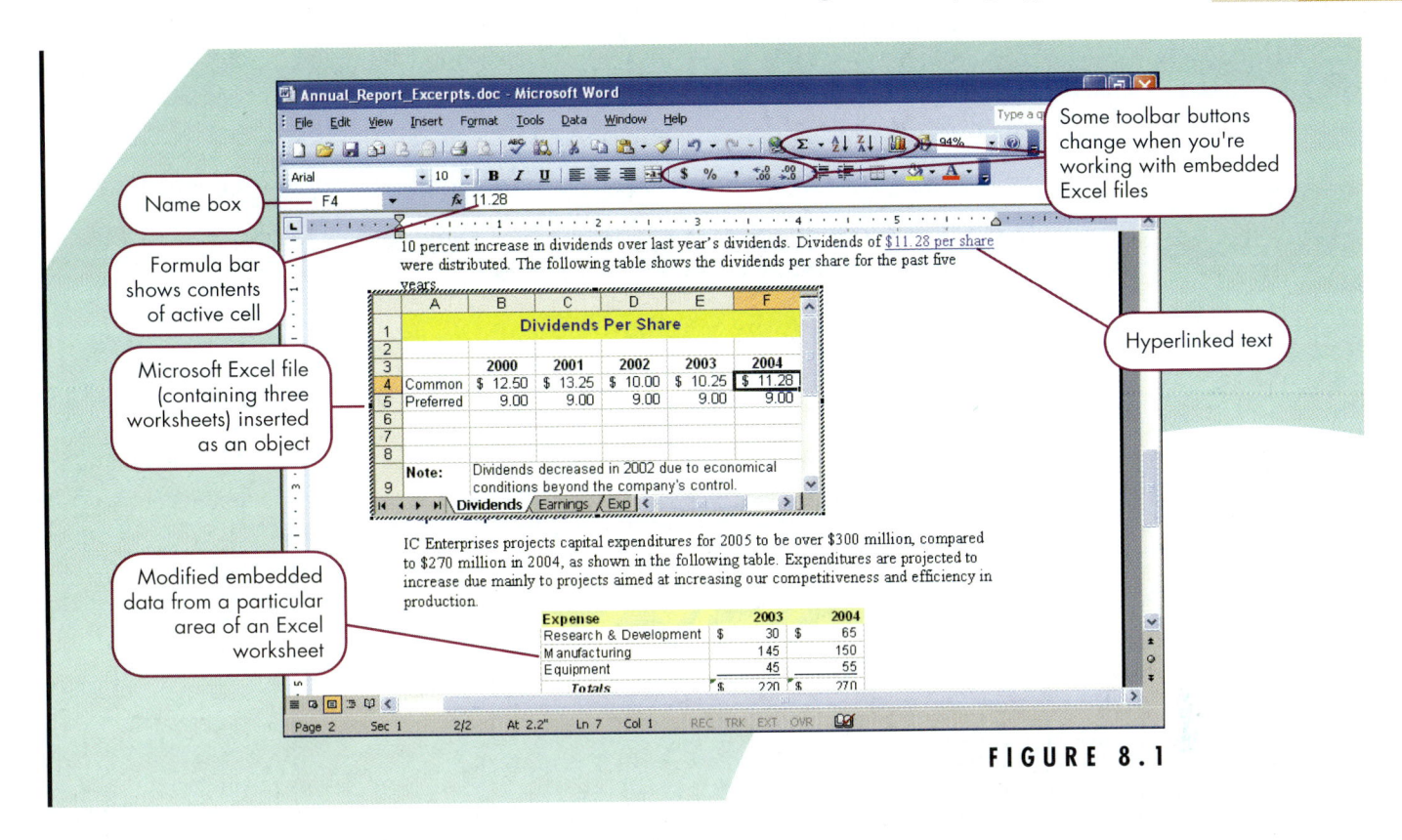

Lesson 1 Inserting and Modifying Hyperlinks   277   LEVEL 2

FIGURE 8.1

Callouts in the figure:
- Name box
- Formula bar shows contents of active cell
- Microsoft Excel file (containing three worksheets) inserted as an object
- Modified embedded data from a particular area of an Excel worksheet
- Some toolbar buttons change when you're working with embedded Excel files
- Hyperlinked text

LESSON 1: Inserting and Modifying Hyperlinks

While working with multiple applications and collaborating with others on various projects, you are likely to encounter a hyperlink that you can click to jump to another location, to open another file, or to start a process such as sending an e-mail or transferring a file. Hyperlinks in Web pages enable you to link to other locations in the current Web site and to other Web sites. You can create your own hyperlinks in Microsoft Office applications that refer to other application files, other locations within the current file, or Internet links. You can format text and graphical images as hyperlinks.

In this lesson, you format text as a hyperlink to open an Excel workbook to see details about stock dividends for your organization. After inserting the hyperlink, you modify it by customizing the ScreenTip that appears when the mouse pointer is positioned over the hyperlink.

Project 8 Using Word with Other Applications

To Insert and Modify a Hyperlink

1 Open *EW2_0801* and save it as `Annual_Report_Excerpts`.
Because you want to format *$11.28 per share* as a hyperlink, you must select it first.

2 In the *Dividends* section, select the words *$11.28 per share*.
Now you need to format the selected text as a hyperlink.

3 Click Insert Hyperlink on the Standard toolbar.
The Insert Hyperlink dialog box opens so that you can specify what you want to link to, where the document or Web page is located, and other hyperlink options (see Figure 8.2).

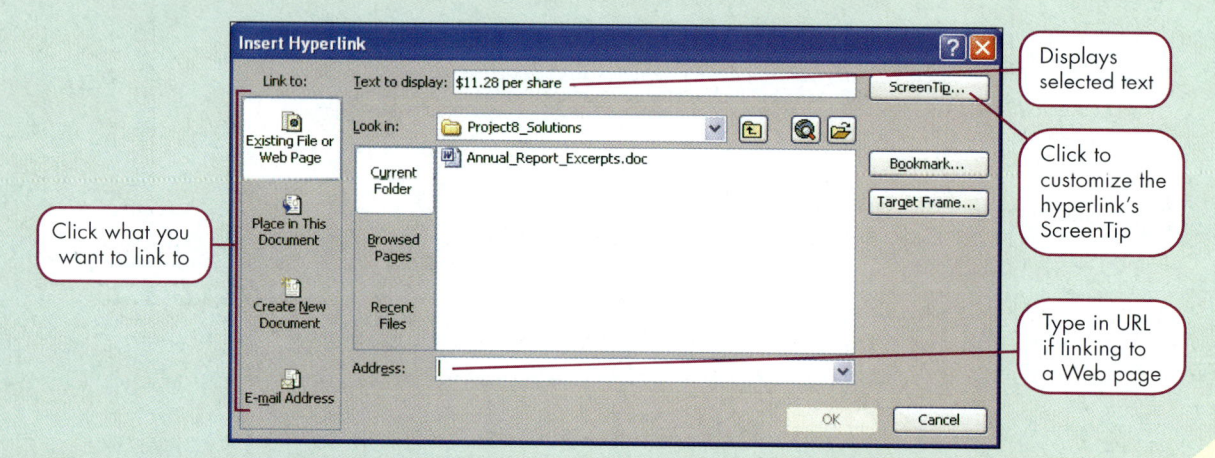

[Insert Hyperlink dialog box shown with callouts:]
- Displays selected text
- Click to customize the hyperlink's ScreenTip
- Type in URL if linking to a Web page
- Click what you want to link to

FIGURE 8.2

4 Make sure the *Existing File or Web Page* option is selected on the left side of the dialog box.
The *Existing File or Web Page* option enables you to link to a file by specifying its path and filename or link to a Web page by specifying its Uniform Resource Locator (URL).

5 Use the *Look in* list to specify the drive and folder location that contains files that accompany this project of this textbook.

If you have problems...

If you type the filename instead of navigating to it, you must type the entire path, filename, and filename extension, such as `C:\Word_2003_Level 2\EW2_Project8_Student\EW2_0802.xls` in the *Address* box. The hyperlink will not work if you do not type the complete path, filename, and filename extension.

6 Select the Excel workbook *EW2_0802*, click OK, and position the mouse pointer over the *$11.28 per share* hyperlink.

Lesson 1 Inserting and Modifying Hyperlinks 279

The text you selected, *$11.28 per share,* appears in Blue font color and is underlined, indicating that this text is a hyperlink. When you position the insertion point over the hyperlink, Word displays a ScreenTip that indicates the file and its hyperlinked location, as well as how to display the linked document (see the sample in Figure 8.3).

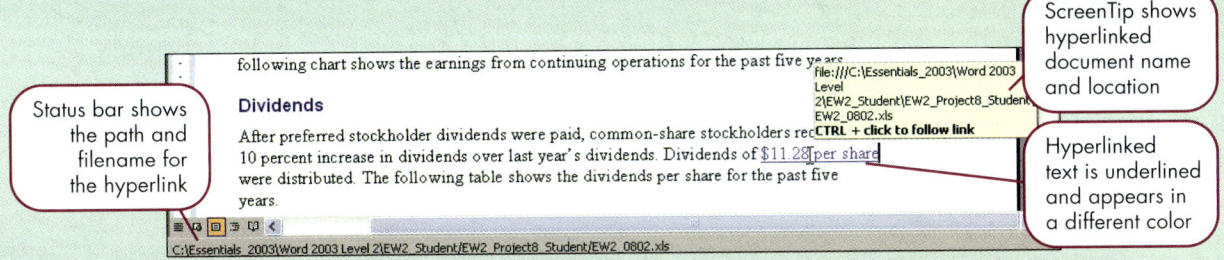

FIGURE 8.3

Now you want to customize the ScreenTip text.

7 Right-click the hyperlinked text, *$11.28 per share.*
You see a shortcut menu of options so that you can edit, select, open, copy, or remove the hyperlink.

8 Choose *Edit Hyperlink* from the shortcut menu.
The Edit Hyperlink dialog box opens and contains options that are identical to those in the Insert Hyperlink dialog box.

9 Click the ScreenTip button in the top-right corner of the dialog box.
The Set Hyperlink ScreenTip dialog box opens so that you can specify the text that appears in the ScreenTip (see Figure 8.4).

FIGURE 8.4

10 Type `Higher Dividends Paid in 2004`, click OK in the Set Hyperlink ScreenTip dialog box, and then click OK in the Edit Hyperlink dialog box.

11 Position the mouse pointer over the hyperlinked text.
Word displays the text you specified in the ScreenTip (see Figure 8.5).

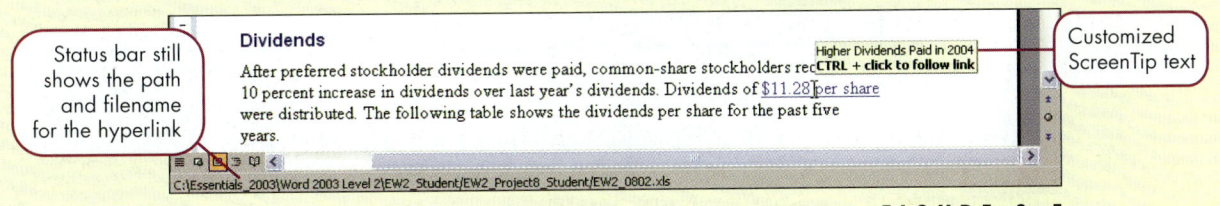

FIGURE 8.5

12 Press Ctrl and click the hyperlinked text.
The Microsoft Excel 2003 program starts, and the *EW2_0802* workbook opens.

13 Leave the *EW2_0802* workbook open, and click the Word button on the Windows taskbar to toggle back to the *Annual_Report_Excerpts* document in Word.
Notice that the color of the hyperlink text changes after you click the hyperlink.

14 Save the *Annual_Report_Excerpts* document and keep it onscreen to continue with the next lesson.

TO EXTEND YOUR KNOWLEDGE...

OPENING THE INSERT HYPERLINK DIALOG BOX
You can also open the Insert Hyperlink dialog box by choosing Insert, Hyperlink or by pressing Ctrl+K.

INSERTING HYPERLINKS TO A WEB PAGE
To insert a hyperlink to a Web page, open the Insert Hyperlink dialog box, type the complete URL, such as `http://www.prenhall.com/essentials/`, in the *Address* box, and click OK.

INSERTING HYPERLINKS TO THE SAME DOCUMENT
When you work with long documents in Word, you might want to create hyperlinks to different sections or topics within that document. Open the Insert Hyperlink dialog box or the Edit Hyperlink dialog box, and click the *Place in This Document* option. The dialog box displays text formatted with heading styles, such as Heading 1, and bookmarks that have been created (see Figure 8.6).

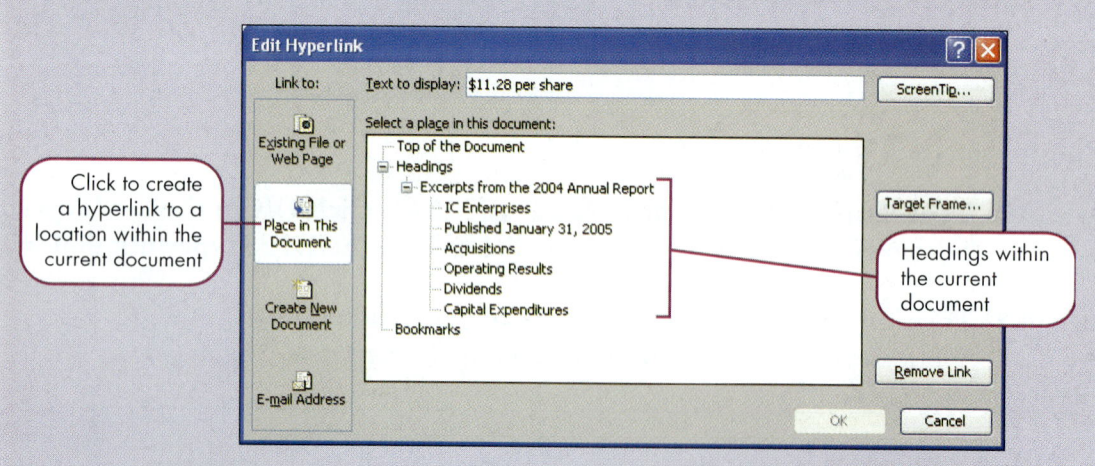

FIGURE 8.6

Click a heading as the destination for the hyperlink, and click OK.

INSERTING A GRAPHICS HYPERLINK
You can create a hyperlink from a graphical object, such as a clip art image, photograph, or drawing shape. You must select the object first before opening the

Insert Hyperlink dialog box. Setting hyperlink options for graphics is the same as setting hyperlink options for text.

REDIRECTING A HYPERLINK
On occasion it may become necessary to redirect a hyperlink to a new location, such as a different location within the same document, a different document, or a different Web page. To redirect a hyperlink, right-click the hyperlink, choose *Edit Hyperlink,* edit the hyperlink's destination or address, and click OK.

COPYING OR MOVING A HYPERLINK
When you edit documents, you might decide to duplicate or move a hyperlink. To copy a hyperlink, right-click the hyperlink, choose *Copy Hyperlink,* position the insertion point where you want to duplicate the hyperlink, and click Paste.

The process of moving a hyperlink is similar to cutting and pasting text or other objects: Select the hyperlink you want to move, click Cut, position the mouse pointer where you want the hyperlink to appear, and click Paste.

CHANGING THE APPEARANCE OF HYPERLINKS
Hyperlinks initially display blue and underlined, which tends to be the standard for links on Web sites, links within e-mail, and so forth. However, you control the appearance of a hyperlink, and you can apply any formatting—font, color, size, shading, and so on. To change the formatting of a hyperlink, select the hyperlink and apply the character and font attributes you desire.

REMOVING A HYPERLINK
To convert hyperlink text to normal text, right-click the hyperlink and select *Remove Hyperlink* from the shortcut menu. To remove a hyperlink and its associated text, select the hyperlink and press Del.

LESSON 2: Inserting an Excel Workbook as an Object

Each Microsoft Office 2003 program is designed to create documents for specific purposes. For example, Word is designed to create and format letters, memos, and reports, and Excel is designed to create electronic spreadsheets to store, format, and calculate values. Although you should use the appropriate program to prepare a specific type of document or output, you might need the same data in another program. For example, you might need to include some Excel data in a proposal that you are creating in Word. The program used to create the original data is called the **source program.** The program that you bring the data into is called the **destination program.**

You can insert a Microsoft Excel workbook as an object within Word without opening the file in Excel. The contents of the entire Excel workbook appear as an object in Word. A workbook may contain multiple pages called worksheets. When you double-click the Excel workbook

Project 8 Using Word with Other Applications

object, Word's interface reflects some of Excel's functionality, and you can choose which worksheet data to display.

In this lesson, you insert a Microsoft Excel workbook as an object within your annual report.

To Insert a Microsoft Excel Worksheet Object

1 In the *Annual_Report_Excerpts* document, position the insertion point on the blank line immediately above the heading *Capital Expenditures*.
You want to insert the Microsoft Excel worksheet object between the paragraph that discusses dividends and the *Capital Expenditures* heading.

2 Choose **Insert**, **Object**, and click the Create from **File** tab.
The Create from **F**ile tab enables you to choose the file you want to use to create the object within Word (see Figure 8.7).

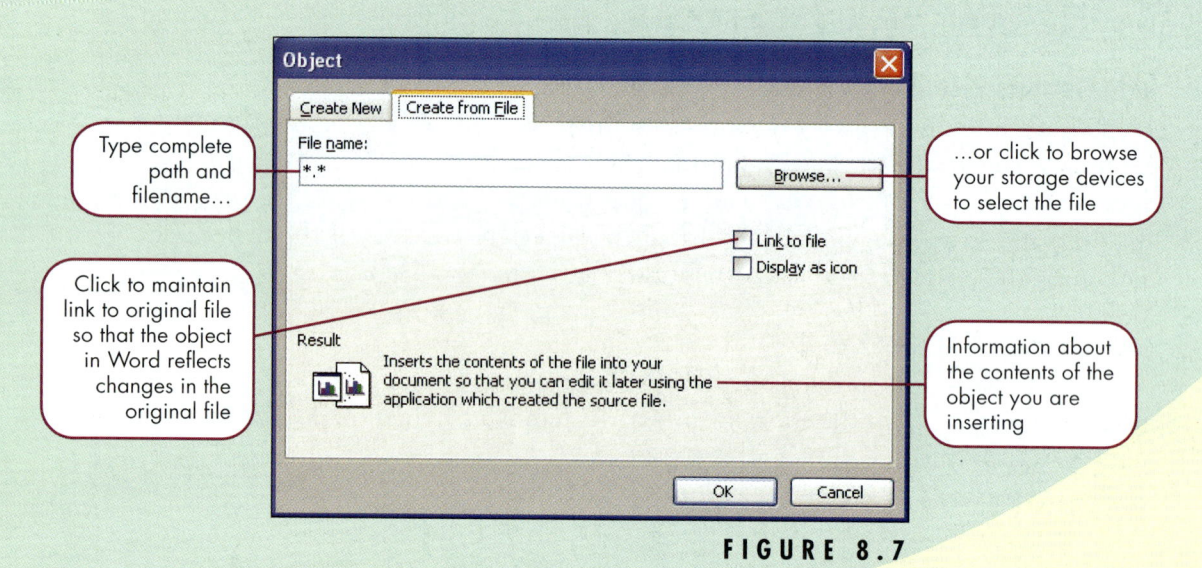

Type complete path and filename...

Click to maintain link to original file so that the object in Word reflects changes in the original file

...or click to browse your storage devices to select the file

Information about the contents of the object you are inserting

FIGURE 8.7

3 Click **B**rowse, browse your storage devices to find and select the *EW2_0802* Excel workbook, and then click In**s**ert in the Browse dialog box.
The *File name* box reflects the complete path and filename of the file you selected in the Browse dialog box.

4 Click OK in the Object dialog box and scroll down to the next page to see the object.
The contents of the active worksheet within the *EW2_0802* workbook appear as an object in Word (see Figure 8.8).

Lesson 2 Inserting an Excel Workbook as an Object

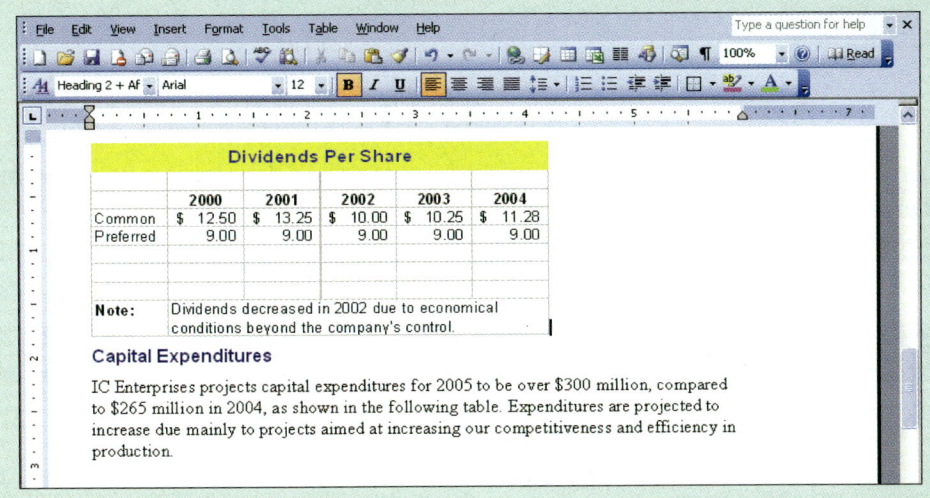

FIGURE 8.8

If you have problems . . .

If your data are different from the data shown in Figure 8.8, another worksheet was active when the Excel workbook was last saved. To display the correct worksheet, complete step 5 and then click the Dividends worksheet tab at the bottom of the embedded object, as shown in Figure 8.9.

5 Double-click the worksheet object.
When you double-click the worksheet object, the Word interface reflects some of Excel's functionality, such as special formatting buttons on the Formatting toolbar (see Figure 8.9).

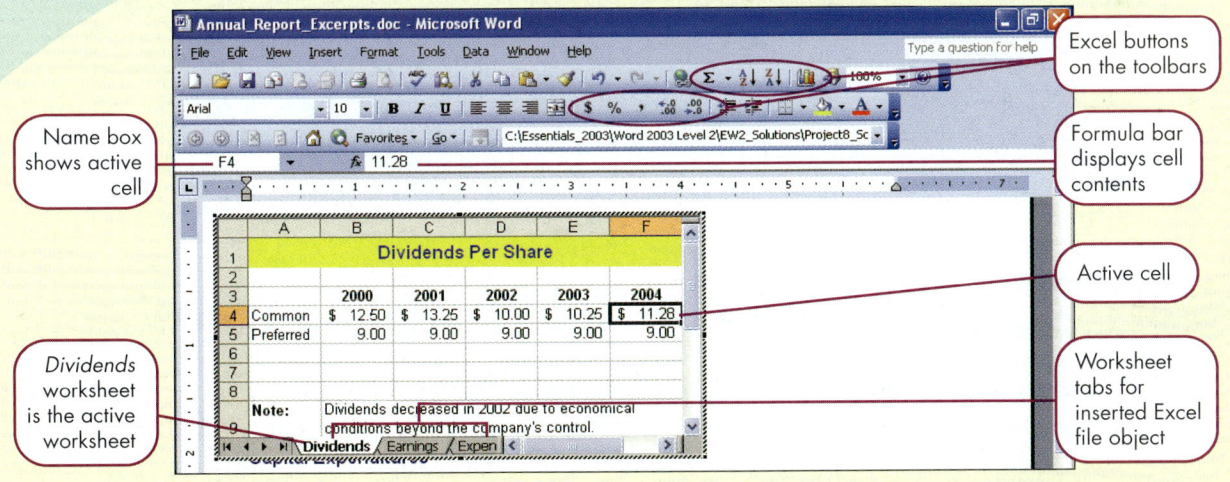

FIGURE 8.9

The Name box displays the *cell reference*—a designation of a cell within a worksheet, typically used to refer to a particular cell while calculating. For example, B1 refers to the cell in the second column (B) in the first row (1).

6 **Click outside the object.**
The menu bar and toolbars no longer reflect Excel functionality when you click outside the object.

7 Save the *Annual_Report_Excerpts* document and keep it onscreen to continue with the next lesson.

TO EXTEND YOUR KNOWLEDGE...

INSERTING A NEW MICROSOFT EXCEL WORKSHEET OBJECT

If you do not have an existing Excel file to insert as an object, you can create a new Microsoft Excel Worksheet object from within Word by using one of two methods: (1) Click Insert Microsoft Excel Worksheet on the Standard toolbar and specify the number of columns and rows you want, just like when you click the Insert Table button; or (2) Choose Insert, Object, click the Create New tab, choose Microsoft Office Excel Worksheet from within the Object dialog box, and click OK.

When you click Insert Microsoft Excel Worksheet on the Standard toolbar, you specify the number of columns and rows from a palette, similar to the way you specify the size for a table when you click Insert Table. When you choose Microsoft Excel Worksheet in the Object dialog box, Word creates an Excel worksheet object and initially displays 7 columns and 10 rows, although you can adjust the viewable area of the object to show more or fewer columns and rows.

CREATING OTHER TYPES OF OBJECTS

You can create other types of new objects or select other types of files to create objects through the Object dialog box. You can create specific objects in Word only if the respective application, such as Excel, is installed on your computer. The *Object type* list box in the Object dialog box reflects the types of objects you can create. For example, in Project 7 you learned how to create and modify a new chart object through the Microsoft Graph Chart application.

LESSON 3: Embedding Excel Data into Word

In the previous lesson, you learned how to insert an Excel workbook as an object within Word. That process inserts the entire workbook contents, which may contain an extensive amount of data stored in several worksheets. Therefore, the object can dramatically increase the size of your Word file.

If you have access to the original Excel workbook, you might want to select only a particular range of cells to insert into the Word document. Thanks to **Object Linking and Embedding**

Lesson 3 Embedding Excel Data into Word   285   LEVEL 2

(OLE), technology that enables you to use objects between programs, you can edit embedded data and objects. ***Embedding*** is the process of importing data that can be edited within the destination program. You typically double-click an embedded object to edit it. Although you inserted an Excel workbook through the Object dialog box in the previous lesson, you actually embedded the workbook contents so that you can edit the object directly within Word.

In this lesson, you embed data from only one worksheet within an Excel workbook that contains three worksheets.

To Embed Excel Data into Word

1 In the *Annual_Report_Excerpts* document, position the insertion point at the end of the document.
Because you want to embed Excel data at the end of the document, you need to position the insertion point in this location.

2 Make sure Excel is running and that the *EW2_0802* workbook is open.

3 Within the *EW2_0802* Excel workbook, click the Expenses worksheet tab at the bottom of the window.
You need to select the range A4:C8. A *range* is a rectangular block of cells in a worksheet. You typically identify the exact range that contains the data you want to embed into your Word document.

4 Position the mouse pointer over cell A4. When the mouse pointer resembles a big plus sign, click and drag down and over to cell C8, which contains the total *$265*.
Figure 8.10 shows the range of cells you just selected.

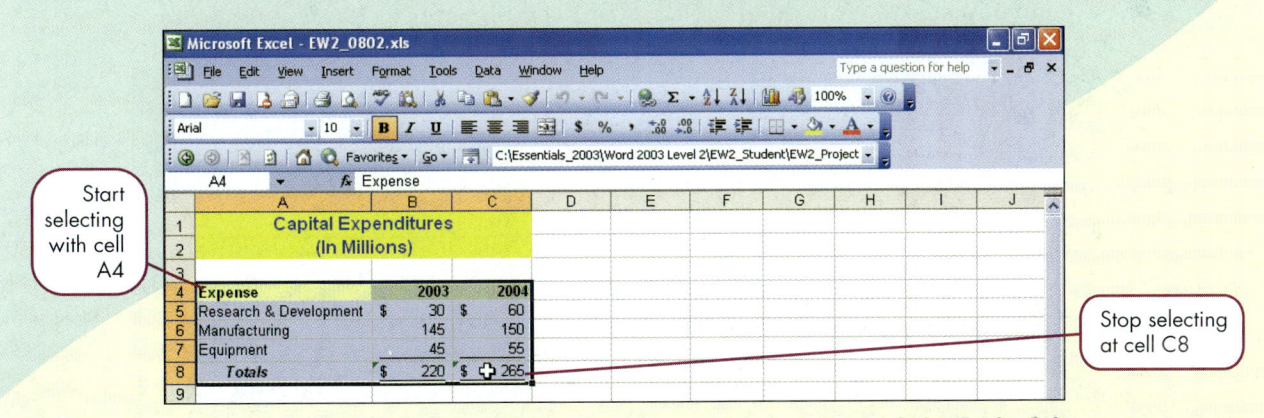

FIGURE 8.10

5 Click Copy on the Excel Standard toolbar.
A *moving border*—a dotted line that moves like lights on a marquee—appears around the selected range you copied. The selected range of data is copied to the

Clipboard. Once the selected range is on the Clipboard, you can paste it in most Windows-based programs.

6 **Click the Word button on the Windows taskbar to toggle back to the *Annual_Report_Excerpts* document in Word.**
Instead of pasting the Excel data, you need to use Paste Special to control how you want the pasted data to appear in Word.

7 **Choose Edit, Paste Special.**
The Paste Special dialog box opens (see Figure 8.11) so that you can choose the type of data you are embedding.

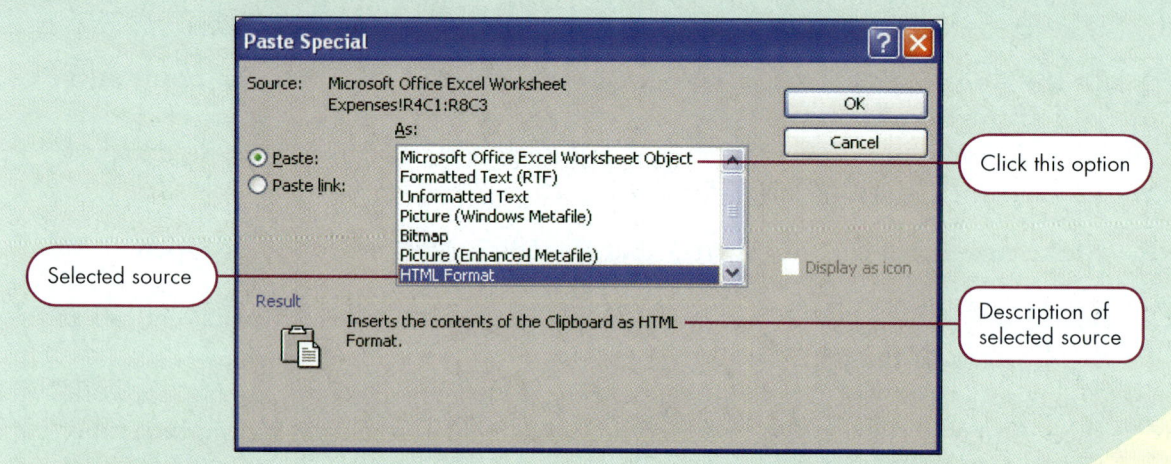

FIGURE 8.11

8 **Click the *Microsoft Office Excel Worksheet Object* option and click OK.**
The range you copied from Excel is pasted as an embedded object within Word.

9 **Click the embedded object.**
When you click an embedded object, sizing handles appear (see Figure 8.12).

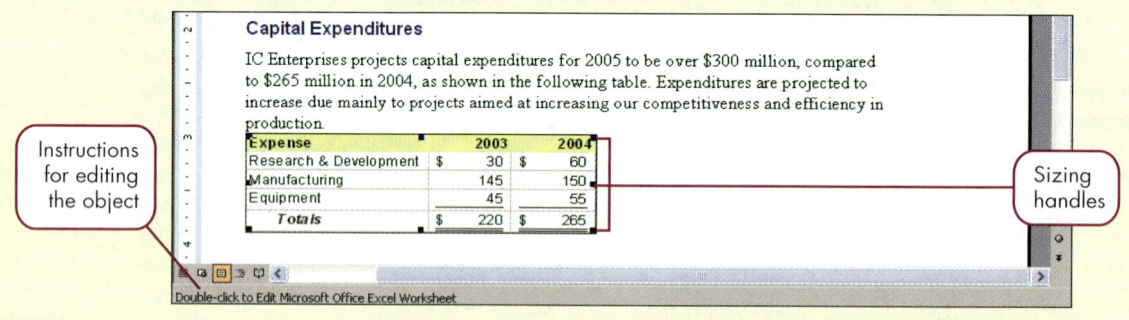

FIGURE 8.12

10 **Right-click the embedded object, and then choose *Format Object*.**
The Format Object dialog box opens, so you can set the object's formats, similar to setting clip art formats.

11 **Click the Layout tab, click the *Square* wrapping style, choose *Center* horizontal alignment, and click OK.**
The embedded object is centered between the left and right margins (see Figure 8.13).

Lesson 3 Embedding Excel Data into Word   287   LEVEL 2

Capital Expenditures

IC Enterprises projects capital expenditures for 2005 to be over $300 million, compared to $265 million in 2004, as shown in the following table. Expenditures are projected to increase due mainly to projects aimed at increasing our competitiveness and efficiency in production.

Expense	2003	2004
Research & Development	$ 30	$ 60
Manufacturing	145	150
Equipment	45	55
Totals	$ 220	$ 265

Embedded object is centered

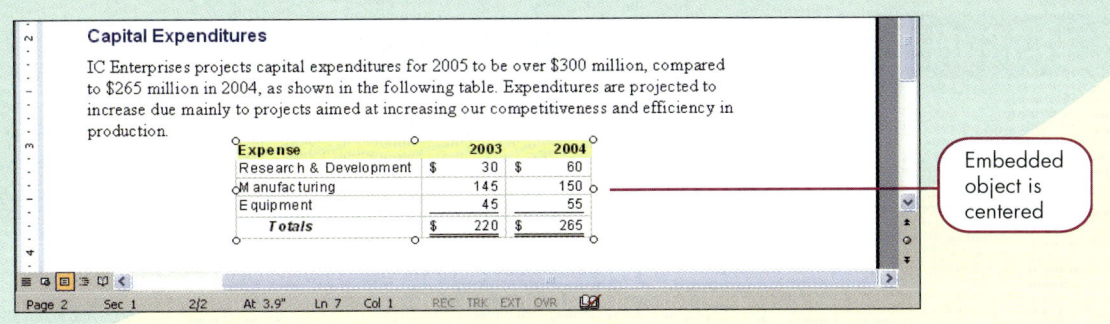

FIGURE 8.13

12 Save the *Annual_Report_Excerpts* document, and keep it onscreen to continue with the next lesson.

TO EXTEND YOUR KNOWLEDGE . . .

COPYING AND PASTING EXCEL DATA

If you use the regular Paste command to paste Excel data into Word, the Excel data are pasted into table cells, instead of as an embedded object. You can then use Table menu options to format the imported table.

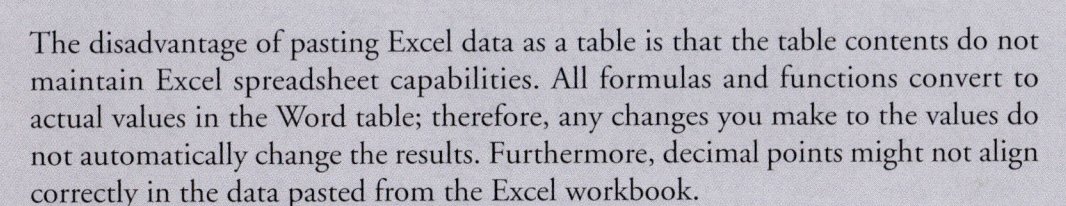

The disadvantage of pasting Excel data as a table is that the table contents do not maintain Excel spreadsheet capabilities. All formulas and functions convert to actual values in the Word table; therefore, any changes you make to the values do not automatically change the results. Furthermore, decimal points might not align correctly in the data pasted from the Excel workbook.

EMBEDDING AN EXCEL CHART

You can embed an Excel chart into a Word document so that you do not have to re-create the chart in Word. Some people prefer creating charts in Excel because Excel contains more charting options than Word. To do this, click the chart within Excel to select it, and copy it to the Clipboard; then in Word, click the Paste button on the Standard toolbar. You do not need to use Paste Special to embed a chart; it is automatically embedded when you use the Paste command.

DRAGGING AND DROPPING A CHART

You have another way to copy and paste a chart from Excel to Word. You can display both the Word and Excel windows side by side, using the *Tile Windows Vertically option.* To do this, right-click a blank space on the taskbar, and choose *Tile Windows Vertically.*

After you select the chart, hold down Ctrl and then drag the chart to where you want to copy it in the Word window. Release the mouse button and release Ctrl. A copy of the chart appears in Word. If you do not press and hold Ctrl during the entire drag-and-drop process, you will move the chart instead of copying it.

LESSON 4: Modifying Embedded Data

You can edit embedded data by double-clicking the object. You see the column and row indicators inside the object window, plus you see Excel buttons and options within the Word window. These options enable you to format the embedded data without exiting the Word program.

When you edit embedded data, you change the data in the destination program (such as Word) only. These changes do not affect the original data in the source program (such as Excel).

In this lesson, you change a value in the embedded object.

To Modify Embedded Data

1 In the *Annual_Report_Excerpts* document, double-click the embedded workbook object in the *Capital Expenditures* section.
Figure 8.14 shows the Excel tools for modifying the embedded object within Word.

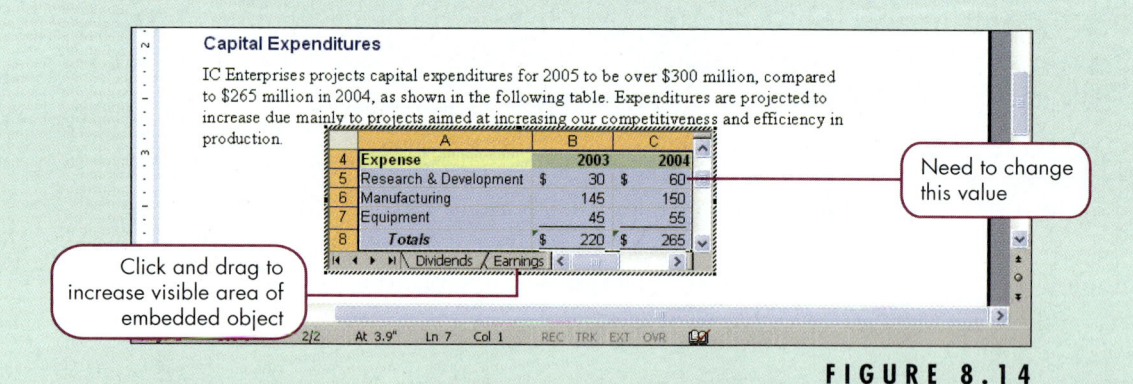

FIGURE 8.14

2 Click and drag the bottom-middle handle to enlarge the height of the worksheet window to see all of the embedded data.

3 Click in cell C8.
The formula bar displays the formula to calculate the total. The formula is =SUM(C5:C7).

4 Click in cell C5, the cell that contains *60*.

5 Type 65 and press ↵Enter.
The total changes to reflect the new value. The new total is *270* (see Figure 8.15).

Lesson 4 Modifying Embedded Data   **289**   LEVEL 2

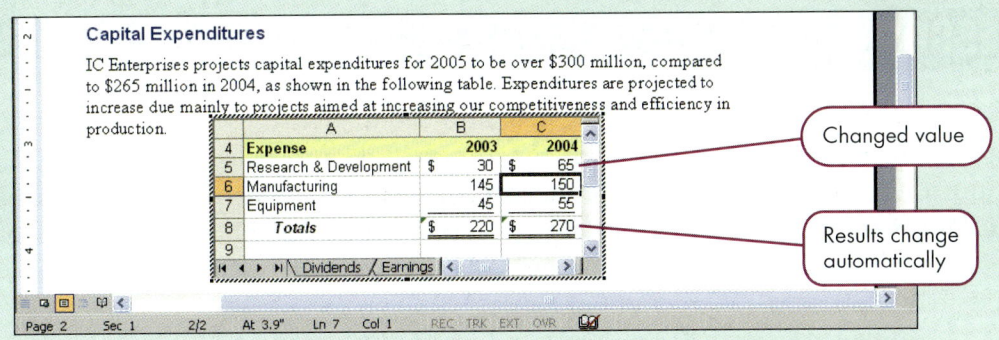

Changed value

Results change automatically

FIGURE 8.15

6 Click outside the embedded object and change *265* to *270* in the last paragraph.

The menu bar and toolbars reflect Word capabilities again.

If you have problems . . .

If the last paragraph wraps on both sides of the embedded worksheet object, display the Format Object dialog box, and click the Layout tab. Click the Advanced button and then click the Text Wrapping tab. Click *Top and bottom* wrapping style, and click OK; then click OK again to close both dialog boxes. *Top and bottom* wrap prevents text from appearing on the left and right sides of the object.

7 Save the *Annual_Report_Excerpts* document, and keep it onscreen to continue with the next lesson.

TO EXTEND YOUR KNOWLEDGE . . .

FORMATTING EMBEDDED DATA

The Format menu contains Excel options when you create and edit an embedded worksheet. Double-click the workbook object and then choose Format, Cells to format worksheet cells. All of Excel's formatting options are available in the Format Cells dialog box. You can choose alignment, underline, and numerical formats for embedded cells. The Formatting toolbar changes to reflect Excel capabilities. For example, you can format data for currency, indent text inside a cell, and so on.

MODIFYING AN EMBEDDED CHART

Double-click an embedded chart to change the values that create the chart. Within the embedded chart window, click the worksheet tab containing the values that create the chart. When you change a value, the chart automatically changes. The original chart in the Excel workbook maintains the original values, however.

LEVEL 2 290   Project 8   Using Word with Other Applications

LESSON 5: Linking Excel Data into Word

Inserting a new object or embedding data into Word are two useful capabilities for importing data. Sometimes, however, you need the imported data to reflect changes in the source program; therefore, you should link the data instead of importing or embedding the data. *Linking* is the process of inserting an object from another program in which the object is connected to the original data. If you change data in the original source program, you can quickly update the data in the destination program.

In this lesson, you complete two sets of hands-on steps. In the first set, you link an Excel chart into Word. In the second set, you change data in the original Excel worksheet, which changes the chart in Excel. You then update the linked chart in Word.

To Link Excel Data into Word

1 In the *Annual_Report_Excerpts* document, position the insertion point on the blank line above the *Dividends* heading.
This is the location where you want to place the Excel chart.

2 Click the Excel button on the Windows taskbar to toggle to the *EW2_0802* Excel workbook.
The moving border remains around the range you copied earlier. You must press Esc to clear the Clipboard and turn off the moving dashed lines; otherwise, you might accidentally enter or paste data over the original data.

3 If the moving border remains on the range you copied earlier, press Esc; save the workbook as `IC_Data`.

4 Click the Earnings tab in the *IC_Data* workbook.
This worksheet contains the chart that you want to link into your Word document (see Figure 8.16).

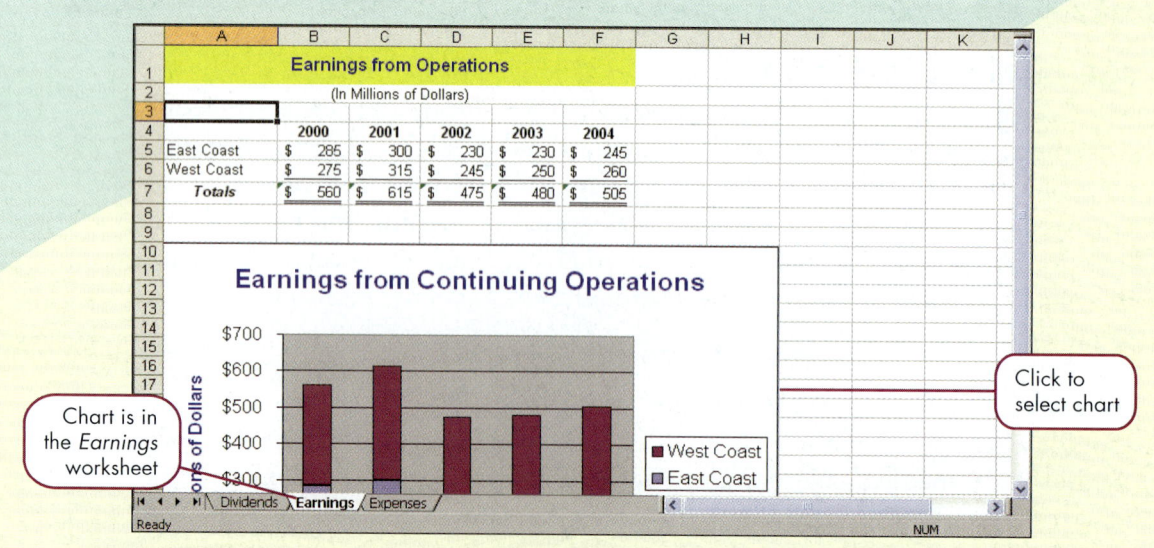

FIGURE 8.16

Lesson 5 Linking Excel Data into Word   **291** LEVEL 2

5 Position the mouse pointer in the white space above the chart and click the chart when you see the *Chart Area* ScreenTip.

If you have problems...

If you click on an element within the chart instead of the entire chart area, your results will not be correct when you use the Paste Special command in Word.

---

6 Click Copy on the Excel Standard toolbar.

7 Click the Word button on the Windows taskbar to toggle back to the *Annual_Report_Excerpts* document.
You are ready to link the chart at the insertion point location.

8 Choose Edit, Paste Special.
When you display the Paste Special dialog box after copying an Excel chart, you have only two options: *Microsoft Office Excel Chart Object* and *Picture (Enhanced Metafile)*.

9 Select the *Microsoft Office Excel Chart Object* option, if necessary; then click the *Paste link* option, and click OK.
The *Paste link* option tells Word to insert the incoming object as a link to the original source data. If you change the original data within Excel, the linked data also change in the Word document when you open the document again in Word.

10 Right-click the linked chart object.
The shortcut menu displays the *Linked Worksheet Object* option (see Figure 8.17). You can edit or open the link if you want.

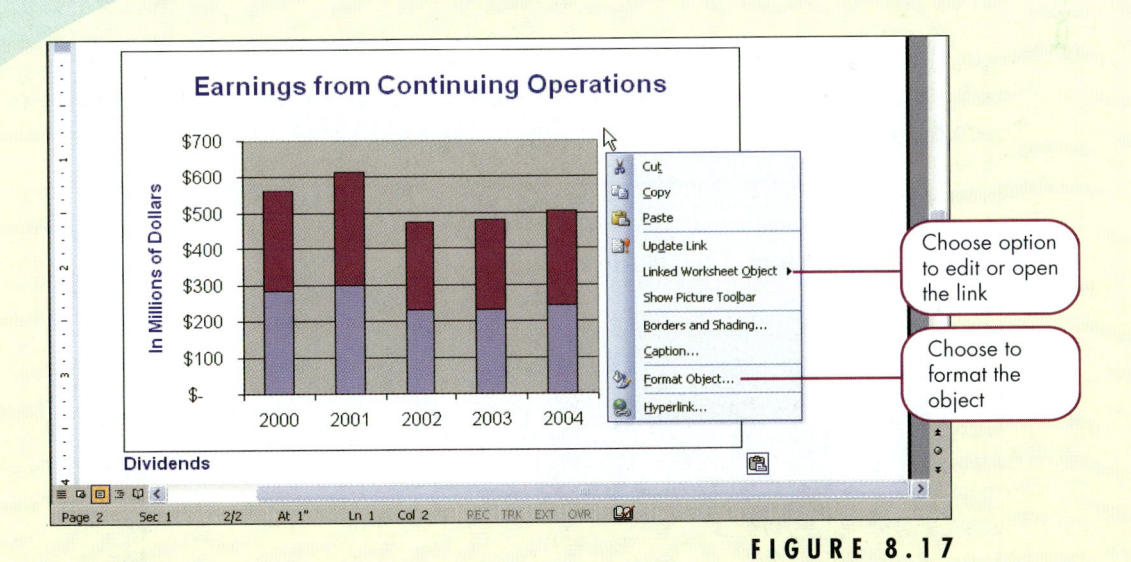

FIGURE 8.17

11 Choose *Format Object,* click the Size tab, type 4.75 in the *Width* box, and click OK.
The chart is smaller so that it fits at the bottom of the first page of your document.

12 Click outside the linked chart object.

13 Save the *Annual_Report_Excerpts* document, and keep it onscreen to continue with the next set of steps.

After reviewing the chart, you realize that some of the values are inaccurate in the Excel worksheet. Because you linked the related chart into Word, you can change the Excel data and instruct Word to update the link from the object to the Excel data.

To Change the Source Data

1 Click the Excel button on the taskbar; then press Esc to clear the Clipboard and turn off the moving dashed lines around the selected chart.

2 Click in cell F5, type 325, and press ↵Enter.
You can see a change in the Excel worksheet and chart. You need to change one more value.

3 Type 350 in cell F6 and press ↵Enter.
The last column in the chart is taller; it is almost at the $700 mark.

4 Save the *IC_Data* workbook, and then exit Excel.
The Word document window is the active window again. Because you kept the Word document open, linked data do not update automatically. You need to instruct Word to update its link to the Excel workbook data. If you had closed the Word document and opened it again, the linked data would be updated.

5 Right-click the chart in Word and choose *Update Link.*
The linked chart object reflects the changes you made in the Excel workbook (see Figure 8.18).

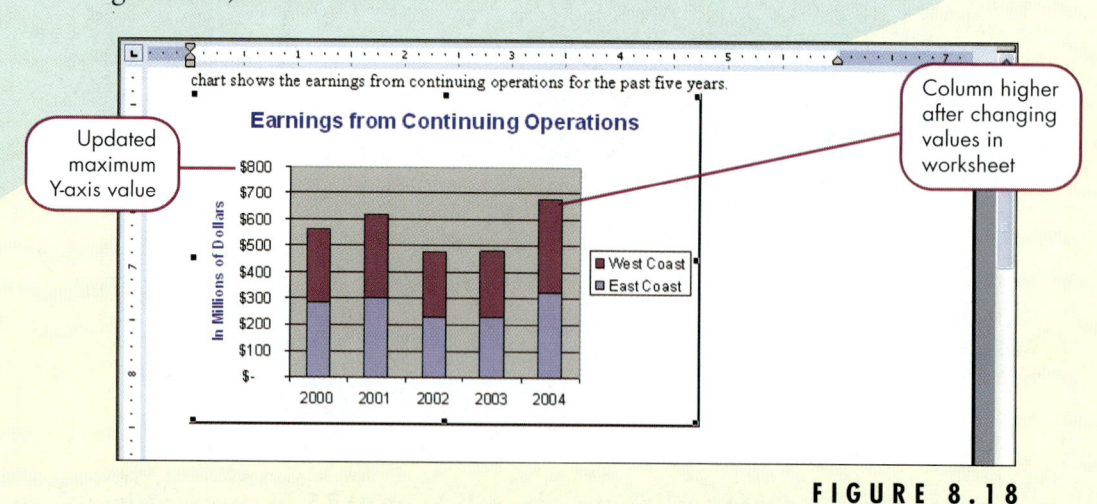

FIGURE 8.18

Now you need to change the paragraph text to reflect the change you made to the linked chart.

Lesson 6 Saving Documents in Different Formats   293   LEVEL 2

6 In the paragraph above the linked chart, change *$505* to **$675**, and then change *5.2* percent to **40.6** percent.

7 Save the *Annual_Report_Excerpts* document and keep it onscreen to continue with the next lesson.

TO EXTEND YOUR KNOWLEDGE...

IMPORTING, EMBEDDING, AND LINKING
You used three methods for inserting Excel worksheet data into Word. Use the following guidelines to determine which method is appropriate for a given situation:

- *Import* when you want a permanent copy of the source data but do not need the data updated within Word.
- *Embed* when you want to insert worksheet data or a chart and be able to modify it *within* Word. Also click the Insert Microsoft Excel Worksheet button to create a blank embedded worksheet within Word.
- *Link* when you want to insert worksheet data that might change in the source worksheet and you want the updates to be reflected in your Word document.

DISPLAYING A LINK AS AN ICON
You can save disk space by inserting the link as an icon instead of displaying the actual linked data. When you are selecting options in the Paste Special dialog box, click the *Display as icon* check box.

You see an icon representing the linked data. The icon represents a worksheet or chart. You can access the source file by double-clicking the icon.

LINKING OTHER DATA
In addition to linking Excel worksheet data and charts into Word, you can also link data from other programs. For example, you can link PowerPoint slides and speaker notes into Word so that any changes you make in the original PowerPoint slide show are reflected in the Word document.

LESSON 6: Saving Documents in Different Formats

When you save files in a particular program, the program saves the files with a particular file format for that particular program. The file's format is indicated by the three-letter filename extension. For example, Word files are indicated by the .doc filename extension, and Excel files are indicated by the .xls filename extension. Although you can open a Word 2003 file in a previous version, such as Word 2002, you might notice that some formatting is lost when you open a Word 2003 file in Word 97. Furthermore, Word documents might not open within other word processing programs.

Project 8 Using Word with Other Applications

If the intended recipient of a file you are creating does not have a major word processing program, such as Microsoft Word or WordPerfect®, you can save a Word document as a plain text file. A *plain text file*—indicated by the .txt filename extension—preserves the main text only; it does not contain any formatting, objects, or tables. All of these features are omitted when you save a document as a plain text file. Therefore, you might prefer to save a document in the *rich text format*—indicated by the .rtf filename extension—which enables you to work with a file in another program or on another platform, such as a Macintosh computer.

In this lesson, you save your current document in rich text format so that workers in your desktop publishing department can open and edit the file on their Macintosh computers.

To Save a File in Another Format

1 In the *Annual_Report_Excerpts* document, choose File, Save As.
The Save As dialog box opens so that you can select a storage location, assign a new filename, or select the file type.

2 Click the *Save as type* drop-down arrow.
You see a list of available file types for saving your document (see Figure 8.19).

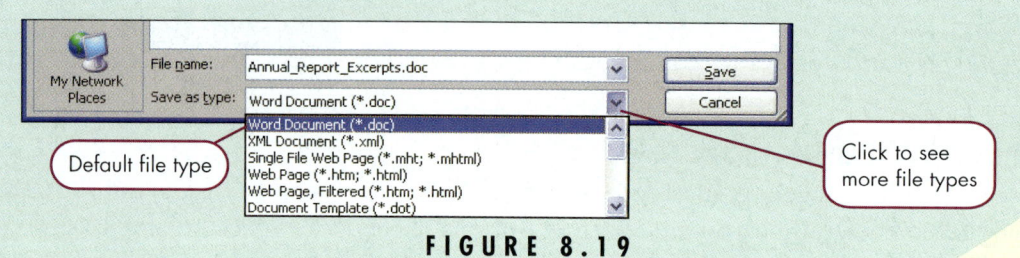

FIGURE 8.19

3 Scroll through the file type list and select *Rich Text Format (*.rtf)*.
Notice that the filename changes to *Annual_Report_Excerpts.rtf* to reflect the new file type.

4 Click Save.
Word saves the document in the rich text format.

5 Close the *Annual_Report_Excerpts* rich text formatted document.

6 If you have access to a Macintosh computer, e-mail the rich text formatted file to yourself, open the e-mail attachment on a Macintosh computer, and observe any formatting changes caused by saving the original file in the rich text format. Then close the document.

TO EXTEND YOUR KNOWLEDGE . . .

FEATURES LOST IN FILE CONVERSION
When you save a Word 2003 document in another file format, some features do not convert correctly. For example, special table formatting, such as a diagonal cell

border, does not appear in a document saved in rich text format. You can type **Results of saving Word 2003 documents in other file formats** in the *Type a question for help* box to learn which Word formats are unavailable in files saved in other file formats.

SUMMARY

In this project you selected text and inserted a hyperlink to an Excel workbook so that the workbook opens when a user holds down Ctrl while clicking the hyperlink. You customized the hyperlink's ScreenTip to show specific text when the mouse is positioned over the hyperlink. You also created a new Microsoft Excel worksheet object from an entire Excel workbook and then you selected a specific range of cells within the workbook, copied it, and then used the Paste Special dialog box to embed the data in Word. After embedding the data, you changed one value within the embedded object to see how the total reflects the change. In addition, you linked an Excel chart within Word so that changes you make in the Excel workbook also change the linked chart within Word. Finally, you saved the document in a different file format for transportability.

You can extend your learning by reviewing concepts and terms, and by practicing variations of skills presented in the lessons. Use the following table as a guide to the numbered questions and exercises in the end-of-project learning opportunities.

LESSON	MULTIPLE CHOICE	DISCUSSION	SKILL DRILL	CHALLENGE	DISCOVERY ZONE
Inserting and Modifying Hyperlinks	4, 7	3	1	1	2
Inserting an Excel Workbook as an Object	1, 5		2		
Embedding Excel Data into Word	2, 3	2	3	2, 4	
Modifying Embedded Data	9	2	3	2	
Linking Excel Data into Word	6	2	4	3	1
Saving Documents in Different Formats	8, 10	1	5	1, 4	

KEY TERMS

cell reference	moving border	rich text format
destination program	Object Linking and Embedding (OLE)	source program
embedding		Tile Windows Vertically option
hyperlink	plain text file	
linking	range	

CHECKING CONCEPTS AND TERMS

MULTIPLE CHOICE

Circle the letter of the correct answer for each of the following.

1. To insert an entire Excel workbook as an object within Word, what should you do? [L2]

   a. Choose File, Open; then click the *Files of type* drop-down arrow, choose *Microsoft Excel Worksheet,* choose the workbook filename, and click Open from within Microsoft Word.

   b. Open the Object dialog box, click the Create from File tab, type the entire path and filename of the Microsoft Excel workbook in the *File name* text box, and click OK.

   c. Select data within an existing Microsoft Excel workbook within Excel, click Copy on the Standard toolbar, and then click Paste within Word.

   d. All of the above

2. When you copy an Excel worksheet and paste it into Word, which of the following is *not* true? [L3]

   a. Formulas are converted to values.

   b. The imported data can be formatted as a table.

   c. Values with decimal points might not align in Word.

   d. You can display the Picture toolbar and then format the pasted data as an object.

3. Which of the following options inserts Excel data in a way that enables you to edit the values in Word, and updates the formula results? [L3]

   a. Copying and pasting

   b. Embedding

   c. Linking

   d. E-mailing

4. Press and hold down _____ as you click a hyperlink within Word to jump to its destination. [L1]

   a. Ctrl
   b. F9
   c. Spacebar
   d. ↵Enter

5. When you double-click an embedded Microsoft Excel worksheet object within Word, the _____ shows the cell reference of the active cell. [L2]

   a. Standard toolbar
   b. Formatting toolbar
   c. Formula bar
   d. Name box

6. Which process should you use to insert Excel data into Word so that any changes you make to the original Excel worksheet are automatically made in Word? [L5]

   a. Copying and pasting
   b. Embedding
   c. Linking
   d. E-mailing

7. To create a hyperlink to a particular Web page, type the Web page's URL in the _____ box in the Insert Hyperlink dialog box. [L1]

   a. Text to display
   b. Look in
   c. Address
   d. Save as type

8. Which format should you use to save a Word file to preserve the document's formats so that it can be opened and edited in different word processing programs on a PC or Macintosh computer? [L6]

   a. Word Documents (*.doc)
   b. Rich Text Format (*.rtf)
   c. Plain Text (*.txt)
   d. Document Template (*.dot)

9. When you change a value in an embedded Microsoft Excel worksheet object within a Word document, what happens? [L4]

   a. The original Excel workbook file reflects the new value.
   b. The results do not recalculate because the embedded object is treated like a table in which the formulas were converted to the original resulting values.
   c. The formulas display the new results in the Excel source workbook but not in the embedded object within Word.
   d. The formulas display the results of changing the value within Word.

10. Which file format saves document text only without its formatting? [L6]

    a. Plain Text (*.txt)
    b. Word Documents (*.doc)
    c. Rich Text Format (*.rtf)
    d. Document Template (*.dot)

DISCUSSION

1. Look at the various *Save as type* options in the Save As dialog box. What are two specific program types in which you can save Word documents? [L6]

2. What should you consider when deciding whether to embed or link Excel data in a Word document? [L3–5]

3. Explain why you would include a hyperlink to a Web page in your document. [L1]

SKILL DRILL

Skill Drill exercises reinforce project skills. Each skill reinforced is the same, or nearly the same, as a skill presented in the project. Detailed instructions are provided in a step-by-step format.

You modify one document named *Personal_Note*. Work through the exercises in sequential order. Be sure to save your changes and close the document if you need more than one work session to complete the desired exercises. Continue working on the *Personal_Note* document instead of starting over with the *EW2_0803* file. Figure 8.20 shows the first page and Figure 8.21 shows the second page of the *Personal_Note* document after completing the first four exercises.

1. Inserting and Customizing a Hyperlink to Send E-Mail

You are writing an update note to tell your family about your semester. You just finished typing the note that you will send as an e-mail attachment, but you want to insert a hyperlink that, when clicked, opens the recipient's e-mail window and displays your e-mail address so that the recipient can send you e-mail.

1. Open *EW2_0803* and save it as **Personal_Note**.
2. Select *send me an e-mail* at the end of the document.
3. Click Insert Hyperlink on the Standard toolbar.
4. With the insertion point in the *Address* text box, type your e-mail address, such as **yourname@school.edu**.

    When you type **@**, Word displays *mailto:* at the front of your e-mail address so that an e-mail program can recognize the hyperlink as an e-mail hyperlink.

5. Click OK.
6. Right-click the hyperlink text and choose *Edit Hyperlink*.
7. Change the *Text to display* contents to **send me weekly e-mail messages**.
8. Click OK.
9. Save the *Personal_Note* document.

Update to my Dear Family

Update on Classes

I'm really enjoying my classes this semester although I keep really busy going to classes, studying, and working. Here is a copy of my schedule so that you can see just how busy I am.

	Monday	Tuesday	Wednesday	Thursday	Friday
9:00	Computer Apps	8:30-9:45 Biology	Computer Apps	8:30-9:45 Biology	Computer Apps
10:00	History	10-11:15 Valuing Diversity	History	10-11:15 Valuing Diversity	History
11:00	Lunch		Lunch		Lunch
12:00	English Comp.	P.E.	English Comp.	P.E.	English Comp.
1:00-4:00	Work	Work	Work	Work	
5:00		Biology Lab		Study	Social Night
6:00	Dinner	Dinner	Dinner	Dinner	
7:00-10:00	Study	Study	Study	Television Night	

I'm taking a computer class to learn Word, Excel, PowerPoint, and Access. Can you believe I can actually use Word and Excel to create and format reports for my other classes? I use Excel to create and maintain a budget to monitor my spending habits. I'm sure you'll be pleased about that!

Update on Expenses

In fact, I created the following table in Excel. Notice how much rent costs each month! And to think I have two other roommates who pay the same amount! Talk about highway robbery!

Expenses	Costs
Rent	$ 500
Utilities	90
Phone	65
Groceries	200
Car	100
Misc.	225
Total	$ 1,180

The pie chart shows the percentage of each major expense in my life. I've actually cut back on eating out as much, so my groceries expense is down from last month.

FIGURE 8.20

Percentage of Budget

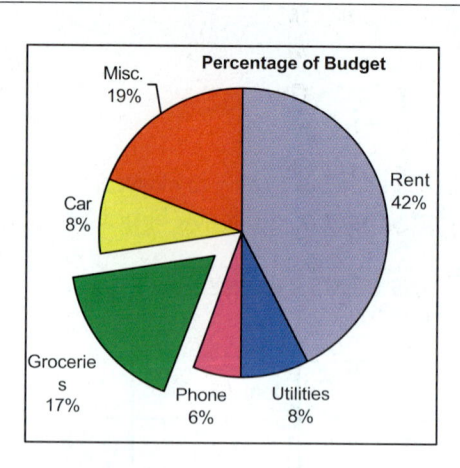

- Misc. 19%
- Rent 42%
- Car 8%
- Groceries 17%
- Phone 6%
- Utilities 8%

Spring Break

Spring break is coming up soon. As you know, I've been saving up money to go to Park City, Utah, to ski! They have some awesome ski slopes there. You probably know where this is headed: Is anyone interested in contributing to this worthy cause? After a week on the slopes, I'll be relaxed and less stressed out to finish the semester. Send cash donations soon please!

My Contact Information

Please call me at 555-4836. I've been trying to watch my phone bill to save money for spring break! You can also send me weekly e-mail messages.

FIGURE 8.21

2. Inserting an Excel Workbook File as an Object

You created an Excel workbook that shows your class, work, and study schedule. You want to insert this workbook file as an object within your note to show your family how busy you are. After inserting the file as an object, you realize that part of the schedule is incomplete, so you need to edit the object within Word.

1. In the *Personal_Note* document, position the insertion point at the beginning of the second paragraph in the *Update on Classes* section.
2. Choose Insert, Object.
3. Click the Create from File tab.
4. Click Browse, browse your storage devices, select the *EW2_0804* Excel workbook, and click Insert.
5. Click OK to close the Object dialog box.
6. With the insertion point blinking after the object, press ⏎Enter twice to insert blank space between the object and the following paragraph.
7. Double-click the Excel object to edit it.
8. Click in cell B4—the cell containing *History* for Monday.
9. Click Copy, click in cell F4, and click Paste.
10. Click in cell B6—the cell containing *English Comp* for Monday—then click Copy, click in cell F6, and click Paste.

11. Click and drag across cells B9 through E9, click the *Fill Color* drop-down arrow on the Formatting toolbar, and choose *Yellow*.
12. Click outside the object.
13. Save the *Personal_Note* document.

3. Embedding and Formatting Excel Worksheet Data

You created a simple budget in Excel and want to embed it into your Word document as an object so that you can format it like you format images. After embedding the Excel data, you want to apply formatting. Specifically, you want to center the object, set its text wrapping style, and add a color border to the object.

1. In the *Personal_Note* document, position the insertion point between the two paragraphs in the *Update on Expenses* section.
2. Start Microsoft Excel and open the *EW2_0805* workbook.
3. Click in cell A3 and drag over and down to cell B10 to select the range that contains the budget data.
4. Click Copy on the Standard toolbar in Excel.
5. Click the Word button on the taskbar to toggle back to the *Personal_Note* document.
6. Choose Edit, Paste Special.
7. Choose the *Microsoft Office Excel Worksheet Object* option and click OK.
8. Right-click the embedded Excel object you just inserted and choose *Format Object*.
9. Click the Layout tab and do the following:
   a. Click the Advanced button.
   b. Click the *Top and bottom* wrapping style option and click OK.
   c. Click the Center horizontal alignment option and click OK.
10. Display the Format Object dialog box again and do the following:
    a. Click the Colors and Lines tab.
    b. Click the *Line Color* drop-down arrow and choose *Sea Green*—the fourth color on the third row of the color palette.
    c. Click the *Style* drop-down arrow, choose *3 pt,* and click OK.
11. Click at the end of the paragraph above the embedded object, and press ⏎Enter once to insert a blank line between the paragraph and the embedded object.
12. Save the *Personal_Note* document.

4. Linking an Excel Chart

Your Excel workbook also contains a pie chart that shows each expense's proportion of your total budget. You want to include it in your personal note. Because you might change the original Excel data and chart, you want to link the chart into Word.

1. In the *Personal_Note* document, position the insertion point on the blank line above the *Spring Break* heading on page 2.
2. Click the Excel button on the taskbar to toggle back to the *EW2_0805* workbook. If needed, open the *EW2_0805* workbook in Excel.
3. Press Esc to clear the moving border around the range of cells, if needed.
4. Position the mouse pointer over the white space within the chart until you see the *Chart Area* ScreenTip; then click the chart to select it, and click Copy on the Standard toolbar.
5. Click the Word button on the taskbar to toggle back to the *Personal_Note* document.
6. Choose Edit, Paste Special, click the *Paste link* option, and click OK.
7. Right-click the linked chart, and choose *Format Object*.
8. Click the Size tab, delete the current value in the *Width* box, type **2.75"**, and click OK.
9. If the chart appears at the top of the document, change the zoom magnification to 50%; then click and drag the chart to the top of page 2, above the *Spring Break* heading. Make sure you have one blank line between the chart and the heading that follows.
10. Save the *Personal_Note* document.

5. Saving a Document in RTF for Transportability

Because you plan to e-mail the Word document to your family and friends, you are concerned that they might not be able to open the file in other word processing programs. Therefore, you decide to save the document in rich text format.

1. With *Personal_Note* onscreen, choose File, Save As.
2. Click the *Save as type* drop-down arrow.
3. Scroll through the list and select *Rich Text Format (*.rtf)*.
4. Click Save, print (optional), and close the *Personal_Note.rtf* document.
5. Close the *EW2_0805* Excel workbook, and close the Excel program.

CHALLENGE

Challenge exercises expand on or are somewhat related to skills presented in the lessons. Each exercise provides a brief narrative introduction, followed by instructions in a numbered-step format that are not as detailed as those in the Skill Drill exercises. You can work through one or more exercises in any order.

1. Inserting Hyperlinks in a Course Syllabus

As an assistant to a college professor, you help prepare course materials. You just finished creating and formatting a syllabus for Dr. Snyder's basic computer applications course. Because you will upload the completed syllabus to Dr. Snyder's FTP site, you want to create hyperlinks to the textbook Web site and to various sections within the syllabus. When you are done, you need to save the document in rich text format so that students can open it within various word processing programs.

1. Open *EW2_0806* and save it as `CIS_1050_Syllabus`.
2. Select the textbook name *Essentials Microsoft Office 2003* and create a hyperlink to `http://www.prenhall.com/essentials`.
3. Edit the hyperlink by displaying a ScreenTip that displays the text `Student data files are available at publisher's Web site.`
4. Delete the asterisk (*) in the *Syllabus Content* section and create a customized bulleted list with these specifications:
   a. Wingdings character symbol 119 from within the Symbol dialog box
   b. Bullet symbol indented at 0.25" from the left margin
   c. Text indented at 0.5" from the left margin
   d. Names of the 10 headings in the document that are formatted with the Heading 3 style
5. Format each bulleted list item as a hyperlink to the respective heading within the same document.
6. Click each hyperlink to make sure it links to the appropriate heading or Web site.
7. Save and print (optional) the *CIS_1050_Syllabus* document.
8. Save the document in rich text format as `CIS_1050_Syllabus.rtf`.

2. Embedding a Mortgage Worksheet into a Letter

Jared Butterfield is the loan officer at your mortgage company. Jared prepared a short mortgage summary in an Excel worksheet for Mr. and Mrs. Rogers that shows the house cost, down payment, amount of the loan, and monthly payment (principal and interest only). You need to embed this worksheet into a letter Jared created. After embedding the object, you need to edit the object to reflect a new interest rate and then edit the paragraph that discusses the information presented in the object. Furthermore, Jared wants you to edit the original Excel worksheet to calculate the monthly payment if Mr. and Mrs. Rogers pay a larger down payment and then use the results to edit the paragraph below the embedded object.

1. Open *EW2_0807* and save it as `Loan_Letter` in Word; then open the *EW2_0808* workbook in Excel.
2. Select and copy the worksheet data (cells A4 through B14).
3. Embed the data as a Microsoft Office Excel Worksheet Object between the first and second paragraphs in your Word document.
4. Apply the *Top and bottom* text wrapping option, and then horizontally center the object between the left and right margins.
5. Make sure you have one blank line before and after the object.
6. Edit the embedded object within Word by doing the following:

a. Change the home price to **195750**. Note: You do not have to type the dollar sign and comma because the cell is already formatted.

b. Change *6.375%* to **6.5%**.

7. Edit the sentence above the object to reflect the new monthly payment amount and the new annual interest rate shown in the embedded object.

8. Complete the following steps to provide information based on Mr. and Mrs. Rogers making a larger down payment:

   a. Toggle back to the *EW2_0808* workbook.
   b. Change the home price to **195750**, change the down payment to **50000** and change the annual interest rate to **6.5%**.
   c. Make a note of the new monthly payment.
   d. Toggle back to *Loan_Letter.doc* and edit the paragraph below the embedded object to reflect the monthly payment based on a larger down payment.

   The embedded object in Word is not changed. The paragraph and the embedded object complement each other. The paragraph below the object provides a what-if explanation—what the monthly payment will be if Mr. and Mrs. Rogers increase their down payment to $50,000.

9. Toggle back to the *EW2_0808* workbook and close it without saving the changes.
10. Save, print (optional), and close the *Loan_Letter* document in Word.

3. Linking and Updating a Linked Excel Chart

You are preparing a report that announces the implementation of new technology for your company. You need to include a chart that was created in Excel. Because you want the chart in Word to reflect changes in the original Excel workbook, you need to link the chart.

1. Open *EW2_0809* in Word, and save it as **CTA_Implementation**.
2. Open *EW2_0810* in Excel, and save it as **CTA_Phases**.
3. Select the chart in Excel, and copy it to the Clipboard.
4. Link the chart at the bottom of the *CTA_Implementation* document in Word.
5. Save and print (optional) the *CTA_Implementation* document.
6. In the *CTA_Phases* workbook in Excel, make these changes:

   a. Phase 1 Hardware value: **1.4**
   b. Phase 2 Software value: **1.0**
   c. Phase 3 Software value: **0.75**
   d. Phase 4 Software value: **0.5**
   e. Phase 3 Training value: **0.5**
   f. Phase 4 Training value: **1.0**

7. Change the chart to a clustered bar chart, similar to the way you change chart types in Word.
8. Change the legend to 10-point size.

9. Select the chart and drag the bottom-middle sizing handle down about three rows to make the chart taller.
10. Save, print (optional), and close the *CTA_Phases* workbook in Excel.
11. Update the linked chart object in the *CTA_Implementation* document in Word.
12. Save, print (optional), and close the *CTA_Implementation* document.

4. Importing Excel Data as a Table and Saving the Document as a Text File

You are preparing a letter that lists several books you believe a particular customer might want to purchase. You started preparing the list in an Excel workbook and need to add four more books to the list. After completing the list, you plan to import it into a letter as a table, format the table, and save the letter. You realize that the customer might not have Microsoft Word, so you decide to also save the document as a plain text file.

1. Open *EW2_0811* in Word, and save it as **Book_Letter_Bestsellers**.
2. Open *EW2_0812* in Excel, and save it as **Book_List**.
3. Find and enter data to complete the workbook using these specifications:
   a. Use the Research tool in Excel to perform an MSN search for current hardcover book bestsellers.
   b. Browse Web sites to locate book titles, authors, ISBNs, and prices for four books.
   c. Type the data below the existing book information in the *Book_List* workbook.
   d. Apply Currency number format to the sale prices.
4. Save the *Book_List* workbook.
5. Import the data in the *Book_List* workbook as a Word table, inserting it between the last two paragraphs in *Book_Letter_Bestsellers* in Word.
6. Customize the imported table with these specifications:
   a. Adjust column widths for all columns.
   b. Horizontally center the table between the left and right margins.
   c. Apply other table formats of your choice, such as borders or shading colors, to the imported table.
7. Save and print (optional) the *Book_Letter_Bestsellers* document in Word.
8. Prepare and save the document as a plain text file by doing the following:
   a. Apply Black font color to the headings on the first row of the table, if needed.
   b. Use Help to learn how to convert a table to tabulated text and then perform the conversion.
   c. Save the Word document in plain text file (*.txt) format.
   d. Close and reopen *Book_Letter_Bestsellers.txt* to see the differences between a regular Word document and a plain text document.
9. Save, print (optional), and close the *Book_Letter_Bestsellers.txt* document.
10. Close the *Book_List* workbook in Excel.

DISCOVERY ZONE

Discovery Zone exercises require advanced knowledge of topics presented in the lessons or self-directed learning of new skills. You can complete the exercises in any order.

1. Preparing Speaker Notes for a PowerPoint Presentation

Camille Davenport, a training consultant, prepared a short PowerPoint slide show to use at an upcoming Microsoft Word 2003 hands-on workshop. She asked you to type some notes that she can use as she conducts her training session. You started typing notes in a Word document. Now you need to finish those notes and import them into the respective Notes windows in PowerPoint.

Open *EW2_0813* in Word and save it as `Training_Notes`; open *EW2_0814* in PowerPoint and save it as `Training_Slide_Show`. Study the content of the Word document and the slide show. Use the same format to type notes in the Word document for the last three slides in the slide show. Correct all spelling errors as you type. Save and print (optional) the *Training_Notes* document in Word.

Although Camille had originally planned to use a one- or two-page Word document for her notes, she decided she wants the notes included with the presentation in PowerPoint. Instead of retyping the notes into PowerPoint, you decide to duplicate the notes from Word into the respective Notes windows in PowerPoint.

Use Word's Help feature to learn how to display and use the Office Clipboard, if necessary. Copy each paragraph individually to the Office Clipboard, but do not copy the bolded slide numbers. Display the Office Clipboard in PowerPoint and individually copy the Clipboard contents into the Notes windows for the respective slides. For slides 2–6, select the content in the Notes windows and apply a bulleted list style. Save the *Training_Slide_Show* presentation in PowerPoint. Customize the slide show by changing any elements and colors in the Slide Master window. Close the *Training_Notes* document in Word.

You realize that you can print the slide show using the *Handouts* option in PowerPoint; however, you know that doing so prints each slide and its notes on a separate page. Instead of wasting so much paper, you want to explore how you can print several slides and notes on a page. You remember your computer applications professor telling you that you can do this through Word.

Type `send slides to Microsoft Word` in PowerPoint's *Type a question for help* box and explore how you can duplicate slides (as thumbnails) with the speaker notes into a Word document. Then perform the steps listed in the Help window to link the slides and notes within a new Word document. Save the document as `Training_Slides_Notes`. Figure 8.22 shows how the first page should look in Word.

Edit some of the notes in the *Training_Slide_Show.ppt* presentation in PowerPoint. Apply the Layers.pot design template and then modify the design colors in the Slide Master to look similar to the colors shown in Figure 8.22. Save and close *Training_Slide_Show.ppt*. Update the linked object in the *Training_Slides_Notes.doc* document in Word to see the changes you made in the presentation. Notice that the notes do not update. Therefore, you need to send the slides from PowerPoint to Microsoft Word again. Save, print (optional), and close the *Training_Slides_Notes.doc* document.

Discovery Zone **307** LEVEL 2

Slide 1

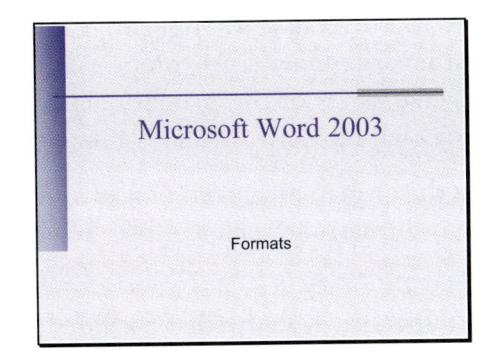

Microsoft Word 2003
Formats

Welcome to the Microsoft Word 2003 training session. Today we're going to explore some basic formatting features that you can use to create documents.

Slide 2

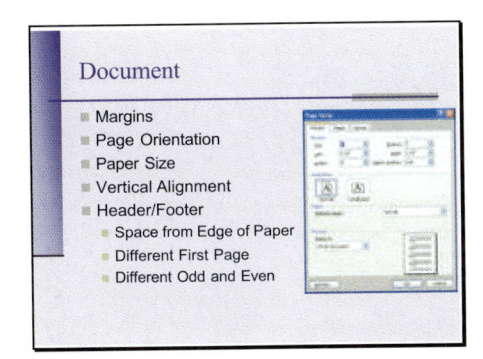

Document
- Margins
- Page Orientation
- Paper Size
- Vertical Alignment
- Header/Footer
  - Space from Edge of Paper
  - Different First Page
  - Different Odd and Even

Define *margins* and why users need to change the margin settings.
Define *page orientation* and show examples of documents in each orientation.
Explain *paper size* options.
Describe *layout* options and show examples of differences in header/footer options.

Slide 3

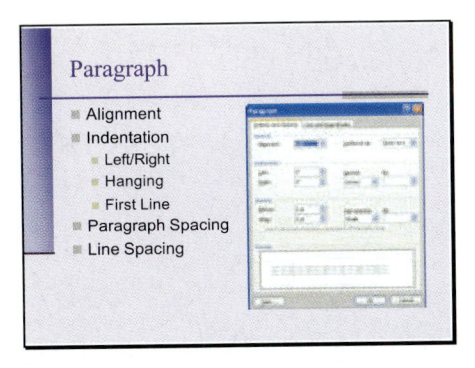

Paragraph
- Alignment
- Indentation
  - Left/Right
  - Hanging
  - First Line
- Paragraph Spacing
- Line Spacing

Show examples of *alignment* settings for individual paragraphs.
Demonstrate use of *indentation* settings, including special settings.
Compare and contrast *line spacing* and *paragraph spacing*.

FIGURE 8.22

2. Creating a Document of Favorite Movies

You and your friends want to compile information on your favorite movies so that you can share this information with each other. You need to start your project by finding information on the Internet for two or three of your favorite movies. As you browse these sites, save images of the DVD covers as bitmap files. Make notes of the primary actors and actresses, DVD release date, genre, and movie rating for each movie.

Create a Word document that includes the bitmap images you saved and type the data for each movie on a separate page. Use consistent formatting, such as tables, for the data. Save the document as `Favorite_Movies`.

Create a hyperlink on each image to a respective Web site that provides more details about the movie. Also include customized ScreenTips for the hyperlinks.

INTEGRATING PROJECTS

Essentials 2003: Microsoft Word (Level 2)

In this section of the text you have the opportunity to use skills illustrated in multiple projects. Each exercise lists the projects you should work through before attempting the exercise. It would be helpful, but is not necessary, to complete exercise 1 before completing exercise 2. You may work through the remaining exercises in any order.

1. CREATING AN INFORMATION SHEET FOR STUDENT VOLUNTEERS

Based on Projects 1, 2, and 3

You are the director of Rolling Meadows, a nursing facility for elderly people. In addition to providing skilled nursing care, Rolling Meadows provides rehabilitation services to people who are affected by injuries or disabilities. Because of the fine reputation of your facility, Rolling Meadows is at 100% capacity and has a waiting list for residents.

Recently, several local teachers have inquired about a volunteer program you established in which their students would participate in activities with the residents at Rolling Meadows. Although most services offered at Rolling Meadows must be performed by certified trained professionals, you believe the presence of young people could help improve the quality of life for your residents.

You drafted a list of activities for student volunteers. Now you need to finish the information sheet by modifying styles, finding and replacing extra spaces, sorting bulleted lists, and hyphenating the document.

IP Exercise Checklist

- Open *EW2_IP1* and save it as **Volunteer_Activities**.
- Apply the Title style to the main title and apply the Heading 3 style to the three headings that are currently bold.
- Edit the Title style by applying Indigo font color and 12-point spacing after paragraphs.
- Edit the Heading 3 style by applying Indigo paragraph shading, White font color, and 3" right indentation.
- Edit the Normal style by applying Bookman Old Style font.
- Find all occurrences of two consecutive paragraph marks and replace them with one paragraph mark.
- Find and replace a period followed by two spaces with a period followed by one space.

- Sort each bulleted list in alphabetical order.
- Edit the bullet style by choosing the Wingdings 2 font character code 168 as the bullet symbol and by applying Indigo font color. Make these changes by *modifying* the style itself rather than using the Bullets and Numbering dialog box.
- Hyphenate the document by applying these specifications: Avoid hyphenating words in all capital letters, limit consecutive hyphens to two, and manually hyphenate appropriate words when prompted.
- Insert nonbreaking spaces as needed in the document.
- Save, print (optional), and close the *Volunteer_Activities* document.

2 COMPOSING A MAIL MERGE COVER LETTER

Based on Projects 3 and 5

You are continuing your role as director of the Rolling Meadows nursing facility. With increasing operating costs, you are pleased with the positive response to your volunteer program from local teachers. Three specific teachers plan to encourage their students to participate.

Instead of composing a separate letter to send along with the information list, you want to prepare a mail merge document to accompany the list of volunteer activities you created in the first exercise. To save time, you decide to use an existing template that one of your assistants created as the starting document.

You need to select the template, compose the message, and complete the Mail Merge task pane steps to prepare the letters.

IP Exercise Checklist

- Open the *EW2_IP2.dot* template.
- If you are using your own home computer, save the template as `Rolling_Meadows_Merge_Letter.dot` in the *c:\Documents and Settings\<your name>\Application Data\Microsoft\Templates* folder on your computer, close the template, open the Templates dialog box, and choose the *Rolling_Meadows_Merge_Letter* template to create a new document.
- Use the template to create a mail merge.
- During the appropriate phase of the mail merge process, create a data source named `Volunteer_Contacts` for the following three teachers:

Mrs. Loretta Owens
Fourth Street Public School
84 South Fourth Street
Emporia, KS 66802

Mr. Terry Vanderbelt
Claussen Street Elementary
240 East Claussen Street
Emporia, KS 66801

Ms. Shirley Davenport
Emporia West Private School
3434 West Lincoln Blvd.
Emporia, KS 66802

- Sort the data source in alphabetical order by teachers' last names.
- Edit the AddressBlock and the GreetingLine fields to reflect a more formal letter format.
- Compose a two- or three-paragraph letter to accompany the volunteer sheet you completed in the first exercise. Include appropriate details and refer to the enclosure. Include all necessary merge fields. Save the main document as `Volunteer_Main_Letter`.
- Perform the mail merge to a new document window and save it as `Volunteer_Letters`.
- Save, print (optional), and close the main and mail merge documents.

3 ADAPTING AN EMPLOYMENT SCREENING AND PLACEMENT DOCUMENT

Based on Projects 1, 3, and 4

You are the assistant to the Affirmative Action/Equal Opportunity (AA/EO) director at Ocean View Community College (OVCC). Your institution is in the process of reviewing employment screening and placement policies and procedures at comparable colleges in the region. You and the AA/EO director will submit a proposed policy and procedure statement to the administrators at your college to replace the current policy.

Recently, you received a document outlining employment screening policies and procedures from Woodward State College. The AA/EO director gave you permission to adapt the document for your college. You decide that this document is very thorough and you want to submit it, with only minor changes, as the proposed new policy and procedure document at OVCC.

You need to use the Find and Replace feature to efficiently change the name of the institution from Woodward State College (WSC) to your institution's name and initials. In addition, you want to create and apply custom styles to format headings.

IP Exercise Checklist

- Open *EW2_IP3* and save it as `Employment_Screening`.
- Create a document version with the comment `Original Version: This version is the original document from WSC.`
- Find all occurrences of a period followed by two spaces and replace them with a period followed by one space.

- Find all occurrences of *Woodward State College* and replace them with **Ocean View Community College**. Also find the original college initials and replace them with your college's initials.
- Modify the Heading 2 style by including these formats: Center horizontal alignment, Dark Blue shading color, White font color, and 16-point spacing before paragraphs.
- Create a paragraph style named **Level 3 Heading** that is based on the Normal style, and include these formats: Arial Narrow, bold, italic, Dark Blue font color.
- Find all occurrences of text formatted with the Heading 5 style and replace these occurrences with the Level 3 Heading style you just created.
- Modify the Normal style by activating the Widow/Orphan control.
- Deselect the *Different first page* option through the Page Setup button on the Header and Footer toolbar, if needed.
- Create a footer for odd-numbered pages with these specifications: **Employment Screening and Placement** text, a space, the Wingdings character code 91 symbol, a space, and the page number field on the right side of the footer. If needed, adjust the right tab to align with the right margin. Apply Arial Narrow font, Dark Blue font color, and a Dark Blue top paragraph line border to the footer.
- Create a footer for even-numbered pages. If you see an existing centered page number field, delete it and then create the footer with these specifications: the page number field, a space, the Wingdings character code 91 symbol, a space, and **Policies and Procedures** text aligned at the left side of the footer. Use the same font, font color, and border specifications as you applied for the odd-numbered page footer. Set a 0″ left indent for the footer.
- Save another document version named **1st Draft: This version reflects our college name. It also includes new styles and footers.**
- Activate the Track Changes feature and make these changes:
    - Select the words *the College* in the first bulleted list item and type **OVCC**.
    - Find forms of the word *administrator* and replace them with forms of the word **department chair**. Review the results of the Find and Replace process. If needed, adjust any replacements that need to be plural, and change the preceding article *an* to the article *a* when necessary.
    - Select the word *employees* in the third item in the second bulleted list and type **faculty members**.
    - In the first paragraph in the *Applicant Evaluation* section, delete the words *full-time permanent* and type **tenure-track**.
    - Remove the Turquoise highlighting color and italicize that sentence.
    - In the *Selective Placement Factor* paragraph, delete *In some instances, a particular job requires* and type **Some specific faculty positions require**.
    - At the end of the *Education and Experience Requirement* paragraph, type the sentence **No exceptions are made to this policy.**
    - In the first paragraph in the *Step 3: Interviews* section, type **designated as** between the words *are* and *the* in the second sentence.
    - Delete the last sentence of the first paragraph in the *Step 3: Interviews* section.
    - In the second paragraph in the *Step 3: Interviews* section, select *is to rate each of the applicants* and type **rates each applicant**.

- In the paragraph above the *Referral, Selection, and Protection* heading, select *Interview scores of each applicant are* and type **Each applicant's interview score is**.
- At the end of the last paragraph in the document, type the sentence **All rating sheets must be destroyed immediately after the official recommendation form is completed.**
- Save a document version with the comment **2nd Draft: This version contains tracked changes.**
- Turn off the Track Changes feature.
- Reject the sentence you added to the last paragraph and reject the change to delete the last sentence in the first paragraph in the *Step 3: Interviews* section.
- Accept the remaining changes you made in the document.
- Save, print (optional), and close the *Employment_Screening* document.

4 CREATING A NEWSLETTER ABOUT DOMESTIC VIOLENCE

Based on Projects 1, 2, 3, 6, 7, and 8

You are the director of a local shelter for women and children who are victims of domestic violence. You are alarmed at the growing number of people who are hospitalized or murdered as a result of domestic violence. While your shelter provides necessary services to victims, you also want to help educate the public about domestic violence.

You and your colleagues decide to start a monthly newsletter to distribute to college students, grocery store customers, apartment tenants, and so on. Your goal in preparing the monthly newsletter is to educate the public so that people can recognize signs of domestic violence and encourage their friends and family members to seek help if they are being abused. In addition, you want to encourage victims to seek help before the violence worsens.

Marie Sanchez, one of your assistants, prepared a masthead for the newsletter and composed some information to include in the first issue. You need to include Marie's masthead and articles to prepare the first issue. Furthermore, you need to conduct some research to complete the newsletter. Your newsletter needs to include a chart that depicts a critical statistic of domestic violence.

IP Exercise Checklist

- Open *EW2_IP4* and save it as **Newsletter_Issue1**.
- Insert a continuous section break at the end of the document and insert the *EW2_IP5* document.
- Format the second document section into two columns.
- Use the Research tool to find a definition of domestic violence through an MSN search. Select, copy, and paste the definition from the online Encarta encyclopedia search result to the first paragraph, between the quotation marks. Apply formatting that is consistent with the rest of the paragraph.
- Insert a column break at the beginning of the *Who Are Victims of Domestic Violence?* heading.
- Use the Research tool to find statistics on domestic violence. Delete the placeholder at the end of the *Who Are Victims of Domestic Violence?* section and create a pie chart that depicts

a startling statistic. Remove the plot border, and apply White plot background color. Display data labels of the percentages inside the respective pie slices, and show the legend below the pie chart. Apply other chart formats of your choice. Type a sentence above the pie chart that explains the chart contents, and cite the source of the statistic.

- Create a hyperlink from the citation to display the Web page where you obtained the information. Provide an appropriate ScreenTip.
- Use the Research tool to find information about causes of domestic violence, and type a paragraph consisting of two or three sentences in the appropriate location.
- In the blank space at the bottom of the first column, insert the "No" AutoShape symbol. Apply Red fill color, and add the text **Domestic Violence Tolerance** on three lines. Increase the font size. Then, if needed, increase the before paragraph spacing on the first line so that all three lines appear vertically centered within the shape, and horizontally center the text within the shape.
- At the bottom of the second column, type **What Will Be in the Next Issue?** and format it with the Heading 3 style. Create the following two-item bulleted list:
  - **Negative Effects on Victims**
  - **Helping Someone Who Is a Victim**
- Hyphenate the document based on rules discussed in Project 2. Limit the number of consecutive hyphens to two.
- Modify the Heading 3 style by applying Red font color.
- Adjust the top and bottom margins as needed so that the newsletter fits on one page.
- Save, print (optional), and close the *Newsletter_Issue1* document.

5 PREPARING A GYM MEMBERSHIP LETTER

CREATIVE SOLUTION

Based on Projects 4, 5, and 8

As an assistant manager of Deluxe Workout Center, a new gym in your city, you are working with Rona Blanchard, the owner/manager, to create a main letter for mass mailing to promote different memberships at your gym. Rona created an Excel worksheet that lists the membership types, month-to-month membership prices, and comparative prepay yearly membership prices.

You composed a draft of the promotional letter last week, and Rona e-mailed it back to you with suggestions indicated by tracked changes and comments. Before you finalize the letter, you need to embed the Excel worksheet data and provide additional suggestions through tracked changes and comments.

IP Exercise Checklist

- Open *EW2_IP6* and save it as **Membership_Promotional_Letter**.
- Read the first comment and make the change indicated. Leave the comment intact and insert your own comment that you made the change.
- Accept the tracked changes in the first, second, and third paragraphs, but leave Rona's comment intact. You will address her comment later.

- Reject Rona's changes to the last paragraph.
- Open the *EW2_IP7* workbook in Excel. Copy the membership pricing information (including column headings and row descriptions). Embed the data as a Microsoft Office Excel Worksheet Object between the last two paragraphs in the *Membership_Promotional_Letter* document. Close the *EW2_IP7* Excel workbook, and then exit the Excel program.
- Apply the *Top and bottom* text wrapping option, and horizontally center the embedded object. Make sure one blank line precedes and follows the embedded object.
- Change the Casual Limited month-to-month membership price to **16.95**.
- Select the numeric values in the last two columns and apply Blue font color and bold.
- Activate the Track Changes feature and make these changes:
  - Add **(DWC)** after *Deluxe Workout Center* in the first paragraph.
  - Address Rona's second comment by inserting a comment that you can use the abbreviation if it is shown after the full gym name in the preceding paragraph.
  - Select the last sentence of the second paragraph and type **For that extra hard workout, sign up to participate in racquetball competitions.**
  - Delete *trained and certified professionals* and type **certified, professional trainers** in the third paragraph.
  - Select *hottest new* in the last paragraph and type **most comprehensive**.
- Turn off the Track Changes feature, and save a document version with the comment **Rona's changes implemented; my changes indicated.**
- Save and print (optional) the *Membership_Promotional_Letter* document.
- Accept all changes in the document and delete all comments.
- Convert the letter into a main mail merge document.
- Create a recipient list containing five records. Type the necessary data into the fields. Save the recipient list as **Membership_Potential_List**.
- Insert the AddressBlock field and GreetingLine field. Make sure you select the colon for the GreetingLine field punctuation.
- Merge the main document and recipient list to a new document window. Save the merged document as **Membership_Promotional_Merge_Letters**. Print (optional) and close the *Membership_Promotional_Merge_Letters* document.
- On the Mail Merge toolbar, deselect *View Merged Data* to see the fields again.
- Save, print (optional), and close the *Membership_Promotional_Letter* document.

6 CREATING A VALENTINE'S DAY DANCE FLYER

Based on Projects 4, 6, and 8

Some local businesses, in conjunction with the high school administrators' approval and guidance, are sponsoring a Valentine's Day dance. This sponsored event is designed to prevent underage drinking and unsupervised dating activities. Local businesses will pay all expenses for the DJ, refreshments, and decorations so students can attend for free.

Because of your extensive experience in using Microsoft Word, you volunteered to create an exciting, eye-catching flyer to place on bulletin boards throughout the school building. You want to include WordArt, a designer page border, an appropriate clip art image, and other shapes.

After creating the flyer, you want to send it as an e-mail attachment to the principal for approval. However, you need to save the flyer in rich text format so the recipient can open the document in another word processing program, if needed. Use Figure IP.1 to help you complete the flyer.

IP Exercise Checklist

- Save a new document as **Valentines_Day_Dance_Flyer**.
- Set 0.75" top, bottom, left, and right margins.
- Apply the art page border shown in the figure.
- Display the Drawing toolbar and create the WordArt object, using the third style on the first row of the WordArt Gallery.
- Apply these settings to the WordArt object:
    - Fire preset gradient fill effect, *Diagonal up* option, and bottom-left variant style
    - Wave 1 WordArt shape
    - *Top and bottom* text wrapping option and Center horizontal alignment
    - 1.5" height
- Create a header with these settings:
    - Clip art image of white cupid on a red heart background
    - Washout color effect (from the Picture toolbar)
    - *Behind Text* wrapping effect
    - 6" height
    - Center horizontal alignment
    - Center vertical alignment (from the Picture Position tab within the Advanced Layout dialog box)
- Create the text box shown in the middle of the figure. Use Comic Sans MS font, 24-point size, and Red font color. Make sure the text is centered within the text box and remove the fill color and border. Horizontally center the text box between the left and right margins.
- Create the Explosion 1 and Horizontal Scroll AutoShapes shown in the figure. Apply Rose fill color to both shapes, and add the text in each shape. The text should be formatted in Comic Sans MS font, appropriate font size, and Dark Red font color.
- Create a 1.9"-wide heart shape in the bottom-left corner. Apply the formats and text shown in the figure. Duplicate the heart in the bottom-right corner and apply the formats and text shown in the figure. Group the shapes together.
- If needed, adjust the position of shapes relative to each other.
- Save and print (optional) the *Valentines_Day_Dance_Flyer* document.
- Save the document in rich text format with the same document name.
- Send the rich text formatted document as an e-mail attachment to the high school principal (or in this case, your instructor).
- Close the *Valentines_Day_Dance_Flyer* document.

Valentine's Day Dance

Cool Music

February 14
9 p.m. to Midnight
Student Center

Refreshments

Free with Student ID

Sponsored by Local Businesses

FIGURE IP.1

FILE GUIDE

Guide to Files in Essentials: Microsoft Word 2003 (Level 2)

Word Level 2	Original Student File	Student File Saved As	Related Solution Notes
Project 1			
P1-L1 thru L7	EW2_0101.doc EW2_0102.doc	Word_Formatting.doc	Use *EW2_0102* in Lesson 5 to demonstrate arranging document windows; do not modify or save *EW2_0102*
P1-SD1 thru SD5	EW2_0103.doc	Training_Proposal.doc	
P1-SD6			Explore the online Research tool
P1-CH1	EW2_0104.doc	Internet_Information.doc	
P1-CH2	EW2_0105.doc	2004_Annual_Report.doc	
P1-CH3	EW2_0106.doc	Headache_Types.doc	Creative Solution exercise; use the Research tool to locate and compose information and to identify and insert synonyms from the online thesaurus; compositions will vary
P1-CH4	EW2_0107.doc	Computer_Terminology	Creative Solution exercise; use the Research tool to locate and compose information; compositions will vary
P1-DZ1	EW2_0108.doc EW2_0109.doc	Design_Information.doc	Use *EW2_0109* to copy a paragraph to *Design_Information*; no changes are made to *EW2_0109*
P1-DZ2	EW2_0110.doc	Stock_Information.doc	Creative Solution exercise; choose 10 stocks and include their current prices
P1-DZ3	EW2_0105.doc	Report_EnglishtoGerman.doc Report_GermantoEnglish.doc	
Project 2			
P2-L1 thru L7 P2-L4	EW2_0201.doc EW2_0202.doc	May_Newsletter.doc	Insert *EW2_0202* into the current document

P = Project   L = Lesson   SD = Skill Drill   CH = Challenge   DZ = Discovery Zone   IP = Integrating Projects

Creative Solution exercises permit individual choices that produce unique solutions

File Guide—Microsoft Word 2003 (Level 2)

Word Level 2	Original Student File	Student File Saved As	Related Solution Notes
P2-SD1 thru 5 P2-SD1	EW2_0203.doc EW2_0204.doc	TMG_Newsletter.doc	Insert *EW2_0204* into the current document
P2-CH1	EW2_0205.doc EW2_0206.doc	IS_Courses.doc	Insert *EW2_0206* into the current document
P2-CH2	EW2_0207.doc EW2_0208.doc	Job_Announcement.doc	Insert *EW2_0208* into the current document
P2-CH3	New document	Publisher_Contacts.doc	
P2-CH4	EW2_0209.doc	Graduation_Newsletter.doc	Creative Solution exercise; create a WordArt image, choose a style, insert an image, and apply formats to the drop cap
P2-CH5	New document	Condominium_Flyer.doc	Creative Solution exercise; choose font, font sizes, and image
P2-DZ1	EW2_0210.doc	PEA_Newsletter_Update.doc	
P2-DZ2	New document	Awards_Banquet_Program.doc	Creative Solution exercise; choose the image for the second page of the document and compose text for the third page

Project 3

P3-L1 thru L3	New document EW2_0301.doc	Announcement_Memo.doc Memo_Heading.doc Cell_Phone_Memo.doc	Use the memohead AutoText entry used in Lessons 2 and 3; use *EW2_0301* in conjunction with the memohead AutoText to create *Cell_Phone_Memo.doc*
P3-L4 thru L8	EW2_0302.doc	Committee_Status_Report.doc Committee_Status_Report_Version2.doc	
P3-SD1 thru SD2	EW2_0303.doc EW2_0304.doc EW2_0305.doc	Jordan_Letter.doc Marjorie_Letter.doc	Do not save *EW2_0303.doc*
P3-SD3	New document	Mortgage_Closing_Fax.doc	
P3-SD4 thru SD5	EW2_0306.doc	Training_Conference_Report.doc	
P3-CH1	New document	Monthly_Calendar.doc	Creative Solution exercise; insert images and text for special occasions within calender table cells
P3-CH2	New document EW2_0307.doc	Customer_Survey_Response.doc	Insert *EW2_0307.doc* within the *Customer_Survey_Response.doc* document

P = Project   L = Lesson   SD = Skill Drill   CH = Challenge   DZ = Discovery Zone   IP = Integrating Projects

Creative Solution exercises permit individual choices that produce unique solutions

Word Level 2	Original Student File	Student File Saved As	Related Solution Notes
P3-CH3	EW2_0308.doc	September_Meeting_Minutes.doc	
P3-CH4	EW2_0309.doc	MG_Minutes.doc	
P3-CH5	EW2_0310.doc EW2_0311.doc	Request_Response.doc Resume_Confirmation_Letter.doc	
P3-DZ1	EW2_0312.doc EW2_0313.doc	January_Minutes.doc	
P3-DZ2	EW2_0314.doc	Tips_Masthead.dot April_Newsletter.doc	
P3-DZ3	EW2_0315.doc EW2_0316.doc	Hart_Letter.doc Willison_Letter.doc	
P3-DZ4	N/A		Delete templates, AutoText, and styles from the Normal template

Project 4

Word Level 2	Original Student File	Student File Saved As	Related Solution Notes
P4-L1 thru L7	EW2_0401.doc EW2_0402.doc	Tablet_PC.doc	Use *EW2_0402.doc* to complete the Compare and Merge feature in Lesson 7
P4-SD1 thru SD5	EW2_0403.doc EW2_0404.doc	Sidewalk_Cafe.doc	Use *EW2_0404.doc* to complete the Compare and Merge feature in SD5
P4-CH1	EW2_0405.doc	Water_Conservation_Plan.doc	
P4-CH2	EW2_0406.doc	Retreat_Agenda.doc	
P4-CH3	EW2_0407.doc EW2_0408.doc	Project_Development_Letter.doc Project_Development_Letter2.doc	Use *EW2_0408.doc* to complete the Compare and Merge feature
P4-CH4	EW2_0409.doc	Halloween_Invitation_1.doc Halloween_Invitation_2.doc Halloween_Invitation_3.doc	Creative Solution exercise; e-mail *Halloween_Invitation_1.doc* to someone; track changes made to another document and e-mail it back to the original sender, who saves it as *Halloween_Invitation_2.doc*; save *Halloween_Invitation_3.doc* as the result of Compare and Merge
P4-CH5	EW2_0410.doc	Fiesta_Lilac_Coffee_Server.doc	
P4-DZ1	EW2_0411.doc	Apartment_Newsletter_October.doc	Insert voice comments if computer has that capability

P = Project   L = Lesson   SD = Skill Drill   CH = Challenge   DZ = Discovery Zone   IP = Integrating Projects

Creative Solution exercises permit individual choices that produce unique solutions

Word Level 2	Original Student File	Student File Saved As	Related Solution Notes
P4-DZ2	EW2_0407.doc	Project_Development_Letter3.doc	Insert ink comments and ink annotations on a Tablet PC if that type of system is available; if not, use Help to learn about these features and visit a computer store to see a demonstration of a Tablet PC

Project 5

Word Level 2	Original Student File	Student File Saved As	Related Solution Notes
P5-L1 thru L6	EW2_0501.doc New document New document New document New document	Conference_Form_Letter.doc Conference_Participants.mdb Conference_Merged_Letters.doc Conference_Form_Labels.doc Conference_Merged_Labels.doc	Save the original document as a main document; in Lesson 2, create the data source through Word and save it with the default .mdb file extension; in Lesson 5, merge the two documents and save the merged document under a different filename; in Lesson 6, create a main label document, merge it with the data source, and save the merged labels under a different name
P5-SD1 thru SD5	EW2_0502.doc New document New document New document New document	Holiday_Form_Letter.doc Holiday_Recipient_List.mdb Holiday_Merged_Letters.doc Holiday_Form_Labels.doc Holiday_Merged_Labels.doc	Save the original document as a main document; in SD2, create the data source through Word and save it with the default .mdb file extension; in SD4, merge the two documents and save the merged document under a different filename; in SD5, create a main label document, merge it with the data source, and save the merged labels under a different name
P5-CH1	EW2_0503.doc New document New document	Application_Form_Letter.doc Application_Recipients.mdb Application_Merged_Letters.doc	Save the original document as a main document; in steps 3–5, create the data source through Word and save it with the default .mdb file extension; in step 10, merge the two documents and save the merged document under a different filename
P5-CH2	New document New document New document	Application_Form_Envelope.doc Application_Recipients.mdb Application_Merged_Envelopes.doc	Create the envelope main document and merge it with the data source created in CH1 or create the data source now; in step 6, merge the documents and save the merged envelopes under a new name
P5-CH3	EW2_0504.mdb EW2_0505.doc New document	Conference_Participants2.mdb Conference_Form_Letter2.doc Conference_Merged_Letters2.doc	In steps 1 and 6, copy the original data source and add records to it; in step 3, use the *Start from existing document* option in Step 2 of the task pane to select the main document; in steps 11 and 13, merge the selected records to a new document window and save it under a new name

P = Project   L = Lesson   SD = Skill Drill   CH = Challenge   DZ = Discovery Zone   IP = Integrating Projects

Creative Solution exercises permit individual choices that produce unique solutions

File Guide—Microsoft Word 2003 (Level 2) **323**

Word Level 2	Original Student File	Student File Saved As	Related Solution Notes
P5-CH4	EW2_0506.doc New document New document New document New document	Scholarship_Recipients.doc Scholarship_Form_Letter.doc Scholarship_Merged_Letters.doc Scholarship_Form_Labels.doc Scholarship_Merged_Labels.doc	Creative Solution exercise; in steps 1–6, use a Word table as the data source; in step 7, compose the content for the main document; create a main label document and a merged label document
P5-DZ1	New document New document New document	Bonus_Form_Memo.doc Bonus_Data_Source.doc Bonus_Merged_Memos.doc	Create a memo main document, a table data source, and perform the merge
P5-DZ2	EW2_0507.xls New document	Emergency_Form_Directory.doc Emergency_Merged_Directory.doc	Use the Excel spreadsheet as a data source and create the directory main document from scratch; use either the Mail Merge task pane or the Mail Merge toolbar; perform the merge and save it under a new name

Project 6

P6-L1 thru L6	EW2_0601.doc	Playground_Sale.doc	
P6-SD1 thru SD5	EW2_0602.doc	Ergonomics_Flyer.doc	
P6-CH1	EW2_0603.doc	School_Flyer.doc	
P6-CH2	New document	House_Drawing.doc	Creative Solution exercise; design the drawing by using various shapes
P6-CH3	EW2_0604.doc	Flower_Flyer.doc	
P6-CH4	EW2_0605.doc	Business_Plan.doc	
P6-CH5	New document	Weekly_Pay_Flowchart.doc	
P6-DZ1	New document	Office_Layout.doc	Creative Solution exercise; design the office layout by using various shapes
P6-DZ2	New document	Conflict_Resolution.doc	Creative Solution exercise; choose and insert a clip art image

Project 7

P7-L1 thru L7	EW2_0701.doc EW2_0702.xls	February_Newsletter.doc	Import *EW2_0702.xls* into *February_Newsletter.doc* in Lesson 5
P7-L8	New document	Color_Diagram.doc	

P = Project   L = Lesson   SD = Skill Drill   CH = Challenge   DZ = Discovery Zone   IP = Integrating Projects

Creative Solution exercises permit individual choices that produce unique solutions

File Guide—Microsoft Word 2003 (Level 2)

Word Level 2	Original Student File	Student File Saved As	Related Solution Notes
P7-SD1 thru SD3	New document	Enrollment_Chart.doc	
P7-SD4 thru SD5	New document	School_Chart.doc	
P7-SD6	EW2_0703.doc	Debt_Reduction_Chart.doc	
P7-CH1	EW2_0704.doc	May_Rentals.doc	
P7-CH2	EW2_0705.doc EW2_0706.xls	Salaries_Memo.doc	Import *EW2_0706.xls* into *Salaries_Memo.doc*
P7-CH3	EW2_0707.doc	Music_Sales_Memo.doc	
P7-CH4	New document	College_Chart.doc	Creative Solution exercise; create organization charts based on own institution's structure
P7-CH5	New document	BIS_Careers_Diagram.doc	
P7-DZ1	EW2_0704.doc	May_Rentals_Pie.doc	
P7-DZ2	EW2_0708.doc EW2_0709.xls	Loan_Letter.doc	Import *EW2_0709.xls* into *Loan_Letter.doc*
P7-DZ3	New document	Food_Pyramid_Guide.doc	

Project 8

P8-L1 thru L6	EW2_0801.doc EW2_0802.xls	Annual_Report_Excerpts.doc IC_Data.xls Annual_Report_Excerpts.rtf	Insert *EW2_0802.xls* into *Annual_Report_Excerpts.doc* as a new object in save *EW2_0802.xls* as *IC_Data.xls* in Excel to link an object to workbook data; in Lesson 6, save the Word document in rich text format (.rtf)
P8-SD1 thru SD5	EW2_0803.doc EW2_0804.xls EW2_0805.xls	Personal_Note.doc Personal_Note.rtf	Insert *EW2_0804.xls* into *Personal_Note.doc* as a new object; embed and link data from *EW2_0805.xls* into the Word document; in SD5, save the document in rich text format (.rtf)
P8-CH1	EW2_0806.doc	CIS_1050_Syllabus.doc CIS_1050_Syllabus.rtf	
P8-CH2	EW2_0807.doc EW2_0808.xls	Loan_Letter.doc	Embed data from *EW2_0808.xls* into *Loan_Letter.doc*
P8-CH3	EW2_0809.doc EW2_0810.xls	CTA_Implementation.doc CTA_Phases.xls	Link data from *CTA_Phases.xls* to *CTA_Implementation.doc*
P8-CH4	EW2_0811.doc EW2_0812.xls	Book_Letter_Bestsellers.doc Book_List.xls Book_Letter_Bestsellers.txt	Creative Solution exercise; select book information and apply appropriate table formats in Word

P = Project   L = Lesson   SD = Skill Drill   CH = Challenge   DZ = Discovery Zone   IP = Integrating Projects

Creative Solution exercises permit individual choices that produce unique solutions

File Guide—Microsoft Word 2003 (Level 2)

Word Level 2	Original Student File	Student File Saved As	Related Solution Notes
P8-DZ1	EW2_0813.doc EW2_0814.ppt	Training_Notes.doc Training_Slide_Show.ppt Training_Slides_Notes.doc	Creative Solution exercise; compose speaker notes and customize the slide design, colors, and so on
P8-DZ2	New document	Favorite_Movies.doc	Creative Solution exercise; compose text, choose your own movies, and insert images of those movies with hyperlinks to Web sites of your choice that provide additional information about each movie

Integrating Projects

IP1	EW2_IP1.doc	Volunteer_Activities.doc	
IP2	EW2_IP2.dot	Rolling_Meadows_Merge_Letter.dot Volunteer_Main_Letter.doc Volunteer_Contacts.mdb Volunteer_Letters.doc	Creative Solution exercise; save the *EW2_IP2.dot* template with a new name; use that template to create the main document; compositions will vary
IP3	EW2_IP3.doc	Employment_Screening.doc	
IP4	EW2_IP4.doc EW2_IP5.doc	Newsletter_Issue1.doc	Creative Solution exercise; save *EW2_IP4.doc* as *Newsletter_Issue1.doc* and then insert *EW2_IP5.doc* into it; use the Research tool to find statistics to compose a paragraph and create a chart; use the Research tool to find information about causes and compose paragraphs
IP5	EW2_IP6.doc EW2_IP7.xls	Membership_Promotional_Letter.doc Membership_Potential_List.mdb Membership_Promotional_Merge_Letters.doc	Creative Solution exercise; create a data source data of your choice; save *EW2_IP6.doc* as with *Membership_Promotional_Letter.doc* and copy/embed pricing information from the Excel file *EW2_IP7.xls*
IP6	New document	Valentines_Day_Dance_Flyer.doc Valentines_Day_Dance_Flyer.rtf	

P = Project   L = Lesson   SD = Skill Drill   CH = Challenge   DZ = Discovery Zone   IP = Integrating Projects

Creative Solution exercises permit individual choices that produce unique solutions

MICROSOFT WORD 2003 TASK GUIDE (LEVEL 2)

A book in the *Essentials* series is designed to be kept as a handy reference beside your computer even after you have completed all the projects and exercises. Any time you have difficulty recalling the sequence of steps or a shortcut needed to achieve a result, find your task in the alphabetized listing that follows. If you have difficulty performing a task, turn to the page number listed in the second column to locate the step-by-step exercise or other detailed description.

Word Task	Page	Mouse	Menu Bar	Shortcut Menu	Shortcut Keys
AutoShape, insert	204	AutoShapes ▼ on Drawing toolbar	Insert | Picture | AutoShapes		Alt+U; press ↓ to select a category; press → to display category palette; press →, ↑, ↓, or ← to highlight shape; Ctrl+↵Enter
AutoText, create	82	New... on AutoText toolbar	Insert | AutoText | New		Alt+F3
AutoText, delete	87	; select entry; Delete	Insert | AutoText | AutoText; select entry; Delete		
AutoText, display toolbar	82		View | Toolbars | AutoText	Right-click toolbar; AutoText	
AutoText, insert	83	All Entries ▼ on AutoText toolbar	Insert | AutoText | AutoText; select entry; Insert		Type AutoText abbreviation; F3
Chart, create	240		Insert | Picture | Chart		
Chart, view or hide datasheet	246	on Microsoft Graph Chart toolbar	Double-click chart; View | Datasheet		
Chart axis, currency type	249	$ on Microsoft Graph Chart Formatting toolbar	Format | Number; Currency	Right-click axis; Format Axis; Number tab; Currency	
Chart axis, decrease decimal places	249	.00→.0 on Microsoft Graph Chart Formatting toolbar	Format | Number; Number; Decimal places	Right-click axis; Format Axis; Number tab; Number; Decimal places	

328 Microsoft Word 2003 Task Guide (Level 2)

Word Task	Page	Mouse	Menu Bar	Shortcut Menu	Shortcut Keys
Chart element, format	248	on Microsoft Graph Chart Standard toolbar	Double-click chart; Format | Selected . . .	Double-click chart; right-click chart element; Format . . .	
Chart object, format	244	on Picture toolbar	Select chart object; Format | Object	Right-click chart object; Format Object	
Chart titles, insert or edit	246		Double-click chart; Chart | Chart Options; Titles tab		
Chart type, change	241	on Microsoft Graph Chart Standard toolbar	Double-click chart; Chart | Chart Type		
Column break, insert	51		Insert | Break; Column break		Ctrl+Shift+Enter
Columns, balance length	54		Position insertion point at end of section containing columns; Insert | Break; Continuous		
Columns, create or revise	46, 48	on Standard toolbar	Format | Columns		
Columns, specify different column widths	49		Format | Columns; deselect Equal column width		
Comments, delete	125	on Reviewing toolbar		Right-click within comment; Delete Comment	
Comments, edit	123	Click inside comment window, edit comment, click outside comment		Right-click within text formatted by a comment; Edit Comment	
Comments, insert	123	on Reviewing toolbar	Insert | Comment		Alt+Ctrl+M
Comments, insert audio	124	on Reviewing toolbar			

Microsoft Word 2003 Task Guide (Level 2)

Word Task	Page	Mouse	Menu Bar	Shortcut Menu	Shortcut Keys
Comments and tracked changes, display Reviewing Pane	121	on Reviewing toolbar			
Comments and tracked changes, printing	128		File	Print; Print what; Document showing markup		
Comments and tracked changes, view by reviewers	132	Show ▼ on Reviewing toolbar; Reviewers			
Compare and merge documents	147		Tools	Compare and Merge Documents		
Datasheet, import data	251	on Microsoft Graph Chart Standard toolbar	Edit	Import File		
Diagram, create	258	on Drawing toolbar	Insert	Diagram		
Diagram, format	259	on Diagram toolbar			
Document summary, create or modify	25		File	Properties; Summary tab		
Document summary, print	27		File	Print; Print what; Document properties		
Drop cap, change format	55		Select drop cap; Format	Drop Cap	Right-click edge of drop cap; Drop Cap	
Drop cap, create	55		Format	Drop Cap; Dropped or In margin		
Drop cap, drop word	57		Select word; Format	Drop Cap; Dropped or In margin		
Drop cap, remove	57		Select drop cap; Format	Drop Cap; None	Right-click edge of drop cap; Drop Cap; None	

Microsoft Word 2003 Task Guide (Level 2)

Word Task	Page	Mouse	Menu Bar	Shortcut Menu	Shortcut Keys
E-mail, current document as an attachment	144	on Standard toolbar	File | Send To | Mail Recipient (as Attachment)		
E-mail, current document for review	142		File | Send To | Mail Recipient (for Review)		
E-mail, route current document	146		File | Send To | Routing Recipient		
Embed, Excel chart	287	on Excel Standard toolbar; on Word Standard toolbar	Edit | Copy (in Excel); Edit | Paste (in Word)	Right-click chart in Excel; Copy; right-click in Word; Paste	Ctrl+C in Excel; Ctrl+V in Word
Embed, Excel data as an editable object in Word	285		Edit | Copy (in Excel); Edit | Paste Special (in Word)		
Embedded worksheet object, edit	289		Double-click embedded worksheet; make changes	Right-click embedded worksheet; Worksheet Object | Edit	
Find and replace, formatting	8		Edit | Replace; More; Format		Ctrl+H; Alt+M; Alt+O
Find and replace, remove formatting options	6		Edit | Replace; click in Find what box; click No Formatting; click in Replace with box; click No Formatting		Ctrl+H; Alt+T; Alt+I; Alt+T
Find and replace, search options	7		Edit | Replace; More; select desired search options		Ctrl+H; Alt+M
Find and replace, special characters	8		Edit | Replace; Special		Ctrl+H; Alt+E
Find and replace text	4		Edit | Replace; type text in the Find what box; type replacement text in the Replace with box; Replace or Replace All		Ctrl+H

Microsoft Word 2003 Task Guide (Level 2)

Word Task	Page	Mouse	Menu Bar	Shortcut Menu	Shortcut Keys
Find text	4		Edit | Find; Type text in the Find what box; Find Next		Ctrl+F
Flowchart, create	261	AutoShapes on Drawing toolbar; Flowchart			
Formatting, display toolbar	91		View | Toolbars | Formatting	Right-click toolbar; Formatting	
Formatting, reveal	91		Format | Reveal Formatting		Shift+F1
Header and footer, different first page	17	on Header and Footer toolbar; Layout tab; Different first page	File | Page Setup; Layout tab; Different first page		
Header and footer, different for odd-numbered and even-numbered pages	15	on Header and Footer toolbar; Layout tab; Different odd and even	File | Page Setup; Layout tab; Different odd and even		
Header and footer, display toolbar	16		View | Header and Footer		
Heading 1 style, apply	90	Normal on Formatting toolbar; Heading 1	Format | Styles and Formatting; Heading 1		Ctrl+Alt+1
Heading 2 style, apply	90	Normal on Formatting toolbar; Heading 2	Format | Styles and Formatting; Heading 2		Ctrl+Alt+2
Heading 3 style, apply	90	Normal on Formatting toolbar; Heading 3	Format | Styles and Formatting; Heading 3		Ctrl+Alt+3
Hyperlink, insert or edit	278	on Standard toolbar	Insert | Hyperlink	Right-click selected text; Hyperlink	Ctrl+K
Hyperlink, remove	281	on Standard toolbar | Remove Link	Insert | Hyperlink; Remove Link	Right-click hyperlink; Remove Hyperlink	Ctrl+K; Alt+R
Hyphenation	57		Tools | Language; Hyphenation		

332 Microsoft Word 2003 Task Guide (Level 2)

Word Task	Page	Mouse	Menu Bar	Shortcut Menu	Shortcut Keys
Import Excel data as a table in Word	287	on Excel Standard toolbar; on Word Standard toolbar	Edit | Copy (in Excel); Edit | Paste (in Word)	Right-click selected cells in Excel; Copy; right-click in Word; Paste	Ctrl+C in Excel; Ctrl+V in Word
Insert Excel worksheet as a new object	284	on Standard toolbar	Insert | Object; Create New tab; Microsoft Excel Worksheet		
Insert Excel worksheet from an existing file	282		Insert | Object; Create from File tab; Browse		
Insert Word file into existing document	284		Insert | File		
Link, update	292		Edit | Update Link	Right-click linked data; Update Link	F9
Link Excel worksheet in Word	290		Edit | Copy (in Excel); Edit | Paste Special; Paste link (in Word)		
List style, apply	90	Normal on Formatting toolbar; List	Format | Styles and Formatting; List		Ctrl+Shift+L
Mail merge, create labels	184	on the Mail Merge toolbar	Tools | Letters and Mailings | Mail Merge; Labels document type; Next: Starting document; Change document layout; Label options		
Mail merge, display toolbar	166		View | Toolbars | Mail Merge	Right-click toolbar; Mail Merge	
Mail merge, using task pane	166; 184		Tools | Letters and Mailings | Mail Merge		
Mail Merge preview	182	on Mail Merge toolbar			Alt+Shift+K
Normal style, apply	90	Normal on Formatting toolbar; Normal	Format | Styles and Formatting; Normal		Ctrl+Shift+N

Word Task	Page	Mouse	Menu Bar	Shortcut Menu	Shortcut Keys
Organization chart, add position	255	Insert Shape on Organization Chart toolbar			
Organization chart, create	253	on Drawing toolbar; Organization Chart	Insert | Diagram; Organization Chart		
Page orientation	43	Double-click blue area of ruler bar; Margins tab; Portrait or Landscape	File | Page Setup ; Margins tab; Portrait or Landscape		
Research tool	21	on Standard toolbar	Tools | Research		Alt and click the term you want to research
Reviewing pane, open and close	135	on Reviewing toolbar			
Save document in different format	293		File | Save As; Save as type		
Section break, continuous	50		Insert | Break; Continuous		
Shape, add text	213			Right-click shape; Add Text	
Shape, change line	217	on Drawing toolbar	Format | AutoShape; Line Style	Right-click line shape; Format AutoShape; Line Style	
Shape, change line color	217	on Drawing toolbar	Format | AutoShape; Line Color	Right-click line shape; Format AutoShape; Line Color	
Shape, change line shadow style	217	on Drawing toolbar			
Shape, draw circle	209	on Drawing toolbar while holding down ⇧Shift			

334 Microsoft Word 2003 Task Guide (Level 2)

Word Task	Page	Mouse	Menu Bar	Shortcut Menu	Shortcut Keys
Shape, draw line	209	\ on Drawing toolbar			
Shape, draw oval	204	○ on Drawing toolbar			
Shape, draw rectangle	207	▢ on Drawing toolbar			
Shape, draw square	209	▢ on Drawing toolbar while holding down Shift			
Shape, draw straight line	207	\ on Drawing toolbar; press and hold Shift and drag mouse to draw line			
Shape, fill color	208	(fill icon) on Drawing toolbar	Format | AutoShape; Fill Color	Right-click shape; Format AutoShape; Fill Color	
Shapes, group	218	Draw ▼ on Drawing toolbar; Group		Right-click selected shapes; Grouping | Group	Alt+D; G
Shapes, layer	218	Draw ▼ on Drawing toolbar; Order		Right-click shape; Order	Alt+D; R
Shapes, position	214	Click and drag to desired location			Select shape; press ←, →, ↑, or ↓
Shapes, regroup shapes	221	Draw ▼ on Drawing toolbar; Regroup		Right-click shape; Grouping | Regroup	Alt+D; O
Shapes, rotate and flip	216	Draw ▼ on Drawing toolbar; Rotate or Flip			Alt+D; P
Shapes, ungroup	221	Draw ▼ on Drawing toolbar; Ungroup		Right-click shape; Grouping | Ungroup	Alt+D; U
Sort lists, paragraphs, and table cells	13	A↓ or Z↓ on Tables and Borders toolbar	Table | Sort		

Microsoft Word 2003 Task Guide (Level 2)   **335**

Word Task	Page	Mouse	Menu Bar	Shortcut Menu	Shortcut Keys
Style, apply	88	**Normal** on **Formatting toolbar**	F**o**rmat | **S**tyles and Formatting; click style name		Ctrl+Shift+S, ↑ or ↓ to select style; Enter
Style, create new style	92; 97	**Normal** on **Formatting toolbar; New Style**	F**o**rmat | **S**tyles and Formatting; New Style		
Style, customize	98	**Normal** on **Formatting toolbar; Show drop-down arrow; Custom; Styles**	F**o**rmat | **S**tyles and Formatting; Show drop-down arrow; Custom; Styles		
Style, delete	96	**Normal** on **Formatting toolbar; Style drop-down arrow; Delete**	F**o**rmat | **S**tyles and Formatting; Style drop-down arrow; **D**elete		
Style, modify	96	**Normal** on **Formatting toolbar; Style drop-down arrow; M**odify	F**o**rmat | **S**tyles and Formatting; Style drop-down arrow; **M**odify		
Style area in Normal view	91		**T**ools | **O**ptions; View tab; Style ar**e**a width		
Style list, full list	90	Press and hold down Shift as you click the Style drop-down arrow			
Styles, copy to Normal template	100		**T**ools | Templates and Add-**I**ns; **O**rganizer; select styles; **C**opy		
Styles, find and replace	92		**E**dit | **R**eplace; **M**ore; Format; **S**tyle		Ctrl+H
Template, attach to current document	103		**T**ools | Templates and Add-**I**ns		
Template, format document with different template	103		F**o**rmat | T**h**eme; **S**tyle Gallery		
Template, save document as	81		**F**ile | Save **A**s; Save as **t**ype drop-down arrow; Document Template (*.dot)		

336 Microsoft Word 2003 Task Guide (Level 2)

Word Task	Page	Mouse	Menu Bar	Shortcut Menu	Shortcut Keys
Template, use to create document	78		File | New; On my computer		
Text boundaries, display	47		Tools | Options; View tab; Text boundaries		
Text effects, add	212		Format | Font; Text Effects tab		Ctrl+D; Alt+X
Track changes, accept all changes	141	on Reviewing toolbar; Accept All Changes in Document			
Track changes, accept one change	137	on Reviewing toolbar		Right-click change; Accept Insertion (Deletion)	
Track changes, activate or deactivate	126	on Reviewing toolbar OR Double-click TRK on the status bar	Tools | Track Changes		Ctrl+Shift+E
Track changes, next change	137	on Reviewing toolbar			
Track changes, options	131	Show on Reviewing toolbar; Options; Track Changes tab	Tools | Options; Track Changes tab		
Track changes, previous change	137	on Reviewing toolbar			
Track changes, reject all changes	141	on Reviewing toolbar; Reject All Changes in Document			
Track changes, reject one change	137	on Reviewing toolbar		Right-click change; Reject Insertion (Deletion)	
Track changes, show markup, final, or original	132	Final Showing Markup on Reviewing toolbar			
Track changes, user information	122		Tools | Options; User Information tab		

Microsoft Word 2003 Task Guide (Level 2)

Word Task	Page	Mouse	Menu Bar	Shortcut Menu	Shortcut Keys
Versions, create document	135		File	Versions		
Versions, delete	141	Double-click ▢ on status bar; Delete	File	Versions; Delete		
Versions, open existing	139	Double-click ▢ on status bar; Open	File	Versions; Open		
View, Full Screen	44		View	Full Screen		
Window, remove split for document window	19	Double-click split bar	Window	Remove Split		Ctrl+Alt+S
Window, split document window into two windows	18	Click and drag split box above the up scroll arrow at the top of the vertical scrollbar	Window	Split; click the horizontal line where you want the split to occur		
Windows, arrange document windows	18		Window	Arrange All		
Windows, compare document windows	20		Window	Compare Side by Side with . . .		

GLOSSARY

All key terms appearing in this book (in bold italic) are listed alphabetically in this Glossary for easy reference. If you want to learn more about a feature or concept, the Index to find the term's other significant occurrences.

Accept Change Option on the Reviewing toolbar or shortcut menu that removes a tracked change revision mark and incorporates the change—insertion, deletion, or formatting—into the document.

AddressBlock field A single mail merge field that produces the inside address (the recipient's address).

anchor The location to which an object or a shape is attached.

arranged windows An onscreen view displaying two or more document windows at the same time.

arrow style Style of the shape—such as an arrowhead, circle, or diamond—chosen from the Arrow Style palette on the Drawing toolbar and attached to the end of a drawn line.

ascending order Text, paragraphs, lists, or table rows arranged in alphabetical (A to Z) or sequential numerical (0 to 10) order. (*See also* **descending order**)

AutoShapes Predefined shapes such as stars and banners that you can create from the Drawing toolbar.

AutoText entry Boilerplate text, graphics, logos, and so on, which you can quickly insert into a document by typing the entry's abbreviation and pressing ↵Enter or by inserting it from the AutoText submenu or from the AutoText tab on the AutoCorrect dialog box.

blind copy A copy of an e-mail message sent to another person, but the other recipients do not know that the identity of a blind copy recipient.

boilerplate text Standard text that appears in a template.

cell reference A designation of a cell within an Excel worksheet, typically used to refer to a particular cell while calculating. For example, B1 refers to the second column (B) in the first row (1).

changed line A vertical line that appears in the left margin when a user adds, deletes, or formats text while the Track Changes feature is active.

character style A style that formats a portion of the text *within* a paragraph. Unlike a paragraph style that can format font, border, language, line spacing, alignment, and indents, a character style can format only fonts, borders, and languages.

chart A visual representation of numerical data that enhances the reader's understanding and comprehension of the values.

chart area The area of a chart that contains all of the chart elements.

chart title Brief description or heading for a chart.

columns Document formatting in which text appears in side-by-side vertical blocks. Text flows down the first column and then continues at the top of the next column.

comment An annotated note or other text that appears onscreen as a ScreenTip but does not affect regular document text. People insert comments to annotate documents or to pose questions for review.

compare and merge documents The process of automatically comparing the contents of two or more documents and displaying markup balloons that show the differences between the documents.

connector lines Special lines that join two shapes in a flowchart or other object and indicate the flow from one process or decision to another. When you move one of the shapes, the connector line remains attached to it and expands or decreases as needed.

continuous section break A division marker that separates a document into sections but continues the next section on the same page instead of starting a new page. Continuous section breaks are helpful to divide pages that contain different column formatting, such as single-column format for a newsletter masthead and two columns for the newsletter text.

curved line A drawn line that contains smooth curves wherever you change directions and click the mouse button to anchor it.

data labels Values that appear with each data series in a chart. For example, data labels typically appear about the columns in a column chart.

data series A series of values in a chart depicting different components of a single category.

datasheet A table containing values and labels with which to create a chart.

data source A document that contains a record of information for each recipient in a mail merge. A data source can be an Access database table, an Excel worksheet, an XML file, or a file created in Word during the Mail Merge process.

descending order Text, paragraphs, lists, or table rows arranged from the

339

highest to the lowest letter (Z to A) or number (10 to 0). (*See also* **ascending order**)

destination program   The program into which you bring external data. For example, Word is the destination program when you embed or link Excel data into a Word document.

diagram   A visual representation that illustrates relationships and processes. Six different types are available in Word: organization chart, Cycle diagram, Radial diagram, Pyramid diagram, Venn diagram, and Target diagram.

document summary   An element that provides descriptive information about a document—such as the author's name, keywords, and comments. Word saves the document summary with the document. You can view it in the Open, Save As, or Insert File dialog boxes by right-clicking a filename, choosing Properties, and clicking the Summary tab.

document type   The type of mail merge document, such as letters or envelopes, that you want to create.

drawing canvas   An area upon which you create and format shapes, such as ovals, rectangles, and lines.

Drawing toolbar   Toolbar containing a collection of drawing tools and options.

drop cap   An oversize character that drops below the current line. A drop cap is often applied to the first character of the first paragraph within a section. Published documents, such as books and magazines, often include drop cap characters.

embedding   The process of importing data that can be edited within the destination program.

fields   Individual components of data in a data source document. Common fields in a data source include first name, last name, address, city, state, and ZIP code.

filter   A set of criteria that each record must meet to be included in the merge process.

floating objects   Objects that are not anchored to a paragraph mark but can be positioned anywhere on a page, overlapping each other as well as document text.

flowchart   A visual representation of shapes that illustrate a process.

form file   A file, also known as a *main document,* containing the information that stays the same for all mail merge recipients.

Free Rotate tool   A green-filled circle above the center handle of a drawing shape that enables the user to click and drag it to rotate the selected shape.

GreetingLine field   A single merge field that produces the salutation—such as *Dear Mrs. Sumpter*—in a mail merge.

gridlines   Lines that guide the eye from the Y-axis values across the columns or bars to help the reader determine the relative value of each data marker.

grouping   The process of selecting objects and treating them as a single object so that you can move and format them together as a group.

gutter   A desktop publishing term that refers to the space between columns of text or the inside margins of a bound book.

hyperlink   An electronic marker that, when clicked, quickly moves the insertion point to a different location within the same document, opens another document, or displays a particular Web page in a Web browser.

hyphenation zone   An area at the end of a line that determines whether a word can potentially be hyphenated. If a word starts on or before the zone and extends past the right side of the zone, Word prompts the user to hyphenate that word. If a word starts after the zone, Word wraps it to the next line.

import   To bring in data from another source application, such as bringing Excel data into a chart datasheet in Word.

ink annotations   Electronic document markups made with a tablet pen on a Tablet PC, similar to using a regular pen to mark up printed documents.

ink comment   A special comment written directly into a markup balloon. You can insert an ink comment by using a tablet pen on a Tablet PC.

landscape orientation   The page orientation that positions text parallel with the long side of the page so that the printed page is wider than it is tall.

layering   The process of stacking graphical objects on top of each other.

legend   A color-coded key that indicates the colors that represent specific regions or data series within a chart.

linking   The process of inserting an object from another program in which the object is connected to the original data. If you change the original data, the linked data also change.

mail merge   A process that combines content from a main document and a data source.

Mail Merge task pane   A series of windows containing steps that guide you through the six major mail merge steps.

main document   A file, also known as a *form file,* containing the information that stays the same for all mail merge recipients.

markup balloons   Colored circles that contain comments, insertions, and deletions in the right or left margin, with a line drawn to where the insertion point was in the document prior to inserting the comment or editing the document.

masthead   The area, also known as the *nameplate,* that contains the title, date, and volume information on the first page of a newsletter.

merge fields   Placeholders of field names stored in the main document. Merge fields specify where data will be inserted from the data source during the mail merge.

Microsoft Graph Chart   An application that enables you to create and format a variety of charts within Word.

moving border   A dotted line that moves like lights on a marquee, appearing around a selected range of cells in an Excel worksheet.

nameplate The area, also known as the *masthead*, that contains the title, date, and volume information on the first page of a newsletter.

Normal template The default template framework that defines the 1.25″ left and right margins, 1″ top and bottom margins, left horizontal alignment, 12-point Times New Roman, and other default settings.

Object Linking and Embedding (OLE) Technology that enables you to use objects between programs.

organization chart A chart showing the hierarchy of positions within an organization.

Organizer A tool that enables you to copy styles, AutoText entries, and other shareable items between two documents or between a document and a template.

page orientation The direction in which printed text appears on a sheet of paper. The two orientations are *portrait* and *landscape*.

paragraph style A style that applies formats to an entire paragraph or to text separated by hard returns. Paragraph styles can include font formats and paragraph formats such as line spacing, indents, alignment, and spacing before and after the paragraph.

placeholders Text and space reserved for entering data into organization charts, templates, and documents.

plain text file A file format that preserves text only and does not contain any formatting, objects, or special features. Plain text files have a .txt filename extension.

plot area The area within a chart that displays the charted data series.

portrait orientation The page orientation that positions text parallel with the short side of the page so that the printed page is taller than it is wide. This is the default page orientation.

propagate labels The process of copying or duplicating the AddressBlock field to the other labels during a mail merge.

range A rectangular block of contiguous cells in an Excel worksheet.

record A group of related fields for a particular person or object in a data source.

regrouping The process of grouping objects together after ungrouping them.

Reject Change Option on the Reviewing toolbar that removes a tracked change revision mark and reinstates the original text, deletes added text, or removes formatting added while the Track Changes feature was active.

Research tool A tool that enables you to conduct research investigations. You can use this tool to locate definitions, synonyms, and Web sites that contain a particular keyword. When you activate the Research tool, the Research task pane appears so that you can specify research topics and locations.

Reviewing Pane A window at the bottom of the screen that displays comments and tracked changes. It appears automatically in Normal view when a user inserts a comment or tracks a change.

revision marks Noticeable onscreen elements that indicate locations where a person added, deleted, or formatted text while the Track Changes feature was active.

rich text format A file format that enables you to work with a file in another program or on another platform, such as a Macintosh computer. Although some formatting might be discarded, most basic formatting and objects are maintained. Rich text formatted files have an .rtf filename extension.

routing slip A list of e-mail recipients and your instructions on whether to send a document to the recipients in sequence or all at the same time.

scribble line The result of using a drawing tool that enables you to draw lines as if with a pencil.

sorting The process of rearranging tabulated text, paragraphs, lists, or table data in a particular order, such as arranging names in ascending order.

source program The program used to create the original data you embed into another file. For example, Excel is the source program when you embed or link Excel data into a Word document.

split document window An onscreen view displaying two different areas of a document at the same time so that you can scroll within each window pane individually.

starting document The document from which you begin creating a mail merge main document, such as the current document, a template, or an existing main document.

style A group of formatting settings that you can apply to characters, paragraphs, tables, or lists. Word contains predefined styles, such as Heading 1, that you can apply to document headings.

style area The space on the left side of the screen that displays style names next to each paragraph in Normal view. You can view the style area by choosing Tools, Options and clicking the View tab and typing a specific setting in the *Style area width* text box.

Style Gallery A window that enables you to select a template, see a preview of how its styles will affect your document, and then apply that template.

Tablet PC A special type of laptop computer that contains additional functionality. A Tablet PC enables people to use a tablet pen to write directly on the screen to annotate documents or to convert handwritten text into typed text.

template A framework of specifications for creating a document, defining the document's formats and often including some text and graphics. (*See also* **Normal template**)

text effect An animation setting that draws attention to onscreen text, although it does not appear on the printed document. Text effects are found in the Font dialog box.

Tile Windows Vertically option Windows option that enables you to display two document windows side by side at the same time.

track changes To track or note all additions, deletions, and formatting changes you make by applying noticeable revision marks and markup balloons in the document.

ungrouping The process of separating grouped objects back into individual objects so that you can format the objects individually instead of as a group.

version A "snapshot" of a document that is marked with the name of the person who saved it, as well as the date and time the version was saved.

wizard A feature that guides you through creating a specific type of document, such as a fax or a letter, by asking questions and having you select from various options.

workbook A Microsoft Excel file. A workbook may contain one or more worksheets.

worksheets A page of data within an Excel workbook.

X-axis A chart's horizontal axis, which typically depicts categories such as time periods (months, years, decades) or regions (cities, states, countries).

Y-axis A chart's vertical axis, which typically displays quantities.

Y-axis title A heading that describes the values or quantities on the left side (Y-axis) of a chart.

Z-axis A three-dimensional chart's vertical axis. Like a Y-axis on a two-dimensional chart, the Z-axis typically displays quantities.

INDEX

A

accepting changes, Track Changes feature, 135–141
adding
    AutoShapes, 204–209, 224–235
    bar codes, 187
    borders to charts, 246
    comments, 121–125, 152, 156, 160–161
    floating objects, 214–216, 232
    hyperlinks, 277–281, 298–308
    ink annotations, 131–132, 160–161
    ink comments, 124, 160–161
    positions to organization charts, 255–257
    records to mail merge data source, 175, 195
    titles to charts, 246–248
    text effects, 212–214, 226
AddressBlock field, 178, 180
addresses, formatting, 181
aligning
    charts, 244–246, 265–266
    shapes, 214–216, 232
anchors, 205
annotations, 128. *See also* **comments**
applying
    breaks, 45
    built-in styles, 88–92, 116
    fill color, 217–218
    line color, 217
    text effects, 212–214, 226
Arrange All (Window menu), 19
arranged windows, 17
arrow styles, 209
ascending orders, 13
attachments
    emailing for review, 142–147, 154
    templates, 103–105, 110
AutoCorrect dialog box, 88
AutoShapes, adding, 204–209, 224–235. *See also* **shapes**
AutoText entries
    creating, 81–83, 108–116
    deleting, 87–88
    editing, 85–87, 108
    inserting, 83–84, 108
axis content
    modifying, 246
    Y-axis
        adding titles, 246–248
        formatting elements, 248–250, 266

B

backgrounds, modifying, 250
balancing column length, 54
bar charts, 243, 273. *See also* **charts**
bar codes, inserting, 187
boilerplate text, 79. *See also* **documents; text**
borders
    adding charts to, 246
    applying to paragraphs, 68
    moving borders, 285, 301–304
boundaries, viewing text, 47
Break command (Insert menu), 50, 52, 54
Break dialog box, 51
breaks
    applying, 45
    deleting, 53
    inserting, 50–54, 65
built-in styles, applying, 88–92, 116
bulleted lists, sorting, 13–15, 32, 37

C

calendars, creating, 112–113
character style, 97–99
chart area, 97
Chart Options dialog box, 247
chart title, 239
Chart Type dialog box, 241
charts, 238
    border, 246
    creating, 240–244, 265–273
    elements, 248–250, 266
    embedding, 289
    Excel
        embedding, 287
        importing, 251–253
        linking, 290–293, 301–305
    flowcharts, 261
    formatting, 244–245, 253
    objects, 244–246, 265–266
    organization
        adding positions, 255–257
        creating, 253–254, 266–271
    titles, 246–248
    updating, 304–305
collaboration
    comments, 121–125, 152–161
    Track Changes feature, 125–128, 153, 158
    accepting/rejecting, 135–141
    comparing/merging documents, 147–148, 155
    customizing, 128–132, 153–154
    e-mailing documents for review, 142–147, 154
    reviewing, 132–135, 153–159
colors
    backgrounds, 250
    drop caps, 55–57, 65
    fill, 217–218
    line, 217
    shapes, 218
columns
    balancing, 54
    breaks, 50–54, 65, 67
    charts, 240–243, 265–269
    deleting, 47
    formatting, 42, 66–68, 70
    newspaper columns, 117
    page orientation, 43–45
    text
        formatting, 45–47, 65
        modifying, 48–49
    viewing, 48
    width, 50
Columns command (Format menu), 49
Columns dialog box, 49
commands
    Edit menu
        Paste Special, 286
        Replace, 4
    File menu
        Page Setup, 44
        Properties, 25
    Format menu
        Columns, 49
        Drop Cap, 55
        Theme, 103
    Insert menu
        Break, 50, 52, 54
        Diagram, 253
        File, 51
        Hyperlink, 280
        Picture, 240, 243, 251, 253
    Table menu
        Sort, 13
    Tools menu
        Compare and Merge Documents, 147
        Language, 58
        Letters and Mailings, 167

344 Index

Mail Merge, 161, 171
  Options, 47, 91, 123, 127–129
View menu
  Full Screen, 44
  Header and Footer, 15
  Mail Merge, 168
  Toolbars, 82
comments
  deleting, 125
  inserting, 121–125, 152–161
  printing, 128
compare and merge documents, 147
Compare and Merge Documents command (Tools menu), 147
Compare Side by Side with command (Window menu), 20
comparing documents, 147–148, 155
connector lines, 212, 232. *See also* **lines**
continuous section breaks, inserting, 54, 64, 67
continuous section breaks, 50. *See also* **breaks; sections**
copying. *See also* **moving**
  Excel, 287
  hyperlinks, 281
  styles, 100–102, 114–115
Create AutoText dialog box, 82
curved lines, 210. *See also* **lines**
Customize Address List dialog box, 174
customizing
  charts
    adding titles, 246–248
    formatting elements, 248–250, 266
    objects, 244–246, 265–266
  document merging, 149
  fields, 174
  headers/footers, 38
  hyperlinks, 277–281, 298–308
  organization charts, 257
  searching, 7
  Track Changes feature, 128–132, 153–154

D

data labels
  formatting, 251
  pie charts, 273
data series, 239
data sources, 164
  fields, 181
  main documents, 182–184, 192–194
  records, 176–177, 190–194
  tables, 175, 196–197
datasheet, 240
Delete dialog box, 252
deleting
  AutoText entries, 87–88
  breaks, 53
  columns, 47
  comments, 125
  drawing canvas, 208
  drop caps, 57
  formatting, 12

hyperlinks, 281
hyphens, 60
sections, 53
styles, 96, 118
templates, 118
versions, 141
descending order, 13
destination programs, 281–284, 300–301
Diagram command (Insert menu), 253
Diagram Gallery dialog box, 253–254
Diagram Style Gallery dialog box, 259
Diagram toolbar, 261
diagrams, 238. *See also* **charts**
  formatting, 258–262, 272–274
  organization charts
    adding positions, 255–257
    creating, 253–254, 266–271
dialog boxes
  AutoCorrect, 88
  Break, 51
  Chart Options, 247
  Chart Type, 241
  Columns, 49
  Compare and Merge Documents, 147
  Create AutoText, 82
  Customize Address List, 174
  Delete, 252
  Diagram Gallery, 253
  Diagram Style Gallery, 259
  Drop Cap, 56
  Edit Hyperlink, 280
  Filter and Sort, 177
  Find and Replace, 4, 6, 11
  Find Font, 10
  Font, 213
  Format Chart Title, 248–249
  Format Object, 244–245
  Greeting Line, 180
  Hyphenation, 58
  Import Data Options, 251
  Insert Address Block, 179
  Insert Hyperlink, 278
  Label Options, 184
  Mail Merge Recipients, 164, 173–175, 177, 185
  Manual Hyphenation, 58–59
  Match Fields, 181
  Merge to New Document, 183
  New Address List, 172
  New Style, 93, 95, 99–100
  Object, 243, 282
  Options, 122, 128–129
  Organizer, 101
  Page Setup, 16, 44
  Paste Special, 286
  Properties, 25–26
  Routing Slip, 146
  Save Address List, 173
  Save Version, 136
  Select Data Source, 185
  Set Hyperlink ScreenTip, 279
  Sort Text, 13–14
  Style, 98–99
  Templates, 78

Templates and Add-ins, 101, 105
Theme, 103
Versions in Tablet_PC.doc, 136
directories, mail merge, 199
document summary, 24–27, 34
Document type, specifying, 166–168, 190, 197–198
documents. *See also* **text**
  comparing and merging, 147–149
  formatting, 36–37
  mail merge
    creating recipient lists, 170–175, 190–191
    formatting main documents, 178–181, 191
    mailing labels, 184–187, 192–193
    merging data sources/main documents, 182–184, 192–194
    sorting records, 176–177, 190–191, 193–194
    starting, 166–168, 190, 197–198
  printing properties, 27
  routing, 146
  saving, 293–294, 302, 305
  splitting, 17–20, 33
  summaries, 24–27, 34
  templates
    attaching, 103–105, 110
    creating, 77–80
    saving as, 81
  workbooks (Excel)
    embedding, 284–287, 301–304
    inserting as objects, 281–284, 300–301
    linking, 290–293, 301–302, 304–305
    modifying embedding, 288–289
downloading templates, 81
drawing
  canvases, 204
    deleting, 208
    resizing, 211
  lines, 209–212, 225–226
  shapes, 204–209, 224–235
  straight lines, 211
Drawing toolbar, 204, 207–208
Drop Cap command (Format menu), 55
Drop Cap dialog box, 56
drop caps, creating, 55–57, 65

E

Edit Hyperlink dialog box, 280
Edit menu commands
  Paste Special, 286
  Replace, 4–5, 9
editing
  AutoText entries, 85–87, 108
  columns, 48–49
  comments, 121, 123–125, 152–161
  records, 176–177, 190–194
  reports, 35
  styles, 96, 116
  Track Changes feature, 125–128, 153, 158
    accepting/rejecting, 135–141
    customizing, 128–132, 153–154

Index **345**

e-mailing documents for review,
142–147, 154
reviewing, 132–135, 153–154,
156–159
effects
shapes, 218
Sparkle Text, 214
text, 212–214
elements, formatting charts, 248–250, 266
e-mail
attachments. *See* attachments
documents for review, 142–147, 154
inserting, 298
routing documents to, 146
E-mail toolbar, 143, 145
embedding Excel worksheets, 284–289, 293, 301–304
ending reviews, 146
envelopes, mail merge, 194
erasing ink annotations, 131
even-numbered pages, creating headers/footers, 15–17, 33
Excel
charts
creating, 269
importing, 251–253
copying/pasting, 287
tables, 305
workbooks
embedding, 284–287, 301–304
inserting as objects, 281–284, 300–301
embedding, 288–289
modifying linking, 290–293, 301–305
explosion object, 217

F

fields
AddressBlock, 178, 180
bar codes, 187
data sources, 181
GreetingLine, 180–181
mail merge, 170
creating main documents, 178–181, 191
customizing, 174
File command (Insert menu), 51
File menu commands
New, 78
Page Setup, 44, 51
Properties, 25
Send To, 142, 144
Versions, 136
files. *See also* **documents; text**
columns, 50–52
inserting, 51, 64, 67
plain text, 294
rich text format, 294
fill color, 217–218
Filter and Sort dialog box, 177
filtering records, 177
Find and Replace dialog box, 4, 6, 11, 92
Find Font dialog box, 10
flipping shapes, 216

floating objects, inserting, 214–216, 232
flowcharts, 212, 232–233, 261–262
Font dialog box, 213
fonts, modifying, 55–57, 65. *See also* **formatting; text**
footers, 15–17
creating for odd- and even-numbered pages, 15–17, 33
customizing, 38
form files, 164. *See also* **documents**
Format Chart Title dialog box, 248–249
Format menu commands
Columns, 49
Drop Cap, 55
Theme, 103
Format Object dialog box, 244–245
formatting. *See also* **customizing**
addresses, 181
built-in styles, 88–92, 116
calendars, 112–113
characters, 97–99
charts, 240–243, 265–273
adding titles, 246–248
elements, 248–250, 266
objects, 244–246, 265–266
columns, 42, 65–68, 70
page orientation, 43–45
text, 45, 47
width, 50
data labels, 251
deleting, 12
diagrams, 258–262, 272–274
directories, 199
documents, 36–37. *See also* documents
saving as different, 293–294, 302–305
summaries, 24–27, 34
templates, 77–80
drop caps, 55–57, 65
embedded data, 289
finding and replacing, 8–12, 32, 35
flowcharts, 261
greetings, 181
headers/footers, 15–17, 33
letters, 113
lines, 209–218, 225–226
mailing labels, 184–187, 192–193
main documents, 178–184, 191–194
mastheads, 64
newspaper columns, 117
objects, 284
organization charts, 253–257, 266–271
paragraphs
creating styles, 92–96, 110–114
viewing, 91
properties, 27
shapes, 204–209, 216–218, 224–235
stars with text effects, 212–214
tables, 117–118
text
AutoText entries, 81–84, 108–110, 115–116
columns, 65
copying styles, 100–102, 114–115
effects, 212–214, 226

replacing, 8–12, 31–32
searching, 8–12, 31–32
Free Rotate tool, 216
Full Screen command (View menu), 44

G

graphics, hyperlinks, 280. *See also* **hyperlinks**
Greeting Line dialog box, 180
GreetingLine field, 178, 180–181
greetings, formatting, 181
gridlines, 239
grouping shapes, 218–221, 231
gutters, 48

H

Header and Footer command (View menu), 15
headers, 15–17
creating for odd- and even-numbered pages, 15–17, 33
customizing, 38
heading styles, applying, 91
Help, 34, 39
hiding legends, 244
horizontal bar charts, 273. *See also* **charts**
Hyperlink command (Insert menu), 280
hyperlinks, inserting, 276–281, 298–308
hyphenating text, 57–60, 66
Hyphenation dialog box, 58
hyphenation zone, 60

I

Import Options dialog box, 251
importing. *See also* **moving**
charts from Excel, 251–253, 293
PowerPoint, 306
tables from Excel, 305
ink annotations. *See also* **comments**
inserting, 131–132, 160–161
understanding, 135
Insert Address Block dialog box, 179
Insert Hyperlink dialog box, 278
Insert menu commands
Break, 50, 52, 54
Diagram, 253
File, 51
Hyperlink, 280
Object, 282
Picture, 240, 243, 251, 253
inserting
AutoShapes, 204–209, 224–235
AutoText entries, 83–85
bar codes, 187
borders to charts, 246
breaks into columns, 50–54, 65
comments, 121–125, 152, 156, 160–161
continuous section breaks, 50, 54, 64
files, 51, 64
floating objects, 214–216, 232
hyperlinks, 277–281, 298–308
ink annotations, 131, 160–161

ink comments, 160–161
positions to organization charts, 255–257
records to mail merge, 175, 195
titles to charts, 246–248
text
  AutoText entries, 81–84, 108, 115–116
  text effects, 212–214, 226

J-K-L

keyboard shortcuts
  built-in styles, 90
  column break, 54
  create AutoText entry, 84
  find, 7
  find and replace, 7
  insert hyperlink, 280
  select entire document, 86
Label Options dialog box, 184
labels
  data
    creating pie charts, 273
    formatting, 251
  mailing, 184–187, 192–193
  propagating, 187
  X-axis, 246
landscape orientation, formatting, 43–45
Language command (Tools menu), 58
layering shapes, 218–221, 231
legends, 239
  viewing, 244
length, balancing columns, 54
Letters and Mailing command (Tools menu), 167
letters, creating, 113. *See also* document; text
line charts, creating, 269. *See also* charts
line color, 217
lines
  creating pyramid charts, 274
  drawing, 209–212, 225–226
  formatting, 216–218
  resizing, 211
linking Excel, 290–293, 301–305
lists
  recipients, 170–175, 190–191
  sorting, 13–15, 32, 37
  styles, 99

M

Macintosh, saving documents as, 293–294, 302–305
mail merge, 164. *See also* e-mail
  directories, 199
  envelopes, 194
  mailing labels, 184–187, 192–193
  main documents
    creating, 178–181, 191
    merging data sources, 182–184, 192–194
  previewing, 192
  recipient lists, 170–175, 190–191
  records
    adding, 195
    sorting, 176–177, 190–194

starting, 166–168, 190, 197–198
Mail Merge command
  Tools menu, 171
  View menu, 168
Mail Merge Recipients dialog box, 164, 173–175, 177, 185
Mail Merge task pane, 166
Mail Merge toolbar, 166, 168–169
mailing labels, formatting, 184–187, 192–193
main documents, 164. *See also* documents
Manual Hyphenation dialog box, 58–59
markup balloons, 121. *See also* comments
mastheads
  formatting, 64
  inserting, 50–52
Match Fields dialog box, 181
matching data source fields, 181
merge fields, 178
Merge to New Document dialog box, 183
merging, 164. *See also* mail merge
merging documents, 147–148, 155
Microsoft Graph Charts. *See also* charts
  creating, 240–243, 265–269, 273
  objects, 244–246, 265–266
  titles
    adding, 246–248
    formatting, 248–250, 266
modifying. *See also* customizing; formatting
  axis content, 246
  background colors, 250
  column text, 48–49
  comments, 121–125, 152, 156–161
  document summaries, 24–27
  embedded data, 288–289
  hyperlinks, 277–281, 298–308
  hyphenation zones, 60
  lines, 209–212, 225–226
  newsletters, 72–73
  page orientation, 64
  properties, 27
  reports, 35–36
  shapes, 204–209, 214–216, 224–235
  source data, 292
  styles, 96, 116
  Track Changes feature, 125–128, 153, 158
    accepting/rejecting, 135–141
    comparing/merging documents, 147–148, 155
    customizing, 128–132, 153–154
    e-mailing documents for review, 142–147, 154
    reviewing, 132–135, 153–159
moving
  borders, 285, 301–304
  charts, 244–246, 265–266
  hyperlinks, 281
  importing charts, 251–253
  object anchors, 205
  shapes, 214–216, 232
  styles, 100–102, 114–115
multiple recipients, routing documents to, 146

multiple sorting, 177
multiple-level sorting, 15

N

nameplates, inserting, 50
New Address List dialog box, 172
New command (File menu), 78
New Document task pane, 78
New Style dialog box, 93, 95, 99–100
newsletters, modifying, 72–73
newspaper columns, creating templates, 117
Normal templates, 77, 81. *See also* templates
  built-in styles, 88–92, 116
  styles, 100–102, 114–115
Normal view, inserting comments, 125

O

Object command (Insert menu), 282
Object dialog box, 243, 282
Object Linking and Embedding (OLE), 285. *See also* embedding
objects
  anchors, 205
  charts, 244–246, 265–266
  creating, 284
  floating, 214–216, 232
  inserting, 243
  organization charts, 257
  regrouping/ungrouping, 221, 231
  selecting, 221
  workbooks (Excel)
    embedding, 284–287, 301–304
    inserting as, 281–284, 300–301
    linking, 290–293, 301–305
    modifying embedding, 288–289
odd-numbered pages, creating headers/footers, 15–17, 33
OLE (Object Linking and Embedding), 284–285. *See also* embedding
options. *See also* customizing; formatting
  charts
    adding titles, 246–248
    formatting elements, 248–250, 266
    objects, 244–246, 265–266
  fields, 174
  headers/footers, 38
  hyperlinks, 277–281, 298, 302–308
  merging, 149
  organization charts, 257
  searching, 7
  Style based on, 96
  text boundaries, 47
  Tile Windows Vertically, 287
  Track Changes feature, 128–132, 153–154
Options command (Tools menu), 47, 91, 123, 127–129, 208
Options dialog box, 122, 128–129
organization charts. *See also* charts
  adding positions, 255–257
  creating, 253–254, 266–267, 270–271

Index

O (continued)

Organizer, copying styles, 100–102, 114–115
Organizer dialog box, 101
Outlook, creating mail merge, 170–175, 190–191. *See also* email

P

page orientation
    formatting, 43–45
    modifying, 64
Page Setup command (File menu), 44, 51
Page Setup dialog box, 16, 44
panes, 17–18, 20, 33
paragraph style, 92
paragraphs. *See also* documents; text
    borders, 68
    drop caps, 55–57, 65
    formatting
        searching/replacing, 12
        viewing, 91
    sorting, 13–15, 32, 37
    styles, 92–96, 110–114
Paste Special dialog box, 286
pasting Excel workbooks, 287. *See also* moving
Picture command (Insert menu), 240, 243, 251, 255
pie charts, creating, 269, 273. *See also* charts
placeholders, 254. *See also* text
plain text files, saving as, 294, 302–305
plot area, 239
portrait orientation, 43
positioning. *See also* moving
    charts, 244, 246, 265–266
    organization charts, 255–257
    shapes, 214–216, 232
PowerPoint, importing, 306
previewing mail merge, 192
printing
    comments, 128
    document summaries, 27
    Track Changes feature, 128
propagating labels, 187
properties
    formatting, 27
    printing, 27
Properties command (File menu), 25
Properties dialog box, 25–26
pyramid diagrams, creating, 274. *See also* charts

Q–R

range, 285
recipient lists, creating, 170–175, 190–191
records, 170–171
    adding, 175, 195
    sorting, 176–177, 190–194
redirecting hyperlinks, 281
reformatting drop caps, 57
regrouping objects, 221, 231
rejecting changes, Track Changes feature, 135–141

Remove Split command (Window menu), 19
Replace command (Edit menu), 4
replacing. *See also* deleting
    styles, 92
    text, 4–12, 31–32
reports
    editing, 35
    modifying, 35–36
Research task pane, 21–24
Research tool, 21–24, 34–39
resizing. *See also* sizing
    drawing canvas, 211
    lines, 211
    shapes, 209
reviewing pane, 121, 135
reviewing, Track Changes feature, 121, 132–135, 153–159
revision marks, 125
revisions
    columns, 48–49
    comments, 121–125, 152–161
    records, 176–177, 190–194
    reports, 35
    styles, 116
    text, 85–87, 108
    Track Changes feature, 125–128, 153, 158
        accepting/rejecting, 135–141
        comparing/merging documents, 147–148, 155
        customizing, 128–132, 153–154
        e-mailing documents for review, 142–147, 154
        reviewing, 132–135, 153–154, 156–159
rich text format (rtf), saving as, 294, 302, 305
rotating. *See also* moving
    shapes, 216
    text, 214
routing documents to multiple recipients, 146
routing slip, 146
Routing Slip dialog box, 146
rows, sorting, 14

S

Save Address List dialog box, 173
Save Version dialog box, 136
saving
    AutoText entries, 84
    documents, 293–294, 302, 305
    templates, 81
    versions, 135–141, 153
scribble lines, 209. *See also* lines
searching
    customizing find and replace, 7
    Research tool, 21–24, 34–39
    replacing. *See* replacing
    styles, 92
    text, 4–12, 31–32
sections
    breaks, 45
    columns, 50–52

    deleting, 53
    drop caps, 55–57, 65
    headers/footers, 17
security, Normal templates, 81
Select Data Source dialog box, 185
selecting objects, 221
Send To command (File menu), 142, 144
series, formatting, 251
Set Hyperlink ScreenTip dialog box, 279
shading colors, applying, 55–57, 65
shapes
    colors, 218
    drawing, 204–207
    effects, 218
    flipping, 216
    flowcharts, 212, 232
    formatting, 216–218, 227
    grouping, 218–221, 231
    layering, 218–221, 231
    lines, 209–212, 225–226
    positioning, 214–216, 232
    resizing, 209
    rotating, 216
    text effects, 212–214, 226
sizing
    charts, 244–246, 265–266
    gutters, 48
    shapes, 204–209, 224–235
Sort command (Table menu), 13
Sort Text dialog box, 13–14
sorting records and text, 13–15, 32, 37, 176–177, 190–194
source data, modifying, 292
source programs, 281–284, 300–301
Sparkle Text effect, 214
specifying Document types 167–168, 190, 197–198
Split command (Window menu), 18
splitting document window, 17–20, 33
stacked column charts, creating, 268–269, 273
stars, formatting, 212–214, 226
starting mail merge document, 166–168, 190, 197–198
straight lines, 211. *See also* lines
style area, 91
Style based on option, 96
Style dialog box, 98
Style Gallery, attaching templates, 103–105, 110
styles. *See also* customizing; formatting
    built-in, 88–92, 116
    characters, 97–99
    copying, 100–102, 114–115
    deleting, 96, 118
    editing, 116
    finding and replacing, 92
    lists, 99
    modifying, 96
    paragraphs, 92–96, 110–114
    tables, 99, 117–118

Styles and Formatting task pane, 91, 93, 95–96, 98
summaries, creating, 24–27, 34

T

Table menu commands, Sort, 13
tables
    charts, 244, 269, 273
    data source, 175, 196–197
    Excel, 305
    sorting, 13–15, 32, 37
    styles, 99, 117–118
Tablet PC, 120, 124
tabulated text, sorting, 14, 32, 35, 37. *See also* text
task panes
    Mail Merge, 166–168, 171–172, 175–187
    New Document, 78
    Research, 21–24
    Styles and Formatting, 91, 93, 95–96, 98
templates
    attaching, 103–105, 110
    AutoText. *See* AutoText entries
    built-in styles, 88–92, 116
    creating, 77–80
    deleting, 118
    downloading, 81
    newspaper columns, 117
    saving, 81
Templates and Add-ins dialog box, 101, 105
Templates dialog box, 78
text
    applying styles, 88–96, 97–99, 110–114, 116
    AutoText entries
        creating, 81–83, 108–110, 115–116
        deleting, 87–88
        editing, 85–87, 108
        inserting, 83–84, 108
    boundaries, 47
    columns
        formatting, 45–47, 65
        modifying, 48–49
    comments, 121–125, 152–161
    drop caps, 55–57, 65
    finding and replacing, 4–7, 31
    formatting, 293–294, 302–305
    hyperlinks, 277–281, 298–308
    hyphenating, 57–60, 66
    inserting, 212–214, 226
    mastheads
        formatting, 64
        inserting, 51–52
    placeholders, 254
    replacing, 4–12, 31–32, 35
    rotating, 214
    searching, 4–12, 31–32
    sorting, 13–15, 32, 37
    templates, 103–105, 110

text boxes, 274
Track Changes feature, 125–128, 153, 158
    accepting/rejecting, 135–141
    comparing/merging documents, 147–148, 155
    customizing, 128–132, 153–154
    e-mailing documents for review, 142–147, 154
    reviewing, 132–135, 153–154, 156–159
    wrapping, 244–246, 265–266
text box, 214
text effect, 212
Theme command (Format menu), 103
Theme dialog box, 103
Tile Windows Vertically option, 287
titles
    adding, 246–248
    formatting, 248–250, 266
toolbars
    AutoText, 82
    Diagram, 261
    Drawing, 204
    E-mail, 143, 145
    Header and Footer, 15
    Ink Annotations, 131–132
    Mail Merge, 166
    Reviewing, 123, 132
tools
    Free Rotate, 216
    Research, 21–24, 34–39
Tools menu commands
    Compare and Merge Documents, 147
    Language, 58
    Letters and Mailings, 167
    Mail Merge, 161, 171
    Options, 47, 91, 123, 127–129
tracking changes, 125–128, 153, 158
    accepting/rejecting, 135–141
    comparing/merging documents, 147–148, 155
    customizing, 128–132, 153–154
    e-mailing documents for review, 142–147, 154
    printing, 128
    reviewing, 132–135, 153–154, 156–159
translate languages, 21, 39
troubleshooting
    Help, 34
    Normal templates, 81
types of objects, creating, 284

U

undoing, 12. *See also* deleting
uneven column width, 50. *See also* columns
ungrouping objects, 221, 231
updating charts, 304–305
user information, 122

V

Venn diagrams, formatting, 258–262, 272–274
versions
    deleting, 141
    saving, 135–141, 153
Versions command (File menu), 136
Versions in Tablet_PC.doc dialog box, 136
viewing
    columns, 48
    comments, 121–125, 152–161
    documents, 17–20, 33
    formatting, 91
    legends, 244
    text boundaries, 47
View menu commands
    Full Screen, 44
    Header and Footer, 15
    Mail Merge, 168
    Toolbars, 82
views, Normal, 125
viruses, Normal templates, 81
voice, inserting comments, 124

W

Web pages, inserting hyperlinks, 280
width, formatting columns, 50
Window menu commands
    Arrange All, 19
    Compare Side by Side with, 20
    Remove Split, 19
    Split, 19
windows, splitting, 17–20, 33
wizards. *See also* templates
    Calendar, 112–113
    Letter, 113
    template, 81
workbooks (Excel)
    charts, 251–253
    copying/pasting, 287
    objects
        embedding, 284–287, 301–304
        inserting as, 281–284, 300–301
        linking, 290–293, 301–305
        modifying embedding, 288–289
worksheets (Excel), importing charts, 251–253
wrapping text, 244–248, 265–266

X-Y-Z

X-axis, 239
    modifying, 246
Y-axis
    adding, 246–248
    describing, 239
    formatting elements, 248–250, 266
Y-axis title, 239
Z-axis, 239